Fundamentals of Japanese Grammar

Fundamentals of Japanese Grammar

COMPREHENSIVE ACQUISITION

Yuki Johnson

University of Hawai'i Press
Honolulu

© 2008 University of Hawai'i Press
All rights reserved
Printed in the United States of America
13 12 11 10   6 5 4 3 2

Library of Congress Cataloging-in-Publication Data
Johnson, Yuki.
   Fundamentals of Japanese grammar : comprehensive acquisition / Yuki Johnson.
     p. cm.
   Includes bibliographical references and index.
   ISBN 978-0-8248-3109-7 (hardcover : alk. paper)
   ISBN 978-0-8248-3176-9 (pbk. : alk. paper)
   1. Japanese language—Grammar. 2. Japanese language—Textbooks for foreign speakers—English.
PL535.J54 2008
495.6'82421—dc22
                                         2007060450

Camera-ready copy has been provided by the author

University of Hawai'i Press books are printed on acid-free
paper and meet the guidelines for permanence and durability
of the Council on Library Resources.

With Many Thanks to Dr. Susumu Kuno
Emeritus Professor of Linguistics
Harvard University

Contents

Preface		XIII
How to Use This Book		XVII
Origin of 仮名		XIX
The Hiragana Chart		XX
The Katakana Chart		XXI
CHAPTER 1	**Japanese Symbols and Their Sounds**	1
	Symbols	1
	Sounds	3
CHAPTER 2	**Structural Features of the Japanese Language**	9
	Japanese as an SOV Language	10
	Other Characteristics of Japanese	13
CHAPTER 3	**Conjugation of Verbs, い Adjectives, and the Copula だ**	20
	Conjugation of Verbs	21
	Conjugation of い Adjectives	29
	Conjugation of the Copula だ	30
CHAPTER 4	**Particles**	33
	は	34
	が	42
	を	51
	に	55
	へ	62
	と	63
	で	67
	も	70
	や	75

	の	76
	から	79
	まで	81
	までに	82
	か	83
	ね	86
	よ	87
	でも	88
CHAPTER 5	**Transitive vs. Intransitive**	90
	Intransitive Verbs	93
	Transitive Verbs: Ditransitive and Transitive	96
CHAPTER 6	**Verbs of Existence: ある・いる**	98
	The Syntax and Semantics of ある and いる	98
	"There Is a Dog in the Yard" vs. "The Dog Is in the Yard"	102
CHAPTER 7	**Tense: る・た in Subordinate Clauses**	105
	Functions of Tense Forms	105
	Tense Forms in "When" Clauses	107
CHAPTER 8	**Dictionary/Plain Form Compounds**	114
	つもり	114
	前に/前は	115
	ところ	117
	ため(に)	118
	間に/間は	120
	うちに/うちは	124
CHAPTER 9	**Stem Form Compounds**	130
	たい	130
	たがる (たい + がる)	132

	やすい / にくい	134
	ながら	135
	方	137
	すぎる	138
	に + Motion Verb	140
CHAPTER 10	**て Form Compounds**	143
	てください	143
	てから	146
	ている	148
	ておく	157
	てある	159
	てみる	162
	てしまう	163
	ていく / てくる	165
	てほしい	168
CHAPTER 11	**た Form Compounds**	172
	た後で	172
	たり〜たりする / たり〜たりだ	174
	たことがある	176
	たところ	178
	たまま	180
CHAPTER 12	**おう Form Compounds and ましょう**	181
	おうと思う	181
	おうとする	183
	ましょう	184
CHAPTER 13	**Demonstrative Pronouns: こ・そ・あ・ど**	187
	The Non-anaphoric (Pointing) Use of こ・そ・あ・ど	187

	The Anaphoric (Referencing) Use of こ・そ・あ	189
CHAPTER 14	**Conjunction Words and Linking Sentence**	193
	The て Form Linkage: そして・それから・それで/だから	194
	Paradoxical Linkage: でも・けれども・しかし	201
	Additive Linkage: それに・その上・しかも	204
CHAPTER 15	**Interrogative Pronouns and Interrogative Sentences**	207
	The Functions of か	207
	The Functions of Interrogative Pronouns	211
CHAPTER 16	**Change of State: する・なる Constructions**	216
	Predicate + する/なる	216
	Verb Dictionary Form/ない + ことにする/ことになる	220
CHAPTER 17	**Modifying Constructions**	223
	Noun-Modifying Constructions	223
	Modifying Verbs: Adverbs	235
CHAPTER 18	**Nominalizers: こと・の**	243
	こと	244
	の	247
CHAPTER 19	**Modal Auxiliaries (Modals): Propositions and Modality Expressions**	253
	Evidential Modals	255
	Suppositional Modals	262
	Explanatory Modals	270

CHAPTER 20	Giving and Receiving	276
	あげる・くれる・もらう	278
	てあげる・てくれる・てもらう	282
	てくれる and てもらう Used in the Request Form	289
CHAPTER 21	Structures of Imperatives/Commands	292
	しろ	292
	なさい	294
CHAPTER 22	Structures of Permission: The ても Form	296
	Permission and the ても Form	296
CHAPTER 23	Structures of Prohibition: The ては Form	301
	The Structure of Sentences of Prohibition	301
	The ては Form with Another Main Clause	303
	The ては Form in Casual Conversation	304
CHAPTER 24	Structures of Obligation	306
	なければならない/なくてはいけない	307
	ないわけにはいかない	309
CHAPTER 25	Terms of Respect: Polite Affixes and Honorific and Humble Forms	312
	丁寧語: The Polite Affixes お and 御	312
	Honorific Statements	314
	Honorific Requests	320
CHAPTER 26	Conditional Sentences: と・たら・ば・なら	323
	と	325
	たら	331
	ば	336
	なら	341

CHAPTER 27	**Comparative Sentences**	345
	Creating a Question Sentence	345
	Answering Question Sentences	346
CHAPTER 28	**Superlative Sentences**	349
	Creating and Answering a Question Sentence	349
CHAPTER 29	**Structures of Suggestions**	352
	たら/ば	352
	方がいい	354
CHAPTER 30	**Potential Sentences**	357
	書ける	358
	Verb Dictionary Form + ことができる	360
CHAPTER 31	**Passive Constructions**	362
	Formation of the Passive	362
	Structure and Meaning of the Passive Construction	363
CHAPTER 32	**Causative Constructions**	375
	Formation	375
	Structure and Meaning: "Make" vs. "Let"	376
CHAPTER 33	**Causative-Passive Constructions**	383
	Formation	383
Bibliography		387
Index		391

Preface

Grammatical competence is among the most important components of language proficiency, especially for adult learners whose mother tongue exhibits a different word order from that of the target language. For example, English exhibits a Subject (S), Verb (V), and Object (O) order, and learning a language that is structured by a S-O-V word order, such as Japanese, may be more difficult than learning a S-V-O language. If one wishes to improve his/her language competence at the highest levels, a thorough knowledge of grammar will definitely help not only in the areas of reading and writing, but also in speaking and listening. This book was written with strong hopes that it would help in the review and recognition of the depth and importance that grammar plays in language acquisition.

This book is a compilation and further development of lectures on Japanese grammar given by the author for students of elementary and intermediate Japanese at Harvard University, International Christian University, the University of Michigan, the University of British Columbia, and the University of Toronto.

The original grammar lecture notes were written according to the order in which textbooks typically introduce grammar items in each lesson. In this book, however, as seen by the categorization of each chapter, grammar items are reorganized in terms of specific grammatical categories, such as particles, *te*-form compounds, passive constructions, conditional sentences, and so forth, and are not organized to accommodate a certain Japanese language textbook. If used as a reference book with a regular language textbook, it is recommended that the course instructor indicate the page number of grammatical items introduced in each chapter in the main textbook found in the index, and the page numbers should be indicated in the syllabus or term schedule.

Thus, this book is intended for learners of Japanese who have already studied basic Japanese grammar, but wish to better organize and expand their knowledge in greater depth and at a higher level. Therefore, if you intend to use this book along with an elementary Japanese language textbook, you need not necessarily learn and understand everything in each chapter, as some explanations may be too detailed for your classroom activities; instead, concentrate on the main concepts of the grammar items.

Looking back upon completion of this volume, I recognize a deep debt of gratitude owed to many individuals. First, I would like to acknowledge my sincere thanks to my Ph.D. advisor, Dr. Wesley Jacobsen, now Director of the Japanese Language Program at Harvard University. Since I was a first-year M.A. student at the University of Minnesota, he demonstrated to me a love for research. I fondly remember the days when I attended all of his grammar lectures for elementary Japanese courses, took notes eagerly, and rehearsed many times in the attempt to model my grammar lectures after his.

I would also like to acknowledge all the insightful questions received from my graduate and undergraduate students at Harvard University, the University of Michigan, and the University of Toronto and instructors at the University of Michigan. I especially would like to thank my graduate students, Jotaro Arimori, Yuri Naito, and Asami Tsuda, as well as the students who took my course "EAS293: Fundamentals of Japanese Grammar" at the University of Toronto for their thorough proofread and insightful comments. Because of their thought-provoking insights on Japanese grammar, I was inspired to keep writing.

Sincere thanks also to Ms. Patricia Crosby and Ms. Ann Ludeman, University of Hawai'i Press. Their extremely professional handling of the publication process helped this book to press with speed and efficiency. Their thoughtful and timely assistance is gratefully acknowledged.

My heartfelt gratitude goes to two great physicists in my life—my father, Dr. Yuzo Endo, and my husband, Dr. Jeff Siewerdsen. Jeff is an exemplary model in every aspect of the personal and scholarly life, especially as to the dedication and diligence required of a researcher. He has been my guide through the pleasures and perils of academia, a better half who shares and inspires a love for scholarly pursuit. To him go my deepest thanks for his unfailing support through all the ups and downs.

Lastly, my deepest appreciation goes to Dr. Susumu Kuno, Emeritus Professor of Linguistics at Harvard University, whose countless original, significant views on Japanese grammar provided constant constructive commentary on my work in linguistics. All of my research and writings are indebted to him and his books, especially *The Structure of the Japanese Language*, published in 1973 by MIT Press. He is a beacon who has unerringly guided me through the most difficult linguistic challenges, and he continually gains my most heartfelt respect. Without his guidance and diligence in research, I would not have been able to complete this volume. For this reason, I dedicate this volume to him. I could never hope to exceed his contributions, but I look up to his work as a guide for my current and future research.

I sincerely hope that this book will be a useful resource and guide for your understanding of Japanese grammar, that your knowledge about the language will improve, and that your knowledge of the language will deepen.

Toronto, Ontario
Yuki Johnson

How to Use This Book

This book is intended primarily for educators and researchers in Japanese studies and the Japanese language, as well as for graduate students and undergraduate students who have already learned basic Japanese grammar through regular language courses. It is assumed that readers know hiragana and katakana, and the basic kanji introduced in two years of language instruction. The following comments cover a few particulars of which readers should be aware prior to using the book.

1. Examples are all written in Japanese (combining kanji, katakana, and hiragana). Words that are normally expressed in kanji are written in kanji with a ruby in hiragana. When a kanji word appears for the first time on a page, it is always accompanied by the ruby, no matter how elementary it may seem, such as 日本. From the second appearance on, the ruby disappears if the usages are on the same page.
2. Examples may be written in the plain or the formal form, assuming that the readers can recognize the forms.
3. A sentence with an asterisk means that the sentence is either grammatically inappropriate or pragmatically awkward.
4. Some examples may seem awkward from the viewpoints of native speakers of Japanese if uttered without any context or any sentence-final particle. The purpose is to show a basic structure without too many frills, so even if the sentence may not be uttered as written, the learners should know that these are given for illustration purposes. A good example may be: 私は母親に人参を食べさせられなかった "I was not made to eat carrots by my mother," an example sentence appearing in the section on "Agglutination" in Chapter 2. The sentence alone may be awkward, and a native speaker of Japanese may understandably question its usage. However, if this utterance is used in a context wherein the speaker is talking about his/her childhood, in which many Japanese parents force their children to eat carrots for nutritional purposes, and such experience does not apply to the speaker, the speaker may say, 私は子供の時母親に人参を食べさせられなかったのよねぇ。だから今でも人参が大嫌いで・・・ "When I was a child, I was

not forced to eat carrots by my mother, so I hate carrots even now." When a sentence is uttered in a certain context and with a certain intonation, nearly any sentence that may seem to be awkward becomes a possible utterance. Thus, please note that one purpose of this book is to provide an explanation of basic sentence structure, and absolute naturalness is sometimes not taken into consideration.

5. Many sections feature reading material and exercises, though the pattern is not consistent throughout the book. Sample dialogues are provided to show how a given grammatical structure is used in context, and the dialogues usually accompany English translation. Some sections include short essays. They are usually presented without English translations and are given as exercises for the reader. In real situations, the ruby is not usually provided, but in this book it is given for the purpose of identifying kanji words. Some vocabulary may be new to readers, and it is recommended that readers use a dictionary when unknown words appear in the reading materials.

6. In the examples throughout the textbook, as well as those in the "sample dialogues" and "sample essays," names and characters of the speakers may or may not be given. Speakers are often identified simply by the letters "A," "B," "C," and so forth and are followed by a colon.

Examples:
本田： どうしたんですか。
松田： ええ、彼女にふられちゃったんです・・・。

A: この人、誰？
B: ああ、この方は先生の御主人ですよ。

女： これ、食べてみてください。
男： え、ああ、今食事したばかりだから・・・。

Lastly, scattered throughout the book are pieces of a story concerning the (hopefully amusing) love triangle between チビ, タビ, and タマ. If you rearrange the dialogues in the right order, the story should be clear. Find them and try!

Origin of 仮名(かな)

漢字(かんじ) to 平仮名(ひらがな)

a →安→あ	i →以→い	u →宇→う	e →衣→え	o →於→お
ka →加→か	ki →幾→き	ku →久→く	ke →計→け	ko →己→こ
sa →左→さ	shi →之→し	su →寸→す	se →世→せ	so →曽→そ
ta →太→た	chi →知→ち	tsu →川→つ	te →天→て	to →止→と
na →奈→な	ni →仁→に	nu →奴→ぬ	ne →祢→ね	no →乃→の
ha →波→は	hi →比→ひ	fu →不→ふ	he →部→へ	ho →保→ほ
ma →末→ま	mi →美→み	mu →武→む	me →女→め	mo →毛→も
ya →也→や		yu →由→ゆ		yo →与→よ
ra →良→ら	ri →利→り	ru →留→る	re →礼→れ	ro →呂→ろ
wa →和→わ	(wi →為→ゐ)		(we →恵→ゑ)	wo →遠→を
				n →无→ん

漢字(かんじ) to 片仮名(かたかな)

阿→ア	伊→イ	宇→ウ	江→エ	於→オ
加→カ	幾→キ	久→ク	介→ケ	己→コ
散→サ	之→シ	須→ス	世→セ	曽→ソ
多→タ	千→チ	川→ツ	天→テ	止→ト
奈→ナ	二→ニ	奴→ヌ	祢→ネ	乃→ノ
八→ハ	比→ヒ	不→フ	部→ヘ	保→ホ
万→マ	ミ→ミ	牟→ム	女→メ	毛→モ
也→ヤ		由→ユ		與→ヨ
良→ラ	利→リ	流→ル	礼→レ	呂→ロ
和→ワ	井→ヰ)		恵→ヱ)	乎→ヲ
				无→ン

There are a total of 48 characters for kana (hiragana and katakana). Kana for the sounds "wi," "wu," and "we" do not exist due to the assimilation of the semivowels into the vowels "i," "u," and "e," respectively. Also, although the term for the currency is spelled "yen," it is pronounced "en" (円). Characters for "wi" and "we" sounds are not used in modern Japanese. This means that a total of 46 characters are used in writing nowadays.

The Hiragana Chart

	W	R	Y	M	P	B	H	N	D	T	Z	S	G	K		
ん	わ	ら	や	ま	ぱ	ば	は	な	だ	た	ざ	さ	が	か	あ	a
	(ゐ)	り		み	ぴ	び	ひ	に	ぢ	ち	じ	し	ぎ	き	い	i
		る	ゆ	む	ぷ	ぶ	ふ	ぬ	づ	つ	ず	す	ぐ	く	う	u
	(ゑ)	れ		め	ぺ	べ	へ	ね	で	て	ぜ	せ	げ	け	え	e
	を	ろ	よ	も	ぽ	ぼ	ほ	の	ど	と	ぞ	そ	ご	こ	お	o
		りゃ		みゃ	ぴゃ	びゃ	ひゃ	にゃ		ちゃ	じゃ	しゃ	ぎゃ	きゃ		ya
		りゅ		みゅ	ぴゅ	びゅ	ひゅ	にゅ		ちゅ	じゅ	しゅ	ぎゅ	きゅ		yu
		りょ		みょ	ぴょ	びょ	ひょ	にょ		ちょ	じょ	しょ	ぎょ	きょ		yo

Characters in the parentheses (ゐ) and (ゑ) are not used in modern standard Japanese.

xx

The Katakana Chart

	W	R	Y	M	P	B	H	N	D	T	Z	S	G	K		
ン	ワ	ラ	ヤ	マ	パ	バ	ハ	ナ	ダ	タ	ザ	サ	ガ	カ	ア	a
	(ヰ)	リ		ミ	ピ	ビ	ヒ	ニ	ヂ	チ	ジ	シ	ギ	キ	イ	i
		ル	ユ	ム	プ	ブ	フ	ヌ	ヅ	ツ	ズ	ス	グ	ク	ウ	u
	(ヱ)	レ		メ	ペ	ベ	ヘ	ネ	デ	テ	ゼ	セ	ゲ	ケ	エ	e
	ヲ	ロ	ヨ	モ	ポ	ボ	ホ	ノ	ド	ト	ゾ	ソ	ゴ	コ	オ	o
		リャ		ミャ	ピャ	ビャ	ヒャ	ニャ		チャ	ジャ	シャ	ギャ	キャ		ya
		リュ		ミュ	ピュ	ビュ	ヒュ	ニュ		チュ	ジュ	シュ	ギュ	キュ		yu
		リョ		ミョ	ピョ	ビョ	ヒョ	ニョ		チョ	ジョ	ショ	ギョ	キョ		yo

Characters in the parentheses (ヰ) and (ヱ) are not used in modern standard Japanese.

CHAPTER 1

Japanese Symbols and Their Sounds

1. Symbols

Japanese has three different types of symbols called 漢字,平仮名, and 片仮名. 漢字 are Chinese characters that were conveyed from Korea (百済 period) around the beginning of 5th century and began to be used in Japan as 万葉仮名 during the 奈良 period (around 700 AD). 万葉仮名 were mainly used by male writers, especially used in a collection of poems called 万葉集. In this collection, only the sound of the 漢字 was borrowed in order to express the poems in writing.

The set of 片仮名 characters was created from 漢字 by taking a part of 漢字 in order for the monks to read Buddhist texts in the 9th century (平安 period). For example, ア was derived from the 漢字 "阿," and イ from "伊." The set of 片仮名 consists of 48 basic characters that have been used mainly to write non-Chinese foreign words, onomatopoeic words, and for emphasis (the equivalent of italic or uppercase text in English, for example). There were originally characters ヰ and ヱ for the sounds "wi" and "we," respectively. No character was assigned for the sound "wu," as it is considered to have assimilated into the vowel "u." Since 1946, due to the change in the Japanese Ministry of Education policy regarding Japanese language reforms, these characters have become obsolete, although they may still be seen in classical Japanese. A total of 46 basic characters, therefore, are commonly used in modern Japanese.

Note that although Japanese does not have "f" and "v" sounds, in order to pronounce the foreign words including these sounds, ファ, フィ, フェ, フォ and ヴァ, ヴィ, ヴ, ヴェ, and ヴォ have been created. Many still prefer to represent words that have a "v" sound with symbols for "b" sounds. Some examples are:

factory	ファクトリー
film	フィルム
fair	フェアー
fork	フォーク
value	ヴァリュー/バリュー
vivid	ヴィヴィッド/ビビッド
velvet	ヴェルヴェット/ベルベット
venice	ヴェニス/ベニス
voice	ヴォイス/ボイス

In addition, in order to express a word such as "tea," a small イ is used in combination with テ as seen in ティーバッグ "tea bag." "T" in "twilight zone," for example, may be spelled トゥワイライトゾーン. Expressing the "th" sound is still a difficult issue, as there is no equivalent sound in Japanese. For example, "think tank" may be expressed シンクタンク, which can be the same as "sink tank." How about a name like "Schwarzenegger?" It is transcribed シュワルツェネッガー.

The expression of foreign sounds using 片仮名 may exhibit some variation depending on the age, educational background, and/or dialect of the individual. Also, the way native speakers of Japanese pronounce foreign words is not always the same. These problems may create confusion or awkwardness among native speakers of that language until one gets used to them.

平仮名 were created by simplifying 漢字 and were first especially used by female writers, but became widespread by the 10th century. In modern Japanese, 平仮名 are usually used for です and ます and Japanese words which are not typically written in 漢字, such as some adverbs, adjectives, and nouns, or in words whose 漢字 may seem obscure. 平仮名 are also used alongside 漢字 to demonstrate pronunciation in materials for children, comic books, foreign language textbooks, and so forth. This function is called ふりがな "ruby."

The 平仮名 ゐ (wi) and ゑ (we) have also become obsolete in modern Japanese, but may be seen in classical Japanese. In addition, the currency unit, 円 (¥), for example, is spelled "yen" in Romanization, but is expressed えん in

平仮名 and pronounced "en." Some foreign words like たばこ "tobacco" have become assimilated into Japanese and are often written in 平仮名.

2. Sounds

Japanese symbols function as phonetic symbols for 漢字 as ふりがな on top of 漢字—漢字. Therefore, if one knows the pronunciation of 平仮名, and they are provided for 漢字, then s/he can pronounce the 漢字. Every 平仮名 (other than the vowels, あ, い, う, え, and お, and ん the "n" sound) consists of a consonant and a vowel when represented in the English alphabet. For example, か is pronounced "ka," which is a combination of the consonant "k" and the vowel "a"; す is pronounced "su," which is a combination of the consonant "s" and the vowel "u."

Each character represents a unit of sound called a "mora," a linguistic term from the Latin for a "period of time." Each mora carries an approximately fixed and equal duration and weight. Japanese is one of the few languages that exhibits this moraic structure, and it uses morae as the basis of the sound system rather than syllables. For example, if one attempts to pronounce あいうえお in a situation, such as where someone teaches the pronunciation to children, the five morae may be pronounced maintaining the same length of time for each mora, just like five eighth-notes ♪♪♪♪♪.[1] If one knows 俳句, s/he may realize that Japanese follows the pattern 5 morae/7 morae/5 morae, rather than 5 syllables/7 syllables/5 syllables. Example: ふるいけや (5 morae) かわずとびこむ (7 morae) みずのおと (5 morae) (古池や、蛙飛び込む、水の音).[2] The mora system works well in teaching/learning Japanese as a foreign/second language. It is especially useful to differentiate words that include a long vowel and double consonants from those that do not. Examples include: おばあさん (5 morae) "grandmother" and おばさん (4 morae) "aunt"; おっと (3 morae) "husband"

---

[1] The length of each mora is not necessarily expressed by one eighth-note, but the point is that each sound occupies the same length of time when pronunciation is attempted in formal settings. In day-to-day conversation, however, due to the involvement of empathy and psychological factors, some morae may be elongated or shortened.

[2] A famous haiku created by a haiku poet, Issa Kobayashi (1763–1827). The equivalent for each segment is: an old pond; a frog jumps into; the sound of water.

and おと (2 morae) "sound"; and じっこう (4 morae) "carrying out" and じこ (2 morae) "accident."

Another remark on Japanese sounds is that Japanese has fewer vowels and consonants than English, Chinese, or Korean, for example. Especially, the lack of an "r" sound is well known. Although 仮名 charts usually employ the symbol "r" to represent the Japanese らりるれろ sounds, this "r" sound is not the same as the English "r." Instead of rolling the tongue toward the back of the throat, one should place his/her tongue behind the upper teeth. The Japanese "r" therefore sounds closer to an "l" or a "d" sound. There are no Japanese sounds that are pronounced by rolling the tongue back in the throat, and it is typical for Japanese speakers to place their tongue behind their upper/lower teeth to pronounce words.

As mentioned above, the "th" sound is also absent from Japanese. The "th" sound in "thriller," for example, is spelled スリラー using the ス (su) sound instead. Some individuals who speak English are sensitive to this issue and make an effort to distinguish the sounds in symbols as well, and the symbol "θ" may sometimes be used, such as θリラー "thriller."

Reducing the number of sounds from one's native tongue is in fact easier than adding sounds one is not accustomed to producing. Therefore, pronouncing Japanese may be easier for some people whose native tongue has many vowels, for example. The difficult aspect, on the other hand, may be found in the moraic characteristics of Japanese.

2.1 音読み and 訓読み

In reading 漢字, there are two common means of pronunciation: 音読み and 訓読み. 音読み is the so-called sound reading, in which Chinese characters are read phonetically. When 漢字 were first introduced, people tried to mimic the pronunciation of Chinese words just as Japanese speakers do today with foreign words. For example, 安 was pronounced "an" and expressed as "an" as a sound reading. Some characters have more than one 音読み because the original Chinese originated from areas with different pronunciations (dialects). This was not only due to the factor of dialect, but also to changes in Chinese pronunciation over the period of many years.

訓読み is a method of reading wherein the original Japanese pronunciation for a word is applied. For example, "person" in Chinese is 人, pronounced "jin"[3] in Chinese. In Japanese the equivalent to "person" is ひと, and this pronunciation is applied to the Chinese character 人.

Some 漢字 compounds are considered 同音異義語 "homophones," which means that the expressed words have the same reading but assign a different meaning. The following are examples for こうえん (音読み) and たつ (訓読み), both of which may be expressed by several different 漢字:

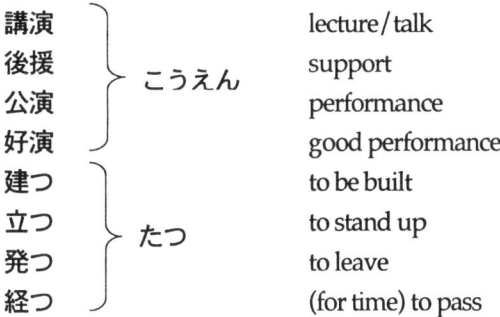

講演		lecture/talk
後援	こうえん	support
公演		performance
好演		good performance
建つ		to be built
立つ	たつ	to stand up
発つ		to leave
経つ		(for time) to pass

The meaning of the words is clear from the use of different 漢字 or the context of the conversation.

2.2 濁音: Voiced sounds

Voicing of the normally voiceless consonants in the たなはまやらわ rows of the 平仮名 chart is indicated by adding two small marks to the 平仮名 in these lines (が、ざ、だ, and ば). In addition, 平仮名 in the は line are pronounced with a "p" sound when a circle is added (ぱ, ぴ, ぷ, ぺ, and ぽ).

---

[3] "Jin" for 人 is in fact not accurate. It is pronounced "ren" and written "ren" in pinyin (a Romanization system for Chinese meaning "spelling.") The Chinese "r" sound is extremely difficult for Japanese to pronounce, and "jin" must have been the closest sound that Japanese people could pronounce. There are many examples of this, not only for Chinese words, but also for foreign words. "R" sounds from Chinese and English are still problematic sounds for Japanese. For example, ライス can be mistaken for "lice" if a native speaker of English hears the word from a native speaker of Japanese who does not know any foreign languages, since Japanese does not have an "r" sound and cannot distinguish the difference between "r" and "l."

In some cases, /g/ in がぎぐげご sounds is weakened to a softer, nasal /η/ tone when occurring within words. For example, が in か<u>が</u>く "chemistry" may be a velar nasal, while が in <u>が</u>っこう "school" is not. This distinction may not be consistent between individuals, or may derive from age, geographic background, social status, and so on. It is often observed that the Tokyo dialect employs a nasal sound, while the Kansai dialect, as it is spoken in the Osaka area, may not. However, this observation takes note of merely a general tendency; actual pronunciation varies among different individuals throughout Japan.

2.3 拗音 (ようおん): Contracted sounds

Contracted sounds are created by the combination of a consonant and a "ya," "yu," or "yo" sound. These contracted sounds are expressed by placing a small や, ゆ, よ next to a 平仮名 (ひらがな), as in きゃ, しゃ, ちゃ, and にゃ. Although the contracted sounds are expressed by two 平仮名, the pronunciation of きや and きゃ are different in that きや is pronounced in two morae, while きゃ is pronounced in one mora. Thus, contracted sounds are all pronounced in one mora. Compare the following:

<u>きゃ</u>く (客: guest) – two morae   vs.   <u>きやく</u> (規約: regulation) – three morae
<u>しょ</u>う (賞: award) – two morae   vs.   <u>しよう</u> (使用: use) – three morae
<u>ひょ</u>う (表: chart) – two morae   vs.   <u>ひよう</u> (費用: cost) – three morae

2.4 促音: Double consonants (assimilated sounds)

促音 (そくおん) is the so-called double consonant where "k," "s," "t," and "p" assimilate the sound of the preceding consonant, marked by a small つ. The double consonant is considered two morae in terms of pronunciation. For example:

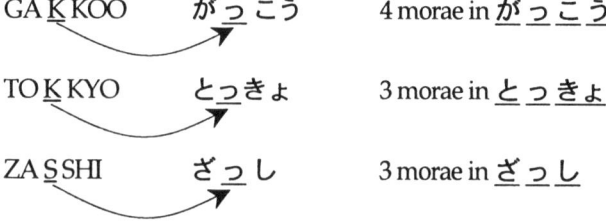

GA <u>K</u> KOO   が<u>っ</u>こう   4 morae in <u>がっこう</u>

TO <u>K</u> KYO   と<u>っ</u>きょ   3 morae in <u>とっきょ</u>

ZA <u>S</u> SHI   ざ<u>っ</u>し   3 morae in <u>ざっし</u>

Fundamentals of Japanese Grammar

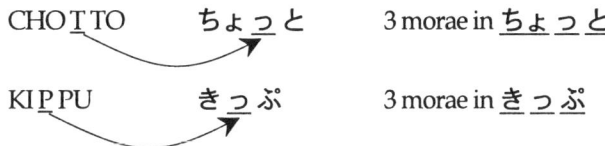

2.5 長音: Long vowels (prolonged sounds)

長音 means that any vowel in a mora is prolonged and becomes a mora written by the vowel in the previous mora. For example, oka a san "mother" includes a 長音 "a" prolonged "a" in "ka." In Japanese, it is written おかあさん, as the alphabet symbolizes. There is no need for reducing its size in writing. All vowels can be prolonged to create long-vowel words. Compare the following examples:

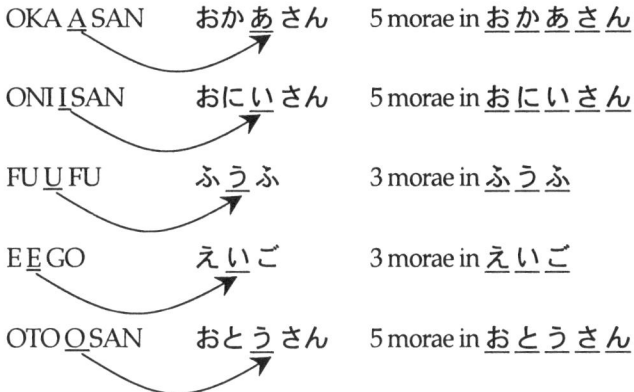

There are two exceptions in the way long vowels are symbolized in 平仮名: case for long "e" and long "o." Lengthening of "e" is primarily expressed by adding the character い instead of a second え, and long "o," by addition of う instead of お. This means that "ee" is written えい and "oo", おう, as in えいが "movie" and べんきょう "study."

However, there are exceptions, for which memorizing the spelling is the best practice. Some of these include: おねえさん (お姉さん) "elder sister," こおり (氷) "ice," and とおる (通る) "to go through."

Sample exercise
Write the following foreign words in 片仮名(カタカナ).

apple	Valentine
birthday card	hot dog
computer	fried chicken
chocolate	condominium
David Johnson	ice cream
flower	jogging
George	road
hospital	volunteer
jacket	dress
skirt	bird watching
McDonald	stage
menu	dream
parking	finance
department store	romance
coffee cup	water
notebook	cell phone
coordinator	executive
California	Dallas
Washington	Dulles
pharmacy	school bus
folk song	rock and roll
fishing	living room
chair	bathroom
control	washing machine
hair dryer	tomorrow
century	yellow
sandwich	fiber
beer	strawberry
cat	hospital
sweet	birthday
think	sink

CHAPTER 2

Structural Features of the Japanese Language

Almost all languages in the world may be identified in terms of three fundamental elements that constitute a basic sentence. They are: *Subject (S); Verb (V);* and *Object (O).*[1] With these elements, there are six possible combinations, but only three of them are frequently found in the languages of the world. In these common combinations, the subject always precedes the object, and this seems to be a universal truth.[2]

SVO	English, French, Italian, Modern Greek, German, Yoruba, Thai, Malay, Swedish, Finnish, Chinese, etc.
SOV	Japanese, Ainu, Korean, Mongolian, Burmese, Tamil, Hindi, and Turkish (verb-final constraint is not observed rigidly in Hindi and Turkish), etc.
VSO	Irish, Hebrew, Arabic, Chinook (spoken by American Indian people of the north shore of the Columbia River at its mouth), Tagabili (Mindanao in the Philippines), etc.
VOS	
OVS	Hizkaryana (Brasil)
OSV	

As can be seen, Japanese is one of the SOV languages, but unlike Hindi and Turkish, the verb-final constraint is observed very rigidly. Since the position of the Verb and Object is in opposition between SVO and SOV languages, these two types of languages create mirror-image structures of one another. Knowing the

---

[1] The term "object" is used to refer to a grammatical object of a sentence throughout the book.
[2] Data are from Kuno (1973).

features of your mother tongue and the language you are going to learn is one of the keys for the efficient and successful acquisition of the language. SOV languages share various characteristics.

1. Japanese as an SOV Language
1.1 Japanese as a postpositional language (position of particles)

Unlike English, Japanese particles are postpositional, and therefore follow the noun.

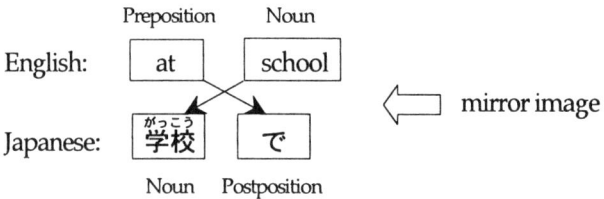

(1) メリーは 東京大学で 日本語を 勉強しています。
   Mary is studying Japanese at the University of Tokyo.
(2) 私は メリーと 日本語で 話します。
   I talk with Mary in Japanese.
(3) ジョンが メリーに 車を あげた。
   John gave Mary a car.
(4) ジョンが メリーと 車で 東京へ 行った。
   John went to Tokyo with Mary by car.

Nouns that constitute a sentence are normally followed by a particle that identifies the function of the noun. For example, を in sentence (1) following 日本語 identifies 日本語 as the object of the predicate 勉強する "to study," and で in sentence (2) identifies 日本語 as a tool for the activity described by the verb 話す "to talk." Thus, particles are used to represent case relationships, or represent the functions that are carried in English by prepositions and conjunctions.

In addition to these particles, there are also sentence-final particles like よ, ね, か, さ, etc., which are placed after a sentence-final verb to represent the speaker's attitude toward the content of the sentence.

(5) 私は松田です<u>よ</u>。
I am Matsuda, you know/I'm telling you.

(6) あの方は松田さんです<u>ね</u>。
That person over there is Ms. Matsuda, isn't she?

(7) あの方は松田さんです<u>か</u>。
Is that person over there Ms. Matsuda?

1.2 Japanese as a left-branching language

"Left-branching" refers to the structural phenomenon where a modifier always precedes a constituent, which means that in horizontal writing, a modifier is placed on the left side of the constituent being modified. A good example is a case of an い adjective that modifies a noun, such as 大きい犬 "a big dog." In Japanese, regardless of the type of constituent (noun, verb, い adjective, な adjective,[3] relative clause, etc.) there are no exceptions to this restriction.

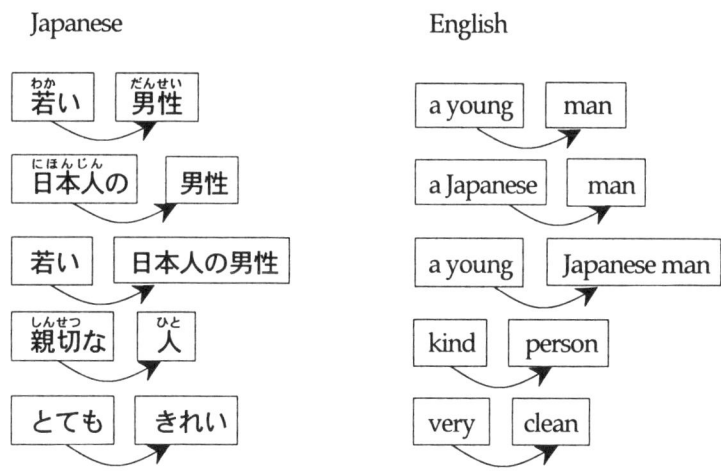

---

[3] Refer to Section 2 in this chapter.

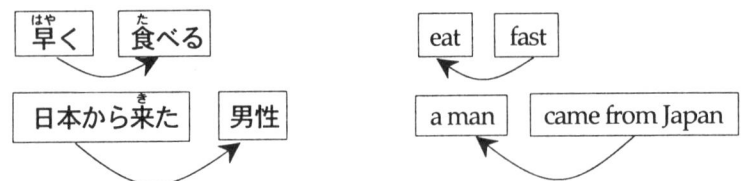

English and Japanese behave the same way with respect to い/な adjectives. However, in English, adverbs can be inconsistent, and relative clauses always follow a noun phrase in English, which is not the case in Japanese.

1.3 The direction of verb phrase deletion

In English, there is a process of deleting all but the first identical verbs or verb phrases in coordinated sentences. In Japanese, due to its rigid SOV structure, all clauses must end with a verb. As shown in the following examples, if the same verb is repeated three times, the first two can be eliminated, but not the last. The particles may also be omitted except for the one in the last clause, as indicated in the parentheses in sentence (8b) and (9b).

(8) a. リサは日本へ行って、ケンは韓国へ行って、トムは中国へ行った。
    Lisa <u>went</u> to Japan, Ken <u>went</u> to Korea, and Tom <u>went</u> to China.
    ↓
    b. リサは日本(へ)、ケンは韓国(へ)、トムは中国へ行った。
    Lisa <u>went to Japan</u>; Ken, Korea; and Tom, China.

(9) a. リサは納豆を<u>食べて</u>、ケンはキムチを<u>食べて</u>、トムはチャーハンを<u>食べた</u>。
    Lisa <u>ate</u> natto, Ken <u>ate</u> kimuchi, and Tom <u>ate</u> fried rice.
    ↓
    b. リサは納豆(を)、ケンはキムチ(を)、トムはチャーハンを<u>食べた</u>。
    Lisa <u>ate</u> natto; Ken, kimuchi; and Tom, fried rice.

1.4 The position of interrogative pronouns

In Japanese, interrogative pronouns do not have to occupy sentence-initial positions. They replace the nouns under discussion without changing their position. A sentence can include more than one interrogative pronoun. The following examples are declarative sentences and interrogative sentences with all the noun phrases in the declarative sentences converted to an interrogative pronoun. Only the questions are translated.

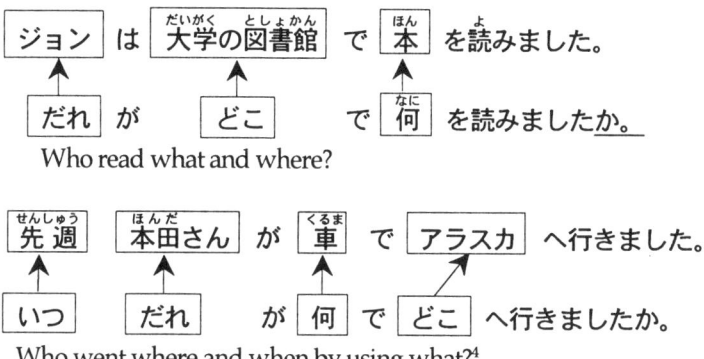

Who read what and where?

Who went where and when by using what?[4]

In daily conversation, a sentence like the above might not be uttered frequently, but if one needs various pieces of information answered all at once, this type of sentence is considered appropriate in Japanese.

2. Other Characteristics of Japanese
2.1 Parts of speech and predicate types

Japanese also has parts of speech, such as verbs, adjectives, nouns, and adverbs.[5] These parts of speech, however, do not necessarily correspond to those of English in terms of their syntactic and/or semantic behavior. For example, there are two types of adjectives, and they are often referred to as い adjectives and な adjectives for the purpose of teaching/learning Japanese.[6] In addition, verbs and

---

[4] When a method of transportation is asked, どうやって "how" may be more commonly used.
[5] Parts of speech also include constituents such as particles, auxiliary verbs, pronouns, conjunctions, and interjections.
[6] The Japanese for い adjectives is 形容詞, and for な adjectives it is 形容動詞. The source of these terminologies stems from the way they modify a noun. While い adjectives modify a noun directly, without any morphemes between the い adjective and the noun, as in おもしろい人 "an interesting person," な adjectives require な between the two parts of speech, such as きれいな人 "a pretty person." This book also employs the terms い adjectives and な adjectives.

い adjectives conjugate,[7] while nouns and な adjectives do not.[8] These parts of speech are all used to form a predicate that describes the subject of a sentence.

In Japanese, sentences comprise three types of predicates: verbal predicates, adjectival predicates, and nominal predicates. Each type of predicate may occur in the plain or the formal form[9]. For example, the verb "to eat" can be expressed either in the plain form—食べる, as in 私はすしを食べる "I'm gonna eat sushi" (uttered to the speaker's close friends/family members), or 食べます as in 本田さんはてんぷらを食べますよ "Ms. Honda is going to eat tempura, you know" (uttered to a stranger/acquaintance). In the case of い adjectives, such as "delicious," おいしい is the plain form, and the polite form is created by adding the copula です—おいしいです. These predicates are often set out in a chart like the following for learners of Japanese at the elementary level. The chart includes only the non-past affirmative and non-past negative and past affirmative and past negative combinations, which are the most basic, simple ones used to create a simple sentence, such as "I do/will go," "I do/will not go," "I went," and "I did not go"; and "is pretty," "is not pretty," "was pretty," and "was not pretty," in both plain and formal forms.[10]

---

[7] For example, the verb 食べる "to eat" and the い adjective おもしろい "interesting" conjugate, producing forms such as, 食べた "ate," 食べれば "if (you) eat," 食べて "eat-and," and おもしろかった "was interesting," おもしろければ "if it is interesting," おもしろくて "interesting-and," respectively. Other forms of verbs are introduced in Chapter 3.

[8] In order for nouns and な adjectives to constitute a predicate, the plain or formal form of the copula だ/です has to follow. For example, the past tense form of きれい "beautiful" is きれいだった, with the copula だ added to きれい in the past tense form だった.

[9] Some other terminologies, such as "casual forms" and "polite forms" equivalent to "plain forms" and "formal forms" may be found in language textbooks. "Plain forms" are normally used in informal and casual settings where one speaks to close friends or his/her family members in a casual manner.

[10] The following are examples of simple sentences based on the chart.

Verb
a. 私は学校へ行く。　　　　　私は学校へ行きます。　　　　　I go/will go to school.
b. 私は学校へ行かない。　　　私は学校へ行きません。　　　　I do/will not go to school.
c. 私は学校へ行った。　　　　私は学校へ行きました。　　　　I went to school.
d. 私は学校へ行かなかった。　私は学校へ行きませんでした　　I did not go to school.

い adjective
a. 天気はいい。　　　　　　　天気はいいです。　　　　　　　The weather is good.
b. 天気はよくない。　　　　　天気はよくありません。　　　　The weather is not good.
c. 天気はよかった。　　　　　天気はよかったです。　　　　　The weather was good.
d. 天気はよくなかった。　　　天気はよくありませんでした。　The weather was not good.

Verb

	Non-past (imperfective)	Past (perfective)
Affirmative formal	〜ます	〜ました
Affirmative plain	〜u/る	〜た
Negative formal	〜ません	〜ませんでした
Negative plain	〜ない	〜なかった

い adjective

	Non-past	Past
Affirmative formal	〜です	〜かったです
Affirmative plain	∅	〜かった
Negative formal	〜くありません	〜くありませんでした
Negative plain	〜くない	〜くなかった

Noun and な adjective

	Non-past	Past
Affirmative formal	〜です	〜でした
Affirmative plain	〜だ	〜だった
Negative formal	〜じゃありません	〜じゃありませんでした
Negative plain	〜じゃない	〜じゃなかった

As mentioned earlier, verbs and い adjectives conjugate and form a predicate either in the plain or the formal form, while な adjectives and nouns do not.[11] They are followed by the copula です, which conjugates. Remember that in a simple sentence in the plain form, an い adjective does not invite だ to it. One

---

Noun and な adjective
a. 彼は親切だ。　　　　　　彼は親切です。　　　　　　He is kind.
b. 彼は親切じゃない。　　　彼は親切じゃありません。　He is not kind.
c. 彼は親切だった。　　　　彼は親切でした。　　　　　He was kind.
d. 彼は親切じゃなかった。　彼は親切じゃありませんでした。He was not kind.

[11] The term "imperfective" means that the event in question has not yet been completed. "Perfective," on the other hand, indicates an event that has already been completed. These notions will be discussed in dealing with Japanese tenses in Chapter 7. They do not work well with stative predicates, such as い adjectives, な adjectives, and nouns, since these are not used to express the completion of events.

may say 親切だ "is kind," 親切だった "was kind," 先生だ "is a teacher," and 先生だった "was a teacher," but *not* おもしろいだ "is interesting" or おもしろいだった "was interesting" in modern standard Japanese. For further discussion of conjugation of these parts of speech, refer to Chapter 3, Section 2.

2.2 Agglutination

Japanese is an agglutinative language. Agglutination is a formation in which words can be divided into separate segments with separate grammatical functions, but function as a unified element of a sentence. Agglutination occurs mostly in conjugation of predicates. See the following agglutinating predicates in the brackets:

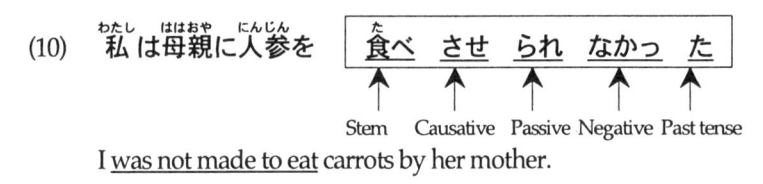

(10) 私は母親に人参を [食べ させ られ なかっ た]
　　　　　　　　　　　↑　　↑　　↑　　↑　　↑
　　　　　　　　　　Stem Causative Passive Negative Past tense
　　I <u>was not made to eat</u> carrots by her mother.

(11) 花子は国へ [帰り たく なかっ た です]
　　Hanako <u>did not want to go back</u> home.

(12) 明日、クラスへ [来 なくて も いい です]
　　It is all right if you don't come to class tomorrow.

(13) 毎日 本を [読ま なければ ならな かった]
　　I had to read books every day.

(14) 私はあなたにそんなことを [言って ほしく なかっ た]
　　I did not want you to say things like that.

Here are some more examples of complex predicates in which more than one semantic element is added to a simple predicate.

	Affirmative form	Negative form
want to read	読みたいです	読みたくありません
want you to buy	買ってほしいです	買ってほしくありません
have written	書いている	書いていない
was created	作られた	作られなかった
made him go	行かせた	行かせなかった
can walk	歩ける	歩けない
had (you) do dishes	お皿を洗ってもらった	お皿を洗ってもらわなかった

2.3 Topic-comment structure

Japanese is a so-called topic language, where any kind of element can be given as a topic and placed at the beginning of a sentence. The topic is marked by the particle は, and a comment regarding that topic follows. In the comment, the subject is marked by the particle が, unless it is contrasted. Typical interpretations of a given topic are "speaking of ~," "regarding ~," and so on. The following illustration is a visualization of the topic-comment structure using a sentence バンクーバーはさけがおいしい "speaking of Vancouver, salmon is tasty" as an example.

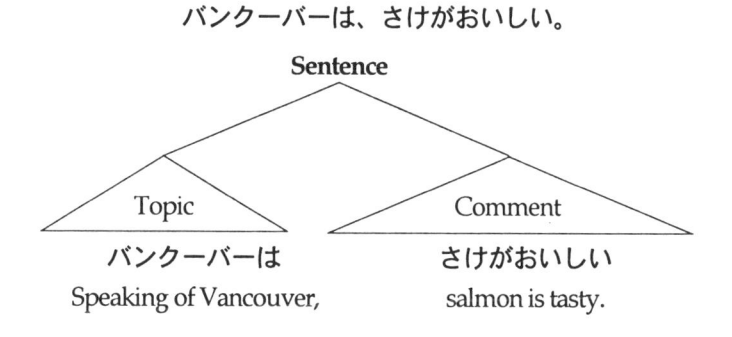

バンクーバーは、さけがおいしい。

Sentence

Topic	Comment
バンクーバーは	さけがおいしい
Speaking of Vancouver,	salmon is tasty.

In the above sentence, the topic バンクーバー "Vancouver" and subject さけ "salmon" in the comment co-exist. The function of these constituents is not identical. バンクーバー does not serve as the subject of the sentence in which おいしい is the predicate, since "Vancouver is tasty" does not make sense. The speaker is designating "Vancouver" as the topic and commenting that salmon caught in Vancouver are good. This is, however, not always the case; there are certainly cases where the topic and the subject are identical, as seen in examples (18) and (19). Let us look at some more examples:

(15) 天気は　　夏がいい
Speaking of weather, summer is good (I like summer).

(16) 日本語は　　弟が大学で学んだ
Speaking of Japanese,　my brother learned at a university.
(This sentence has a different meaning from that of "弟は大学で日本語を学んだ" where 弟 is given as the topic of the sentence.)

(17) 映画は　　アクション映画がおもしろい
Regarding movies, action movies are interesting.

The following are cases where the topic and subject are identical.

(18) 彼は　　(彼が)ハーバード大学の学生だ
Speaking of <u>him</u>, <u>he</u> is a student at Harvard University.

(19) 妹は　　(妹が)ピザが好きだ
Speaking of <u>my sister</u>, (<u>she</u>) likes pizza.

When a word functions as the topic and the subject of a sentence, you may not need to state the topic specifically. A sentence like "speaking of me, I am a student" can simply be stated "I am a student" in English.

2.4   Propositions vs. modality expressions

Japanese makes a syntactic and semantic distinction between propositions and modality expressions. A proposition is a statement of facts or the substance of a case expressed in a sentence. Modality expressions are constituents of a sentence that are used to indicate a speaker's opinion or psychological attitude toward a proposition. Unlike in English, propositions and modality expressions in Japanese are relatively easy to distinguish, as modality expressions usually follow the tense markers.

Proposition	Modality Expression
彼は日本へ行く	にちがいない
He goes to Japan;	it must be the case.

⇩

He must go to Japan.

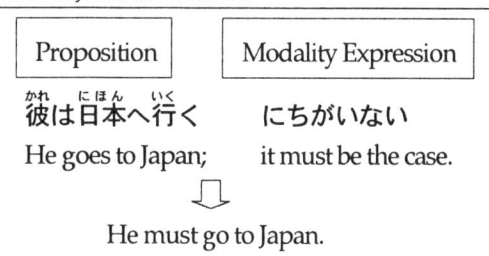

The English sentence "he must go to Japan" can be considered semantically ambiguous since "must" can carry two different meanings: a speaker's confidence in the truth of the proposition, and the notion of "obligation." In Japanese, there is no modal auxiliary that represents two different meanings.

True modal auxiliaries include そう "I hear, it appears to be," らしい "I hear, it seems like," よう/みたい "it looks like," はず "it must be," にちがいない "it must be," だろう "it probably is," かもしれない "it may be," のだ "it is that," わけ "it is the case that," and so forth. There are some combinations of these modal auxiliaries that may elongate a sentence, such as だろうと思う "I think it is probably the case that ~," and so forth. This writing style is one of the techniques used to express an author's opinion or attitude toward a proposition more implicitly, as writers often tend to avoid a strong-sounding, definite statement in Japanese. For detailed discussion on modality, refer to Chapter 19.

CHAPTER 3

Conjugation of Verbs, い Adjectives, and the Copula だ

As mentioned in Chapter 2, in Japanese, verbs and い adjectives conjugate,[1] but nouns and な adjectives do not. Nouns and な adjectives are followed by the copula だ, and this copula conjugates. Each part of speech and the copula conjugate for non-past/present (する), past (した), imperative (しろ), cohortative (しよう), continuative (し), gerundive (して), conditional (すれば), and other factors.

In learning Japanese as a second or foreign language, however, the first form introduced in textbooks is typically the verb formal form ending in ます and a noun with the copula in the formal form, です. This is attributed to the fact that learners of Japanese can immediately create simple single sentences on the first day of class using these parts of speech, such as 私はすしを食べます "I eat sushi" and 私は本田です "I am Honda." Then, learners acquire the structures to negate the sentence (私はすしを食べません "I do not eat sushi") and state the sentence in the past context (私はすしを食べました "I ate sushi" and 私はすしを食べませんでした "I did not eat sushi"). The same thing applies to the copula です following a noun. The conjugation of い adjectives is usually introduced shortly after the conjugation of these parts of speech.

---

[1] In language, grammatical conjugation is the creation of derived forms of a verb from the word root by regular alteration according to rules of grammar, called inflection. (For further information, please refer to *http://open-encyclopedia.com.*) Conjugation may be affected by person, gender, tense, voice, or other language-specific factors. For example, in English, the main verb of an English sentence conjugates according to the subject, as in "I walk" and "s/he walks." In Japanese, verbs do not conjugate based on these factors, but conjugate for tense (する "I do" and した "I did," negation (しない "I do not do" and しなかった "I did not do"), and aspect (している "I am doing/I have done.").

In this chapter, conjugation is introduced in a manner appropriate to learners of Japanese at the college level. Conjugation of verbs is first introduced along with the categories of verbs, followed by い adjectives. Then comes the copula だ with nouns and な adjectives.

1. Conjugation of Verbs
1.1 Verb categories

Before introducing verb conjugations, one important issue—the verb categories—needs to be discussed. When conjugating Japanese verbs, there are three categories to consider: consonant, vowel, and irregular.[2] As for irregular verbs, there are only two: します "to do" and 来ます "to come." Remember that the pronunciation of the irregular verbs changes depending on the form, such as する and した and 来る, 来ない and 来た, respectively. All other verbs belong to either the consonant verb (CV) category or the vowel verb (VV) category. There are some verbs whose stem ends in "i," but these are exceptions and are included among the vowel verbs. Although there are many exceptions, there is no rule to tell you which ~i-masu verb is an exception for learners of Japanese. Native speakers of Japanese intuitively know by forming the negative form—if it is i/e-nai, such as tab-e-nai (食べない), oshi-e-nai (教えない), and m-i-nai (見ない), ok-i-nai (起きない), then the verb is a vowel verb. If it is ~a-nai, such as ik-a-nai (行かない), then the verb is a consonant verb. However, in order to apply such rules, the ない form has to be acquired, so there is no easy way for learners to know.

---

[2] In different books, consonant and vowel verbs may also be referred to as う and る verbs or type I and type II verbs, respectively. The reason they are called consonant verbs and vowel verbs may become easy to understand when the conjugation of the verb is visualized in the following manner. (The conjugation patterns are basic ones for demonstration purposes.)

書く	"to write"	食べる	"to eat"
kak-u	"will write (plain)"	tabe-ru	"will eat (plain)"
kak-i-masu	"will write (formal)"	tabe-masu	"will eat (formal)"
kak-e-ba	"if you write"	tabe-reba	"if one eats"
kak-e	"write"	tabe-ro	"eat"
kak-oo	"let's write"	tabe-yoo	"let's eat"

The unchanged segment of the verb is called the stem. For example, the stem of 書く ends in the consonant "k," while the stem of 食べる ends in the vowel "e." This is why 書く is called a consonant verb, whereas 食べる is a vowel verb.

One recommendation is simply to memorize them as the exceptions are introduced. The figure below illustrates the verb categories.

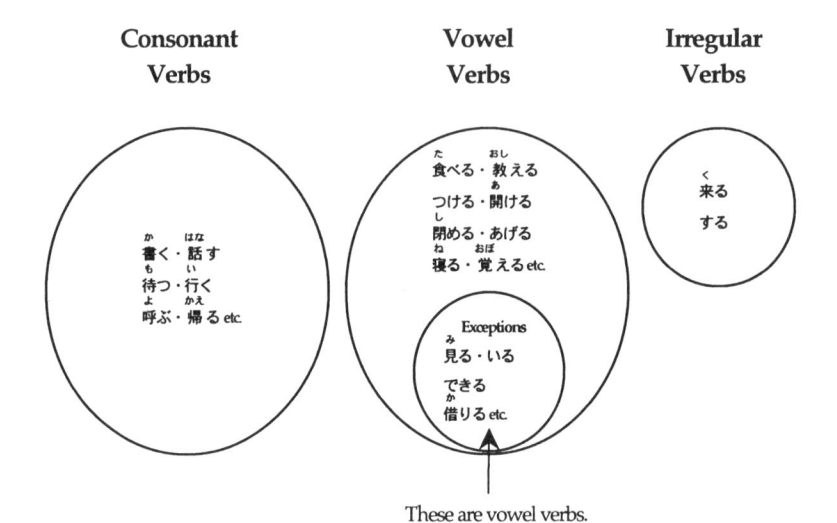

Consonant Verbs

書く・話す
待つ・行く
呼ぶ・帰る etc.

Vowel Verbs

食べる・教える
つける・開ける
閉める・あげる
寝る・覚える etc.

Exceptions
見る・いる
できる
借りる etc.

These are vowel verbs.

Irregular Verbs

来る
する

Examples of consonant verbs:

聞きます	kik-i-masu	"to ask/listen"
話します	hanash-i-masu	"to talk/speak"
立ちます	tach-i-masu	"to stand up"
死にます	shin-i-masu	"to die"
呼びます	yob-i-masu	"to call/invite"
読みます	yom-i-masu	"to read"
帰ります	kaer-i-masu	"to return"

Examples of vowel verbs:

食べます	tabe-masu	"to eat"
教えます	oshie-masu	"to teach"
寝ます	ne-masu	"to sleep"
見ます	mi-masu	"to see/look" (memorize)
借ります	kari-masu	"to borrow" (memorize)

In a simple sentence with a verb at the end, the verb is either in the plain or the formal form.[3] The English equivalents for these two forms are exactly the same. The plain form of "to eat" is 食べる, and the formal form is 食べます. The plain form is used in casual communication, such as when a speaker talks to his/her friends, family members, or someone with whom the speaker feels relaxed about being informal. On the other hand, the formal form is used in situations where the speaker needs to pay attention to the age difference, social status, and his/her degree of intimacy with the interlocutor. For example, one may utter, using the plain form, 今日、何する？ "What are you gonna do today?" to a friend, while 今日何をしますか "What are you going to do today?" to someone whom s/he has not yet registered as a friend, to a person who is older than the speaker, or to someone who is in higher status in terms of social rank. In the latter sentence, if it is addressed to someone who is older than the speaker or occupies a higher social rank, even honorific language may be employed (see Chapter 20). However, the ます form alone can carry a formal enough impression if uttered in a polite manner.

The plain and the formal forms of verbs conjugate in two tense forms, ます (non-past) and ました (past), each with its own affirmative and negative. To illustrate this concept, part of the chart introduced in Chapter 2 is repeated below.

	Non-past (imperfective)	Past (perfective)
Affirmative formal form	～ます	～ました
Affirmative plain form	Dictionary form	～た
Negative formal form	～ません	～ませんでした
Negative plain form	～ない	～なかった

The plain form of the formal ます is often called the dictionary form, since this is the form one needs to know to look up the Japanese verb in a dictionary. The た

---

[3] See Chapter 2, note 8, for examples of equivalent terminologies used in various textbooks. When a verb is used in a subordinate clause, it is usually in the plain form. Example: 映画を見る前に食事をしましょう "Before watching a movie, let's have a meal." In this sentence, the plain form is used in the subordinate clause with 前, but not the formal form. If the formal form ます were used, then it would indicate the end of the sentence.

form is the plain past affirmative counterpart to the formal ました. The form in ない is the plain counterpart to the non-past negative formal form ません, whereas なかった is the plain form of the past negative formal ませんでした. In the following sections, rules for deriving the dictionary form, the gerundive (て form), the past tense (た form), the negative (ない form), and the cohortative (おう form) are introduced.[4]

1.2   The dictionary form

The dictionary form, equivalent to the infinitive in English, is an informal alternative to the ます form and is used (a) in very informal situations where friends and family talk to each other or (b) in conjunction with other phrases.

	W	R	Y	M	H	N	T	S	K	
ん	わ	ら	や	ま	は	な	た	さ	か	あ
		り		み	ひ	に	ち	し	き	い
		る	ゆ	む	ふ	ぬ	つ	す	く	う
		れ		め	へ	ね	て	せ	け	え
	を	ろ	よ	も	ほ	の	と	そ	こ	お

→あ row→ない form
→い row→ます form (for CV & some VV)
→う row→**Dictionary form**
→え row→ます form (for VV)
→お row→おう form

1.2.1   Consonant verbs (CV)

In order to create the dictionary form, the "i" preceding ます is always replaced by a syllable from the "u" row of the above ひらがな chart.[5]

ます form		Dictionary form		
書きます	kak-**i**-masu	書く	kak-**u**	to write
話します	hanash-**i**-masu	話す	hanas-**u**	to talk
待ちます	mach-**i**-masu	待つ	mats-**u**	to wait
帰ります	kaer-**i**-masu	帰る	kaer-**u**	to go home

---

[4] Others, such as conditional forms, are introduced in the chapter dealing with conditionals (Chapter 25).
[5] The dictionary form may be introduced first in some textbooks, and learners may have to extrapolate the ます form from it. This may be done by changing the vowel in the stem from "*u*" to "*i*" and adding ます to it.

Change the following verbs into the dictionary form:

乗ります	( )	to ride
会います	( )	to meet
飲みます	( )	to drink
読みます	( )	to read
探します	( )	to search
呼びます	( )	to invite

1.2.2 Vowel verbs (VV)

For the dictionary form, just add る to the stem of the vowel verb.[6]

ます form		Dictionary form		
食べます	tabe-masu	食べる	tabe-ru	to eat
教えます	oshie-masu	教える	oshie-ru	to teach
つけます	tsuke-masu	つける	tsuke-ru	to turn on
開けます	ake-masu	開ける	ake-ru	to open
あげます	age-masu	あげる	age-ru	to give
借ります	kari-masu	借りる	kari-ru	to borrow
起きます	oki-masu	起きる	oki-ru	to wake/get up
見ます	mi-masu	見る	mi-ru	to see/look

1.2.3 Irregular verbs

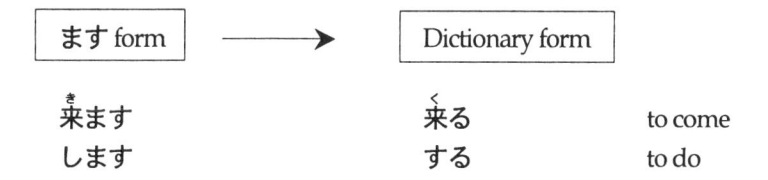

ます form	Dictionary form	
来ます	来る	to come
します	する	to do

1.3 The て form

The て form itself does not have any meaning or tense, but attaches a verb to some constituent following the て form of that verb; together, the て form of the

---

[6] From the dictionary form to the formal form, る is replaced by ます.

verb preceding the constituent creates meaning according to the verb and constituent. For example, a request "please do ~" is formed by attaching the constituent ください to the て form of a verb. The next section describes rules of formation of the て form.

1.3.1 Consonant verbs

First, look at the dictionary form. If the dictionary form of a verb ends in either う、つ、or る、these syllables become って; the syllables ぬ、む、or ぶ、become んで; す becomes して; the syllable く turns into いて; and ぐ turns into いで. The verb 行きます offers the only exception: its て form is 行って, not 行きて.[7]

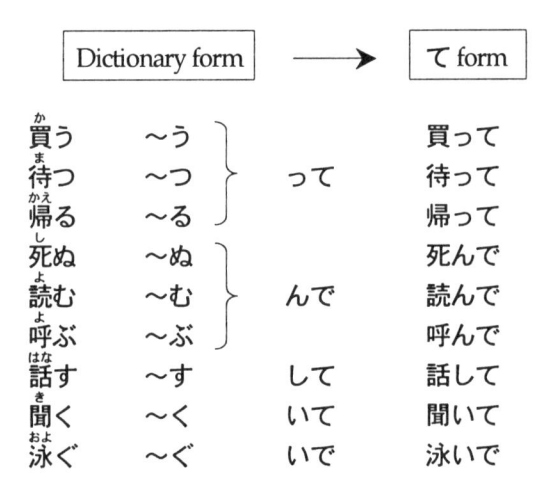

Dictionary form			て form
買う	～う		買って
待つ	～つ	って	待って
帰る	～る		帰って
死ぬ	～ぬ		死んで
読む	～む	んで	読んで
呼ぶ	～ぶ		呼んで
話す	～す	して	話して
聞く	～く	いて	聞いて
泳ぐ	～ぐ	いで	泳いで

Exception: 行く → 行って

1.3.2 Vowel verbs

For the て form of vowel verbs, simply add て to the stem form:

食べます	食べて
教えます	教えて
つけます	つけて

---

[7] The song "Santa Claus Is Coming to Town" can be sung with the て form lyrics.♪♪うつる　って、ぬむぶ　んで、す　して、く　いて、ぐ　いで、する　して、くる　きて、いく　いって♪♪

開<ruby>あ</ruby>けます	開けて
閉<ruby>し</ruby>めます	閉めて
見<ruby>み</ruby>ます	見て
います	いて
借<ruby>か</ruby>ります	借りて
起<ruby>お</ruby>きます	起きて
できます	できて

1.3.3 Irregular verbs

来<ruby>き</ruby>ます	来て
します	して

1.4 The た form

The た form, which is the plain equivalent of ～ました, is based on the て form. Simply change て to た.

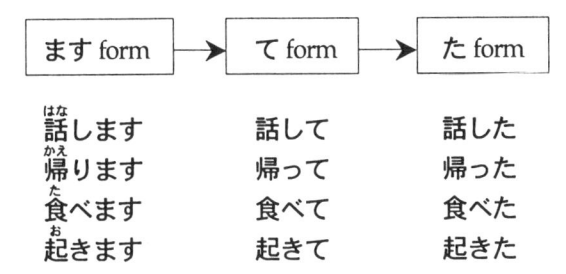

ます form → て form → た form

話<ruby>はな</ruby>します	話して	話した
帰<ruby>かえ</ruby>ります	帰って	帰った
食<ruby>た</ruby>べます	食べて	食べた
起<ruby>お</ruby>きます	起きて	起きた

1.5 The ない form

The ない form is the plain form of ません. Note that the ない form is morphologically an い adjective. Accordingly, the past tense of ない is なかった, which is the plain form of ませんでした.

1.5.1 Consonant verbs

For consonant verbs, the vowel "i" in the stem form turns into "a," and ない is attached.[8]

---

[8] If created from the dictionary form, "*u*" in the stem turns into "a," as in 書く "kak-u," which becomes 書かない "kak-a-nai."

書きません	kak-i-masen	書かない	kak-a-nai
話しません	hanash-i-masen	話さない	hanas-a-nai
待ちません	mach-i-masen	待たない	mat-a-nai
呼びません	yob-i-masen	呼ばない	yob-a-nai
読みません	yom-i-masen	読まない	yom-a-nai
帰りません	kaer-i-masen	帰らない	kaer-a-nai

For consonant verbs ending in う, such as 買う、会う、and 言う, う becomes わ and ない follows, as shown in the following.

買う	kau	kaWanai	買わない
会う	au	aWanai	会わない
言う	iu	iWanai	言わない

1.5.2 Vowel verbs
Simply add ない to the stem to form the negatives.

食べません	食べない
教えません	教えない
あげません	あげない
見ません	見ない
いません	いない
借りません	借りない

1.5.3 Irregular verbs

来ません	来ない
しません	しない

1.6 The おう form
1.6.1 Consonant verbs

The おう form is created by changing the "u" of the dictionary form (from the う row, as in kak-u, 書く) to "o" as in the お row (as in kak-o, 書こ) and adding う (to yield kak-o-o, 書こう).

話す	hanas-u	話そう	hanas-o-o

呼ぶ	yob-u	呼ぼう	yob-oo
読む	yom-u	読もう	yom-oo
帰る	kar-u	帰ろう	kaer-oo

1.6.2 Vowel verbs
Drop る from the dictionary form of a vowel verb and add よう.

つける	tsuke-ru	つけよう	tsuke-yoo
あげる	age-ru	あげよう	age-yoo
見る	mi-ru	見よう	mi-yoo
いる	i-ru	いよう	i-yoo
借りる	kari-ru	借りよう	kari-yoo
起きる	oki-ru	起きよう	oki-yoo

1.6.3 Irregular verbs
| 来る | | 来よう | |
| する | | しよう | |

2. Conjugation of い Adjectives

Conjugation of い adjectives is not as complicated as that of verbs. The stem of い adjectives is the part preceding い, as in おもしろ(い) "interesting" and むずかし(い) "difficult." Thus, おもしろ and むずかし are the stems of these い adjectives, and い changes with the different forms. First observe some of the conjugation patterns to see how the stem alters. The い adjective たかい "expensive" serves as a regular example.

Non-past	たか–い	taka-i	"is expensive"
Past	たか–かった	taka-kat-ta	"was expensive"
Gerundive	たか–くて	taka-kute	"is expensive and"
Conditional	たか–け–れば	taka-ke-reba	"if it is expensive"
Negative	たか–く–ない	taka-ku-nai	"is not expensive"

Now observe the following chart, which shows the formal and plain forms of い adjectives, taking たかい as an example.

	Non-past	Past
Affirmative formal	たかいです	たかかったです
Affirmative plain	たかい	たかかった
Negative formal	たかくありません	たかくありませんでした
Negative plain	たかくない	たかくなかった

Note that the plain form of たかくありません is たかくない, which is morphologically an い adjective (as are most words that end in い) in the plain form. Therefore, たかくない can invite the copula です to alter its formality. Thus, たかくありません and たかくないです are at the same formal level, and so are たかくありませんでした and たかくなかったです. Which one to use depends on individual preference, but たかくありませんでした may sound slightly more formal and polite.

In the negative of the plain and formal forms, the い in たかい turns into く. This form in fact functions as an adverb when an い adjective modifies a verb and illustrates one of the differences between い adjectives and な adjectives: な adjectives must take に when they modify a verb, as in きれいに書く "write neatly." The following are some examples:

(1) 朝早く起きましょう。　　　"Let's get up early in the morning."
(2) うちの犬はよく食べます。　　"My dog eats well."
(3) 屋根を赤く塗りました。　　　"I painted the roof in red."

3. Conjugation of the Copula だ

Although nouns and な adjectives do not conjugate, the copula だ that follows the plain form of な adjectives and nouns does. Note that です, the formal form of だ, can follow an い adjective, such as たかいです "is expensive," but the plain form, だ, cannot. たかいだ is not accepted in standard Japanese. Neither is たかかっただ or たかくなかっただ. This feature is one of the differences between い adjectives and な adjectives.

The Japanese copula has many forms, among them だ, な, で, and です. だ and です are used to form a predicate by following a noun or a な adjective, while な and で are used in sentences to modify or link another constituent. These forms of the Japanese copula are never used by themselves, but are completely dependent. If someone asks saying 本田さんは先生ですか "Is Mr. Honda a teacher?" one always has to include the whole predicate in the answer: はい、先生です. はい、です is never considered an appropriate response. First, observe some of the conjugation patterns of the plain form of the copula だ. The noun 先生 "teacher" is included in parentheses to create a more realistic example.

Non-past	(先生)だ	"is a teacher"
Past	(先生)だった	"was a teacher"
Gerundive	(先生)で	"is a teacher and"
Conditional	(先生)で－あれば/な－らば	"if one is a teacher"
Negative	(先生)では－ない/じゃ－ない	"is not a teacher"

ではない is a polite/formal equivalent of じゃない and is often used on rather formal occasions, for example, in a public speech. In daily conversation, じゃない is the principal negative form of だ. Now observe the following chart, which shows the formal and the plain forms of nouns and な adjectives, using the な adjective 元気 "healthy/cheerful" as an example:

	Non-past	Past
Affirmative formal	元気です	元気でした
Affirmative plain	元気だ	元気だった
Negative formal	元気じゃありません	元気じゃありませんでした
Negative plain	元気じゃない	元気じゃなかった

When the plain form of a noun and a な adjective are used to form a question sentence, だ has to be deleted. In a casual situation, sentences such as 本田さんは元気か "Is Mr. Honda doing well?" or 本田さんは先生か "Is Mr. Honda a teacher?" may be heard (producing a somewhat masculine sound), but 本田さんは元気だか or 本田さんは先生だか does not occur in standard Japanese.

The differences between nouns and な adjectives are (a) that な adjectives are not genuinely nouns and therefore cannot be used as subjects and objects in sentences, and (b) that な adjectives can modify a verb, while nouns cannot. Nouns can modify another noun, but not a verb, while な adjectives can modify both nouns and verbs, as the following examples demonstrate.

a. 英語 の 本　　　　noun + noun　　　　"an English book"
b. 親切 な 人　　　　な adjective + noun　　"a kind person"
c. 親切 に 振舞う　　な adjective + verb　　"behave kindly"

Compare the usage of い adjectives:
d. 速い ∅ 車　　　　い adjective + noun　　"fast car"
e. 速く 走る　　　　い adjective + verb　　"run fast"

The above examples demonstrate that the attributes of な adjectives and nouns are not the same—な adjectives share some features that nouns and い adjectives have. Upon learning new vocabulary, learners should also know the type of the part of speech so that creating and modifying a simple sentence are done appropriately.

Sample exercise

Convert the following English sentences into Japanese.

(1) I am not a student.
(2) This book is not new.
(3) This book was not expensive last year, but it is expensive now.
(4) Mr. Honda was a schoolteacher.
(5) Mr. Toyota wears the same shirt every day.
(6) I am going to wear this shirt today.
(7) Ms. Suzuki will not come.
(8) Ms. Suzuki usually does not come to the meeting.
(9) My room was not clean yesterday, but it is clean now.
(10) This dictionary is not very handy (convenient).
(11) I do not watch TV, but I see movies every weekend.
(12) Mr. Toyota went to school yesterday, but I did not.
(13) The weather was not very good yesterday, but it is good today.
(14) Ms. Matsuda used to be famous.
(15) I was busy last week, but this week I have free time.

CHAPTER 4

Particles

Particles play a significant role in language use in that they specify the function of the noun or noun phrase that they follow. In this sense, they share some of the functions of English prepositions such as "at," "to," "on," "in," and "with." For example, "eat at Hiro" and "eat with Hiro," although both contain the words "eat" and "Hiro, " have very different meanings. The "at" in "eat *at* Hiro" identifies Hiro as a location where the eating activity takes place, while the "with" in "eat *with* Hiro" identifies "Hiro" as a person with whom the speaker carries out the eating activity. Thus, changing the preposition in English can alter the meaning of the entire sentence.

The same concept is true of Japanese particles. The crucial difference is that the particles are post-positioned to a noun or a noun phrase in Japanese. There are many particles; some consist of just a simple particle, such as は, が, を, に, で, と, and も; others consist of more than one particle, such as から, まで, and までに. Some of them have a clear English equivalent, such as と "with," に "to, at," and で "at, by"; others have no English equivalent, such as は, が, and を.

Observe the following sample sentence that includes some of the representative particles:

昨日 (は) 鈴木さん (が) レストラン (で) すし (を) 食べました。

Speaking of yesterday, Ms. Suzuki ate sushi at a restaurant.

In the sentence above, the particle は identifies 昨日 as the topic of the sentence; similarly, が identifies 鈴木さん as the subject, で marks レストラン as the location where the activity takes place, and を denotes すし as the object she ate.

Changing even one particle to a different particle alters the meaning of the entire sentence. For example, if で and を are switched (レストランをすしで食べました), the sentence no longer makes sense, implying that "Ms. Suzuki ate a restaurant using sushi."

The following sections present explanations of each particle in terms of its fundamental use.

1. は

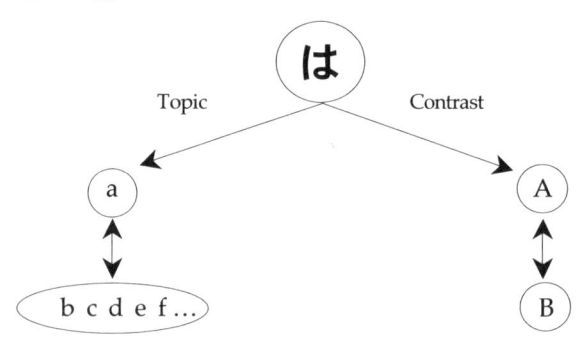

```
              は
         Topic   Contrast
          ↙         ↘
         a           A
         ↕           ↕
      b c d e f...   B
```

The inherent nature of はis to *single out* the noun phrase marked by は from other sets of elements for discussion. Other elements can be either all possible candidates for a subject of conversation (topic), or a particular set of elements that are divergently compared to the はmarked noun in discourse (contrast). The meaning of はis usually identifiable from the content and the environment of the conversation in which the speaker and the listener are engaged.

> 1. 「は」 as a topic marker: "speaking of X."
> 2. 「は」 for contrast: "I eat X, with the implication that I do not eat Y, for example)."

1.1　「は」 as a topic marker

The use of は can turn any noun or noun phrase into the topic of a sentence. It focuses attention on what follows.

1.1.1 What is "topic"?

Topic as a concept is the entity, whether animate or inanimate, that provides the point of departure for conversation in certain contexts. In a sentence, the topic is a noun phrase drawn from the body of the sentence and placed at its beginning to draw the attention of the individuals who are engaged in the communication.

Also, the topic must be something that has previously been mentioned in the flow of conversation or is already known/registered in an individual's mind. Therefore, the topic is shared knowledge and is often considered "old information." In 田中さんは学生です "Speaking of Ms. Tanaka, she is a student," for example, 田中さん is given as the topic of conversation and is shared, old information that the speaker and the listener have already registered in their minds. What the listener would like to hear is then more information about 田中さん, which, in this case, is 学生です.

In Japanese conversation, unlike in English, one may mention a noun phrase about which one is going to talk (as a topic) at the beginning of the sentence, then give a comment on the topic. This type of structure for conveying information is the so-called topic-comment structure. Other languages, such as Korean and Chinese, also exhibit this structure.

For example, in 私は昨日すしを食べました "Speaking of me, I ate sushi yesterday" 私 "I" is presented as the topic of discussion, and 昨日すしを食べました as the comment on the topic. The implication is that "I am going to tell you about *me*; I ate sushi yesterday." However, if the speaker is going to talk about sushi, then すし will be singled out for discussion, as in すしは、昨日食べました "Speaking of sushi, (I) ate (it) yesterday." Thus, in the course of conversation, the speaker structurally promotes "sushi" by bringing it to the beginning of the sentence in order to signal to the listener that the speaker is going to tell the listener about "sushi."

The following is a visualization of the topic-comment structure for both 私は昨日すしを食べました "Speaking of me, I ate sushi yesterday" and すしは、昨日食べました "Speaking of sushi, (I) ate (it) yesterday" as examples.

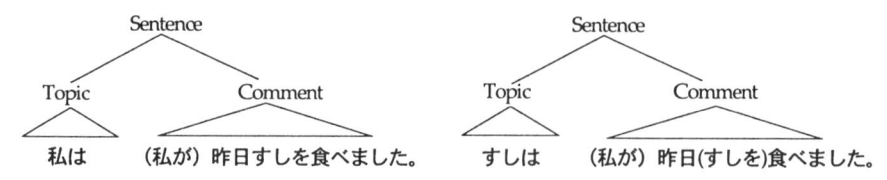

```
        Sentence                              Sentence
       /        \                            /        \
    Topic     Comment                    Topic      Comment
    /\         /\                         /\          /\
  私は    (私が) 昨日すしを食べました。    すしは    (私が) 昨日(すしを)食べました。
```

As one may see immediately from the sentences in the diagrams above, while the topics of the sentence are "I" and "sushi," the subject of the sentence is "I" for both sentences. This difference demonstrates that the topic does not always coincide with the subject of the sentence. The subject refers to a noun phrase that performs an action or is in a state expressed by the predicate. In 私は(私が)昨日すしを食べました "Speaking of me, (I) ate sushi yesterday," "I" is the person who performed the eating activity. "I" is given as the topic as well as the subject of the sentence. In this case, the topic and the subject are identical.[1]

On the other hand, in すしは、昨日食べました "Speaking of sushi, (I) ate (it) yesterday," while "sushi" is given as the topic, "I" is the subject of the sentence, so that the topic and the subject are not identical. If one identifies "sushi" as the subject, s/he is saying that "sushi ate (something)"!

Let us now observe how nouns within a sentence can be identified as a topic, using a sample sentence with five noun phrases and a verb. Note that は can replace the particles を and が (e.g., すしを can become すしは), but it cannot replace other particles, such as に、で、へ、から、and so on. は is added to those particles (e.g., ここで becomes ここでは).[2]

---

[1] There are many cases where the topic and subject are identical entities. For example, in the sentence 私は学生です (Speaking of me, I am a student = I am a student), 私 is presented as a topic and, at the same time, functions as the subject of the sentence. If the topic and the subject are identical entities, as in this sentence, then it is not necessary to provide "speaking of ~" in the English translation.

[2] For example, 鈴木さんは英語を教えます and 鈴木さんには英語を教えます express two different meanings. The former sentence means "Ms. Suzuki teaches (someone) English," whereas the latter sentence means "Speaking of Ms. Suzuki, someone teaches her English." In addition, も is a thematic particle, and is on par with は. は does not replace も because は and も are mutually exclusive.

<ruby>今日<rt>きょう</rt></ruby> <ruby>鈴木<rt>すずき</rt></ruby>さんが <ruby>家<rt>うち</rt></ruby>で <ruby>弟<rt>おとうと</rt></ruby>に <ruby>英語<rt>えいご</rt></ruby>を <ruby>教<rt>おし</rt></ruby>えます。
  1   2   3   4   5   verb

Mr. Suzuki will teach my brother English at our house today.

In the following examples, the underlined noun phrase is the one singled out for discussion and given as a topic:

(1) <u>今日は</u> 鈴木さんが 家で 弟に 英語を 教えます。
Speaking of today, Mr. Suzuki will teach my brother English at our house.

(2) <u>鈴木さんは</u> 今日（鈴木さんが）家で 弟に 英語を 教えます。
Speaking of Mr. Suzuki, (he) will teach my brother English at our house today.

(3) <u>家では</u> 今日 鈴木さんが 弟に 英語を 教えます。
Speaking of at our house, Mr. Suzuki will teach my brother English (there) today.

(4) <u>弟には</u> 今日 鈴木さんが 家で 英語を 教えます。
Speaking of to my brother, Mr. Suzuki will teach (him) English at our house today.

(5) <u>英語は</u> 今日 鈴木さんが 家で 弟に 教えます。
Speaking of English, Mr. Suzuki will teach (it) to my brother at our house today.

鈴木さん is the subject of all five sentences above (since 鈴木さん is the performer of the predicate 教えます), and the underlined noun phrase is not, except in sentence (2), where the topic and the subject are identical. Based on this basic function, は is usually called a topic marker and が a subject marker. (Refer to section 2 for a discussion of が.)

If the topic and the subject in a sentence are not identical, but the relationship between the two is such that the subject belongs to and/or is dependent upon the topic (in a possessive relationship), then the sentence can be restated. In such cases, the X は Y が construction can become the X の Y が construction. Observe the following examples:

(6) 松田さんは目がきれいです。 → 松田さんの目はきれいです。
Speaking of Ms. Matsuda, her eyes are pretty.
= Ms. Matsuda's eyes are pretty.

(7) あの店はすしがおいしいです。 → あの店のすしはおいしいです。
Speaking of that restaurant, the sushi is delicious.
= That restaurant's sushi is good.

(8) この本は説明がだめです。 → この本の説明はだめです。
Speaking of this book, the explanations are not good.
= The explanations in this book are not good.

The subjects of sentences (6) through (8), 目, すし, and 説明, all belong to 松田, あの店, and この本, respectively, and the sentences can be reframed with 松田さんの目, あの店のすし, and この本の説明 using the possessive marker の without changing the basic meaning of the sentence. However, if the relationship of the given topic and subject of the sentence is not a possessive relationship, then restating the sentence using the possessive particle の does not work. For example, in the sentence バンクーバーは、雨がたくさん降る "Speaking of Vancouver, it rains a lot there," the subject "rain" does not belong to or depend on the topic "Vancouver"; therefore, this sentence does not make sense or expresses a different meaning if it is restated as バンクーバーの雨がたくさん降る "Vancouver's rain falls a lot."

Another important point regarding the use of は as a topic marker is that since は signals the listener about the emphasis of the speaker's upcoming remark, the listener focuses his/her attention to what follows は. Therefore, when a predicate consisting of an interrogative noun, such as 何ですか "what is it?" いつですか "when is it?" or だれですか "who is it?" constitutes a sentence, only は is appropriate to mark the noun preceding the interrogative. This noun serves as the topic (as exemplified in それは in sentence [9], below). The particle が is never used in this type of construction.

(9) それは何ですか。
Speaking of the thing near you, what is it?
(これは)雑誌です
This is a magazine.

(10) 本田さんの家(うち)はどこですか。

Speaking of Mr. Honda's house, where is it?

(本田さんの家は)東京(とうきょう)です。

(His house) is (in) Tokyo.

(11) あの人(ひと)はだれですか。

Speaking of that person over there, who is she?

(あれは)私(わたし)の妹(いもうと)です。

(The person over there) is my sister.

(12) 今日(きょう)は何曜日(なんようび)ですか。

Speaking of today, what day is it?

(今日は)月曜日(げつ)です。

(Today) is Monday.

1.2 「は」 as a contrast marker

In contrasting, two groups of entities are compared in order to identify their dissimilarities. The groups of entities are usually in opposition in the speaker's mind.

A contrasted meaning in language may be stated, or is implied, depending on the speaker's environment. Whether は is used as a topic marker or as a contrastive marker depends on the context surrounding the speaker, although it is normally the case that the first は marked noun phrase in a sentence is given as a topic,[3] and the second is given as a contrasted element (as are the third, fourth, and so on if given).

For example, when the contrasted element is stated, the sentence may be one like スミスさんはお茶(ちゃ)は飲(の)みますが、コーヒーは飲みません "Mr. Smith drinks tea, but does not drink coffee." In this sentence, お茶 is contrasted with コーヒー, as signified by the use of が "but" at the end of the first sentence and the use of the negative form of the verb "to drink." In this case, even if the second half of the sentence were not made explicit, the use of が would signify that Mr. Smith

---

[3] Under certain circumstances in daily communication, there are obviously cases where the first は implies a contrasted meaning. For example, the use of the first は in スミスさんは、お茶は飲みます can imply "Mr. Smith, but not Mr. Johnson, for example" depending on context. The whole sentence, then, can express that "Mr. Smith (not Mr. Johnson) drinks tea (not coffee)."

does not drink something else, though what the "something else" is that he does not drink would not be completely clear. Due to this ability of contrastive は to imply opposition, in daily conversation は is often used to convey the intended contrast without actually completing the sentence.

(13) a. 私はのりが好きです。
I like seaweed.
b. 私はのりは好きですが・・・。
I like seaweed (implies that I don't like natto, for example).

(14) a. 母はすしを食べました。
My mother ate sushi.
b. 母はすしは食べました。
My mother ate sushi (implies that she did not eat eel, for example).

(15) a. 彼は英語を話します。
He speaks English.
b. 彼は英語は話します。
He speaks English (implies that he does not speak Spanish, for example).

In sentence (13b), for example, the implied meaning is what the speaker actually intends/wants to convey. By marking "seaweed" with は in stating that the speaker likes seaweed, s/he tries to hint as to the real intention, in this case, that the speaker does not like something else that may be under discussion. In daily conversation, one may often hear a sentence like 明日ですか、明日は・・・ "Tomorrow? Tomorrow is. ..." The use of は here is intended to let the listener know that tomorrow is not quite convenient for the speaker, without saying exactly that. Thus, the use of は can be a practical communication device.

There are also cases where は appears multiple times in a sentence. In such cases as well, the first は normally indicates the topic and the rest of the occurrences of は indicate a contrast, either explicit or implicit. For example, the interpretation of the sentence 私は会社ではコーヒーは飲みます is most likely "Speaking of me, I drink coffee (but not tea) at work (but not at home)." In this sentence, the items being contrasted are not "work" and "coffee." As indicated in the phrase in parentheses, "work" is contrasted with other places such as home, and "coffee" is contrasted with other beverages such as tea. Therefore, if the contrasted elements were to be explicitly stated, the sentence might look like: 私(わたし)は家(うち)ではなく会社(かいしゃ)で、お茶(ちゃ)ではなくコーヒーを飲(の)みます "I drink coffee, not tea, at work, not home."

In addition, because of its contrastive function, は is often used when the statement is negative.[4]

(16)　(私は)家にはねこ<u>は</u>いません。
　　　I do not own cats (but may own dogs).
(17)　(私は)中国語(ちゅうごくご)<u>は</u>わかりません。
　　　I do not understand Chinese (but may understand other languages).
(18)　(私は)お茶(ちゃ)<u>は</u>飲みませんでした。
　　　I did not drink tea (but may have drunk coffee).
(19)　ここには電話(でんわ)<u>は</u>ありません。
　　　There is no phone here (but something else may available).

As is the case for the topic marker は, the contrastive は can replace the particles を and が, but cannot replace other particles, such as に, で, へ, から, and so on; rather, は is added after those particles.

(20)　(私は)てんぷら<u>は</u>食(た)べますが、[5] すし<u>は</u>食べません。
　　　(I) eat tempura, but (I) don't eat sushi.

---

[4] This is due to the idea that negative sentences generally occur where the corresponding affirmative has been mentioned or contemplated, or when the speaker believes that the interlocutor tends toward the affirmative. Negative statements cannot be effective without reference to corresponding affirmative statements. A negative predicate is usually used when a speaker uses some "understood" fact(s) to obliquely convey information more obviously expressed by an affirmative form of the statement. If one does not possess the information expressed by the affirmative form, the negative form cannot play its role. In this sense, negative statements are contrastive in nature to affirmative statements.

[5] If no contrastive meaning were involved, then the sentence would be 私はてんぷらを食べます "I eat tempura" with the object marker を.

(21) 電話はオフィスにはありますが、教室にはありません。

Speaking of a phone, there is one in the office but none in the classroom.

(22) (私は)図書館では勉強しますが、家ではしません。

I study at the library, but I do not study at home.

(23) (私は)大阪へは行きますが、東京へは行きません。

(I) will go to Osaka, but (I) won't go to Tokyo.

2. が

> 1. 「が」as a **subject** marker for new information
>   a. used to mark the subject in a sentence of neutral description[6]
>   b. used to mark the subject as exhaustive-listing
> 2. 「が」as an **object** marker
>   When a predicate is stative[7]-transitive, the function of the が marked noun is an object.

2.1　「が」as a subject marker for new information

The primary function of が is to mark a noun or a noun phrase as the subject of a sentence and to present the が marked noun as a new piece of information.

2.1.1　What is a subject?

In language/linguistics, "subject" refers to a major constituent of a sentence or clause structure, usually associated with the performer of an action, as in "The cat caught a fish," or with a state expressed by the predicate, as in "The cat is fat."

---

[6] The terms "neutral description" and "exhaustive listing" are from Kuno (1973). The concepts employed here are also based on Kuno's premise presented in the same book.

[7] The term "stative" here is used to refer to states of affairs, rather than action. It offers a concept of static that is the opposite of dynamic. A static state (that is said to express stativity) continues unless some kind of outside force is added to change the state. Stative predicates include verbs such as いる, できる, わかる, い adjectives (including negative forms of all parts of speech followed by ない), な adjectives, and nouns.

In order to find the subject of a single sentence in Japanese, one needs to observe the predicate (which comes at the end of the sentence in SOV languages) and see who/what performs the action described by the predicate or what is described by the predicate. Observe the following topic-comment sentences.

(1) 秋は魚がおいしいです。
    Speaking of autumn, <u>fish</u> is tasty.
(2) その魚は私が食べました。
    Speaking of that fish, <u>I</u> ate (it).

In sentence (1), the subject of the sentence is found in the comment: what tastes good is fish, not autumn. "Autumn" is presented as the topic of the sentence and is shared information; it does not serve as the subject. The same observation is true of sentence (2). The person who ate is I, not the fish. In neither case is the topic identical with the subject, and there is a subject for each predicate.

2.1.2 「が」for neutral description

While は can present any noun as a topic of a sentence, as may be seen in examples (1) through (5) in the は section, が's *primary* function is to present a noun or noun phrase as the subject of a sentence (except for the cases where the predicate is stative-transitive, as discussed in section 2.2. It is always associated with the predicate of a sentence.

Some predicates that let us envision the existence of an entity, a state coming into being, or a situation approaching closer to the speaker usually coincide with a subject marked by が (unless the subject is topicalized or contrasted). These predicates are most often used to present *a neutral description[8] of actions or temporary states,* and the sentence is considered to be introducing a new piece of information. The following are some examples:

(3) あそこに銀行があります。
    There is a bank over there.

---

[8] "Neutral description" here means that the sentence does not have any particular reference to prior discourse.

(4) 部屋にねずみみたいな犬がいます。
There is a dog that looks like a rat in the room.

(5) 帰国の日が近づきました。
The day I would return to my country draws near.

(6) アメリカの大統領が日本に来ます。
The president of the United States will come to Japan.

(7) 雨が降ります。
Rain is going to fall.

(8) ドアが閉まります。
The door will close./The door closes.

Sentences (3) through (8), concerned with neutral description, are usually uttered in situations where the whole sentence is presented as a new piece of information that has not previously been registered in discourse. The following examples in a brief dialogue should clarify the use of these sentences.

(9) A: あの、図書館へ行きたいんですが・・・。
Excuse me, I would like to go to the library but… (would you tell me how to get there?)
B: ほら、あそこに銀行がありますね。あの銀行の角を左に曲がるとすぐですよ。
Look, there is a bank over there, right? If you turn left at the corner of the bank, the library is right there.

(10) A: あれ、部屋にねずみみたいな犬がいますよ。
Look, there is a dog that looks like a rat in the room.
B: ああ、あの犬はジョンソン先生のチワワですよ。
Ah, that's Professor Johnson's chihuahua.

(11) A: 帰国の日が近づきました。もうすぐお別れですね・・・。
The day I return to my country draws near. I have to say good-bye shortly.
B: え!そうなんですか・・・。それは知りませんでした。いつ帰るんですか。
Is that right! I did not know that. When are you going back?

(12) A: 来週、アメリカの大統領が日本に来ますよ。
The president of the United States is coming to Japan next week, you know.

B: そうなんですか。どこに泊まるんでしょうね。
Is that so? I wonder where the president is going to stay.

(13) A: 明日の天気はどうでしょう。
How will the weather be tomorrow, do you know?

B: 明日は雨が降りますよ。
It's going to rain tomorrow.

A: そうですか。いやですねえ。
Is that so? How disgusting.

(14) At a platform of a train station, there is an announcement saying:
ドアが閉まります。お足下に御注意ください。
The door will close. Please watch your steps.

Sentences in examples (3) through (8) are embedded in the short conversation given in (9) through (14). が is used to mark the subject of the sentence, and the whole sentence is presented as a new piece of information in the conversation.

However, the subject of the sentence can also be an interrogative noun, such as 何 "what" and 誰 "who," as in 部屋に何がいますか "What is in the room?" and 日本に誰が来ますか "Who is coming to Japan?"[9] The answers, then, may be (部屋に) ねずみみたいな犬がいます "There is a dog like a rat (in the room)" and アメリカの大統領が(日本に)来ます "The U.S. president is coming (to Japan)," respectively. These answers are exactly the same as the ones used in examples (10) and (11), although those examples did not imply any indication of a question previously asked, but simply present new information.

When answering the question 誰が日本に来ますか "Who is coming to Japan?" only アメリカの大統領 "The president of the United States" is given as a new piece of information; 来ます "is coming" is a repeated part of the question

---

[9] は never follows a question word that is in the position of a subject in normal situations. For example, the equivalent of "Who opened the door?" is 誰がドアを開けましたか, and not 誰はドアをあけましたか, since は puts a focus on what follows. The question focuses on the question word 誰 and contradicts the function of は.

sentence. The speaker knows that someone is coming to Japan, but does not know who. Such providing of complete information is called "exhaustive-listing" (a complete list of information) in this textbook, following the term introduced by Kuno (1973).

The discussion above demonstrates that the interpretation of the subject with が can be either neutral description or exhaustive-listing. When a predicate represents an action, existence (not state) or a temporary state, the sentence can be interpreted as either a neutral description or an exhaustive-listing.[10]

On the other hand, if the predicate is a static, stable state (described by a noun, an い adjective, a な adjective, or a stative predicate), the subject with が receives only the exhaustive-listing interpretation. For example: あの人がカナダ人です "It is that person over there who is a Canadian"; さけがおいしいです "It is salmon that is delicious"; この辞書が便利です "It is this dictionary that is handy"; and たろうがテニスができます "It is Taro who can play tennis." This idea is discussed below.

2.1.3 「が」 for exhaustive-listing: It is X that ~

"Exhaustive-listing" here means listing a complete set of entities that serves as an answer to a question sentence. For example, when the question "Who is a student?" is asked, the answer may be "Tom is a student" or "Tom, Lisa, and David are students." Either model answer is given as one that includes the complete set of people who are students. In addition, "Tom" and "Tom, Lisa, and Tim" are marked by が in Japanese, as in トムが学生です and トムとリサとティムが学生です, respectively. When the predicate describes a state, the sentence including the が marked subject is susceptible only of the exhaustive-listing interpretation.

In spoken English, the speaker may put stress on the answer, but in writing or without context, it is impossible to distinguish clearly between the two Japanese equivalents of "Tom is a student," トムが学生です or トムは学生です. That is, the difference in が (new information) and は (old information) cannot be differentiated without a clear context. To emphasize that the information is new, the closest English equivalent for exhaustive-listing is "It is X that/who. ..." For example, "It is Tom who is a student" allows us to imagine that a question has

---

[10] This discussion is found in Kuno (1973, 60).

been asked, to identify which person in a group of people is a student. "Tom," in this case, is presented as new information that corresponds to a question asked with "who."

Below are other examples that may distinguish the notions of neutral description and exhaustive-listing, both of which are considered to present a new piece of information, and both of which include a が marked subject.

(15) サルが木から落ちた。
A monkey fell from the tree./It is a monkey that fell from the tree. (neutral or exhaustive)

(16) 太郎がハンサムです。
It is Taro who is handsome. (exhaustive only)

In sentence (15), サル "a monkey" can represent a new piece of information either as a neutral description or as exhaustive-listing. If it is a neutral description, the sentence as a whole is presented as a new piece of information, as if to say "Look! A monkey fell from the tree!" If it is considered an exhaustive-listing, offering an answer to a question "What fell from the tree?", then "monkey" is presented as a new piece of information, as in "It is a monkey that fell from the tree."

Contrary to these two possible readings of sentence (15), sentence (16) presents 太郎 as a new piece of information and receives an exhaustive-listing interpretation only, implying that the question 誰がハンサムですか "Who is [considered handsome] (among these people)?" was asked (or at least considered). If the sentence is describing a natural attribute of 太郎, the sentence should be 太郎はハンサムです. The difference between the following sentences should be clear.

(17) a. 私は本田です。
Speaking of me, I am Honda.
b. 私が本田です。
It is I who am Honda.

(18) a. リサの足は長くて細いです。
Speaking of Lisa's legs, they are long and skinny.

b. リサの足が長くて細いです。
   It is Lisa's legs that are long and skinny.

(19) a. 太郎のペットは死にました。
   Speaking of Taro's pet, it died.

   b. 太郎のペットが死にました。
   It is Taro's pet that died./Taro's pet died.

(20) a. 銀行はあそこにあります。
   Speaking of the bank, it is over there.

   b. あそこに銀行があります。
   It is a bank that is over there./There is a bank over there.

While sentence (17b) and (18b) receive only an exhaustive-listing interpretation—"It is I who is Honda" and "It is Lisa's legs that are long and skinny," respectively—the interpretation of sentences (19b) and (20b) is ambiguous. Each can be either an exhaustive-listing or neutral description, depending on the environment. All these sentences, however, present a new piece of information, either as a whole sentence or as a が marked noun phrase, demonstrating the primary function of the particle が.

2.2 「が」 as an object marker[11]

2.2.1 What is an object?

An "object" in language/linguistics is the entity that is acted upon or affected by an agent who performs an action. The verb is usually an activity verb where the subject of a sentence directly consumes or affects something else. For example, when one says "I eat an apple," "an apple" is the object that is directly consumed and affected by the person who carried out the eating activity. When one says "I like her," "her" is the object who is affected by the person who feels an emotion for the female individual. In English, grammatical objects are usually unaccompanied by any prepositional phrases, as in "I like *Japan*," but not "I went *to Japan*." In Japanese, the particle を follows a noun to identify it as the object of the sentence (discussion of the particle を appears in section 3).

---

[11] Much more detailed discussion of this issue is found in the following articles: Kuno and Johnson (2004, 2005).

Thus, a grammatical object is usually tied to activity verbs. In Japanese, however, there are a handful of predicates that are considered stative-transitive predicates, as originally defined by Kuno (1973). Although these are stative predicates, they can still invite a constituent that behaves like the object of an activity verb. To mark this constituent, が is used, not を (since を is strictly tied to objects of activity verbs). The types of stative-transitive predicates which are concerned with human attributes include non-intentional perception, competence, internal feeling, desire, and necessity and possession. The attributes expressed by these predicates are beyond a speaker's volitional control, and the predicates, as statives, behave differently from regular activity verbs such as 食べる "to eat," 行く "to go," 泳ぐ "to swim," and so on.

The following are representative stative-transitive predicates:

わかる	(私は/私に/私には)日本語がわかります。
	I understand Japanese.
見える	(私は/私に/私には)富士山が見えます。
	I can see Mt. Fuji.
聞こえる	(私は/私に/私には)音楽が聞こえます。
	I can hear music.
できる	(私は/私に/私には)テニスができます。
	I can play tennis.
いる	(私は/私に/私には)お金がいります。
	I need money.
ある	(私は/私に/私には)お金があります。
	I have money.
好き	(私は)音楽が好きです。
	I like music.
嫌い	(私は)漢字が嫌いです。
	I dislike kanji.
ほしい	(私は)お金がほしいです。
	I want money.

こわい	(私 は)犬がこわいです。[12]
	I am afraid of dogs.
とくい	私はテニスがとくいです。
	I am good at tennis.
上手	ジェフはゴルフが上手です。
	Jeff is good at golf.
苦手	私はお世辞を言うのが苦手です。
	I'm not good at flattering people.
下手	弟は嘘をつくのが下手だ。
	My brother is bad at lying.

As can be seen from the above examples, some stative-transitve predicates can take は, に, or には to mark the topic/subject of the sentence, while some take only は (unless they are in the form of a question or express an exhaustive-listing meaning).[13] The tendency of such usage seems to be attributed to the observation that when the sentence describes an objective fact (such as わかる, できる, and 聞こえる), then は, に, or には is optional, whereas for a stative-transitive predicate more related to an animate entity's emotion and characteristics, the use of に and には becomes unacceptable or awkward (as in 好き, ほしい, and こわい).[14]

In addition to the predicates listed above, there are two types of compound predicates that also take an object marked by the particle が. They are the potential compound (書ける) and the desiderative compound (飲みたい).

---

[12] こわい can describe either the speaker's feeling toward an object (stative-transitive predicate) or the attributes of the subject (い adjective). When the subject is, for example, この犬 "this dog," in この犬はこわい, then the sentence means "This dog is scary." Thus, the interpretation of the predicate depends on the subject.

[13] If the sentence is in the form of a question, then it would be だれが音楽が好きですか "Who likes music?" and if the sentence expresses an exhaustive-listing meaning, then it would be 私が音楽が好きです "It is I who like music." In either case, が is used.

[14] This assumption, however, may be accepted differently from individual to individual. Some may say that the use of に alone in 私に日本語がわかります "I understand Japanese," for example, sounds awkward and that には in 私には日本語がわかります is much more acceptable. In general, the use of には may be more common than the use of just に. However, in certain contexts, に is fine, and it is never ungrammatical.

書ける	(私は/私に/私には)漢字が書けます。
	I can write kanji.
飲みたい	(私は)お茶が飲みたいです。
	I want to drink tea.

For these compound predicates, either が or を is possible because of the partial involvement of the activity verb, 書く and 飲む. The involvement of an activity verb may bring out the activity predicate by emphasizing its verbal aspect as in "I want to *drink* coffee" and "John can *write* 100 kanji." On the other hand, が may emphasize the meaning expressed by the suffix, such as "I *want* to drink coffee" and "John *can* write 100 kanji." However, this is a grammatical distinction, and in daily conversation, various factors affect the speaker's immediate choice of a particle. For other, purely stative predicates, however, only が is the proper grammatical choice.

(21) 私は漢字　が/を　書けます。
　　　I *can write* kanji.

Cf.　私はテニス　が/*を　できます。
　　　I can play tennis.

(22) 私はお茶　が/を　飲みたいです。
　　　I *want to drink* tea.

3.　を

The fundamental function of the particle を is to mark a noun or a noun phrase being acted upon by the agent (performer of the action) of the activity described by the predicate. This function is generally called "object marking," and therefore を is an object marker. "Being acted upon" includes cases in which an agent directly consumes the object, as in すしを食べる "eat sushi" and コーヒーを飲む "drink coffee," and cases in which an agent makes an approach to an object in some way, as in 本を読む "read a book," 木を切る "cut a tree," and 映画を見る "see a movie." The objects in these sentences (marked by を) are all *affected and involved* in some way by the performer of the activity.

> 1. 「を」as an object marker for transitive predicates (including stative-transitive predicates)
> 2. 「を」as a place noun marker when the predicates (volitional intransitive predicates) describe motion

3.1 「を」as an object marker

The most frequent use of を is with an activity verb, that is, a transitive verb,[15] to mark an object. Observe the following examples.

(1) 鈴木さんは毎日日本語を勉強します。
     Mr. Suzuki studies Japanese everyday.
(2) (私は)昨日日本語の辞書を買いました。
     I bought a Japanese dictionary yesterday.
(3) (私は)豊田さんを３０分待ちました。
     I waited for Ms. Toyota for 30 minutes.
(4) この漢字を書いてください。
     Please write this kanji.
(5) 毎朝シャワーを浴びます。
     I take a shower every morning.
(6) タクシーを呼びます。
     I am going to call a taxi.
(7) 鈴木さんは豊田さんを紹介しました。
     Mr. Suzuki introduced Ms. Toyota (to someone).

を can also mark an object when the predicate is a stative-transitive predicate. See section 2.2, which describes が as an object marker.

(8) 私はコーヒーが/を飲みたいです。　I want to drink coffee.
(9) ジョンは漢字が/を100書けます。　John can write 100 kanji.

---

[15] Stative predicates (such as いる "exist," ほしい "want," 聞こえる "can hear") and non-volitional intransitive verbs (such as 開く in ドアが開く "the door opens" and 消える in 電気が消える "the lights turn off") do not invite an object.

3.2 「を」 as a place noun marker indicating a "path"[16]

As mentioned previously, the fundamental meaning of the particle を is to mark a noun or the noun phrase acted upon by the agent of the action described by the predicate. This function allows some motion verbs (usually volitional *intransitive* verbs) to take a place noun just as if it were an object. This usage arises from the fact that the place, such as a street, is actually acted upon by the agent walking on it. However, since motion verbs are not considered transitive verbs, the を marked place noun is *not* exactly the same as the object of a transitive verb. With motion verbs, を is used to indicate that the motion taking place covers the whole dimension or some portion of the place. The following diagrams (adapted from 日本語表現文型中級 I [1983]) help illustrate which motion verbs have this function. The circle represents the dimension in which the motion takes place, and the arrow represents the type of motion performed by the agent.

歩く　　よくこの道を歩いた。
　　　　I often <u>walked along</u> this street.

走る　　毎日公園を走った。
　　　　I <u>ran through</u> the park every day.

登る　　富士山を登った。
　　　　I <u>climbed</u> Mt. Fuji.

下る　　富士山を下った。
　　　　I <u>climbed down</u> Mt. Fuji.

渡る　　その橋を渡った。
　　　　I <u>crossed</u> the bridge.

泳ぐ　　川を泳いだ。
　　　　I <u>swam across</u> the river.

飛ぶ　　空を飛んだ。
　　　　I <u>flew across</u> the sky.

---

[16] This notion was first presented by Kuroda (1978) and has not yet been challenged.

Note that when the place noun is marked by を, the arrow represents a motion that goes through it. If the motion takes place within/inside the dimension (as in "I took a walk in the park") or the motion takes place from one point to another (as in "I climbed up to the summit of Mt. Fuji"), a different particle should be employed. Refer to sections 4 and 7, where に and で are discussed, for further clarification.

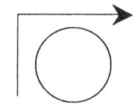

曲がる　公園の角を曲がった。
I turned the corner of the park.

回る　柱の周りを回った。　　I circled around the pillar.

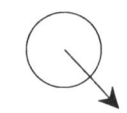

出る　3時に家を出た。
I left home at 3 o'clock.

卒業する　去年大学を卒業した。
I graduated from college last year.

降りる　バスを降りる。
I will get off the bus.

離れる　船が港を離れた。
A ship left the harbor.

辞める　昨日会社を辞めた。
I quit the company yesterday.

を in the third figure communicates the notion of "from" in English, and the equivalent から in Japanese may be able to replace を. However, if the motion is depicted rather as an abstract manner, then から cannot replace を. For example,

卒業する and 辞める represent abstract concepts; therefore, 大学から卒業する and 会社から辞める would be inappropriate, while バスから降りる、船が港から離れる are concrete, visualizable activities; therefore, the use of から in these sentences is appropriate.

4. に

The fundamental concept of に describes a *unidirectional* situation with a focus on the result or goal of the directional activity rather than on the process of the activity. Therefore, に is often used to designate a single place or a specific time out of the wider scope of location or time. Unidirectional motion is at the root of all the uses of に. It allows に to possess many functions, such as marking an indirect object, a location, the source of an action, and so on.

> 1. 「に」 marking an indirect object
> 2. 「に」 marking a place noun
> 3. 「に」 marking a time noun and indicting frequency
> 4. 「に」 marking the source of an action: "from" or "by"
> 5. 「に」 for listing noun phrases

4.1 「に」 marking an indirect object

Transitive verbs, such as 食べる、見る、飲む, take one object, and the object is specified as the direct object of these verbs. There are also transitive verbs called "ditransitive" that can take two objects—a direct object marked by を and an indirect object marked by に. An indirect object usually lets us envision a recipient and/or a benefactor of the action described by the verb. The recipient and/or benefactor of an action is generally an animate entity that is capable of receiving an action.[17] Some tests to check whether a verb is transitive or ditransitive may be:

---

[17] This is, however, not absolute. Plants, for example, can be the recipients of water, as in 母は植木に水をあげた "My mother gave a plant water."

a. If the question "to whom/what?" is considered appropriate.
b. If an English equivalent "someone does *someone something*" is applicable (as in "my father taught *me English*.")

Some representative ditransitive verbs are 教える "teach," 売る "sell," 貸す "lend," 見せる "show," 買う "buy," and 渡す "hand in." Observe the following examples:

(1) 私は妹に英語を教えました。
I taught my sister English.

(2) 豊田さんは鈴木さんに車を売りました。
Mr. Toyota sold Ms. Suzuki a car.

(3) 先生は学生に本を貸しました。
The teacher lent a student a book.

(4) 豊田さんは鈴木さんに写真を見せました。
Mr. Toyota showed Ms. Suzuki a picture.

(5) 私は妹におみやげを買いました。
I bought my sister a souvenir.

(6) 学生は先生に宿題を渡しました。
Students handed the teacher their homework.

In the examples above, the recipients/benefactors of the action described by the verb are all marked by に. Also, the activities described by the ditransitive verbs can be captured in terms of the notion of unidirectionality. Just like the example in sentence (1), where English instruction went from the speaker to his/her sister, movement of some entity from one place or person to another can be easily envisioned. Note that a causative sentence also involves an indirect object, such as in 母親は子供ににんじんを食べさせました "I made my son eat carrots." (Refer to Chapter 32, Section 2 for more examples.)

The indirect object marked by に usually precedes the direct object, but in conversation, this grammatical restriction is not strictly observed. As long as a correct particle is used, the word order need not be a concern. For example, you may say:

(7)　車を本田さんは豊田さんにあげました。
　　　Mr. Honda gave Mr. Toyota a car.

4.2　「に」marking a place noun

There are a number of predicates that require a place noun to describe where things are or where activities take place. The representative ones are verbs of existence and some motion verbs. Observe the following examples:

(8)　a.　銀行の前に郵便局があります。
　　　　There is a post office in front of the bank.
　　b.　教室に学生が50人います。
　　　　There are 50 students in the classroom.
　　c.　来年から日本に住みます。
　　　　I will live in Japan starting next year.

(9)　a.　川崎さんは去年中国に行きました。
　　　　Ms. Kawasaki went to China last year.
　　b.　米国の大統領が日本に来ました。
　　　　The U.S. president visited Japan.
　　c.　本田さんはもう家に帰りました。
　　　　Mr. Honda has already gone home.
　　d.　飛行機はもうすぐ成田に着きます。
　　　　The airplane will arrive at Narita shortly.
*　　e.　毎日大学に歩きます。
　　　　I walk to the university everyday.
　　　　(毎日大学まで歩きます or 毎日大学に歩いて行きます)
*　　f.　川の反対側に泳ぎます。
　　　　I will swim to the other side of the river.
　　　　(川の向こうまで泳ぎます or 川の向こうに泳いで行きます)

In sentences (8) and (9), に marks the specific spot or location of the subject. This function is also reflected in sentences with motion verbs. The compatibility or incompatibility of に with motion verbs is decided by how these verbs are perceived: 行く, 来る, and 帰る are perceived to include the idea of a goal that the motion reaches and therefore are compatible with a place noun marked by に, while 歩く and 泳ぐ are process-oriented motion verbs and are less compatible with place nouns marked by に.[18] に with the verb 住む "to live" in sentence (8c) can be considered a result of the motion of settling into a place.

4.3　「に」 marking a time noun and indicating frequency

に marks a specific point relative to the broader concept of time. For example, January might be considered a narrower target when considering a yearlong time frame, while it may be considered a longer duration of time compared to Sunday. The concept of "specific point in time" is therefore relative to the time frame to which the speaker is referring. Note that 昨日 "yesterday," 今日 "today," 明日 "tomorrow," 毎日 "every day" 先週 "last week," etc., are not marked by に regardless of how they compare to the time frame the speaker has in mind. Also, a phrase that indicates frequency requires the use of に (such as once a week, twice a year, etc.). Observe the following examples:

(10) (私は)毎日朝8時に起きます。
I get up at 8:00 A.M. every day.

(11) (私は)6月に日本に来ました。
I came to Japan in June.

(12) 弟は2004年に生まれました。
My brother was born in 2004.

(13) 月曜日にオフィスに来てください。
Please come to my office on Monday.

(14) (私は)一日に5時間勉強します。
I study five hours a day.

(15) 閏年は4年に1度来ます。
A leap year comes once every four years.

---

[18] A more appropriate manner of describing the same situation is suggested in the parentheses. For example, まで, which means "as far as" involves the notion of process and is compatible with 歩く and 泳ぐ. The equivalent of "go on foot" or "go by swimming" are other alternatives.

4.4 「に」 marking the source of an action: "from" or "by"

Since に illustrates a unidirectional concept, the source of an action or event can also be marked by に. It is similar to the use of "from" and "by" in the passive construction (refer to Chapter 31, the passive construction, for further explanation). に in the former function tends to occur with a verb that offers a passive atmosphere and/or is beneficial to the receiver, such as 習う "to learn," 借りる "to borrow," and もらう "to receive." When a verb describes a situation that is considered active, aggressive, not necessarily beneficial to the receiver, such as "to obtain something by force," から is the only choice; に cannot be used. Sentences (16) to (20) are cases where に and から are interchangeable, while sentences (21) and (22) are cases where only から is used.

(16) (私は)川崎さんに/から[19]日本語を習います。
I will learn Japanese from Ms. Kawasaki.

(17) 弟は父に/から時計をもらいました。
My brother received a watch from his father.

(18) 友達に/から本を借りました。
(I) borrowed a book from my friend.

(19) 友達に/からひどい事を言われました。
(I) was told a terrible thing by my friend.

(20) 友達に/から頼まれました。
(I) was asked by my friend.

Sentences (19) and (20) are passive sentences: から is not always interchangeable with に in the passive construction.

(21) a. 強盗は老人からお金を盗んだ。
A robber stole money from an old man.

  * b. 強盗は老人にお金を盗んだ。

---

[19] Since に offers the same function as "from," から is also a choice, but に is more frequently used. Also, since に can also mark recipient of an action, whether the use of に indicates the goal or the source of action/event depends on the meaning of the verb. For example, 先生に聞きました can be interpreted either "I asked the teacher (the teacher is the recipient of the question)" or "I heard from the teacher (the teacher is the source of information." In case of the latter, から should be used to clarify the meaning.

(22)　a.　山田さんから小包みを受け取った。
　　　　　I received (obtained) a package from Ms. Yamada.
　*　b.　山田さんに小包みを受け取った。

When the source of an action or event is an inanimate entity, that source cannot be marked by に. This restriction exhibits that に is strongly related to an animate entity where the source of an action/event is involved.

(23)　a.　図書館から本を借りました。
　　　　　I checked out a book from the library.
　*　b.　図書館に本を借りました。
　　c.　銀行からお金を借りました。
　　　　　I borrowed money from the bank.
　*　d.　銀行にお金を借りました。[20]
(24)　a.　大学から奨学金をもらいました。
　　　　　I received a scholarship from the University.
　*　b.　大学に奨学金をもらいました。
(25)　a.　バターはミルクから作られる。
　　　　　Butter is made from milk. (passive sentence)
　*　b.　バターはミルクに作られる。

4.5 「に」 for listing noun phrases

When *more than two items* are listed, に may be used to mark noun phrases and may seem similar to the use of the particle と. While と has a function that brings two noun phrases to connect, に is used to simply single out noun phrases as a list of items. Let us observe the following sentences to see the differences and similarities.

---

[20] In our daily conversation, this type of sentence may be heard. In such case, the given place noun is used as a personification giving an impression that the place noun is representing a person who provides the object.

(26) a. だれが学生ですか。
　　　　Who is a student?
　　b. ジョンとメリーとトムが学生です。
　　　　John, Mary, and Tom are students.
　　c. ジョンにメリーにトムが学生です。
　　　　John, Mary, and Tom are students.
(27) a. だれが結婚しますか。
　　　　Who is getting married?
　　b. ジョンとメリーが結婚します。
　　　　John and Mary are getting married (meaning John and Mary are united as a legal couple).
　? c. ジョンにメリーが結婚します。[21]
　　d. ジョンにメリーにトムが結婚します。
　　　　John, Mary, and Tom are getting married (each person to a different partner).
　　e. ジョンとメリーとトムが結婚します。
　　　　John, Mary, and Tom are getting married.
(28) a. お昼ご飯は、何を食べましたか。
　　　　Speaking of lunch, what did you eat?
　　b. すしとうなぎとうどんを食べました。
　　　　I ate sushi, eel, and noodles.
　　c. すしにうなぎにうどんを食べました。
　　　　I ate sushi, eel, and noodles.

In a situation where に and と are interchangeable, と usually prevails over に in daily conversation. に may be more commonly seen in writing. Also, に gives an impression that the items are listed on top of the previous one, and conjunction words, such as それから and それに may be used more frequently than they are with と.

---

[21] Since marriage is a mutual contract that requires two individuals, it is difficult for this sentence to receive an interpretation of listing two individuals, each of whom is getting married to a different partner. The sentence should be ジョンとメリーが結婚します "John and Mary are getting married." Sentence (27d), on the other hand, may easily be construed as listing people who are getting married to different partners, since it lists more than two people.

(29)　すしに・・・うなぎに・・・、それからうどんを食べました。
　　　Well, let's see what I ate. I ate sushi . . . eel, and . . . oh yes, noodles.

In addition to these functions of に, there are some fixed expressions that use に as an indicator of unidirectionality. Examples of such phrases are: 妹は父に似ている "My sister resembles my father," 学生は先生の指示に従うといい "Students are advised to follow the teacher's instructions," and この理論は物理学の理論に基づいている "This theory is (derived) based on the theory of physics." In fact, the concept of unidirectionality is well reflected in the use of に with these verbs. For example, "resemble" is a case where one person or thing looks similar to another. In this case, と can also be used if the speaker intends to say that two entities look like each other, though に is the primary use. 従う "to follow" also indicates a unidirectional act, in this case by abiding by another person's rule; the concept of 基づく is to be derived from something. The use of に in these examples makes sense under the concept of unidirectionality.

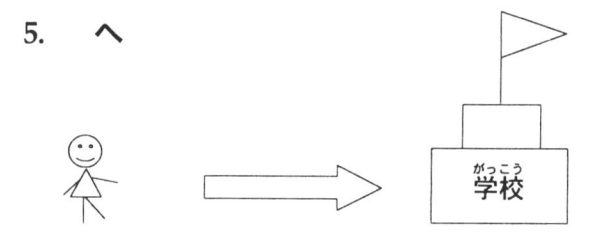

5.　へ

The particle へ marks a place noun and indicates a direction where the place noun is located. It occurs only with *a motion verb*. In this sense, に and へ are interchangeable: both 学校へ行きます and 学校に行きます are interpreted as "I am going to school." The difference is that, while the function of に can be boiled down to point to the specific destination or time of an event, the へ covers a broader dimension of the place where a motion occurs. This is why へ cannot be used to mark a time noun, while に can. When へ is used in a sentence, に can replace へ (without changing the meaning of the sentence too much), but not vice versa. Observe the following examples:

(1)　a.　本田さんはもう家へ戻りました。
　　　　Mr. Honda has already returned home.

b. 本田さんはもう家に戻りました。
   Mr. Honda has already returned home.

(2) a. ブッシュ氏が日本へ来ました。
   Mr. Bush came to Japan.

　　b. ブッシュ氏が日本に来ました。
   Mr. Bush came to Japan.

(3) a. 弟はアメリカへ旅行します。[22]
   My brother will travel to the United States.

　　b. 弟はアメリカに旅行します。
   My brother will travel to the United States.

(4) a. 弟はアメリカに住みます。
   My brother will live in the United States.

　* b. 弟はアメリカへ住みます。

(5) a. この本は図書館にあります。
   This book is at the library.

　* b. この本は図書館へあります。

(6) a. 毎朝6時に起きます。
   I get up at 6 o'clock every morning.

　* b. 毎朝6時へ起きます。

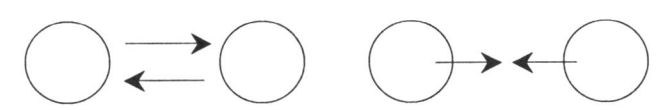

6. と

The function of と is to bring states, activities, and events into a mutual and reciprocal position. The fundamental meaning of と is bi-directional. In this sense, it is contrary to the function of に that offers a unidirectional concept. The concept of

---

[22] If you travel covering a certain portion of the United States, the sentence should be アメリカを旅行します。 If you intend to say that you go to the United States and do some traveling there, you would say アメリカで旅行します。 The particle thus always plays a role in changing the meaning of the sentence.

mutuality develops particularly and clearly into two of the following three functions:[23]

> 1. 「と」 indicating a mutual action: "with each other"
> 2. 「と」 linking multiple noun phrases: "and"
> 3. 「と」 as quotation marks : "that~"

6.1 「と」 indicating a mutual action: "with each other"

The use of と depends on the meaning of the verb: some verbs can be perceived as an event mutually conducted between two entities and allow the use of と, while some verbs are considered only a unilateral event. In the latter case, に is employed. Some verbs can take either と or に, while some verbs can employ only one particle. Verbs, such as 話す "to speak," 会う "to meet," and 相談する "to consult" can occur with either と or に indicating a slightly different meaning. Verbs such as 交換する "to exchange," 結婚する "to get married," and 遊ぶ "to play" are compatible only with と due to the meaning of the verb, while verbs such as 話しかける "to speak to" and 聞く "to ask (a question)" are not compatible with と since they are perceived as unilateral communication. Observe the following examples:

(1) a. 川崎さんは先生と話しました。
       Ms. Kawasaki spoke with the teacher.
    b. 川崎さんは先生に話しました。
       Ms. Kawasaki spoke to the teacher.
(2) a. 川崎さんは先生と会いました。
       Ms. Kawasaki met with the teacher.
    a. 川崎さんは先生に会いました。
       Ms. Kawasaki met the teacher.

---

[23] と also has the same function as the quotation marks in "He said, 'I will come,'" or "that" in "He said *that* he would come," followed by a verb, such as 言う "to say," 思う "to think," 聞く "to hear," and so on. The function of this と as "noun complementizer" is similar to the function of と as linkage. See section 6.3 below.

(3) a. 川崎さんは先生と相談しました。
　　　 Ms. Kawasaki consulted with the teacher.
　　b. 川崎さんは先生に相談しました。
　　　 Ms. Kawasaki consulted the teacher.
(4) a. 本田さんは豊田さんと車を交換しました。
　　　 Ms. Honda exchanged a car with Mr. Toyota.
　* b. 本田さんは豊田さんに車を交換しました。
(5) a. 本田さんは豊田さんと結婚しました。
　　　 Ms. Honda got married to Mr. Toyota.
　* b. 本田さんは豊田さんに結婚しました。
(6) a. 本田さんは豊田さんと遊びました。
　　　 Ms. Honda played with Mr. Toyota.
　* b. 本田さんは豊田さんに遊びました。
　　　 Ms. Honda played to Mr. Toyota.
(7) * a. 学生は先生と話しかけました。
　　　 A student spoke to the teacher.
　　b. 学生は先生に話しかけました。
　　　 A student spoke to the teacher.
(8) * a. 学生は先生と聞きました。
　　　 A student asked (a question) with the teacher.
　　b. 学生は先生に聞きました。
　　　 A student asked (a question) to the teacher.

6.2 「と」linking multiple noun phrases:[24] "and"

と links noun phrases to create a unit. In English, "and" is required only between the last two noun phrases, but in Japanese, と is required between each pair of noun phrases (unless they are on the list). Observe the following examples:

(9) 　レストランで何を食べましたか。
　　　What did you eat at the restaurant?
　　　てんぷらとすしとうどんを食べました。
　　　(I) ate tempura, sushi, and noodles.

---

[24] There are two more particles, に and や, that connect noun phrases.

(10) 日本で、どこへ行きましたか。
　　 Where did you go in Japan?
　　 東京と京都と大阪と奈良へ行きました。
　　 (I) went to Tokyo, Kyoto, Osaka, and Nara.
(11) どんなボールがいいですか。
　　 What kind of balls do you like?
　　 大きいのときれいなのがいいです。
　　 (I) like big ones and pretty ones.
(12) 趣味は何ですか。
　　 What are (your) hobbies?
　　 食べることと寝ることです。
　　 My hobbies are eating and sleeping.

Remember that と comes between noun phrases, and when parts of speech other than nouns are linked by と, they have to be in nominalized form, as in 大きい の "big one," きれいな の "pretty one," and 食べる こと "eating."

6.3 「と」 as quotation marks: "that ~"

と has yet another function: it is used as quotation marks or "that" in "She said *that* ~." This function is called "sentence complementation." と links a quotation and a verb of thinking, reporting, and the like. In this usage, と functions to link the verb with the content of the action described by the verb.

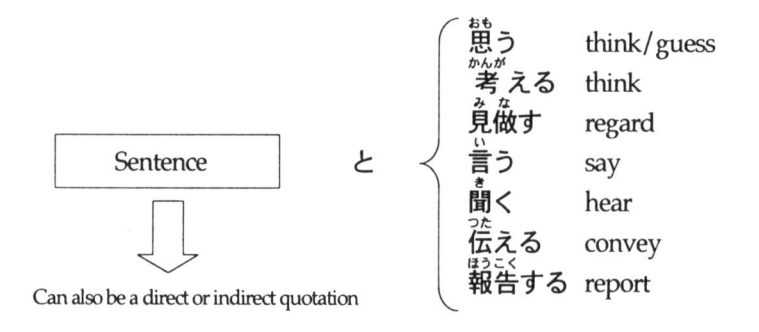

Sentence	と	思う	think/guess
		考える	think
		見做す	regard
		言う	say
		聞く	hear
		伝える	convey
		報告する	report

Can also be a direct or indirect quotation

(13) 私はこの答が正しいと思うが、友達は間違っていると言う。
I think that this answer is correct, but my friend says that it is wrong.
(14) 今度のオリンピックはバンクーバーであると聞いた。
I heard that the next Olympics will be held in Vancouver.
(15) 「来週編入試験を受けなさい」と先生に言われた。
I was told by the teacher, "Take the placement exam next week."
(16) 「にほんご」は漢字で「日本語」と書きます。
You write "Japanese language" as "日本語" in kanji.

7. で

The fundamental function of で is to limit or restrict the range of the targeted entity. It can be a location, an activity, a reason, a time, or a quantity. When で marks a place noun, it indicates that the activity designated by the verb takes place within the location. When で marks a noun phrase, it limits the possible range of entities to mean "using" or "by means of," a possible reason, or a possible time or quantity.

> 1. 「で」 marking a place noun where an activity or event takes place
> 2. 「で」 marking a noun phrase indicating an entity as a tool
> 3. 「で」 marking a noun phrase indicating a cause of the activity or event in the main clause
> 4. 「で」 marking a noun phrase indicating time or quantity

7.1 「で」 marking a place noun

で is used to indicate the location where an activity is performed. "Place noun + で" occurs only with a verb that is perceived as an activity. Observe the following paired sentences in which で is compared to に.

(1) a. 友達の家で電話をかけます。
I will make a phone call at my friend's house. → The activity takes place at the house of my friend.

b. 友達の家に電話をかけます。
　　 I will call my friend's house. → The destination of the call is the house of my friend.

(2) a. ここで名前を書いてください。
　　 Please write your name here. → Requests that an activity take place in this place.

b. ここに名前を書いてください。
　　 Please write your name here. → The final location of you name is here (on this paper).

(3) a. 友達の家でパーティがありました。
　　 There was a party (held) at my friend's house. → A party took place at the house of my friend.

* b. 友達の家にパーティがありました。
　　 A party existed at my friend's house.

(4) a. トムは日本で3年住みました。
　　 Tom lived in Japan for three years. → Tom actively lived life for three years in Japan.

b. トムは日本に3年住みました。
　　 Tom lived/stayed in Japan for three years.

As clearly seen, the use of で and に creates a different interpretation of the sentence. In sentence (3a), ある is considered an activity verb meaning "to hold (a party)" and で is the appropriate particle in this case. When に is used, it implies that the party is a static entity, so it is incompatible with the meaning of the sentence. The verb 住む is compatible with either で or に, though general preference is given to に when the sentence simply tells where one lives. 日本で 住む implies the various activities that make up life, while 住む in 日本に 住む gives us a composite picture of living in general. Thus, not only the meaning of the verb, but also the abstract picture that the verb creates affect the use of the particle and the meaning of the sentence.

7.2 「で」 marking a noun phrase indicating an entity as a tool

A noun phrase marked by で presents a "tool" through the meaning "using," "by means of," "with a tool," etc. Observe the following examples:

(5) (私は)毎日 車 で大学へ通っていますが、今日は自転車で来ました。
 (I) commute to school by car every day, but today I came by bicycle.
(6) 答えは鉛筆で書いてください。日記は日本語で書いてください。
 Please write answers using a pencil. Speaking of the diary, please write it in Japanese.
(7) すしは手で食べますが、スパゲティはフォークで食べます。
 Speaking of sushi, you eat (it) with your fingers, whereas spaghetti you eat with a fork.
(8) (私は)母と電話で話しました。その後、弟 と英語で話しました。
 (I) spoke with my mother on the phone. After that, (I) spoke with my brother in English.
(9) そのニュースは新聞で読みましたが、テレビでは見ませんでした。
 Speaking of that news, (I) read it in the newspaper, but (I) did not see it on TV.

For a method represented by a verb, the て form of the verb is used to link with the main verb.

(10) 次の駅まで歩いて行きましょう。
 Let's walk to the next station.
(11) いえ、私は走って行きます。
 No, I will run (to the next station).

In sentences (10) and (11), 歩く "to walk" and 走る "to run" are the method that the agent chooses for going to a designated location. When combining two verbs in this manner, the first verb is in the て form.

7.3 「で」 marking a noun phrase indicating a cause of the activity or event in the main clause

The English equivalent of this phrase is "because of" or "due to."

(12) 事故でクラスに遅れました。
I was late for class due to an accident.

(13) かぜでクラスを休みました。
I missed class due to a cold.

(14) 雨で試合が中止になりました。
The game was canceled because of rain.

(15) 急用で家へ帰らなくてはなりません。
I have to go home due to urgent business.

7.4 「で」 marking a noun phrase indicating time or quantity

The English equivalent of this phrase is usually "within," "in," or the like. The use of で delimits the time frame or the number of an entity.

(16) この論文は3日で書き上げました。
I wrote up this term paper in three days.

(17) 期末試験は今週の金曜で終わります。
The final exam will end on this Friday (after continuing from a day preceding the Friday).

(18) 子供が一人で飛行機に乗っていました。
(I saw) a child was riding an airplane alone.

(19) みんなで一緒に勉強しませんか。
Why don't we all study together?

8.　も

The fundamental function of も is to indicate that the marked item is given in relation to another phrase in terms of their status. Another phrase may be implied or stated, depending on the environment of the communication. For example, in 山田さんはすしを食べました。それに、うどんも食べました "Ms. Yamada ate sushi. On top of that, she ate a bowl of noodles, too," うどん is presented as an object that is given in relation to すし (which is stated in this case). すしandうどん are in equal status in that both are eaten by 山田さん. The same observation applies to a negative predicate, as in 山田さんはすしを食べませんでした。それに、うどんも食べませんでした "Ms. Yamada did not eat sushi. Not only that, she did not eat noodles, either."

も following a noun phrase or a verb stem form has various meanings, such as "also," "both A and B," "neither A nor B," "not even," "as many as/fewer than ~." Note that も can replace only the particles は, が, and を. も is added after the particle, as in でも, にも, and からも. も is also used in the permission construction following a gerundive form, as in 行ってもいい "you may go." Please refer to Chapter 22 on structure of permission .

---

1. Noun phrase + 「も」
2. Verb stem + 「も」
3. い adjective or く / な adjective で + 「も」

8.1 Noun phrase + 「も」
8.1.1 「も」meaning "also," "both A and B," or "neither A nor B"

(1) a. 私は日本語の先生です。田中さんも日本語の先生です。
I am a Japanese language teacher. Mr. Tanaka is also a Japanese language teacher. (Mr. Tanaka is compared to the speaker in terms of his being a Japanese language teacher.)

b. 田中さんも私も日本語の先生です。
Both Mr. Tanaka and I are Japanese.

c. 田中さんも私も学生じゃありません。
Neither Mr. Tanaka nor I is a student.

(2) a. 山下さんは台湾へ行きました。韓国へもいきました。それから、香港へも行きました。
Ms. Yamashita went to Taiwan. She also went to Korea. And, she also went to Hong Kong. (Taiwan, Korea, and Hong Kong are compared in terms of Ms. Yamashita's visits to those places.)

b. 山下さんは台湾へも韓国へも、(それから)香港へも行きました。
Ms. Yamashita went to Taiwan and Korea, as well as Hong Kong.

Cf. 山下さんは台湾と韓国と香港へ行きました。

(3) a. 電話は一階にはありません。二階にもありません。
Speaking of the telephone, it is not on the first floor. It is not on the second floor, either. (The 1st floor and 2nd floors are compared in terms of not having a telephone.)

b. 電話は一階にも、二階にもありません。
Speaking of the telephone, it is neither on the first nor the second floor.

8.1.2 「も」 meaning of "as many/fewer than," "not even"

(4) a. 若者がコンサートに 5,000 人来ました。
5,000 young people came to the concert.

b. 若者がコンサートに 5,000 人も来ました。
As many as 5,000 young people came to the concert.

(5) a. 学生は試験を受けませんでした。
Speaking of the students, they did not take the exam.

b. 学生は 10 人も試験を受けませんでした。
Speaking of the students, not even ten students took the exam (out of 40, for example).

(6) a. 最近の若い人は漢字が書けません。
Speaking of present-day young people, they cannot write kanji.

b. 最近の若い人は漢字も書けません。
Speaking of present-day young people, they cannot even write kanji.

Sometimes the compared entity is greater or less than the given or implied item. For example, the difference between 若者がコンサートに 5,000 人来ました "5,000 young people came to the concert" and 若者がコンサートに 5,000 人も来ました "As many as 5,000 young people came to the concert" in sentence (4) is that the former presents a simple fact without any implication, while the latter implies that the speaker's original expectation was *less than 5,000* (i.e., an implied, compared item) and tends to express a feeling of unexpectedness (either favorable or unfavorable). The same is true of sentence (5b), where a negative predicate is used. The speaker in this sentence expected that many students would turn out (implied expectation compared to the actual number of students who turned out), but the result was *fewer than 10* against the speaker's original expectation. Sentence (6b) implies that the speaker has some other compared item in mind; it directly follows an additional item that young people cannot do, such as making proper use of honorific forms to older people. (See Chapter 17, Section 2.7 on しか〜ない.)

8.1.3 Interrogative noun + も + negative predicate indicating "no ~"

も can follow an interrogative noun indicating "nothing," "no one," and "nowhere. The following are the basic interrogative nouns that occur with も to express these meanings. Note that a particle may be required between the interrogative noun and も to explicate the meaning of a sentence.[25]

何		
誰	も + negative predicate	none/nothing
どこ		no one
どう		nowhere
		nothing

(7) a. 何か食べましたか。
     Did you eat something?
   b. 何も食べませんでした。
     I did not eat anything.
(8) a. 誰かと話しましたか。
     Did you speak with someone?
   b. 誰とも話しませんでした。
     I did not speak with anyone.
     If と is forgotten, the meaning of the sentence changes to:
 * c. 誰も話しませんでした。
     No one spoke.

---

[25] Note that いつも "always" is not used in this pattern.

(9) a. どこかへ行きましたか。
Did you go anywhere?
b. どこ(へ)も行きませんでした。
I did not go anywhere.
(*Note that the use of へ is grammatical and desirable, but in conversation, as long as the meaning is clear, it may be omitted.)

(10) a. 財布はどこかにありましたか。
Speaking of the wallet, was it somewhere?
b. どこにもありませんでした。
It was not anywhere.
* c. どこもありませんでした。[26]
Nowhere existed.

(11) a. どうかしましたか。
Did something wrong happen?
b. どうもしませんでした。
Nothing wrong happened.

8.2 Verb stem + 「も」

Verb phrases can also serve as additional entities. If the entity is an affirmative addition, する follows the stem form of a verb with も, as in 骨を食べもする "(he) even eats bones." If the entity is a negative addition, する follows the stem form of a verb with も, as in 水を飲みもしない "(he) does not even drink water." The following are some examples:

(12) うちの犬はこの3日間、ご飯を見もしない。
My dog has not even looked at food for three days.

(13) 私は逃げも隠れもしないつもりだ。
I intend to neither escape nor hide.

(14) 彼は手紙を読みもしないで、捨てた。
He threw the letter away without even reading it.

---

[26] どこも as an individual word means "everywhere," and can be used in a sentence like どこもセールをしています "A sale is going on everywhere."

(15) 山田さんは英語を読む。それに書きもする。
Ms. Yamada reads English. In addition, she writes English.

8.3 い adjective く or な adjective で + 「も」

An い/な adjective phrase can serve as an entity with も, as in "it is not even delicious." In such cases, the く form of an い adjective and the て form of a な adjective precedes も. The following are some examples:

(16) 魚は嫌いだ。見たくもない。
I dislike fish. I do not even want to see it.
(17) 忙しくもないのに、いつも疲れている。
Though not even busy, I am always tired.
(18) 彼はじょうずでもないのに、ゴルフができることを自慢する。
He brags about being able to play golf even though he is not good.
(19) おもしろくもないのに、専攻のため毎日クラスに出なければならないのは苦痛だ。
It is painful to attend class every day because of my major, and the class is not even interesting.

9. や

The particle や, like と and に, is used to list nouns. The difference is that や refers to partial lists, implying the existence of more items. For example, in the picture below, saying "B や G" implies the existence of the rest of the items in the circle; hence the meaning "B and G, and so forth." や can be replaced by とか in colloquial conversation (though とか cannot always be replaced by や).[27]

---

[27] Note that when you list things you did (described by a verb), the たり〜たり construction should be used (see Chapter 11). E.g., 日本で旅行したり友達に会ったりしました "I did activities, such as traveling and meeting a friend in Japan." Also, や may appear at the end of a sentence as a sentence final particle like よ, ね, and か as in まあ、いいや "Well, it's okay. ..." No explanation of this function is provided in this book.

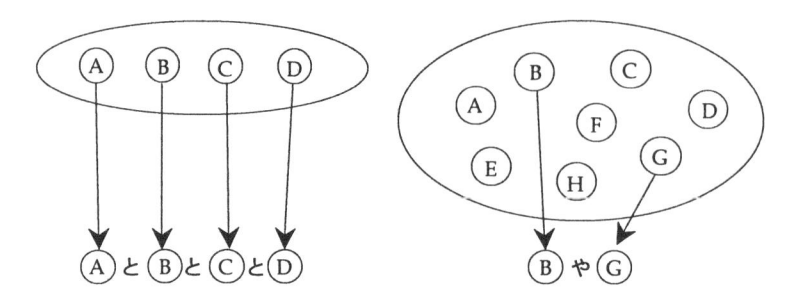

(1) a. レストランで何を食べましたか。
What did you eat at the restaurant?
b. すきやきやてんぷらを食べました。
I ate food, such as sukiyaki and tempura.
(2) a. 日本ではどこを旅行しましたか。
Where did you travel in Japan?
b. 京都や奈良や大阪を旅行しました。
I traveled to places such as Kyoto, Nara, and Osaka.

10. の

> 1. 「の」 linking noun phrases
> 2. 「の」 marking a subject in a relative clause

10.1 「の」 linking noun phrases
10.1.1 「の」 expressing a possessive relationship

の links multiple noun phrases and identifies the relationship of the phrases. One of the most frequently observed functions is "possession" —the phrase following の belongs to the preceding noun phrase. Observe the following examples and compare to English to see how the relationship is represented in a structurally consistent manner in Japanese. (See also noun-modifying constructions in Chapter 17.)

A describes B

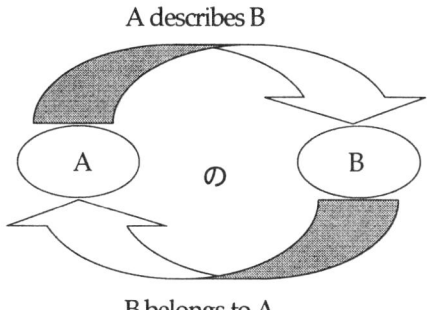

A の B

B belongs to A

(1) a. 私の友達
my friend, a friend of mine
b. 友達の写真
pictures of a friend, a friend's picture
c. 私の友達の写真
a picture of my friend, my friend's picture
d. アメリカのミシガン
Michigan in America
e. アメリカのミシガンの大学
a university in Michigan in America
f. アメリカのミシガンの大学の先生
a teacher at a university in Michigan in America
g. アメリカのミシガンの大学の日本語の先生
a Japanese language teacher at a university in Michigan in America

Noun phrases linked by の become a longer noun phrase which can be a topic, subject, direct object, or indirect object.

(2) 私の友達 は アメリカのミシガンの大学 へ行きました。
     NP   NP

My friend went to a university in Michigan in America.

(3) アメリカのミシガンの大学の日本語の先生 に会いました。

I met a Japanese language teacher at a university in Michigan in America.

10.1.2 「の」 expressing an appositional relationship

When two phrases are of equal status rather than standing in a hierarchical order, the relationship between the phrases is said to be appositional. In English, a comma is usually used between such phrases. In Japanese, の is used to describe the appositional relationship. In this case, の is not connecting two noun phrases so that the first noun phrase is modifying the second, but is simply linking them in a parallel manner. Remember that the main noun is always stated at the end of all the phrases when の is used to link noun phrases. (The main noun in the following examples with の is underlined.)

(4) a. 私の友達 ⓪ ジョンは来年日本へ行きます。
My friend John is going to Japan next year.
b. 私の友達、ジョンは来年日本へ行きます。
My friend John is going to Japan next year.

(5) a. 社長 ⓪ 田中氏がホワイトハウスでブッシュ氏に会った。
President Tanaka met Mr. Bush at the White House.
b. 田中社長がホワイトハウスでブッシュ氏に会った。
President Tanaka met Mr. Bush at the White House.

(6) a. 日本人 ⓪ 私たちもお米をよく食べます。
We, (who are) Japanese people, eat rice a lot, too.
b. 私たち、日本人もお米をよく食べます。
We Japanese people eat rice a lot, too.

(7) a. アメリカ人 ⓪ ジョンも日本人と一緒に行きました。
John, (who is) an American, went with Japanese people.
b. アメリカ人、ジョンも日本人と一緒に行きました。
An American, John went with Japanese people.

10.2 「の」 marking a subject in a relative clause (RC)

The particle の can mark a subject only in a relative clause. の and が are in this case interchangeable. Observe the following examples:

(8)　鈴木さんは[本田さんが/の買った][豊田の車]を運転した。
　　　　　　　　⎵⎵⎵⎵⎵⎵⎵⎵⎵⎵⎵⎵⎵　⎵⎵⎵⎵⎵⎵⎵
　　　　　　　　　　　　　RC　　　　　　　HN

Ms. Suzuki drove [a Toyota car][28] that [Mr. Honda purchased].

(9)　(私は)[あなたが/の言う][事]が信用できません。
　　　I cannot trust [what] [you say].
(10)　[あなたが/の好きな][人]にこのプレゼントをあげてください。
　　　Please give this present to [a person] [whom you like].
(11)　[木村さんが/の昨日行った][レストラン]で食事をしましょう。
　　　Let's have a meal at [the restaurant] where [Mr. Kimura went yesterday].

11. から

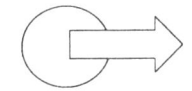

The fundamental meaning of から is to indicate the source or beginning point of an event physically, temporally, and spatially. から indicates the point where an event takes place, but it also refers to the notion of the continuation of the event. から expresses various meanings, such as "from," "since," and "after." The meanings "since" and "after" are usually expressed by the use of the て form of a verb. Observe the following examples:

(1)　a.　会議は10時から始まります。
　　　　　The meeting runs from 10 o'clock (implies that the meeting goes until 12 o'clock, for example).
　　　b.　会議は10時に始まります。
　　　　　The meeting starts at 10 o'clock.
(2)　a.　飛行機は成田から出ます。
　　　　　The airplane leaves from Narita (goes somewhere else).

---

[28] "A Toyota car" in this sentence functions as a "head noun (HN)." A head noun is a noun or a noun phrase that is modified by a relative clause. For further discussion, see Chapter 17, Section 1.4.

b. 飛行機は成田を出ます。
The airplane leaves Narita.

(3) 隣の部屋から音楽が聞こえます。
I can hear music from the next room.

(4) 父は出張から戻りました。
My father returned from the business trip.

(5) バターはミルクから作られます。
Butter is made from milk.

(6) a. 松田さんからうわさを聞きました。
I heard the rumor from Ms. Matsuda.

b. 松田さんにうわさを聞きました。
I heard the rumor from Ms. Matsuda.

(7) a. 大学から奨学金をもらいました。
I received a scholarship from the university.

* b. 大学に奨学金をもらいました。

(8) a. 図書館から本を借りました。
I checked out a book from the library.

* b. 図書館に本を借りました。

Note that when the source of an event is not an animate entity, only から can be used. (Refer to section 4 in this chapter about に.)

(9) 日本に来てから２０年になります。
It has been 20 years since I came to Japan.

(10) コップに一杯水を飲んでから寝ます。
I go to bed after I drink a glass of water.

から can also be used as a sentence-final conjunction meaning "and so." Refer to Chapter 14, Section 1.1.3.

12. まで

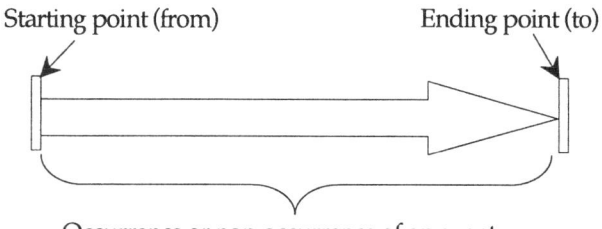

Starting point (from) → Ending point (to)

Occurrence or non-occurrence of an event

The particle まで is used to indicate that the occurrence or non-occurrence of an event continues up to a certain point, and not beyond that point. It emphasizes the continuation of the event rather than goal (usually indicated by に). It is often used with から to indicate the source of an event. When から does not occur, it is usually implied.

(1) 今日は10時から12時まで大学で化学の試験があります。
Today, I have a chemistry exam from 10 to 12 at the university.

(2) 成田からデトロイトまで飛行機で約12時間かかります。
It takes approximately 12 hours from Narita to Detroit by airplane.

(3) 7月から9月まで雨がぜんぜん降りませんでした。
It did not rain at all from July to September.

(4) あなたの家まで車で送ってさしあげましょう。
I shall give you a ride to your home.

(5) ここまで来ればもう大丈夫でしょう。
Since we have come this far, we will be OK (we will no longer need to worry).

(6) あなたがそこまで言うなら、私も一言言いましょう。
If you speak up to that point, I will say a word, too.

In certain context, まで is used to emphasize the meaning of "even," which is similar to も. This use of まで is derived from the concept "until," in that some state has been reached to influence someone or something to be or act in a certain way. Observe the following examples:

(7) a. あなたまでそんな事を言うのですか。
   Even you come to say things like that?
   b. あなたもそんな事を言うのですか。
   You *too* come to say things like that?
(8) a. あの建物まで壊されてしまいます。
   Even that building will unfortunately be demolished.
   b. あの建物も壊されてしまいます。
   That building *too* will unfortunately be demolished.

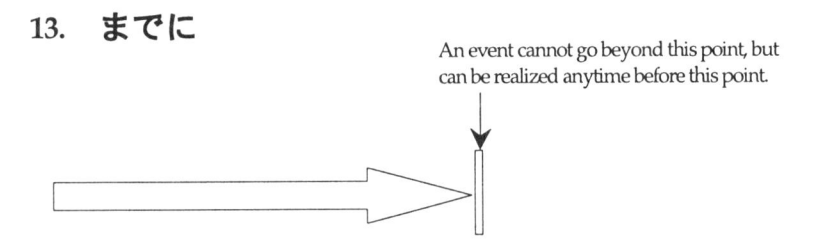

13. までに

An event cannot go beyond this point, but can be realized anytime before this point.

までに, a combination of まで and に, generally follows a time noun, indicating that an event ought to be realized before the point described by the time noun. に in までに indicates the specific time before which the event is supposed to be realized, and まで indicates a duration of time to which the event may extend. For example, 4時までに来てください means that a speaker is requesting the listener to visit the speaker anytime before 4 o'clock, but not beyond. までに is used to indicate that an event is to be realized either "in time" or "on time." Observe the following examples:

(1) 7時までに家へ帰らなければなりません。
   I have to go home by 7 o'clock.
(2) 6月15日までに日本へ行くことになっていますが、まだ切符を買っていません。
   I am supposed to go to Japan by June 15th, but I have not yet purchased a ticket.
(3) 何時までに電話をすればいいですか。
   By what time shall I call you?

14. か

The sentence-final particle か has three main functions, listed below.

> 1. Sentence-final 「か」 as a question marker
> 2. 「か」 indicating "or"
> 3. 「か」 with an interrogative noun creating a word: "some ~"

14.1 Sentence-final 「か」 as a question marker

Instead of using a question mark, Japanese uses か to mark a sentence as a question.[29] か may appear at the end of a sentence or in an embedded sentence.

(1) a. あの方は日本人ですか。
   Is that person Japanese?
   b. ハーバード大学はどこにありますか。
   Where is Harvard University located?
   c. 試験の結果はどうでしたか。
   What was the result of the exam?
   d. 明日も雨が降るでしょうか。
   I wonder if it will rain tomorrow, too.

The following are cases where か appears in an embedded sentence. When a question becomes embedded, か remains to maintain the interrogative status of the original, but follows a plain form of the predicate. Sentences (2a) and (2b) include an interrogative.

(2) a. 鈴木さんの誕生日はいつですか。教えてください。
   When is Ms. Suzuki's birthday? Please let me know.
   ↓
   鈴木さんの誕生日はいつか教えてください。
   Please let me know when Ms. Suzuki's birthday is.

---

[29] See also Chapter 15, Section 1.3.

b. 豊田さんはどんな車が好きですか。知っていますか。
What kind of car does Mr. Toyota like? Do you know?
↓
豊田さんはどんな車が好きか知っていますか。
Do you know what kind of car Mr. Toyota likes?

If the original sentence is interrogative, かどうか is used, as shown in the following examples:

(3) 本田さんは来月日本へ帰りますか。聞いてみてください。
Is Ms. Honda returning to Japan next month? Please ask and find out.
↓
本田さんは来月日本へ帰るかどうか聞いてみてください。
Please ask Ms. Honda and find out if she is returning to Japan next month.

(4) この電話は使えますか。試してください。
Is this phone usable? Please try.
↓
この電話は使えるかどうか試してください。
Please try to see if this phone is usable.

14.2 「か」 indicating "or"

か can also be used to express the meaning "or." It follows a phrase or sentence. The equivalent of "A or B" is "A か B か." When か is used with two noun phrases, it seldom follows the second noun phrase.

(5) a. すしかてんぷら(か)を注文しましょう。
Let's order either sushi or tempura.
b. 土曜日か日曜日(か)に、釣りかハイキング(か)に行きませんか。
Wouldn't you like to go fishing or hiking on either Saturday or Sunday?
c. 行けるか行けないか、まだわかりません。
I do not know yet if I can go or not.
d. 部屋がきれいかきたないかはここでは問題ではありません。
The room's being clean or not is not an issue here.

(6) a. これは本田さんの車ですか、(それとも)³⁰ 鈴木さんのですか。
Is this Mr. Honda's car or Mr. Suzuki's?
b. このドレスは日本製ですか、(それとも) 韓国製ですか。
Was this dress made in Japan or in Korea?

14.3 「か」 with an interrogative noun creating a word: "some ~"

When か is added to an interrogative word, such as 誰、どこ、何, and so on, the word is no longer an interrogative. It instead expresses a "some ~" meaning.

誰		誰か	someone/anyone
いつ		いつか	sometime
何	か	何か	something/anything
どこ		どこか	somewhere/anywhere
どう		どうか	somewhat/in some way
どうして		どうしてか	some reason
なぜ		なぜか	some reason

(7) A: 今日は誰かに会いましたか。
Did you meet anyone (particular) today?
B: いいえ、誰にも会いませんでした。
No, I did not meet anyone.
(8) A: いつか一緒に韓国へ旅行しませんか。
Won't you go on a trip with me to Korea sometime?
B: ええ、いつか・・・。
Yes, sometime....
(9) この問題はどうか (なんとか) しなければならない。
Speaking of this problem, we must do it in some way/we must do something about it.
(10) なぜか彼は最近静かだ。
For some reason, he has been quiet recently.

---

³⁰ The conjunction それとも "or" is often used after か.

15. ね

ね is used most commonly in casual/colloquial speech and communication. It occurs at the end of a phrase or a sentence when the speaker is looking for agreement from the listener.[31] ね has many variations in intonation. Depending on the prosody, it can create various nuances. There is also interaction between the intonation and the pragmatics of ね and other sentence particles, such as よね and ねぇ. The main use of ね, however, is as a tag question, such as in "The food was delicious, *wasn't it?*" where the speaker is confirming the appropriateness of the sentence with the listener. The strategy of ね is certainly that the speaker is trying to involve the listener in the conversation, but if the speaker wants to elicit agreement from the listener, the よね pattern may be more commonly used. The よね pattern offers the speaker's idea, belief, opinion, knowledge, and so forth, then awaits the listener's agreement and/or confirmation. The particle ね, on the other hand, may simply seek the listener's agreement and/or confirmation

(1) a. 暑いですね。
   It's hot, isn't it?
   b. 暑いですよね。
   I feel hot. Don't you feel so too?

(2) a. 試験は難しかったですね。
   The exam was hard, wasn't it?
   b. 試験は難しかったですよね。
   I think that the exam was hard. Don't you think so too?

(3) a. 会議は10時に始まりますね。
   The meeting will start at 10:00, right?
   b. 会議は10時に始まりますよね。
   I believe that the meeting starts at 10:00, but am I right?

(4) a. 昨日は欠席でしたね。
   You were absent yesterday, right?
   b. 昨日は欠席でしたよね。
   I thought that you were absent yesterday. Isn't that correct?

---

[31] Cf. Kamio (1990, 1994, 1997b).

(5) 試験、すごく難しかったよねぇ。
The exam was extremely difficult, wasn't it?

In ねぇ, the vowel "e" in "ne" is prolonged and pronounced "nee." This may create a feminine sound, as it is often used by female language speakers. ね is also used to indicate a speaker's statement as confirmation, such as "O.K." or "all right" as shown in the following examples:

(6) 車の運転に気をつけてね。
Please drive safely, O.K.

(7) 元気でね。
Please take care, O.K.

(8) 私は彼の意見には反対ですね。
I tell you that I disagree with his opinion.

Sample dialogue

ひどいわよねぇ

洋子: ねえ、ちょっと聞いてよ。
Say, listen.

友子: どうしたの？
What happened?

洋子: 彼ったら、ひどいのよ。「君、最近太った？」なんて言うのよ！
My boyfriend is terrible. He says, "Did you gain weight lately?"

友子: そんなこと言ったの？ それはひどいわねぇ。
Did he say that? That's terrible, isn't it!

洋子: そうよね。ひどいわよねぇ。普通はそういうこと言わないわよね。
I think so too. It's terrible. People usually don't say things like that, don't you think.

友子: ねぇ！
They don't, do they!

16. よ

よ may be used to state a sentence assertively and/or to soften the tone of the voice. English equivalents may be, "you know" and "I'm telling you," but these equivalents may not be applicable in all よ sentences. The nuance created by よ is subtle and depends on the environment of the communication. In general, just like ね, よ is often used to involve the listener in the communication or to respond to the speaker's invitation to communication. For this reason, よ often occurs in response to questions. The sentences in parentheses in the following examples are given to show the difference in what よ sentences may imply.

(1) A: 失礼ですが、日本の方ですか。
        Excuse me, but are you Japanese?
     B: ええ、そうですよ。
        Yes, I am (but what can I do for you?).
     A: この日本語、英語に訳せますか。
        Can you translate this Japanese into English?
     B: ええ、できますよ。
        Yes, I can (so do you want me to do it?).

(2) A: 昨日の会議に出ませんでしたよね。
        I believe that you did not attend yesterday's meeting. Isn't that correct?
     B: いいえ、出ましたよ。
        Your statement is wrong; I attended the meeting, you know.

(3) A: あ、そこは危ないですよ。
        Wow, that place is dangerous, you know.
     B: そうなんですか。
        Is that right?
     A: そうですよ。気をつけてくださいよ。
        Yes, I'm telling you. Please be careful, O.K.

17. でも

でも, meaning "~ or something/someone," is used when a speaker is not necessarily particular about the preceding noun. It can replace various particles, such as を, へ, と, に. For example, お茶を飲みませんか means that the speaker is asking the interlocutor whether or not s/he is interested in having some tea, while in お茶でも飲みませんか, the drink can be something other than tea. The focus is on the activity, and not on the noun. でも is often used in invitation structures, such as ませんか, ましょう, ましょうか.

すしを食べませんか　　　　　すしでも食べませんか。
　　　　　　　　　　　　　　Would you like to eat sushi or something?
喫茶店へ行きましょうか。　　喫茶店へでも行きましょうか。
　　　　　　　　　　　　　　Shall we go to a coffee shop or something?
公園で話しましょうか。　　　公園ででも話しましょうか。
　　　　　　　　　　　　　　Shall we talk at a park or somewhere?

Sample dialogues
デートに誘うときは
チビ:　あのう、タマさん、ちょっとミルクでも飲みませんか。
タマ:　あなたねぇ、もうちょっと気の利いた誘い方できないの？(Can you be a bit more tactful?) そういうの、「決まり文句」っていうのよ。(That's called "a fixed phrase.")
チビ:　そうですか。すみません。あの、じゃあ、鳥でも見ませんか。
タマ:　それも同じ。
チビ:　あ、そう・・・。じゃ、「木でも登りませんか」はどうですか。
タマ:　それも同じでしょう。あのねぇ、「〜でも」を使うと真剣味に欠けるのよねぇ。(Lack of seriousness when you use でも.)
チビ:　・・・。

何もできない日
男:　今日は料理でもするか。（と言って冷蔵庫を開ける）
　　あれ、何もない・・・。じゃ、買い物にでも行くか。（と言って財布を開ける）
　　あれ、お金がない。じゃ、まずお金でもおろしに行くか。（と言って車に乗る）
　　あれ、ガソリンがない。しかたない、家でテレビでも見るか。（と言ってテレビをつける）
　　あれ？　停電だ。(power outage) もう・・・。
　　何もできないじゃないか。じゃ、寝よう〜っと。

CHAPTER 5

Transitive vs. Intransitive

Describing verbs as transitive or intransitive is one of the most basic and common ways to characterize them. "Transitive" refers to a verb that takes an object, while "intransitive" refers to verbs that do not. In other words, the transitive structure is SOV, while the intransitive structure is SV. In English, many verbs can serve both as transitive verbs (v.t.) and intransitive verbs (v.i.), for example, "open" in "I open the door" vs. "the door opens," or "change" in "I changed the rule" vs. "the rule changed." This distinction is marked morphologically in Japanese, and different verbs are used to express transitivity and intransitivity. The Chinese characters used to transcribe the verbs may be the same and pronunciation of the verbs may be similar, but there is no single rule for the formation of transitive and intransitive verbs (see Jacobsen, 1992). The following examples exhibit the basic structures of transitive and intransitive verbs:

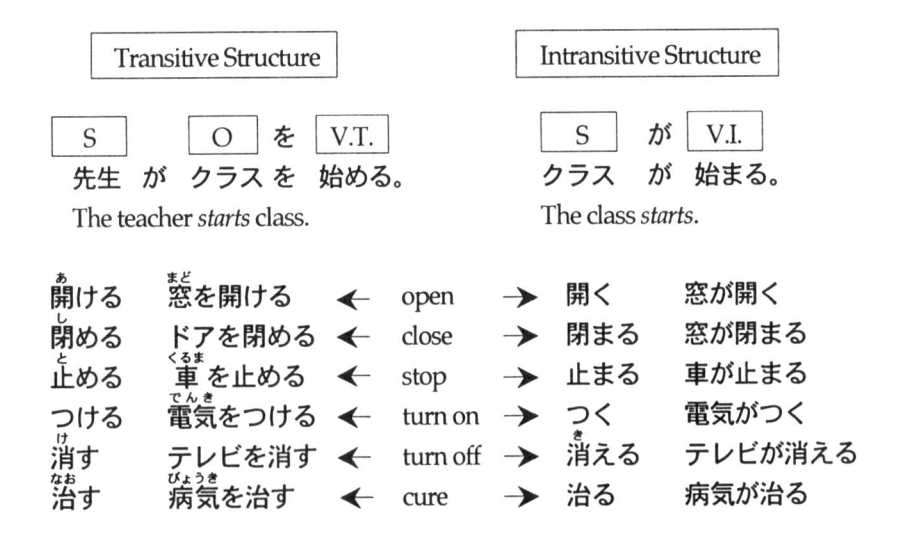

Transitive Structure	Intransitive Structure
S　O を V.T.	S が V.I.
先生 が クラス を 始める。	クラス が 始まる。
The teacher *starts* class.	The class *starts*.

開ける	窓を開ける	←	open	→	開く	窓が開く
閉める	ドアを閉める	←	close	→	閉まる	窓が閉まる
止める	車を止める	←	stop	→	止まる	車が止まる
つける	電気をつける	←	turn on	→	つく	電気がつく
消す	テレビを消す	←	turn off	→	消える	テレビが消える
治す	病気を治す	←	cure	→	治る	病気が治る

落とす	財布を落とす	←	drop	→	落ちる	財布が落ちる
腐らす	野菜を腐らす	←	spoil	→	腐る	野菜が腐る
変える	名前を変える	←	change	→	変わる	名前が変わる
壊す	時計を壊す	←	break	→	壊れる	時計が壊れる
集める	お金を集める	←	gather	→	集まる	お金が集まる
乾かす	服を乾かす	←	dry	→	乾く	服が乾く

Each English verb above serves both transitive and intransitive functions, but has two different equivalents in Japanese. Other English verbs may have a different way to form the intransitive equivalent. Here are some more examples:[1]

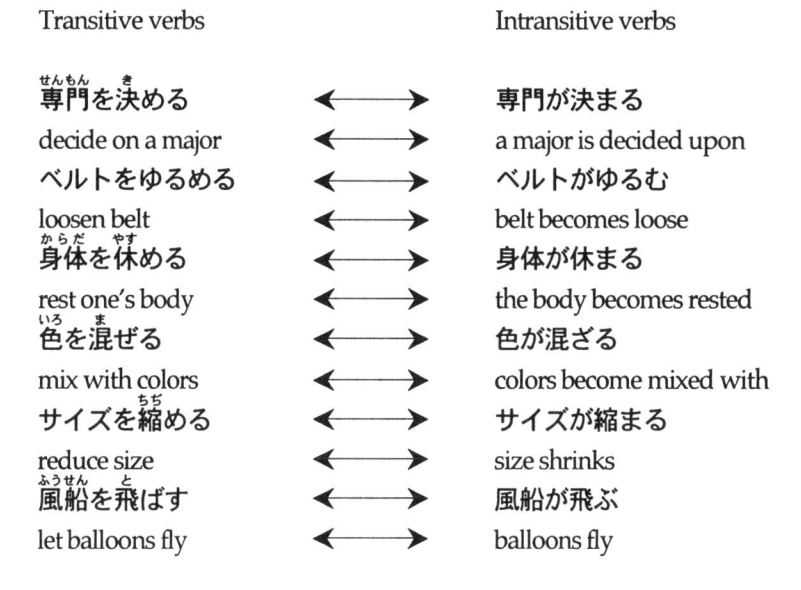

Transitive verbs		Intransitive verbs
専門を決める	←→	専門が決まる
decide on a major	←→	a major is decided upon
ベルトをゆるめる	←→	ベルトがゆるむ
loosen belt	←→	belt becomes loose
身体を休める	←→	身体が休まる
rest one's body	←→	the body becomes rested
色を混ぜる	←→	色が混ざる
mix with colors	←→	colors become mixed with
サイズを縮める	←→	サイズが縮まる
reduce size	←→	size shrinks
風船を飛ばす	←→	風船が飛ぶ
let balloons fly	←→	balloons fly

A semantic feature commonly seen in transitive verbs is that the subject (agent) is most often an animate entity which operates and controls the situation, activity, or event described by the verb by its own volition. Contrarily, when a situation is described by an intransitive verb, the situation is usually one that is not under the control of an animate entity; rather, it describes what happens to the subject. Therefore, an intransitive verb tends to express a situation that results from the

---

[1] Refer to Chapter 4 for explanations of the usage of each particle.

action of an animate entity, but indicating a resultative state. For example, in ドアを開けた "I opened the door" versus ドアが開いた "the door opened," it is envisioned that the door opened as a result of someone's having opened the door. An animate entity's volitional control tends to be behind the generation of a sentence with an intransitive verb.[2]

Among events described by intransitive verbs, however, there are many that an animate entity can control by its own will. These are called "volitional-intransitive verbs" in this book.[3] Also, among transitive verbs, there are verbs called "ditransitve" and "stative-transitive." Ditransitive verbs can take both direct and indirect objects. Stative-transitive verbs are not volitionally controllable, but can take an object. The figure shows the categories of these verbs and where they belong.

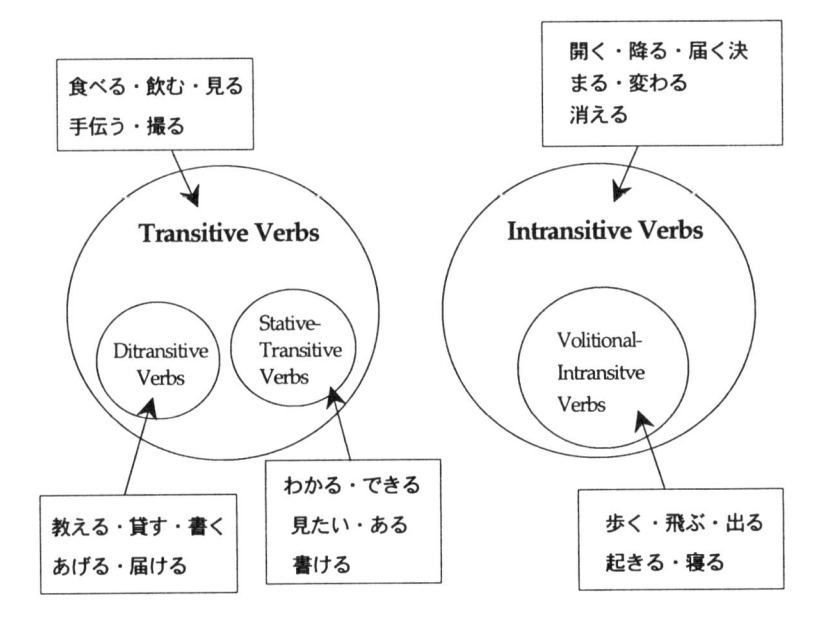

食べる・飲む・見る
手伝う・撮る

開く・降る・届く決まる・変わる
消える

Transitive Verbs

Intransitive Verbs

Ditransitive Verbs

Stative-Transitive Verbs

Volitional-Intransitve Verbs

教える・貸す・書く
あげる・届ける

わかる・できる
見たい・ある
書ける

歩く・飛ぶ・出る
起きる・寝る

---

[2] Natural phenomena are exceptions since they are not caused by an animate entity, such as 風が吹く "the wind blows" and 雨が降る "the rain falls."

[3] The classification of intransitive verbs used here (intransitive verbs and volitional-intransitive verbs) is based on two categories: unaccusatives and unergatives (as opposed to accusatives for transitive verbs). This linguistic classification is covered, e.g., in Perlmutter (1978), Levin and Rappaport Havov (1995), and Johnson (2001, 2002).

1. Intransitive Verbs
1.1 Volitional-intransitive verbs
1.1.1 Standard volitional-intransitive verbs that take the particle 「を」

Let us first look at some standard verbs, such as 歩く "to walk," 走る "to run," 飛ぶ "to fly," 泳ぐ "to swim," 渡る "to cross," 曲がる "to turn the corner"[4] in addition to motion verbs, such as 行く "to go," 来る "to come," and 帰る "to go home." These volitional-intransitive verbs normally do not take an object, but are often used for a movement from one place to another. In this case, the place noun in which the movement occurs is marked by the particle を, as if the verb is transitive. The use of the particle を in these contexts is not exactly the same as its usage when used with a transitive verb, such as すしを食べる "I eat sushi," but it is similar, in that the place marked by を with volitional-intransitive verbs is acted upon by an agent, either conceptually or physically.[5] Let us look at the following examples:

(1) a. サリーは公園まで歩いた。
    Sally walked as far as the park. (公園 is the goal of the motion.)
   b. サリーは公園を歩いた。
    Sally walked the park. Sally took a walk in the park. (公園 is the place where the motion "to walk" occurred.)

---

[4] The transitive counterparts for these verbs are 歩かす, 走らす, 飛ばす, 泳がす, 渡す, and 曲げる, respectively.

[5] The difference between the object marker を and the を that marks the path is identified when, for example, the predicate accompanies the desiderative form たい. When を in 山を登る "climb a mountain" is changed to が in the desiderative sentence 山が登りたい "I want to climb a mountain," the change creates an awkward expression, while the object marker を in 水を飲む "drink water" can be changed to が in the desiderative sentence 水が飲みたい "I want to drink water" without causing any awkwardness. The degree of acceptability for sentences like 山が登りたい, 川が泳ぎたい "I want to swim in the river," and 空が飛びたい "I want to fly through the sky" may be different depending on context and from individual to individual, but the tendency is for を to prevail over が in the desiderative construction and the use of が to be considered inappropriate. For a review of the particle を, refer to Chapter 4, Section 3.

c. サリーはてんぷらを食べた。
     Sally ate tempura. (てんぷら is an object upon which the agent/subject acted.)
(2) a. トムはキャンパスに向かって走った。
     Tom ran toward the campus. (キャンパス is the goal of the motion.)
  b. トムはキャンパスを走った。
     Tom ran through the campus. (キャンパス is the place where the motion "to run" occurred.)
(3) a. ジェリーは川で泳いだ。
     Jerry swam in the river. (The activity 泳ぐ took place in the river.)
  b. ジェリーは川を泳いだ。
     Jerry swam through the river (and went to the other side of the river.) (川 is the place Jerry acted upon.)
(4) a. シルベスターは富士山に登った。
     Sylvester climbed Mt. Fuji (and reached a certain location on the mountain.)
  b. シルベスターは富士山を登った。
     Sylvester climbed Mt. Fuji. (富士山 is the place where the climbing took place.)

The verbs in sentences (a) in (1) through (4) are used to express intransitivity without an accompanying object. On the other hand, the same verbs in sentences (b) in (1) through (4) are used to express a different meaning. In these examples, the places linked to the verbs are all acted upon and affected by the agent. For example, to the unidirectional use of the particle に, 富士山に登る indicates that the agent reached the summit of the mountain, while 富士山を登る indicates that the climbing itself is the focus of communication.

The following are cases that do not have different interpretations. Only を marks the place noun in a way that makes sense, since one cannot say 空で飛んだ, for example, because 空 is an unlimited dimension. The same applies for 橋で渡る, since 渡る itself describes a crossing activity, and not an activity occurring inside a limited dimension.

(5) トゥイティは空を飛んだ。
Tweety flew through the sky. (空 is the place where the flying took place.)
(6) ジェフは橋を渡った。
Jeff crossed the bridge. (橋 is the place where the crossing took place.)

1.1.2 Verbs of leaving
Verbs of leaving, such as 出る "to get out," 卒業する "to graduate," and 離れる "to leave," can be represented by this schematic: ⤴. They are also considered volitional-intransitive verbs[6] when some kind of an entity causes the event. The place noun the agent leaves is marked by を, though again, the function of を is not exactly the same as that of the を that marks the object of a transitive verb; it is the same as for standard volitional-intransitive verbs.

(7) 花子は3時に家を出た。
Hanako left home at 3 o'clock.
(8) 太郎は去年大学を卒業した。
Taro graduated from college last year. (から is not appropriate, even though it is the normal equivalent to "from.")
(9) 智子は結婚して、実家を離れた。
Tomoko got married and left her parents' home.

1.1.3 Verbs of non-voluntary physical events
There are verbs that express spontaneous, non-voluntary physical events, such as "snore," "yawn," and "sneeze." In English these verbs are considered intransitive verbs that do not take an object. In Japanese, however, "yawn" and "sneeze" can be expressed by either a transitive or an intransitive verb (あくびをする/あくびが出る and くしゃみをする/くしゃみが出る, respectively). "Snore," on the other hand, is expressed only by a transitive verb, as in いびきをかく. When such events are expressed by an intransitive verb, they are presented as non-voluntary physical events, while transitive verbs give an impression that the events are caused by the subject's voluntary acts. See the following examples.

---

[6] See Chapter 4, Section 3 about the particle を. The transitive counterparts of these verbs are 出す, 卒業させる, and 離す, respectively.

(10) 夫は一晩中いびきをかくので、私は睡眠不足なんです。
Because my husband snores all night, I cannot get enough sleep.
(11) a. 授業中にあくびをするのは失礼だ。
It is rude to yawn during class.
b. あの先生の講義はあくびが出る。
That professor's lectures make me yawn.
(12) a. くしゃみをしたら、すっきりした。
When I sneezed, I felt good.
b. 胡椒が鼻に入って、くしゃみが出た。
Pepper got into my nose, and a sneeze came out.

2. Transitive Verbs: Ditransitive and Transitive
2.1 Ditransitive verbs

Verbs that take both direct and indirect objects are called "ditransitive verbs," and this ability plays a crucial role for some grammatical categories, such as てくれる, てあげる, and てもらう, which express giving and receiving of an activity. The indirect object is usually the recipient of an event described by the verb. If a question "what and to whom?" can be formed, the verb is usually ditransitive.

(1) 田中さんは｜アメリカ人に｜日本語を｜教えています。

田中さんは　　｜誰に｜　　｜何を｜　教えていますか。
　　　　　　Indirect Obj.　Direct Obj.

(2) その両親は子供にいいお手本を見せた。
Those parents showed a good example to their children. (Those parents were good role models.)
(3) 私はお世話になった先生に手紙を書いた。
I wrote a letter to my teacher to whom I am indebted.
(4) すみません、(私に)塩を渡してくださいませんか。
Excuse me, please pass me the salt, won't you?
(5) 友達に(お金を)1,000円貸しましたが、結局返してもらえませんでした。
I lent 1,000 yen to my friend, but did not get it back after all.

2.2 Stative-transitive predicates (some verbs and い/な adjectives)

Since stative-transitive verbs (as proposed by Kuno 1973), including い and な adjectives, are stative predicates, they are not supposed to take an object. However, there are a handful of stative predicates that behave like transitive verbs and do take an object. These predicates are usually related to a state of mind or an ability, and the subject is usually an animate entity. An object of these stative predicates is marked by が. Only when the predicate is a compound involving an activity verb, such as 書ける(書く+できる) "can write," may を also be an option. See the following examples.

(6) ジェリーさんは日本語がわかります。(わかる is a stative verb.)
　　Jerry understands Japanese.

(7) トムさんはテニスができます。(できる is a stative verb.)
　　Tom can play tennis.

(8) 太郎は花子が好きだ。(好き is a な adjective.)
　　Taro likes Hanako.

(9) 私が犬が怖い。(怖い is an い adjective.)
　　I am scared of dogs.

(10) 私は新車が欲しい。(欲しい is an い adjective.)
　　 I want a new car.

(11) 私はすしとてんぷらが/をおもいきり食べたい。(食べたい is a compound verbal predicate from 食べる "to eat" and the desiderative form たい "want.")
　　 I want to eat sushi and tempura to my heart's content.

(12) トムさんは漢字が/を 1,000 字書けます。(書ける is a compound verb phrase.)
　　 Tom can write 1,000 Chinese characters.
　　 (書ける is formed from the activity verb 書く "to write" and the potential morpheme ~e-ru "can.")

CHAPTER 6

Verbs of Existence: ある・いる

In Japanese, there are two verbs, ある and いる, whose approximate equivalent is "to exist" in English. ある alternates with いる depending on whether the existing entity is animate or inanimate. In general, when the entity is animate, いる is used; when the entity is inanimate, ある is used. Note that verbs of existence are inherently engaged with a place or a substance to which the entity belongs. The place or the substance that the entity belongs to is marked by the particle に (は may follow in order to create a contrastive meaning or to mention the noun marked by に as a topic). First, let's observe how ある and いる sentences are constructed.

1. The Syntax and Semantics of ある and いる

There is Y located in/belongs to X:

$$\boxed{X} \; に \; \boxed{Y} \; が \; \begin{cases} いる \text{ (animate entity)} \\ ある \text{ (inanimate entity)} \end{cases}$$

公園に子供がいる。
There are children in the park.

公園にベンチがある。
There is a bench in the park.

When numbers need to be referenced, they are placed in front of the verb like adverbs, as in the following:

(1) a. 公園に子供が3人いる。
        There are three children in the park.
   *b. 公園に子供が3人ある。
    c. 公園にベンチが3つある。
        There are three benches in the park.
   *d. 公園にベンチが3ついる。

Sentences (1a) and (1c) represent very basic formations of いる and ある sentences. When what exists is children, いる is used to mean "children [animate entity] exist," while if the entity is a bench, ある is used meaning "bench [inanimate] exists." Now let's observe some more examples:

(2)   a.   私にはポルシェがある。
            There is a Porsche that belongs to me.
            = I have a Porsche.
   *b.   私にはポルシェがいる。
   c.   私には子供が3人いる。
            There are three children that belong to me.
            = I have three children.
   d.   私には子供が3人ある。[1]
            There are three children that belong to me.
            = I have three children.

In sentences (2a) and (2b), where an inanimate entity is the entity of existence, only ある is appropriate. Sentence (2c) offers a standard use of いる, but ある is also applicable for an animate entity under certain circumstances. In day-to-day communication, preference may be given to いる, but more formal settings may privilege ある. This means that the animate-inanimate dichotomy of ある and いる does not necessarily apply to a situation where the subject of the sentence is itself an animate entity. In such cases, if the person owns the entity, the meaning is equivalent to "I have/own ~." The subject of both sentences (2c) and (2d) is 私, who owns three children, and the interpretation of these sentences is "I have three children." In this case, the animate nature of the owned entity does not always demand the use of いる.

The following figure illustrates the use of いる and ある. Some examples are given as well.

---

[1] The validity of the use of ある for a sentence involving an animate entity can also be supported by the use of honorific forms of the verb ある. One may say either 先生にはお子様が3人おありになります or 先生にはお子様が3人いらっしゃいます.

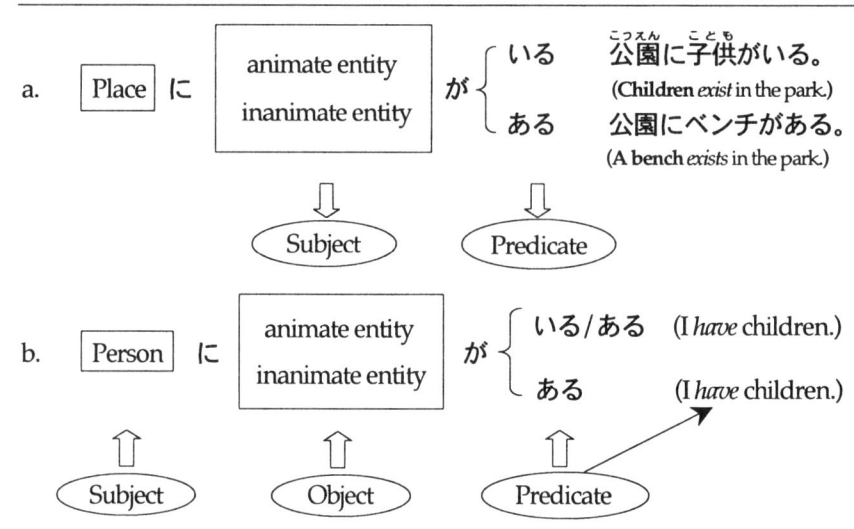

a. [Place] に { animate entity / inanimate entity } が { いる / ある }

公園に子供がいる。
(**Children** *exist* in the park.)
公園にベンチがある。
(**A bench** *exists* in the park.)

⇓ Subject   ⇓ Predicate

b. [Person] に { animate entity / inanimate entity } が { いる/ある (I *have* children.) / ある (I *have* children.) }

⇑ Subject   ⇑ Object   ⇑ Predicate

(3) a. 駐車場に人が3人いる。
There are three people in the parking lot.
b. 駐車場には車が3台ある。
There are three cars in the parking lot.
c. 隣の家に猫が3匹いる。
There are three cats at the neighbor's house.
d. 隣の家にプールがある。
There is a pool in the neighbor's yard.

(4) a. メリーには兄弟が3人いる。
Mary has three siblings.
b. メリーには兄弟が3人ある。
Mary has three siblings.
c. メリーには車が3台ある。
Mary has three cars.
d. 隣の家に猫が3匹いる。
My neighbor has three cats.
e. 隣の家にプールがある。
My neighbor has a pool.

As is evident from example sentences (3a) and (3b), when an animate/inanimate entity is located in a place, the sentence is concerned with the existence of the entity at the location; therefore, the interpretation for sentence (3a) 駐車場に人が3人いる, for example, is "three people exist in the parking lot," and "three people" becomes the subject of the sentence. Accordingly, 人がいる and 車がある mean "a person exists" and "a car exists," respectively.

On the other hand, as can be seen in sentences (4a)–(4c), when a noun marked by に is an animate entity, the noun cannot be interpreted as a location. Instead it becomes an entity that owns the が marked object. For example, メリー in sentence (4a), メリーには兄弟が3人いる, *cannot* be considered a location, but *can* be considered the subject, who has three siblings. Therefore, this sentence consists of the subject (メリー), the object (兄弟), and the predicate (いる). The nature of the に marked noun phrase exhibits different characteristics in terms of the interpretation of the syntax and semantics of the sentence.

Regarding sentences (3c), (3d) and (4d), (4e), 隣の家 can be viewed as a place noun (the neighbor's house) or as a person (the neighbor), and depending on the speaker's intention, the sentence can be interpreted either way. This is why these sentences are repeated as examples. There are many more examples like these in daily situations.

Another point is that ある is not unique in demonstrating inconsistency in terms of its agreement with an animate or inanimate entity. The verb いる also exhibits inconsistent usage depending on the perception of the speaker. Such is the case when an entity is moving or moved by human control. See the following examples:

(5) あ、あそこにタクシーがいる。呼ぼう。
Look, there is a taxi over there. Let's call him.

(6) エレベータはまだ45階にいるみたいだ。もう少し待ってみよう。
It looks like the elevator is still on the 45th floor. Let's wait a little longer.

These sentences demonstrate that a moving entity is not situated stably in a location. The avoidance of ある also shows a secondary characteristic of ある, namely, that it is used when the existence is conceived of as stable. On the other hand,

いる can represent an entity's existence that may be dynamic and/or fluid. This observation is supportable, since いる itself can be used to express a sense of stability, as when it occurs with ください in sentences like ここにいてください "please stay here." This also indicates the idea ここで待ってください "Please wait here."

2. "There Is a Dog in the Yard" vs. "The Dog Is in the Yard"

Thus far we have identified certain usages of いる and ある. In figure (a) in the section preceding, where an entity belongs to a place, the equivalent of the sentence is *"There is ~ located in ~ place/~ exists in ~ place."* In figure (b), where an entity belongs to a person, the equivalent of the sentence is *"The person has ~."* When the pattern represented in (a) is used, the subject is presented as new information, in the same way that "a dog" in "There is a dog over there" is new information in English. For example, one may point and say, "Look, there is a dog over there," as the first recognition of the dog. Thereafter, when one mentions the same entity, it is no longer *"a dog,"* but *"the dog,"* since the word has been introduced and has become registered/shared information between the speaker and the listener. "A dog/The dog" may be used in the following manner:

(1) Outside Shibuya station, there is *a* statue of *a* dog called Hachi-koo. *The* statue is built in honor of *the* dog who died in front of the station after waiting for his master many years.

(2) Once upon a time, there were *an* old man and *an* old woman living in a small village. The village had *a* mountain and *a* river. One day, *the* old man went to *the* mountain to collect wood, and *the* old woman went to *the* river to wash clothes. (Translate into Japanese as your exercise.[2])

Figure (a) also corresponds to the use of "a" and "the" in English. Look at the figure below and the accompanying examples:

---

[2] Sample answer (1) 渋谷駅の外に、ハチ公という犬の銅像がある。その銅像は、飼い主を何年も待ち続けた後、駅の前で死んだハチ公を記念して建てられた。(2) 昔、昔、ある小さい村におじいさんとおばあさんが住んでいた。その村には山と川があったある日、おじいさんは山へ芝刈りに、おばあさんは川へ洗濯にでかけた。

Diagram

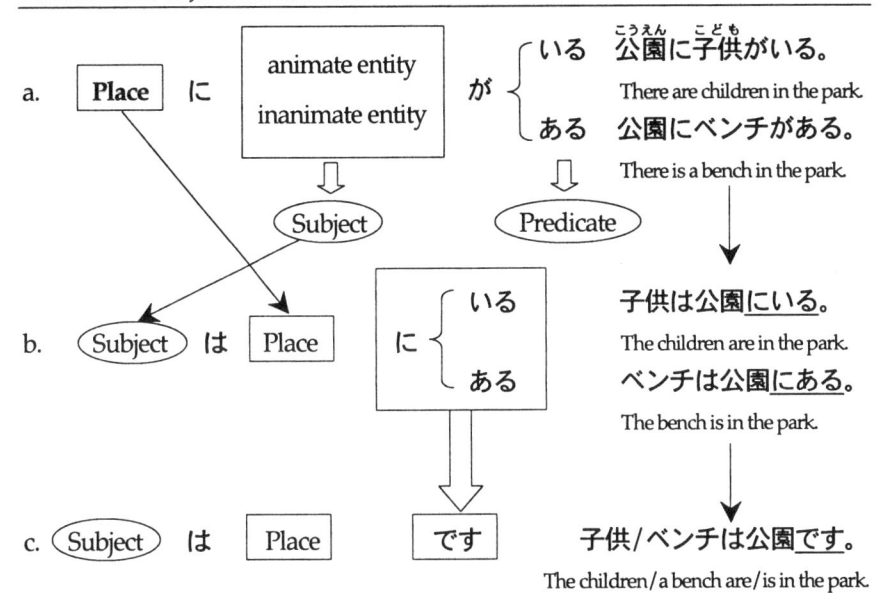

a. [Place] に { animate entity / inanimate entity } が { いる / ある }

公園に子供がいる。
There are children in the park.
公園にベンチがある。
There is a bench in the bench.

(Subject) (Predicate)

b. (Subject) は [Place] に { いる / ある }

子供は公園にいる。
The children are in the park.
ベンチは公園にある。
The bench is in the park.

c. (Subject) は [Place] です

子供／ベンチは公園です。
The children/a bench are/is in the park.

The figures demonstrate how sentences may be transformed depending on whether the speaker and the listener share the same information. In figure (c), the particle は is used to indicate that 子供 and ベンチ are shared information and given as a topic (also the subject) at the beginning of the sentence. Also, にいる／ある can be replaced by です, as in 子供は公園です "the children are in the park." Note that this sentence does not mean "the children *are* the park," as would be the case if です were used as the copula in the sentence pattern "X is equal to Y." Here です represents sort of a contracted form of にいる／ある, and its meaning is identified from context. The following are some more examples that demonstrate different semantic features of です:

(3) 先生は日本人です。
Our professor is Japanese.

(4) a. 先生はオフィスです。
The professor is in his office./*The professor is the office.

b. 先生はオフィスにいます。
The professor is positioned in his office.

(5) a. 犬は庭です。
The dog is in the yard./*The dog is the yard.
b. 犬は庭にいます。
The dog is positioned in the yard.
(6) a. トイレはどこですか。
Where is the bathroom?
b. トイレはどこにありますか。
Where is the bathroom located?

If you are in a place where the existence of a bathroom may not be expected, but you would like to find one, you may ask saying この辺にトイレが ありますか "Is there a *bathroom* in this vicinity?" This sentence indicates that not only the speaker, but also the listener, may not possess the information from the speaker's viewpoint. On the other hand, if you are in a mall, where there must be at least several bathrooms, people's knowledge lets them say トイレは どこですか "Where is *the* bathroom?" without prior conversation. Thus, the pattern "place に 〜があります" is the equivalent to "there is ~" for new information, and the pattern "〜は〜にあります（です）" "the ~ is located in ~" expresses a different meaning depending on whether or not a piece of information is shared. In these situations, the use of が and は plays the crucial role.

CHAPTER 7

Tense: る・た in Subordinate Clauses

1. Functions of Tense Forms

Japanese has two tense forms for each part of speech. The tense forms constitute a predicate agglutinatively, referring to the time when the event described by a verb is realized and the time when the event is in the state described by an い adjective, な adjective, or noun.

In Japanese, these tense forms for activity verbs do not necessarily correspond to present, future, and past in English. The る form, for example, is used to describe a situation where the event has not yet been realized/completed, and it can be used to describe an event occurring in the past. For this reason, the term "imperfective" is often employed to describe the use of る accurately. The た form is termed "perfective" and is used to describe situations where an event has been realized/completed. It can also be used to describe an event in the future; therefore た is not necessarily a past tense form.[1]

Note that the interpretation of the る form differs depending on whether the predicate is an activity or a stative verb. Let us take 食べる and いる as examples.

(1) a. 私は今晩 8 時に夕飯を食べる。
 I <u>will eat</u> dinner at 8:00 PM tonight.
 b. 私は毎日 8 時に夕飯を食べる。
 I <u>eat</u> dinner at 8:00 PM <u>every day</u>.

---

[1] Please note that the notions "imperfective" and "perfective" do not apply to stative predicates, such as い adjectives, な adjectives, nouns, and stative verbs, including stative-transitive verbs. This is due to the fact that such predicates are not concerned with the completion/realization of the event, but express a static and/or everlasting state.

* c. 私(わたし)は今夕飯(いまゆうはん)を食(た)べる。→ 私は今夕飯を食<u>べている</u>。
       I eat dinner now.   I <u>am eating</u> dinner now.

(2) a. 明日(あした)は３時(さんじ)までオフィスにい<u>る</u>。
       I <u>will be</u> in my office until 3 o'clock tomorrow.
    b. 毎日(まいにち)オフィスにい<u>る</u>。
       I <u>stay</u> in my office <u>every day</u>.
    c. 今オフィスにい<u>る</u>。
       I <u>am</u> in my office now.

As is evident from the above example sentences, the activity verb 食べる expresses either a future or a habitual event, but not an event that is currently going on. For current activity, the aspectual form ている[2] must be used.[3] This is attributed to the fact that 今 "now" is used to point to a current moment during which some event is progressing or continuing. In order for 食べる to describe such a situation, an animate entity has to be in the middle of eating, which is expressed by the use of ている. On the other hand, the stative verb いる "to stay" can express a future, a habitual, or a present event. For the present, on-going event, unlike 食べる, the use of ている is unnecessary. This is because いる is concerned with an internal situation of a time expanse, rather than the starting point and/or an ending point of the described event. いる therefore can point to any point in time during the time いる continues.

Now observe the following conjugation table with the plain forms of parts of speech.

Verb

	Past (perfective)	Non-past (imperfective)
Affirmative	食べた	食べる
Negative	食べなかった	食べない

---

[2] Refer to Chapter 10, Section 3 for further discussion of ている.
[3] 今夕飯を食べる may be heard in day-to-day communication, although it is not a proper use of the verb form. However, it usually occurs with ところ or (食べ)ようとする "about to," indicating the starting point from which the speaker is going to realize the event. Even if the speaker does not employ these grammatical devices, the listener understands that the speaker meant to say "I am about to eat" for sentence (1c).

い adjective

	Past	Non-past
Affirmative	おもしろかった	おもしろい
Negative	おもしろくなかった	おもしろくない

な adjective/Noun

	Past	Non-past
Affirmative	元気だった/学生だった	元気だ/学生だ
Negative	元気じゃなかった/学生じゃなかった	元気じゃない/学生じゃない

The past (perfective) tense is commonly expressed by た for all parts of speech, while the non-past (imperfective) tense is expressed by the plain form in る. As will be mentioned in the following section about the 時 "when" clause, the notion of imperfective and perfective plays a significant role in deciding when and where an activity in the main sentence occurred.

2. Tense Forms in "When" Clauses

The morpheme 時 "at the time when," used in a subordinate clause,[4] indicates the specific point in time when the event described by the predicate in the main clause is realized. The difference between this and the "when" meaning expressed by the conditional forms と and たら, for example, is that the 時 clause, especially with an activity verb, is closely related to notions of "before" and "after," depending on the form of the verb. For example, 風が吹くとドアが開く "the door opens when the wind blows" indicates a natural consequence of the wind's blowing against the door, and 風が吹いたら、ドアが開く "if the wind blows, the door will open" is used to indicate that the main event will realize on condition of the wind's blowing. 風が吹く時、ドアが開く "the door opens at the time when the wind blows" is used to indicate a specific time when the door opens.

---

[4] In language and linguistics, the term "subordinate" includes various kinds of patterns and grammatical forms. In this book, "subordinate clause" is used in a rather limited sense in that it refers to a sentence that is considered structurally secondary to the main clause. Subordinate clauses include constructions, such as "when ~," "before ~," "after ~ ," " if ~," "because ~," and "since ~."

Although the English equivalent of both of these morphemes can be "when," the speaker differentiates the use of these morphemes in order to convey a subtle nuance behind the sentence.

Now let us look at the construction of 時 sentences. A 時 clause may be formulated by using one of each of the parts of speech shown in the following chart (representing only non-past tense forms):

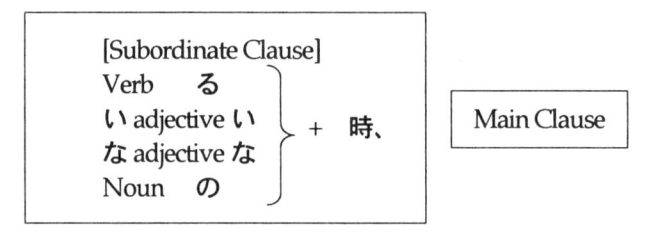

```
[Subordinate Clause]
Verb     る
い adjective い    + 時、    Main Clause
な adjective な
Noun     の
```

Main clause in non-past context
(1) a. 日本へ行く時、プレゼントを買います。
        When I go to Japan, I will buy a present.
    b. 日本へ行った時、プレゼントを買います。
        When I arrive in Japan, I will buy a present.
    c. 天気がいい時、よくバーベキューをします。
        I often barbecue when the weather is nice.
    d. 暇な時、テレビを見ます。
        I watch TV when I have time.
    e. 信号が赤の時、道路を渡ってはいけません。
        You are not supposed to cross the street when the traffic light is red.

Main clause in past context
(2) a. 日本へ行く時、プレゼントを買いました。
        When I went to Japan/Before I went to Japan, I bought a present.
    b. 日本へ行った時、プレゼントを買いました。
        When I arrived in Japan, I bought a present.
    c. 天気がいい/よかった時、よくバーベキューをしました。
        I used to barbecue often when the weather was nice.
    d. 暇な/だった時、テレビを見ました。
        I watched TV when I had time.

e. 子供の/だった時、よく父に叱られました。
   When I was a kid, I was often scolded by my father.

When an activity verb is used in the subordinate clause, either the imperfective or the perfective form may occur, regardless of the tense in the main clause, to indicate when/where the event in the subordinate clause actually occurs/occurred.

However, stative predicates do not behave in the same fashion. When the main sentence is in a non-past context, only the imperfective form is used, and when the main sentence is in the past context, either the imperfective or the perfective form may be used. This arises from the nature of stative predicates. The notion of stativity is captured not as a specific point in time, but as a situation in an expanse of time without a clear beginning and end point. The internal situation captured in such an expanse is perceived as the same regardless of whether the situation is in past context or future context. Time does not affect the interpretation of stativity. One subtle difference between 子供の時よく父に叱られた and 子供だった時よく父に叱られた may be that the latter gives an impression that the event is remote, emphasizing a psychological distance between the time of speech and the event, while the former may not generate a similar psychological distance with regard to the past event. Of the two expressions, 子供の時 may be heard more frequently, and generally, imperfective forms may be more common for stative predicates.

When 時 follows the imperfective form of an activity predicate, the 時 clause functions in a similar fashion to the notion of "before," and when 時 follows the perfective form, the 時 clause is similar to the notion of "after."[5] This is due to the fundamental function of imperfective and perfective, the "not-yet-realized or incomplete" and the "realized or completed" situation, respectively. The following timeline demonstrates how these notions play a role in determining the meaning of 時 sentences. In 時 sentences, tense is expressed in the main clause.

---

[5] Interpretation of imperfective and perfective in this way is applicable to subordinate clauses with 前 "before" and 後 "after." 前 is compatible only with the imperfective form of a verb, since 前 indicates a not-yet-realized or complete situation, and 後 with the perfective form, since 後 indicates a realized or completed situation.

(3) a. 学校へ来る時先生に会った。
I met my teacher on the way to school.

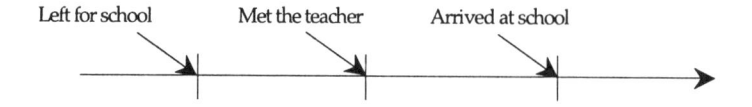

```
Left for school    Met the teacher    Arrived at school
      ↓                  ↓                   ↓
──────┼──────────────────┼───────────────────┼──────────→
```

b. 学校へ来た時、先生に会った。
I met my teacher when I arrived at school.

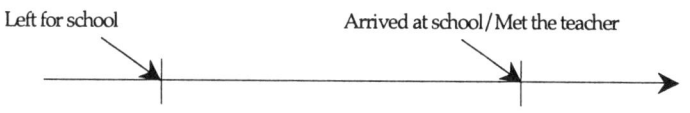

```
Left for school                Arrived at school/Met the teacher
      ↓                                    ↓
──────┼────────────────────────────────────┼──────────→
```

(4) a. 学校に行く時、友達に電話をかける。
I will call my friend before I leave for school.

```
              Leave for school
Call my friend      ↓                Arrive at school
      ↓                                    ↓
──────┼─────────────┼───────────────────────┼──────────→
```

b. 学校に行った時、友達に電話をかける。
I will call my friend after I arrive at school.

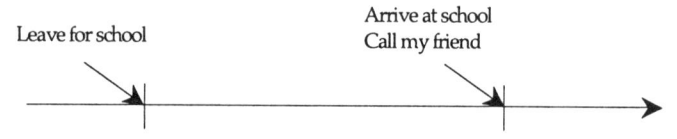

```
                                    Arrive at school
Leave for school                    Call my friend
      ↓                                    ↓
──────┼────────────────────────────────────┼──────────→
```

(5) 本を読む時、めがねをかける。
I wear glasses when I read a book.

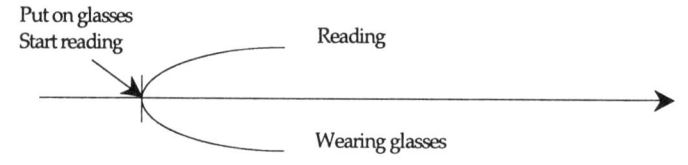

```
Put on glasses
Start reading        Reading
      ↓
──────┼──────────────────────────────────────────────→
                     Wearing glasses
```

(6) 頂上に着いた時、プロポーズした。
When I arrived at the summit of the mountain, I proposed to her.

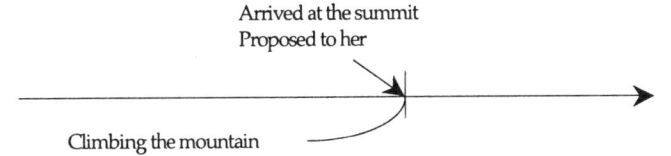

Arrived at the summit / Proposed to her

Climbing the mountain

When a stative predicate is used in past context, just like other stative predicates (い adjective, な adjective, noun), exchanging る and た does not affect the meaning of the sentence, as is shown in sentence (7). For the non-past context, the perfective form is not applicable. Compare sentence (8).

(7) 日本にいる/いた時、英語を教えていた。 I was teaching English when I was in Japan.
(Tense agreement is unnecessary when a predicate in a 時 clause is a stative predicate and the whole event is described in past context.)

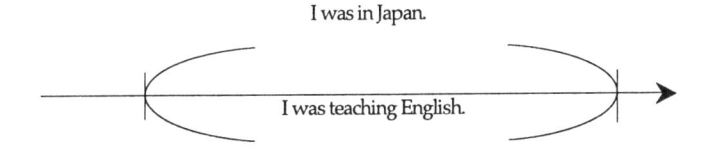

I was in Japan.
I was teaching English.

(8) 時間がある/*あった時は、ピアノの練習をする。
(Tense agreement is *necessary* when a predicate in a 時 clause is a stative predicate and the whole event is described in non-past context.)

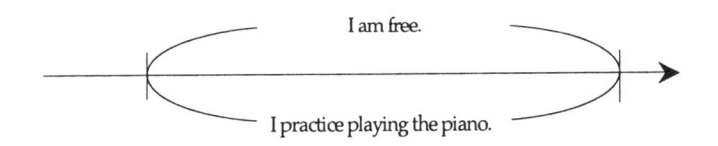

I am free.
I practice playing the piano.

Some sentences make sense only when either る or た is used. See the following examples:

(9) a. 朝起きた時に、歯をみがきます。
        I brush my teeth after I get up.
  * b. 朝起きる時に、歯をみがきます。
        I brush my teeth before I get up. (nonsensical)

Sentence (9b) is nonsensical, since getting up in the morning and brushing your teeth cannot occur simultaneously. You will do so after getting out of bed.

(10) a. 地震が来た時は、机の下にもぐります。
        When/after an earthquake comes, we crawl underneath the desk.
  * b. 地震が来る時は、机の下にもぐります。
        Before an earthquake comes, we crawl underneath the desk.

Sentence (10b) is pragmatically awkward, because the time when an earthquake will come is unpredictable. You would not crawl underneath the desk before the earthquake.

(11) a. 夫は死ぬ時に、遺言を残した。
        My husband left his will when/before he died.
  * b. 夫は死んだ時に、遺言を残した。
        My husband left his will at the time of his death.

Since leaving a will cannot take place at the moment of death, sentence (11b) is pragmatically awkward.

Sample dialogues
かばんはどこで買えばいいでしょうか
雅子: イタリアへ行った時、グッチ (Gucci) のかばんを買おうと思っているんです。日本では高いですから。
葉子: あら、それなら、帰る時に買った方がいいですよ。空港の免税店 (duty free shop) の方が安いですから。
雅子: あ、そうなんですか。それはいいことを聞きました。ありがとう。

Where is 雅子 going to buy a Gucci bag? Be very specific.

帰った時じゃなくて、帰る時に連絡してください

松田：　　アメリカへ帰る時は必ず連絡してくださいね。
スミス：　ええ、必ずご連絡します。

[1ヶ月後、スミスさんから電話がかかってくる。]
A month later, Matsuda receives a phone call from Smith.

スミス：　あ、松田さん、スミスです。日本ではほんとうにお世話になりました。
松田：　　あ、スミスさん、今どちらですか。
スミス：　アメリカです。先週戻って来ました。それで、連絡しなくちゃと思って。
松田：　　え、もうアメリカへ帰ってしまったんですか。帰る時に連絡してほしいとお願いしたのに・・・。お土産を渡したかったんです。
スミス：　ああ、それはどうもすみませんでした。お気を使ってくださって、本当にありがとうございます。
松田：　　お土産、どうしましょうか・・・。
スミス：　あ、そうですね・・・。あの、来週弟もこちらに帰って来ることになっているんです。
松田：　　じゃ、弟さんが帰る時に預けますから、受け取ってくださいね。
スミス：　すみません、色々と御迷惑をおかけしてしまって・・・。

From where did Mr. Smith contact Mr. Matsuda and why?
Who is going to get the souvenir for Mr. Smith?

CHAPTER 8

Dictionary/Plain Form Compounds

As is explained in Chapter 7 in the discussion of tense, for action verbs, the fundamental notion of the る form is imperfective, meaning that the event described by the る form has not yet been completed. Such a notion is applicable if the event occurred in the past or if it will have been completed in the future. In this sense, the る form does not necessarily act as the future tense form, but creates a notion similar to "before." Thus, the る form may be used to describe a past or a future event, either imperfective, regardless of the tense of the predicate in the main clause.

Some of grammatical patterns treated in this chapter require the dictionary form of the verb (the plain form of ます), including the negative form, to form a compound predicate. These patterns all indicate that the event described by the verb has not yet been realized or completed.

1. つもり

つもり is a dependent noun that always follows an activity verb and expresses a speaker's intention. When つもり is attached to a phrase, the whole phrase becomes a noun phrase. Negation, when it occurs, occurs within the verb, as in 行かないつもりです "I intend not to go."

(1) A: 大学を卒業したら、どうするつもりですか。
What are you going to do after you graduate?
B: まず修士号(M.A.)を取って、それから博士号 (Ph.D.)を取るつもりです。
First, I intend to obtain an M.A. degree, then a Ph.D.

(2) 今日の会議には出席しないつもりだ。
I intend not to attend today's meeting.

(3) 小泉(こいずみ)さんはどこへ行(い)くつもりか、だれにもわからない。
No one knows where Mr. Koizumi intends to go.
(4) A: ずいぶんひどいことを言(い)うのですね。
You say terrible things.
B: すみません、そんなつもりはなかったのですが・・・。
I am sorry. I did not mean to (hurt your feelings), but . . .

In a negative expression, although つもり may follow the ない form of a verb, expressing "intend not to~," つもり may itself be followed by a negative form. つもりはない or つもりじゃない means "I do not mean to do ~." For example, 言わないつもりだ means "I intend not to say" and 言うつもりはない means "I do not mean to say it." Both of these communicate the same result: the speaker will not mention something. When this situation occurs in a past context, although the sentences lead to the same result, the use of つもり + negative creates a counter-factual meaning, as may be seen in sentence (4b).

If the た form is used instead of the dictionary form, the meaning becomes "pretend to have done ~." For example, 食(た)べたつもり means "I pretend that I had eaten." See the section regarding た forming compounds.

2. 前に/前は

Since 前(まえ) means "before," it is logical that only the imperfective (dictionary) form can occur with it. It can also follow a noun linked by の. 前 can be followed by either に or は (前に/前は). 前に usually invites an activity verb that focuses on the sequentiality of events. It does not occur with a stative predicate in the main clause, while 前は can be followed by a stative predicate in the main clause. When 前は invites an activity verb in the main clause, the flavor created is contrastive or habitual. See the following examples:

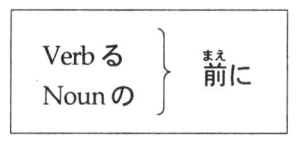

```
Verb る  }  前(まえ)に
Noun の   }
```

出(で)かける前に掃除(そうじ)する   clean before leaving
映画(えいが)の前に食事(しょくじ)をする   eat before the movie

(1) A: 映画を見る前に食事をしましょうか。それとも映画を見てから食事をしましょうか。
Should we eat before the movie, or eat after seeing the movie?

B: 私おなかがすいているんです。ですから、映画を見る前に食べませんか。
I am hungry now, so why don't we eat before going to see the movie?

C: 私は食事の前にちょっと買い物がしたいんですが、いいですか。
I would like to do some shopping before eating, is it O.K.?

B: あ、じゃあ、買い物をする前に食事をしてしまいましょうよ。
Well, then, let's eat before doing some shopping.

(2) a. 映画を見る前はおなかがすいていなかったのですが、今急におなかがすいてきました。
Before watching the movie, I was not hungry, but suddenly I became hungry.

b. 公園の前にマンションが建つ前は、この辺は静かでした。
Before the condominiums were built in front of the park, it was quiet in this vicinity.

c. 食事をする前は、たいていコップに1杯お水を飲みました。
Before I had a meal, I usually drank a glass of water.

d. 試験を受ける前は、ちゃんと寝ます。
Before I take an exam, I have a good sleep.

前は would be awkward for all the sentences in (1), while 前は in sentences (2) are all compatible with the predicate. Predicates in sentences (2a) and (2b) are stative predicates, and those in sentences (2c) and (2d) express a habitual activity and a contrastive meaning, respectively. This difference created by the use of particles is due to the fundamental meaning of に, which points to a specific point in place/time. When a predicate is a stative predicate involving a duration of time, it becomes incompatible with a specific time, and with に. 前に, therefore, does not occur with a stative predicate.

3. ところ

ところ is used to indicate a specific point in time or space. When following the various forms of verbs, it shows the point at which the event or action is about to happen, is happening, or has just happened. For example, るところ means that the activity is going to happen right at the time of speech; ているところ means that the activity is continuing at the time of speech, and たところ means that the activity has just been completed.[1]

(1)　これから食事をするところです。
　　　I'm about to have a meal now.
(2)　今食事をしているところです。
　　　I'm in the middle of having a meal now. (on-going)
(3)　父がアメリカへ来ているところです。
　　　My father is at the point where he has visited America. = My father is in America. (resultative)
(4)　今ちょうど友達の家へ出かけるところなんです。また後で電話してください。
　　　I am about to leave for my friend's house, so please call us later.
(5)　クラスへ行くところです。
　　　I am on the way to class.
(6)　今試験を受けるところです。
　　　I am about to take the exam now.

Although ところ generally follows a verb, you may notice that some adjectives may also be used, for example, この映画、今おもしろいところなのよ "This movie is right in the middle of being interesting." In this case, the attribute おもしろい is captured as expressing a time expanse, and the speaker recognizes a point within that time expanse.

　　ところ originally means "place" or "spot," and it can also be used in a variety of ways to indicate physical location. Here are some examples:

---

[1] For たところ, see Chapter 11, Section 4.

(7) ここにお所(ところ)とお名前(なまえ)を書(か)いてください。
Please write your address and name here.

(8) 先生(せんせい)の所でパーティをしましょう。
Let's have a party at the teacher's place.

(9) わからないところがあったら聞(き)いてください。
Ask me if there are any places you do not understand.

(10) 黒板(こくばん)の所に先生が立(た)っています。
The teacher is standing at the blackboard.
(黒板に先生が立っています means that the teacher is standing on the blackboard.)

Sample dialogue

都合(つごう)が悪(わる)いので、また後(あと)で連絡(れんらく)してください

チビ: もしもし、タマさん、もしよかったら、ちょっと外(そと)へ出(で)て来(こ)ない？星(ほし) (stars) がとってもきれいなんだ。

タマ: まあ、それはロマンチックね。でも今(いま)だめなの。

チビ: どうして？

タマ: 映画(えいが)を見(み)るところなのよ。

チビ: そんなの、ビデオにとっておいて、後(あと)で見ればいいじゃないか。

タマ: それだけじゃないの。洗濯(せんたく)もしているところなの。

チビ: そんなの機械(きかい)に任(まか)せればいいじゃないか。(You should let the machine take care of it.)

タマ: あ、それにね、今ちょうど父(ちち)が来(き)たところなのよ。

チビ: え、お父(とう)さんが？　そう、じゃ、また電話(でんわ)するよ。

タマ: 悪(わる)いけど、そうしてね。

4. ため(に)

The word ため alone means "benefit/usefulness" as in ためになる話 "beneficial/useful story." Eventually it came to be used to express "for the purpose of ～," with the underlying meaning of bringing one a benefit. ため follows the dictionary form of the verb, or a noun that often indicates the purpose or benefit. But when an event preceding ため influences negatively, the interpretation of the whole sentence ため may be interpreted as expressing "cause" or "reason." Observe the following examples:

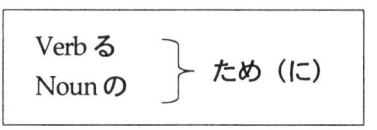

```
Verb る  ⎫
Noun の  ⎬ ため（に）
         ⎭
```

コンテストに出るために、練習する。
Practice in order to attend the contest.
コンテストのために、練習する。
Practice for the contest.
たばこを吸いすぎるため、医者に禁煙命令を出された。
Due to too much smoking, I was told not to smoke by the doctor.
雨のため、試合が中止になった。
Due to rain, the game was cancelled.

(1) A: 私は生きるために食べます。
　　　I eat in order to live.
　　B: 私は食べるために生きます。
　　　I live in order to eat.
(2) 日本へ行くためにパスポートを取りました。
　　I obtained a passport in order to go to Japan.
(3) 毎月貯金するために、無駄使いを減らしています。
　　I am restraining my impulse to buy in order to save money every month.
(4) あなたのために作ったんですから、食べてください。
　　I made this for (the benefit of) you, so please eat it.
(5) 日本語ができないため、雇ってもらえなかった。
　　Because I cannot communicate in Japanese, I could not get hired.
(6) 洪水のため、家を失った。
　　Due to the flood, I lost my house.

Sample dialogue

あなたのためなら何でもします

タビ: タマさん、これ、双眼鏡 (binoculars) です。鳥を見るの (bird watching) に使ってください。これ、ぬいぐるみ (stuffed animal) です。夜一緒に寝てください。そして、これはまぐろのかんづめ (a can of tuna) です。おなかがすいた時に食べてください。
それから、これ、新しいお皿 (dish) です。使ってください。

タマ: まあ・・・、タビさん・・・。これ、みんな私に？

タビ: ええ、みんなあなたのために見つけて来たんです。
あなたに好きになってもらうためなら、僕、何でもします。

タマ: 私贈り物に弱いのよねえ (I have a weak spot for presents)・・・。
ありがとう、タビさん。あなたってやさしいのね・・・。

5. 間に/間は

The morpheme 間 literally means "an interval," "duration," or "time expanse." It follows the non-past form of a predicate and governs a subordinate clause. (The tense of the whole sentence is identified by the tense of the predicate in the main clause.) 間 can also occur with the affirmative or the negative form of the non-past. Since 間 means "duration of time," it commonly occurs with on-going ている and stative predicates, such as い and な adjectives, which also involve an expanse of time either physically or conceptually.

With respect to particles, 間 can take either に or は, depending on the nature of the predicate in the main clause. に tends to be used with 間 when the predicate in the main clause is an action predicate that can be contrasted as a single occurrence (or sequence of single occurrences). On the other hand, は tends to follow 間 to create a contrastive implication when the predicate in the main clause may be construed as expressing state of being represented by, for example, an い/な adjective, stative verb, and so forth. This arises from the nature of the predicate in the main clause. Because it expresses a duration of time, it cannot be reconciled with the fundamental meaning of に, that is, to designate a specific point in time/place. If no particle follows, then the event in the main predicate might be perceived as if the event were continuing during the time expressed by 間. Here are some examples:

(1)　となりに安売りの店がある間は、うちの店はもうからない。[2]
While a discount shop is next to us, our shop would not do well (implying that the shop would do well if the discount shop were gone).

(2)　ガソリンが高い間は、あまり車に乗らなかった。
While gas was expensive, I did not drive the car very often (implying that I drove regularly when gas was not expensive).

(3)　テレビを見ている間に何回も勧誘電話がかかってきた。
While I am / was watching TV, I received many phone calls from tele marketers.

(4)　仕事が暇な間に、旅行の計画を立てておいた。
While work was not busy, I made plans for the trip.

(5)　僕が勉強している間、彼女はずっと電話で話していた。
While I was studying, my girlfriend was talking on the phone throughout the entire time.

Another unique feature of 間 is that the translation of 間 is "while," which is the same as the ながら construction (see Chapter 9). But the ながら construction requires that the subject of the subordinate clause and the main clause be identical, whereas 間 does not. This observation is supported by the examples (1) through (5) above. Diagrams (6) and (7) capture the essence of 間.

(6)

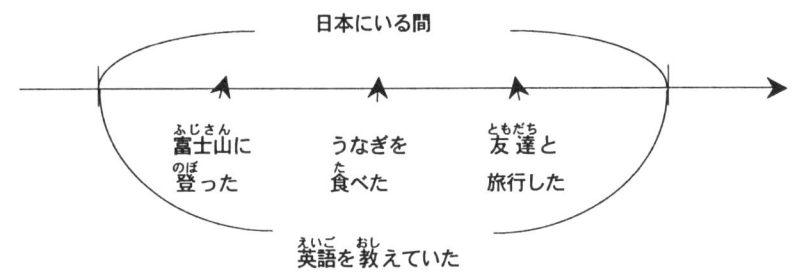

日本にいる間

富士山に登った　　うなぎを食べた　　友達と旅行した

英語を教えていた

Diagram (6) represents a situation in which the speaker carried out several activities while in Japan. Examples are:

---

[2] The negative form of a predicate is morphologically an い adjective, which is a stative predicate.

a. 日本にいる間に、富士山に登った。[3]
   While I was in Japan, I climbed Mt. Fuji.
b. 日本にいる間に、うなぎを食べた。
   While I was in Japan, I ate eel.
c. 日本にいる間に、友達と旅行した。
   While I was in Japan, I traveled with my friends.
d. 日本にいる間(は)、英語を教えていた。
   While I was in Japan, I was teaching English.

While the use of に is appropriate for sentences (6a) through (6c), it is not for (6d). When the predicate in the main clause is stative, then は becomes optional and has the sense of expressing a contrasting meaning. Diagram (7) below is a case where the subjects of the subordinate clause and the main clause are not identical.

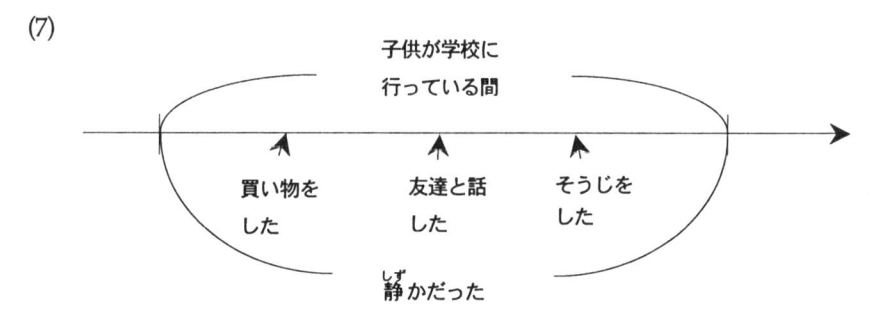

(7)

```
             子供が学校に
             行っている間
      ↑        ↑        ↑
    買い物を   友達と話   そうじを
    した      した      した
             静かだった
```

The diagram above describes both a situation where the speaker carried out several activities and the state of a period during which the child was away for school. Examples are:

a. 子供が学校に行っている間に、買い物をした。
   While my child was at school, I did shopping.
b. 子供が学校に行っている間に、友達と話した。
   While my child was at school, I spoke with my friend.

---

[3] Some people might say 日本にいた間, using the past form of いる. Tense is decided by the predicate in the main sentence, and the past tense form is not considered appropriate. 時, on the other hand, may be used with the past tense.

c. 子供（こども）が学校（がっこう）に行（い）っている間（あいだ）に、そうじした。
   While my child was at school, I cleaned.
d. 子供が学校に行っている間(は)、静（しず）かだった。
   While my child was at school, it was quiet.

Again, action predicates in main clauses are compatible with the particle に in subordinate clauses, while the stative predicate 静か "quiet" is not. Since 静か does not pinpoint a time/place, either no particle or は is more appropriate.

間に/間は is used to place focus on an expanse of time during which a certain situation is maintained. This emphasis on the duration is the difference between 時（とき） and 間 subordinate clauses. 日本（にほん）にいる時, for example, means "*at the time* I was in Japan" while 日本にいる間 means "*during the time* I was in Japan." The former looks at the speaker's stay in Japan as a single temporal point, whereas the latter focuses on the internal situation of the expanse of time. Also, the tense form used in the 時 clause varies, affecting the interpretation of the sentence, but for the 間 construction, the grammatical form is uniformly non-past.

Another possible point of confusion for learners may lie in the use of 間に/間は and うちに/うちは (which is discussed in section 6, immediately below). うちに/うちは is used to express meanings equivalent to "while" and "before." When a "while" meaning is intended, the sentence can make use of either the 間に/間は or the うちに/うちは construction. The うちに/うちは construction tends to prevail over 間に/間は when the negative form of a predicate is used in the subordinate clause. This is attributed to the fact that ないうちに carries a sense of urgency that the situation is going to change shortly to the state described in the corresponding affirmative form and communicates the "before" meaning. In the following examples, (8a) and (8b) are both equally appropriate; (9b) may be more commonly used than (9a); (10b) sounds more natural than (10a). But again, the preference is up to the individual.

(8) a. 日照（ひで）りが続（つづ）く間は、作物（さくもつ）が育（そだ）ちにくい。
       While hot sunny days continue, crops are not easy to grow.
    b. 日照りが続くうちは、作物が育ちにくい。
       While hot sunny days continue, crops are not easy to grow.

(9) a. 知らない間に、雨が降り始めていた。
　　　　While I was unaware, it had started to rain.
　　b. 知らないうちに、雨が降り始めいた。
　　　　While I was unaware/Before I realized it, it had started to rain.
(10) a. 歯医者に行かない間に、歯がどんどん悪くなっていった。
　　　　While I was avoiding the dentist, my teeth got worse and worse.
　　b. 歯医者に行かないうちに、歯がどんどん悪くなっていった。
　　　　While I was avoiding the dentist, my teeth got worse and worse.

間 may share some meanings with 時 and うち subordinate clauses, but the use of 間 specifically focuses on the time duration. The duration may be described by the simultaneous occurrence of an event or may be given as the time frame for the occurrence of a certain event.

6.　うちに/うちは[4]

The subordinate clause pattern うち, when it occurs with the particle に or は, as a whole means "while" (i.e., "while something is in a particular state") or "before" (i.e., "before something happens"). うち can follow some different words/forms, such as ている, ない, or the plain, non-past form of a stative predicate. It creates a subtle shade of meaning for "while" and "before." First, let's observe a few examples:

(1)　ている + うちに/うちは
　　a. 晴れているうちに、買い物に行っておこう。
　　　　I should go shopping while the weather is sunny.
　　b 晴れているうちは、みんなが外で日光浴をしていた。
　　　　Everyone was tanning outside while it was sunny.
　　c. 怖い映画を見ているうちに、だんだん気分が悪くなってきた。
　　　　While I was watching a scary movie, I started to feel sick.
　　d. 怖い映画を見ているうちは、トイレにも行けなかった。
　　　　While I was watching a scary movie, I could not even go to the bathroom.

---

[4] See Johnson (1998a, 2004a, and 2004b) for further discussion.

(2) い/な adjective + うちに/うちは
  a. 天気がいいうちに、車を洗ってしまおう。
     I should wash the car while the weather is good.
  b. 天気がいいうちは、出店のものもよく売れた。
     Things at the kiosk sold well while the weather was good.
  c. 有名なうちに、たくさん稼いで貯金しておくといい。
     You should make lots of money and save while you are popular.
  d. 有名なうちは、毎日カメラマンにつきまとわれた。
     I was stalked by cameramen every day while I was popular.

(3) ない + うちに/うちは
  a. 雨が降らないうちに、買い物に行っておこう。
     Before it starts raining, I should go shopping.
  b. 雨が降らないうちは、バーベキューができる。
     Before it rains, we can barbecue.
  c. クラスに行かないうちに、落ちこぼれてしまった。
     While I was absent from class, I fell behind.
  ? d. クラスに行かないうちは、家で勉強していた。
     While I was absent from class, I was studying at home.

(4) Noun + の + うちに/うちは
  a. 1ヶ月のうちに、仕上げてしまわなければならない。
     I have to finish it up within a month.
  b. 1ヶ月のうちは、特に何の問題も起こらなかった。[5]
     No particular problem occurred in a month.

The difference in the use of the particles に and は is similar to that of に and は with 間. Just like 間は, うちは is compatible with a stative predicate in the main clause. The situation described by the stative predicate holds in concert with the situation described by the うちは subordinate clause. Also, just like 間に, うちに is compatible with non-stative, action predicates in the main clause, since the fundamental function of に is to designate a specific point in time/place.

---

[5] Both sentences (3d) and (4b) are much more acceptable with 間.

As may be seen from the English equivalents of the examples above, うちに/うちは sentences are generally interpreted in three different ways, depending on the preceding predicate. うちに/うちは following ている and an い adjective in sentences (1a) through (1d) and (2a) and (2b) emphasize "during the period that something is in a particular situation" and receives a "while" interpretation. When a noun occurs with うちに/うちは in sentences (4a) and (4b), the うちに/うちは clause becomes an adverbial phrase with a meaning such as "during a certain period of time." Only when うちに/うちは follows the negative suffix ない in sentences (3a) through (3d), does it emphasize "before something happens" or "before the situation changes." In these cases, it receives either a "while" or a "before" interpretation.

What then is the difference in meaning between "while" and "before" as expressed by うちに sentences? Sentences (1a) and (3a) have the same main clause; their difference lies in the use of ている and ない in the うちに subordinate clause. There is a psychological motivation for choosing one expression over the other. While sentence (1a), 晴れている "to be sunny," has a situation that is already realized and is being maintained, sentence (3a) does not. Instead it implies what the situation is like before a certain event is realized. This is why the sentence is interpreted as "before." This "before" means that the situation has not yet entered a different state, but it is very close to entering it. Sentence (3a) implies that, at any moment, the given situation will change into the situation expressed by the affirmative form, 雨が降る "it rains." ないうちに sentences are thus often used to suggest some kind of warning in preparation for a change in a situation. The content of the change is clearly indicated in the corresponding affirmative form of the predicate.

However, as may be seen in example (3c), there are cases where ないうちに expresses a "while" meaning. In this case, the main sentence usually describes a situation in which a change takes place in the main clause in temporal concert with an interval of time defined by the subordinate clause.

As for ているうちに in sentence (1a), it does not imply that any major urgent change is expected, especially in comparison to a negative form combined with うちに. 晴れているうちに implies, with a sense of urgency, that the situation will change from a sunny to a non-sunny weather pattern. This could be any type of weather: cloudy, snowy, windy, or rainy—as long as it is not sunny.[6] 晴れているうちに is not as clear as 降らないうちに in terms of what kind of change may be approaching a situation. Where 晴れているうちに implies some change, but not any particular change, 降らないうちに additionally implies a particular result, in this case that the situation will change from not raining to raining.

However, as may be seen in example (3c) クラスに行かないうちに、落ちこぼれてしまった "While I was absent from class, I fell behind," there are cases where ないうちに expresses a "while" meaning. In this case, the main sentence usually describes a situation in which a change takes place in the main clause along with an interval of time defined by the subordinate clause.

(5) ているうちに has two different meanings depending on the main clause:
    a. 学生が期末試験を受けているうちに宿題の採点をしてしまった。
       <u>While</u> students were taking the final exam, I finished grading their homework.
       During a situation described by the subordinate clause, a one-time event occurs in the main clause.
    b. 毎日コーヒーを飲んでいるちにだんだん歯が黄色くなってきた。
       <u>While</u> I was drinking coffee every day, my teeth gradually became yellow.
       Within a passage of time occurring in a situation described by the subordinate clause, the change expressed in the main clause takes place.

(6) ないうちに also expresses two meanings which differ depending on the main clause:
    a. 子供が起きないうちに自分の仕事を済ませた。
       <u>Before</u> the child woke up, I finished my own work.
       Before a change occurs in the subordinate clause, the one-time event of the main clause occurs.

---

[6] The opposite of a given negative form is generally considered its affirmative, but the opposite of a given affirmative is not necessarily the corresponding negative. An affirmative form is certainly more likely to have a greater number of viable opposites.

b. しばらく会わないうちに/間にずいぶん大きくなったね。
   While I was not seeing you, you grew up a lot, didn't you?

   The second meaning is the same as the second meaning of ている
   うちに: a change takes place in the main clause during an interval
   defined by the subordinate clause.

Thus, while ているうちに subordinate clauses are generally interpreted as expressing a "while" meaning, ないうちに subordinate clauses carry a "before" meaning. However, ないうちに sentences can also be interpreted as expressing a "while" meaning in certain circumstances. ているうちは and うちは following い/な adjectives are generally interpreted as expressing a "while" meaning.

Last, since うちに shares the meaning "while" with 間に and the meaning "before" with 前に some confusion may exist about the appropriate use of these constructions. Sentences (7) through (9) offer cases where うちに can be rephrased with 間に, and sentences (10) and (11) present cases where うちに can be rephrased 前に.

(7) 知らないうちに/間に、となりの犬がうちの犬と仲よくなっていた。
    While I was unaware, my neighbor's dog became on good terms with my dog.

(8) クラシック音楽を聞いているうちに/間に、眠くなった。
    While I was listening to classical music, I became sleepy.

(9) 明るいうちに/間に、ドラキュラの城に着いた。
    While it was light outside, we arrived at Count Dracula's castle.

Note that none of the above examples indicates a sense of urgency. Both 間に and うちに are appropriate, and the choice is up to the speaker.

(10) 台風が来ないうち/来る前に、ドアを補強しておこう。
     Before a typhoon comes, we should board up the doors.

(11) 映画が終わらないうちに/終わる前に、ポップコーンを買った。
     Before the movie ended, I bought popcorn.

Although both うちに and 前(まえ)に in the examples above express a "before" meaning, うちに certainly indicates urgency and gives an impression that the speaker is rushing to do the activity described in the main clause before the situation changes. 前に does not create such a sense of urgency; rather 前に describes the sequential events indicated in the subordinate and main clause objectively.

CHAPTER 9

Stem Form Compounds

1. たい

たい is an adjectival suffix which, when attached to the stem form of an activity verb, expresses first-person desire. For example, 飲みたい "I want to drink" is considered a compound い adjective (verb stem 飲み + suffix たい), and it conjugates the same way as an い adjective.

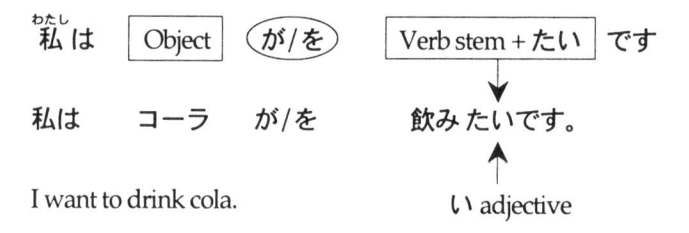

私は [Object] が/を [Verb stem + たい] です

私は　コーラ　が/を　飲みたいです。

I want to drink cola.　　　　い adjective

In the desiderative construction, an object can be marked either by が or by を, due to the syntactic features of the たい form (a stative predicate that takes an object). In theory, the noun phrase marked with が is related to the たい part of the sentence (I *want* to drink cola), putting more emphasis on the speaker's desire (state of mind), whereas the noun phrase marked with を is related to the 飲む part of the sentence, putting more emphasis on the activity (I want to *drink*).[1]

When the sentence is negated, は is often used, as it creates a contrastive implication. Remember that the たい form cannot be used to express third-person desire. Also, a たいですか question addressed to a second or third person,

---

[1] Also, を may be preferred over が if there are more phrases between the grammatical object and the たい phrase. For example: すしが食べたいです "I wan to eat sushi" vs. すしをおなかがくるしくなるまで思いきり食べたいです "I want to eat sushi to my heart's content and until my stomach feels completely stuffed."

such as 先生、パーティへ行きたいですか "Professor, would you like to go to the party?" should not be used as *an invitation* to a superior or person who is older than you are. If it is an invitation, パーティへいらっしゃいませんか is the most appropriate expression.[2]

(1) 私は すし が/を ｛ 食べたいです。
I want to eat sushi.
食べたかったです。
I wanted to eat sushi.

私は すし は ｛ 食べたくありません。
I do not want to eat sushi.
食べたくありませんでした。
I did not want to eat sushi.

Note that only an object is marked by either が or を. For other noun phrases, the particle is the same as the one used in the declarative sentence.

(2) 僕は来年日本へ帰りたいです。
I want to go back to Japan next year.

(3) 私はアメリカにいたいです。
I want to stay in America.

(4) 日本にいる友達に会いたいです。
I want to see my friend in Japan. = I miss my friend in Japan.

(5) 一度京都を旅行したいです。
I want to travel in Kyoto once.

(6) カリブ海で泳いでみたいです。
I want to swim in the Caribbean and see how it is.

(7) もっと早く手紙が書きたかったです。
I wanted to write a letter much sooner.

---

[2] If you want to ask what your teacher wants, for example, you may use a ~たい sentence in the honorific form. E.g., 先生、日本へお帰りになりたいですか "Professor, do you want to go back to Japan?" This is not an invitation, but the speaker is asking the professor's desire.

(8) 怖い映画は見たくなかったのですが・・・。
I did not want to see a scary movie, but...

Sample essay[3]

葉子さん、お元気ですか。御家族のみなさんもお元気ですか。もっと早くメールを出したかったんですが、今日まで毎日試験があって、時間がありませんでした。ごめんなさい。12月16日にクラスが終わりますから、その後、18日から日本へ行きたいと思っています。もしよかったら、一緒に京都を旅行しませんか。取り急ぎ御連絡まで。またメールします。

ジェーン

2. たがる (たい＋がる)

Verb stem + たい "I want to do ~" is exclusively used for first-person desire and cannot be used to express a second or third party's desire. In order to express a desire that is not that of the speaker, the suffix がる is attached to the desiderative adjective 欲しい or the desiderative suffix たい to form 欲しがる or たがる。

がる is a verbal suffix that makes the entire predicate into a verb. It usually expresses a habitual or general desire of a second or third person. If the desire is a current, *affirmative* situation, ている is attached. For example, the equivalent of "John wants to eat sushi right now" is ジョンはすしを食べたがっている。 Observe the following sentences:

(1) 姉のジェーンは日本へ行きたがっている。
My sister Jane wants to go to Japan.

(2) 妹はよくバービーを欲しがった。
My sister used to want to have a Barbie doll.

(3) 日本の若い女の子たちはブランド物を買いたがる。
Young Japanese girls want to buy brand-name stuff.

(4) 弟は英語を話したがらない。
My brother does not want to speak English. = He resists speaking English.

---

[3] This sample essay is an e-mail message. Rubies are provided in order to assist learners, although they are not likely to be used so extensively in reality.

(5) 今の子供たちは外で遊びたがらない。
Young kids nowadays do not like to play outside.

Although たがる is usually understood as a grammatical device to express someone else's desire, not that of the speaker, pragmatically it can often be used to describe things that people in general want, or at least the desire of people who belong to the speaker's group (Johnson 2007).[4] In daily communication, たがる may not be used or may be inappropriate to describe the desire of people who have a hierarchical relationship with the speaker. For example, 先生は日本へ帰りたがっている "The teacher wants to go back to Japan" may be considered less appropriate or polite if you are his/her student. Even if がる is employed to describe another person's state of mind, it is still necessary to modify a statement about someone who has a psychological distance from the speaker. The best way to do this may be by using a modal or the like at the end of the statement. For example:

(6) 先生は日本へ帰りたい そうだ。
I hear that the teacher wants to go back to Japan.
(7) お隣の奥さんは息子さんをハーバード大学へ入れたい ようだ。
It looks like my neighbor's wife wants to send her son to Harvard University.
(8) 社長はたばこを辞めたい と言っている。
Our president is saying that he wants to quit smoking.
(9) 課長は会社を辞めたがっている らしい。
I hear that our section chief wants to quit the company.

---

[4] The "speaker's group" means the territory or domain for which the speaker feels a sense of belonging. This group may include the speaker's family, the place the speaker works, some social assembly to which the speaker belongs, or the country in which the speaker was born. When one recognizes his/her group, that group is considered as "in-group," and it is distinguished from the "out-group." This distinction depends on how strongly the speaker feels that s/he is a member of the group. This notion is especially important in grammatical patterns of "giving" and "receiving" which are discussed in Chapter 20. Detailed discussion of the concepts of in- and out-group is found in Makino (1992).

(10) 本田さんはレストランへは行きたがらないと聞いている。
I heard/learned that Ms. Honda does not like to go to a restaurant.

3. やすい/にくい

When something or someone is easy or difficult to handle physically or mentally, or something happens easily or with difficulty, the い adjectives やすい/にくい are used as auxiliaries to describe the situation. For example, when one finds a pen easy to handle physically, このペンは書きやすい is used to express that circumstance. Also, the target of being easy or difficult can be a person, as when one indicates that he/she is easy to talk to, for example. やすい and にくい function in this way only when they are used as auxiliaries. When an answer is requested, the whole phrase has to be repeated. Observe the following examples:

(1) A: そのくつは歩きやすいですか。
     Is that pair of shoes easy to walk in?
     B: いいえ、歩きやすくありませんよ。
     No, they are not easy to walk in.
   * C: (いいえ、やすくありません。)
     No, it is not cheap.

(2) 箸は、慣れると使いやすいです。
    Chopsticks are easy to use once you become accustomed to them.

(3) カクテルは甘くて飲みやすいので、ついたくさん飲んでしまいます。
    Cocktails are sweet and easy to drink, so I often overdrink unintentionally.

(4) このチーズは溶けやすいので、ピザには最適です。
    This cheese is easy to melt, so it is best suited for pizza.

(5) この本はひらがなばかりで、読みにくいです。
    This book contains nothing but hiragana and is difficult to read.

(6) 本田さんはとても話しやすいけど、豊田さんは近づきにくいです。
    Mr. Honda is easy to talk to, but Mr. Toyota is difficult to get close to.

(7) 松田さんの顔はブラピに似ているので、覚えやすいですよ。
    Mr. Matsuda's face resembles Brad Pitts' and is easy to remember.

4. ながら

(妹は)電話で話しながら	(妹は)運転します
Subordinate clause	Main clause

My sister talks on the phone while *she* drives. → Same subject

The fundamental meaning of ながら is that one person does two different activities simultaneously or alternately during the same period of time, so ながら is not always the same as "while" in English. Also, although ながら is used to describe two activities engaged in by the same subject (performer of the event) at the same time, since it is a subordinate clause, the main event comes at the end of the sentence. For example, 小泉さんは運転しながら煙草を吸う "Mr. Koizumi smokes while he drives" is pragmatically awkward in Japanese as it gives an impression that the person is paying more attention to smoking than to driving. An appropriate expression should be 煙草を吸いながら運転する, where 運転する is considered the main activity. The following are some examples of cases whereながらis used.

(1) a. 本田さんはテレビを見ながら勉強します。
   Mr. Honda watches TV while he studies.
   b. 松田さんは音楽を聞きながら勉強します。
   Ms. Matsuda listens to music while she studies.
   c. 私は勉強しながら食べます。
   I eat while I study.

(2) 朝はコーヒーを飲みながらパンを食べる。
   In the morning, I drink coffee and eat bread.

(3) a. 日本では電話で話しながら運転すると、罰金を取られます。
   In Japan, if you talk on the phone while you drive, you will be fined.
   b. 日本では煙草を吸いながら道を歩くと、罰金を取られます。

(4) アメリカの大学生はたいていアルバイトをしながら大学で勉強しますが、日本の大学生は大学で勉強しながらアルバイトをして、よく海外旅行をします。
Students in America usually study at university and have a part-time job, but students in Japan have a part-time job while they are at university and often travel abroad.

Although ながら is usually translated as "while" in English, as is the case for 間 (に/は), 間 (に/は) does not require the subject (the performer of the event) of the subordinate and the main sentence to be identical. 間 (に/は) means "while a certain situation is maintained," and two different entities can be employed as the subject of the subordinate and main sentence. Compare the following examples:

(5) a. 妻が買い物をしている間に、フットボールの試合を見た。
While my wife was shopping, I watched a football game.
 * b. 妻が買い物をしながら、フットボールの試合を見た。
While my wife was shopping, she watched a football game.
(6) a. 子供が寝ている間は、部屋は静かだった。
While the child was sleeping, the room was quiet.
 * b. 子供が寝ながら、部屋は静かだった。
(7) a. 晴れている間に、洗濯をしてしまおう。
Let's do the laundry while it is sunny.
 * b. 晴れながら、洗濯をしてしまおう。

As may be seen from the unacceptability of the sentences that use ながら, when the subject of events in the subordinate and the main clause is not the same, ながら creates either a different interpretation, as seen in (5b), or a nonsensical meaning. The subject performing the action in the subordinate clause and the main clause must be identical. This restriction applies strictly to the use of ながら.

Another point to note about ながら is that it has a different function that indicates the same meaning as けれども "though." It is used in sentences such as 貧しいながらも、楽しい我が家 "Though poor, my family is cheerful" and だ

めだと知りながらも、試してみた "Though I knew that it would not work, I tried anyway." It usually accompanies も, but も is optional.

5. 方

The suffix 方 is derived from the word 方法 "method" and means the way things are done. When attached to the stem form of a verb, the whole phrase becomes a noun. Any verb that can be described as turning into a method can be accompanied by 方.

覚える	+	方	=	覚え方	how to memorize
食べる	+	方	=	食べ方	how to eat
行く	+	方	=	行き方	how to get there
作る	+	方	=	作り方	how to make
考える	+	方	=	考え方	a way of thinking

(1) 漢字のいい覚え方を知っていますか。
   Do you know a good way to memorize kanji?

(2) みそ汁の作り方は母に教えてもらいました。
   I had my mother teach me how to make miso soup.

(3) お宅へ伺いたいんですが、行き方を教えてくださいますか。
   I would like to visit you. Could you tell me how to get to your home?

(4) 人に迷惑をかけない死に方がいいです。
   Dying in a way that does not cause a problem to others would be good.

Sample dialogues

主婦1: 近ごろの日本の親たちは、子供を全然叱りませんね。どうしてなんでしょう。
   Recent Japanese parents do not scold their kids at all. I wonder why.

主婦2: 叱らないというより、叱り方を知らないのかもしれませんね。
   Rather than the fact that they don't scold, they may not know how to scold (their kids).
   小学校に入れば、学校でしつけをしてくれると思っているのかもしれません。
   They may think that the school will discipline their kids once they get in.

主婦1: 私達のころとは育て方がずいぶん違いますね。
The way they raise their children is quite different from the way we had.

主婦2: 本当に。
Indeed.

食べ方は知りませんが、においでわかります

男: わ、なっとうだ。
Wow, natto, isn't it!

女: そんないやな顔して・・・。食べ方、知ってるの？
Don't be disgusted. Do you know how to eat it?

男: 知らない。
I don't know.

女: じゃあどんな味かわからないでしょう。
Well, then you don't know what it tastes like, do you?

男: 食べなくても、においでわかる。
I can tell by the smell without tasting it.

6. すぎる

すぎる suffixed to the stem form of a verb, い adjective, or な adjective means "to exceed," and the situation described by the preceding predicate has passed some standard limit. For example, "went too far" is 行きすぎた, where the activity "to go" passed the expected boundary.

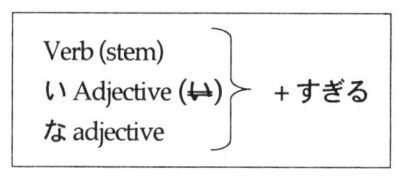

Verb (stem) </br> い Adjective (⥫) + すぎる </br> な adjective	食べすぎる　　eat too much </br> 甘すぎる　　　too sweet </br> 不便すぎる　　too inconvenient

働きすぎる　　　　work too hard
行きすぎる　　　　go too far
早すぎる　　　　　too early
速すぎる　　　　　too fast
暇すぎる　　　　　have too much free time

重すぎて持てない　　　　　　too heavy to carry
疲れすぎて動けない　　　　　too tired to move
(コーヒーを)飲みすぎて眠れない　drink too much (coffee) to sleep

(1) 食べ放題の店でおすしを食べすぎた。おなかが苦しくて死にそうだ。
I ate too much at an all-you-can-eat restaurant. I'm so stuffed and feel like I'm going to die.
(2) カレーはおいしいけど、私にはからすぎて、あまりたくさん食べられない。
Curry is tasty, but it is too spicy for me and I cannot eat very much.
(3) 松田さんは元気すぎて、一緒にいると疲れる。
Ms. Matsuda is too lively (talks too much, etc.) and I get tired when I am with her.
(4) うちの子は朝起きるのが遅すぎて、いつも学校に遅刻する。
My child gets up too late, therefore is always late for school.
(5) 東京は物価が高すぎて、住みにくい。
The price of things is too high in Tokyo and it is difficult to live there.

Sample dialogue
きのう飲みすぎたので・・・
A: おかしいなぁ・・・。先生の家、この辺なんだけどなぁ。
B: 住所は？
A: 230。
B: ここは280だよ。ちょっと来すぎたんだ。(We've come too far.)
A: そうか、じゃ戻ろう。
B: ここは180。あれ、今度は戻りすぎた。
なんだよ、しっかり番地を見ろよ。
A: ごめん、きのうビールを飲みすぎて、二日酔い (hang over) なんだ。
あ、あった！ここだ。

先生: まあ、二人ともいらっしゃい。
学生: すみません、遅くなって。他の学生はもう来ていますか。

先生: 　ええ、とっくに (long time ago)。だから、食べるもの、もうないわよ・・・。
学生: 　やっぱり遅すぎたか・・・。

7.　に + Motion Verb

The verbs 行く "to go" and 来る "to come" are used in a way that is always speaker-centered. When an activity or temporal phenomenon is going away from the speaker, 行く is used, while 来る is used when an activity or temporal phenomenon is approaching the speaker. When a person comes or goes with the purpose of engaging in some kind of activity, the verb (following the stem form of the activity verb) is followed by に. There are also some other motion verbs that can be used in this construction, such as 帰る "to return," 出かける "to leave," 歩く "to walk," and 走る "to run." Observe the following examples:

私は警察に行きました。　→　purpose　→　落し物を届ける
　　　　　　　　　　　↓
私は警察に落とし物を届けに行きました。
I went to a police station <u>to turn in lost property</u>.

(1)　松田さんは私の所へ書類を取りに来ました。
　　　Mr. Matsuda came to my place to pick up some documents.

(2)　アメリカの大統領が首相と会談をしに日本へ来ました。
　　　The American president came to Japan to confer with the prime minister of Japan.

(3)　今晩韓国料理を食べに行きませんか。
　　　Would you like to go eat Korean food tonight?

(4)　あなたに会いにお宅まで行きます。
　　　I will come to your home to see you.

(5)　新しい本が図書館に入りましたから、借りに行きましょう。
　　　New books arrived in the library, so let's go borrow them.

(6)　大学のオフィスに忘れ物を取りに走った。
　　　I ran to the university office to get the stuff I forgot to pick up.

When a noun that can accompany する, thereby changing into a verb, is used with に来ます or に行きます, then する is not needed, and に来ます or に行きます can follow the noun immediately. Some examples are: 買い物 "shopping," 食事 "eating," 旅行 "travel," 観光 "sight-seeing," テニス "playing tennis," and ゴルフ "golfing."

(7) 妻は今食事に行っています。子供は買い物に出かけています。私は一人です。

My wife has gone to eat. My kid has gone shopping. I am alone.

(8) 先週妹夫婦がアメリカへ旅行に来ました。今週はコロラドへスキーに行っています。

Last week, my sister and her husband came to America (where I am) to travel. They have gone to Colorado to ski this week.

Sample dialogues

財布は空でした

松田: やあ、本田さん、どちらへ？

Mr. Honda, where are you going?

本田: ちょっと近くの交番 (police station)まで行くんですよ。

I am going to a police station nearby.

松田: え、私もですよ。でも、またどうして？

Me too. But why?

本田: いえね、きのうあのあたりで、財布を落としたから、届いていないかなと思って・・・。

I lost my wallet in that area yesterday, and was wondering if it may have been turned in.

松田: え、財布？財布ってもしかしてこれですか？

Wallet? Is this it by any chance?

本田: えー？ そうそう、これですよ。どうして松田さんが？

Yes, this is it. Why do you have this?

松田: きのう拾ったんですけど、だれのかわからないでしょう。
それで交番に届けに行こうと思って・・・。
I found it yesterday, but don't know whose it is, so I thought that I should turn it in to the police.

本田: 松田さんが拾ってくださったんですか。なんて偶然なんだ。
どうもありがとう！
You found it? What a coincidence! Thank you so much.

松田: よかったですねえ、中が空から (empty) で・・・。
You are lucky since it was empty.

本田: え・・・？ええ、まあ・・・。
What? Ah . . . yeah . . . .

口座にお金を入れておいてください

男: あのう・・・すみません。お金をおろしに来たんですけど、機械がキャッシュカードを読めないようなんです・・・。
Excuse me. I came to withdraw some cash, but the machine does not seem to be able to read the card.

銀行員: そうですか。ちょっとカードをお貸しください。
Is that so? May I have your card, please?

ああ、お客様の口座には現在 50 円しかございません。ですから、1,000 円はおろせないのです。お金を入れに来ていただけますか。
Well, your account has only 50 yen now. So, you cannot withdraw 1,000 yen. Could you please come deposit some money?

男: あ、そう・・・。どうもすみませんでした。
Is that so?. . . I am sorry.

CHAPTER 10

て *Form Compounds*

The て form, as in 食べて, おもしろくて, きれいで, and 学生で, does not by itself assign any particular meaning.[1] The て form of these parts of speech is used to combine sentences; in this usage, it expresses the meanings "and," "and then," or "and so."[2] For example, when combining two adjectival phrases, such as 安いです "cheap" and おいしいです "delicious," the first い adjective has to alter its form into the て form to combine with おいしいです. 安くておいしいです means "cheap and delicious." Verbal phrases, as for example 遅くなる "to be late" and すみません, may also be combined using the て form to create a sentence like 遅くなってすみません "I'm late, so I'm sorry, i.e., I'm sorry for being late." Another type of example concerns two activities that occur one after the other: お風呂に入って、テレビを見た "I took a bath, then watched TV."

In addition to its function as a sentence/phrase linkage, the て form is commonly used with a variety of auxiliaries to constitute compound predicates, as in てから, ておく, てある, and ている. The attached auxiliary usually gives the meaning of the phrase. The constructions discussed in this chapter are basic ones in Japanese.

1. てください

ください is used when a speaker requests the listener to give him/her something. お水をください, for example, means "please give me (a glass of) water." Requesting something, however, is not limited merely to entities, but it also extends to an activity as in "please give me something, that is, to teach me Japanese." ください still plays a role in this construction by following the て form of a verb:

---

[1] Except when it is used as a casual form of てください, such as これ、食べて "Eat this."
[2] For explanation of the て form, refer to Chapter 14, section 1.

日本語を教えてください "Please teach me Japanese." In this construction, however, the meaning in practice communicates the concept of "command," and it can be rude, especially when used to an older individual. For example, 先生、ここに漢字を書いてください "Professor, please write the kanji here" is pragmatically the same as "write the kanji here" (though sometimes the tone of voice may rectify the impression that the speaker is giving) and much less appropriate than the polite equivalent ここに漢字を書いてくださいませんか "Could you please write the kanji here?" Also, てください is often seen on signs at various places and is heard in public announcements.

(1) お年よりに席をゆずってください。
Please offer your seat to an elder.
(2) ゴミはくずかごに捨ててください。
Please put garbage in the trash can.
(3) ここに名前と住所を書いてください。
Please write your name and address here.
(4) 猿にえさをやらないでください。
Please do not feed (give food to) the monkeys.
(5) すみません、お水を持ってきてください。
Excuse me. Please bring me (a glass of) water.
(6) 皆さん、一列に並んでください。
Everyone, please form a line.
(7) ドアによりかからないでください。
Please do not lean against the door.

In order to make a request polite and socially acceptable, ますか or ませんか may be added to てください. (For degrees of politeness in requests, see section 9 in this chapter.)

(8) 先生、宿題を見てくださいませんか。
Professor, could you please check my homework?
(9) こちらに座ってくださいますか。
Could you have a seat here?

Sample dialogue

私が作ったケーキ、どうぞ
友子: あの、これ、食べてください。
　　　Please eat this.
トム: え、何ですか、これ。
　　　What is this?
友子: 私が作ったケーキです。その後でこれを飲んでください。
　　　It's a cake I made. After eating it, please take this.
トム: え、これは何ですか。
　　　What is this?
友子: 胃の薬です。
　　　This is stomach medicine.
トム: え、やだなあ。食べませんよ、そんなケーキ！
　　　There is no way I'm going to eat such a cake!
　　　Why is Tom refusing to eat the cake?

動物園で
弟: お姉ちゃん、ぼくにもホットドッグちょうだいよ。[3]
　　Sis, give me a hot dog, too.
姉: だめよ。
　　No.
弟: どうして？　お母さんがぼくたちに買ってくれたんだよ。
　　Why not? Mom bought them for us.
姉: だめよ。ほら、あそこのサインを見てちょうだい。
　　No. Look, see the sign.
　　「サルにえさをやらないでください」って書いてあるでしょ。
　　It says "Do not feed the monkeys," right?
弟: おかあさ〜ん！お姉ちゃんがいじめるぅ！
　　Mom! Sis bullies me!
　　Why does the little brother think that his sister is bullying him?

---

[3] ちょうだい is a casual/informal equivalent of ください。Therefore, 見てちょうだい expresses the same meaning as 見てください。

2. てから

When two sequential activities need to be mentioned, てから may be used to combine two sentences into one sentence. Although the て form of the verb can itself express the sequential activity "and then," when から is added, the sequentiality is strongly emphasized, indicating that one activity comes first, then is followed by a second. The meaning is similar to that of た後で. てから can also be used to express "since," as in "Fifteen years have already passed *since* I came to America." In this sentence too, two ordered events are described, though the emphasis is not on their sequentiality. Tense is always identified in the main verb.

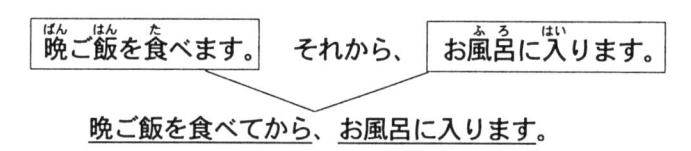

晩ご飯を食べます。　それから、　お風呂に入ります。

晩ご飯を食べてから、お風呂に入ります。

Observe the following examples:

(1) 日本へ行ってから、日本語を習います。
　　I go to Japan, then will learn Japanese.

(2) ひらがなを学んでから、カタカナを学びました。
　　I learned hiragana first, then learned katakana.

(3) a. 映画を見てから食事をしましょう。
　　　Let's see a movie first, then have a meal.

　　b. 映画を見た後で、食事をしましょう。
　　　Let's have a meal after seeing a movie.

(4) a. アメリカに来てから15年過ぎました。
　　　Fifteen years have passed since I came to America.

 * b. アメリカに来た後で15年過ぎました。
　　　Fifteen years passed after I came to America.

Sentence (1) of the above examples may normally be presented 日本へ行って、日本語を習います "I go to Japan and learn Japanese." When てから is used, the sentence emphasizes the order in which the actions occur. Sentence (1) thus implies that the speaker does not have any intention of learning Japanese before going to Japan.

Since てから emphasizes the sequentiality of events, てから and た後で are usually interchangeable when two activities occur one after the other. However, as (4a) demonstrates, てから can invite a phrase that is not controlled by the speaker: 15年過ぎた "fifteen years have passed." た後で is appropriate only when two events occur that are under the volitional control of an agent. The inappropriateness of sentence (4b) is attributed to the fact that 過ぎました cannot be a volitionally controlled event.

Note that when sequential activities are considered normal occurrences in daily life, the use of てから may become awkward. For example, people brush their teeth after they get up (not while they are in bed). The activities expressed in 朝起きます。それから、歯を磨きます "I get up in the morning. Then I brush my teeth" are understood as normal sequences, and there is no need to emphasize their sequentiality using てから. The て form may be used alone in such cases: 朝起きて、歯を磨きます "I get up in the morning **and** brush my teeth."

Sample dialogue
ある夫婦の会話
女： あなた、今日は何をしましょうか。
　　 Honey, what shall we do today?
男： フットボールを見るんだ。それから、シャワーを浴びて、テレビ。
　　 I'm going to watch a football game. Then, take a shower, and (watch) TV.
女： そう・・・フットボールを見てからまたテレビ・・・。
　　 Well, after watching the football game, then (I) watch TV again ...
　　 自分の好きなことばかりね。
　　 Nothing but your favorite activities.
男： 君はどうするの？
　　 How about you? What are you going to do?
女： 私は買い物に行ってから食事して、それから映画を見るの。
　　 I'm going to go shopping, then eat, then watch a movie.
男： え、誰と？
　　 Hah? With whom?
女： さあね・・・。
　　 None of your business.

3. ている

ている is called an "aspectual form," and it is used to express the continuation of a situation either in a dynamic or a static state. It expresses a situation that involves a duration of time expressed in sentences, like "is/has been ~ing" and "is/have ~ed." The former expresses an *on-going state*; the latter, a *resultative* state in which something has been done, and the result of that action remains unchanged; something is in the state of having come to an end. An on-going state involves a period of time in which an activity is in a dynamic situation (is ~ing). A resultative state involves a situation wherein the activity is completed by the animate entity and the state resulting from the completion of the activity remains as static (have ~ed). ている can be interpreted as expressing "~ing" or "have ~ed" in English, and therefore is not exactly an equivalent to the English "~ing" construction (see Johnson 2004).

Although it is true that ている in general can be used to express either an on-going meaning or a resultative meaning, there are some verbs that can express either meaning depending on the environment, while other verbs with ている may be able to yield only a resultative meaning. For example, 見ている can be interpreted as expressing either "I am watching" or "I have watched," whereas 死んでいる can only mean "(something) is dead (= in the state of having died)" and *cannot* mean "(something) *is dying*," unlike in English. The meaning of ている sentences depends on the type of verb, and there is quite a difference the way that ている is used compared to the English progressive "~ing" form. Therefore, as mentioned, a ている sentence does not immediately translate into an English progressive ("~ing") sentence.

In Japanese, activities that are controlled by a animate entity's volition can often be perceived as repetitive activities, either conceptually or concretely. For example, for some activities, such as 歩いている "walking" and 食べている "eating," the notion of repetition is visualizable, and the action can be more concretely recognized as a repetitive action (alternating legs moving ahead and bringing food to mouth to eat, respectively). Some actions, however, may be conceptual and abstract, such as 買っている "is buying" and 聞いている "is listening." However, there is a commonality in these activities, that is, the constant *energy input* required from the animate entity to maintain the situation. In other words:

> If the attribute of a verb is perceived as satisfying "volitionally controllable," "visually or conceptually repetitive," and/or "requires energy input to maintain the situation," then the ている phrase expresses either an on-going state or a resultative state.

Let's do a test using the following verbs:
Table 1

	Volitional control	Repetition	Energy input
泳ぐ	✓	✓	✓
泣く	✓	?	✓
買う	✓	??	✓
(雨が)降る	X	✓	X

The verb 降る in 雨が降る satisfies only one category, repetition, but is the same type as 泳ぐ, for example, in terms of the interpretation of the construction with ている. The interpretation "on-going" for this type of natural phenomenon expressed by the ている form usually prevails over the "resultative" interpretation in normal communication. It is certainly possible for a resultative interpretation to be appropriate, as in 今年はたくさん雨が降っている "It has rained a lot this year." Although natural phenomena occur without respect to human volition, these phenomena are often personified as if indicating that nature has its own power and volition to drop rain on us and blow wind at us.

On the contrary, non-volitional activities, which are often expressed by intransitive verbs, can be perceived as one-time events changing the subject. Since they are non-volitional, energy input by the animate entity is lacking from the event. Also, the change cannot be viewed as a repetition of some event; rather, it occurs once to the subject. 死ぬ "to die," for instance, is a good example of a one-time event. One does not reach death, by dying over and over again. The situation approaches the point of death not by repeating it, but by progressing. This progression to the point of change can be described by "~ing" in English, but not by ている in Japanese. As discussed, 死んでいる expresses a situation where something reached the point of death; the state after the death has occurred is an unchanging one (is dead). Likewise, non-volitional intransitive verbs, such as 着く "to arrive," 済む "to finish," and 焼ける "to be baked" express only a resultative meaning when ている is attached. In other words:

> If the attribute of a verb is perceived as "one-time occurrence to bring a change into a subject," "non-volitional event," and/or "non-repetitive event," then the ている phrase expresses only a resultative state.

Let's do a test using the following verbs:

Table 2

	Volitional control	One-time event	Energy input
結婚する	✓	✓	X
住む	✓	✓	??
持つ	✓	✓	??
知る	??	✓	X

Comparing this with table 1, we can see that "volitional control" is not the key to differentiate between verbs when determining aspectual category. The key seems to be the combination of the concepts of "repetition" and "energy input."

結婚する "to get married" and 住む "to live," for example, are perceived as expressing human volition. However, they express only a resultative meaning when ている is attached. This is due to the fact that neither of them can be perceived as repeating the actions 結婚する and 住む to reach the point of realization of the events. "I'm getting married" cannot be perceived as "I repeat the marriage to reach married standing." In Japanese, 結婚している means "I'm married," and not "I'm getting married." In order to say "I'm getting married," 私は結婚します "I will get married" is the appropriate expression. In the following sections, further explanation about these types of verbs is given.

3.1 Verbs of volition, repetition, and/or energy input

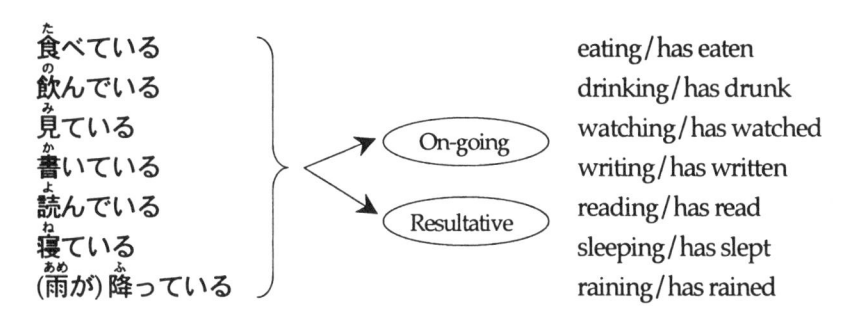

食べている   eating/has eaten
飲んでいる   drinking/has drunk
見ている   watching/has watched   → On-going
書いている   writing/has written
読んでいる   reading/has read   → Resultative
寝ている   sleeping/has slept
(雨が)降っている   raining/has rained

When activity verbs, such as 食べる "to eat," 飲む "to drink," 読む "to read," 書く "to write," 歩く "to walk," 降る "to fall/to rain," and 話す "to talk" are used in the non-past form, they express either a future or a habitual event, but they cannot express an on-going event. 食べる, for example, can be used to express either "I will eat" or "I (habitually) eat," but not "I will be/am eating (tomorrow/now)." In order for these activity verbs to express an on-going meaning, ている must be attached. To express the equivalent of "I *am eating*"[4] or "I *will be eating*," 食べている has to be used. When ている is attached to these verbs, however, the sentence can express not only an on-going state (is ~ing), but also a resultative state (have ~ed), depending on the context. This is attributed to the fact that a resultative state also lets us envision a duration of time from completion of the action to the moment of speech. The following generic timeline depicts the meaning of ている in a more comprehensive manner:

---

[4] 食べている "I am eating" can also be considered a habitual activity as, for example, when it indicates that someone is eating from 6:00 to 6:30 every day. The difference between the habitual meaning expressed by 食べる "I eat" and that expressed by 食べている "I am eating" is subtle. Theoretically, the former is used when one observes the situation in its entirety, while the latter is used when one observes the situation closer to the internal situation of the event, perhaps putting a little more focus on the ongoing aspect of the event within the given time frame.

(1)

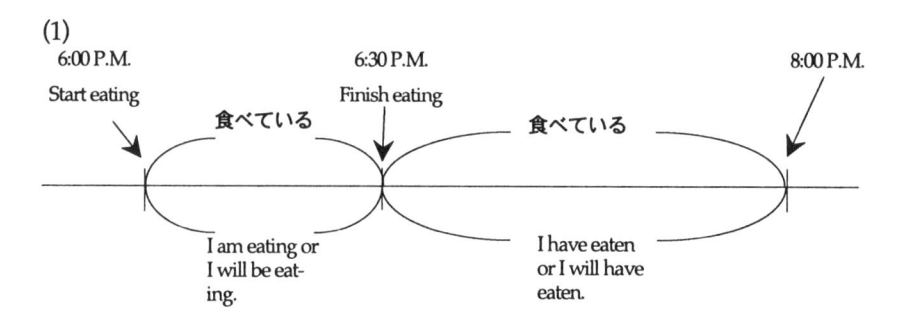

```
6:00 P.M.              6:30 P.M.                    8:00 P.M.
Start eating           Finish eating
         食べている                 食べている
    ↓         ⌒          ↓          ⌒          ↓
────────┤         ├─────────┤          ├────────
              I am eating or       I have eaten
              I will be eat-       or I will have
              ing.                 eaten.
```

(Note that the time of speech is 8:00 if "I have eaten" is the meaning to be expressed. The time of speech is some time before 6:00 P.M. on the timeline if "I will have eaten" is the meaning to be expressed.)

In the above timeline, the non-past form is used as an example, but if the event occurs in a past context, る is simply changed to た, as shown in sentences (3a) and (3b), below. Also, the ambiguity caused by 食べています (is eating or have eaten) is clarified by the surrounding context and/or by the use of adverbs such as 今 and もう. These adverbs play a crucial role in explicating the meaning. See the following examples:

(2)   a.   今晩6時から6時半まで晩ご飯を<u>食べています</u>。
          I <u>will be eating</u> dinner from 6:00 to 6:30 tonight.
   b.   (8時に夫が帰る時は)(もう)晩ご飯を<u>食べています</u>。⁵
          (When my husband returns home at 8:00,) I <u>will have (already) eaten</u> dinner.

If the event occurs in a past context, the past tense form is used as exemplified in the following:

(3)   a.   6時から6時半まで晩ご飯を<u>食べていました</u>。
          I <u>was eating</u> dinner from 6:00 to 6:30.
   b.   (8時に夫が帰った時は)(もう)晩ご飯を<u>食べていました</u>。
          (When my husband returned home at 8:00,) I (already) <u>had eaten</u> dinner.

---

[5] 食べています can be interpreted as expressing "I will already be eating" in daily conversation. However, the grammatical Japanese equivalent would be もう晩ご飯を<u>食べ始めています</u> "I will already start eating."

晩ご飯を食べていました alone, without context, can be interpreted either as "I was eating" or "I had eaten." Here are some more examples:

(4) 飲んでいます。
   I am drinking./I have drunk. (ambiguous)

(5) a. 今映画を見ている。
   I am watching a movie now.
   b. その映画はもう見ている。
   Speaking of that movie, I have already seen it.

(6) a. その本は今読んでいる。
   Speaking of that book, I am reading it now.
   b. その本はもう読んでいる。
   Speaking of that book, I have already read it.

(7) a. 今論文を書いている所だ。
   I am writing a term paper now.
   b. 論文はもう書いている。
   I have already written a term paper.

(8) a. 今雨が降っている。
   It is raining now.
   b. 今年はたくさん雨が降っている。
   We have had a lot of rain this year.

(9) a. 隆は今隣の部屋で静かに寝ている。
   Takashi is sleeping peacefully in the next room now.
   b. 隆は昼間たくさん寝ているから、夜なかなか眠れないのだ。
   The reason Takashi cannot fall asleep easily is that he has slept a lot during the day.

3.2 One-time events ⟶ ⟨Resultative⟩

As mentioned above, one-time events are perceived as events or situations that occur once and only once to bring about a physical and situational change in the subject. Also, the change is not realized by the repetition of the same event. For example, reaching the point of arrival may be realized by a gradual progression, but not by repeating the arrival itself. Events described by non-volitional intransitive verbs are mostly perceived as one-time events. These verbs, when attached to ている express *only a resultative meaning*. They do not express an on-going meaning as, for example, in "an airplane is arriving" in English. 着いている in Japanese exhibits only a resultative meaning that is equivalent to "an airplane has arrived (is in the state of having arrived at the airport)." This is an important difference found between English and Japanese. "An airplane is arriving" is then expressed simply by the non-past form 着きます "will arrive" or some different sentence patterns, such as 着くところです "is about to arrive." Compare the difference between the use of ている with a repetitive event and a one-time event:

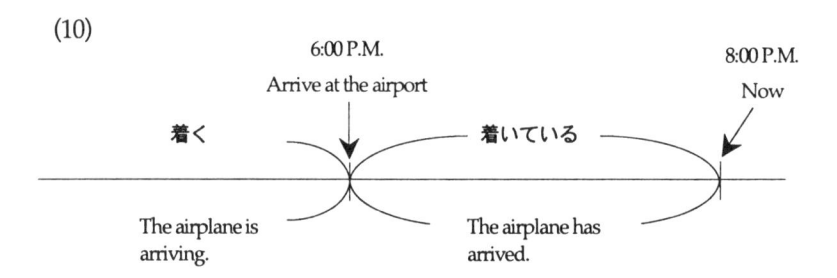

(10)

```
            6:00 P.M.                          8:00 P.M.
         Arrive at the airport                   Now
  着く                    着いている
─────────────┼──────────────────────┼─────────
   The airplane is          The airplane has
   arriving.                arrived.
```

Typical verbs that describe one-time events are:

(11) 死ぬ　　　　　　　　　あ、リスが死んでいる！
　　　Meaning:　　　　　　A squirrel is in the state resulting from having died.
　　　English expression:　Look, a squirrel is dead!

(12) 知る　　　　　　　　　私はジョンを知っている。
　　　Meaning:　　　　　　I am in the state resulting from having come to know John.
　　　English expression:　I know John.

(13) 持つ　　　　　　　　　本田さんはトヨタの車を持っている。
　　　Meaning:　　　　　　Mr. Honda is in the state resulting from having owned a Toyota car.
　　　English expression:　Mr. Honda has a Toyota car.

(14) 結婚(けっこん)する　　　　先生(せんせい)は結婚している。
　　　Meaning:　　　　　　　The teacher is in the state resulting from having gotten married.
　　　English expression:　　The teacher is married.
(15) 行(い)く　　　　　　　田中さんは日本(にほん)へ行っている。
　　　Meaning:　　　　　　　Mr. Tanaka is in the state resulting from having gone to Japan.
　　　English expression:　　Mr. Tanaka is in Japan./Mr. Tanaka has gone to Japan.
(16) 来(く)る　　　　　　　母(はは)が日本から来(き)ている。
　　　Meaning:　　　　　　　My mother is in the state resulting from having come from Japan.
　　　English expression:　　My mother has arrived from Japan./My mother is here.

The verbs 行く and 来る with ている are perhaps among the most difficult to comprehend in terms of why 行っている and 来ている are used to express only a resultative meaning. Most learners of Japanese immediately construe 行っている as "someone is going" which means "someone is on the way to somewhere" (if not expressing a habitual meaning)[6] and 来ている as "someone is on the way here." 行く and 来る in Japanese are not perceived as "walking," but are strongly associated with the notion of "achievement" that can be treated in the same way as 着(つ)く "to arrive." They are in fact perceived as one-time events.

The following are some more examples of verbs that express only a resultative meaning when ている is attached.

開(あ)く　　　　ドアが開いている。
　　　　　　　　The door is open.
消(き)える　　　電気(でんき)が消えている。
　　　　　　　　The light is turned off.

---

[6] If a habitual meaning is meant to be conveyed, words such as 毎日(まいにち) "every day" make the meaning clear. 息子(むすこ)は毎日学校(がっこう)に行(い)っている "My son goes to school every day" is different from 息子は学校に行っている "My son is at school."

着く	飛行機は空港に着いている。	
	The airplane has arrived at the airport.	
焼ける	ケーキが焼けている。	
	The cake has been baked.	
落ちる	財布が落ちている。	
	A wallet has fallen (and been found on the road).	
太る	うちの猫は太っている。	
	My cat is fat.	
できる	夕飯ができている。	
	Dinner is ready.	
始まる	その映画はもう始まっている。	
	The movie has already begun.	
帰る	父はもう家へ帰っている。	
	My father has already returned home.	
届く	荷物が届いている。	
	The parcel has arrived.	
こぼれる	テーブルに水がこぼれている。	
	Water is spilled on the table.	

Sample reading

ピザ急いで届けます

I will deliver pizza quickly

僕は高校を卒業して、今年からハーバード大学の学生になった。工学 (engineering) を専攻したいと思って、今頑張って勉強している。予習や復習も毎日している。そして論文ももういくつか書いた。けれども、自分で学費 (tuition) を払っているので、働かなくてはならない。平日はクラスがあって忙しいので、週末だけピザを届ける仕事を始めた。

　その日は朝から雪が降っていて、あまり運転したくなかったが、いつもよりたくさんの注文が入った。僕はピザを箱に入れて、急いである家へ持っていった。

その家の玄関に着いてベルを鳴らした (rang the bell) が、だれも出てこない。もう一度鳴らしてみたが同じだ。変だと思って、裏 (backyard) へ行ってみた。電気は消えている。僕は大きい声で「すみません！」と呼んでみたが、やはり返事はない (there was no answer)。それで、住所を間違えていたのだと思い、車に戻って確かめることにした。

するとその時、地下室 (basement) に電気がついていることに気がついた。「あれ、人がいるのかな・・・」と思って、小さい窓から中を覗いてみた。中は暗かったが、椅子が見えた。そして、その椅子には女の人が座っていた。ところがよく見ると、その女の人は縄で縛られているではないか！(to my surprise, she was tied up with rope!) そして、椅子のそばにはナイフが置いてあるし、女の人は血を流しているようだ。僕は驚いて、急いで車に戻り、警察 (police) に電話した。「すぐに来てください。人が死んでいます。」10分後に警察官が来た。事情を説明すると (when I explained the circumstance)、彼らは家のドアを開けて、中へ入っていった。

ちょうどその時、その家の人 (owner of the house) が帰って来た。「いったい何があったのでしょうか」とその家の人が言うと、警察官は「人が死んでいるという電話があったのです」と答えた。主人は急いで地下室へ下りていった。1分後、家の中から声が聞こえて来た。「おーい、あれはマネキン (mannequin) だ。この家のご主人は芝居の道具を作る人 (theater prop maker) で、あれは小道具 (prop) なんだよ。血はケチャップだ。」

僕は何も言えなかった。そして、ピザを届ける家は隣の家だったこともわかった。でもその時はピザはもう冷たくなっていた。

Excerpt sentences of aspect and provide a meaning for each sentence indicating either an on-going or a resultative meaning.

4. ておく

おく means "to place something somewhere." When attached to the て form, it refers to an activity that has been done (placed) in advance for future use, purpose, and/or preparation. Since ておく is used to express the preparation of some event, the verb has to be an activity verb performed with the speaker's intention.

For example:

日本へ行く前に Before I go to Japan
    パスポートを取っておきます。
    I will obtain a passport in advance.
    日本語を勉強しておきます。
    I will study Japanese in preparation.
    おみやげを買っておきます。
    I will buy some souvenirs in advance.

パーティの前に Before I have a party.
    部屋を掃除しておきます。
    I will clean the room.
    飲み物を買っておきます。
    I will buy some drinks.
    食べ物を作っておきます。
    I will make some food.

Sample dialogue

母: まあ、どうしたの、掃除なんかして。いつもは一年に一度くらいでしょ？どういう風の吹き回し？
What happened? Why are you cleaning? You usually do it once a year or so, right? What made you do this?

息子: お母さん、それはひどいよ。ぼくだってたまには掃除くらいするよ。
Mother, that's mean. Even I occasionally clean the room.

母: わかった！美々子さんが来るんでしょう。
Got it! Mimiko is coming, isn't she?

息子: いや、美々子はもう来たんだ。僕の部屋を見てびっくりして・・・ふられちゃった。だから次の彼女のために掃除しておくんだよ。
No, Mimiko has already been here. She was surprised to see my room, and I got dumped. So I am cleaning my room in advance for the next girl friend.

母: まあ、それなら、その鼻のピアスも取っておくといいわよ・・・。
If that is the case, you should remove the nose pierce too (before you meet the girl).

5. てある

てある means that an intended action has been undertaken and that the resulting situation continues up to the present moment. The function of てある and ている is somewhat similar in that both are used to describe a resultative state, that is, something in the state of having been done. The difference is that てある is used when someone intended to cause the state that has resulted. Therefore, てある can accompany only an activity verb.[7] The diagram below helps capture the similarities and differences between ている and てある.

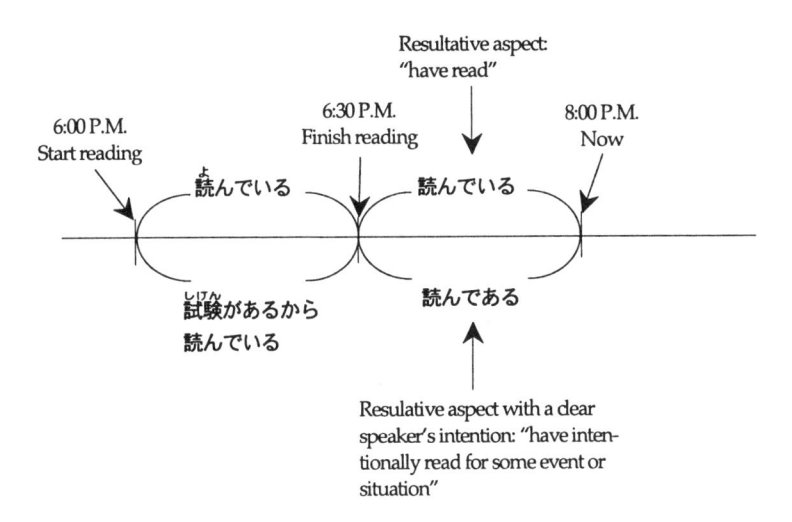

```
                         Resultative aspect:
                            "have read"
                                ↓
                         6:30 P.M.           8:00 P.M.
    6:00 P.M.           Finish reading          Now
   Start reading              ↓                  ↓
        ↓         読
                  ん
           ─── で ───        ─── 読んでいる ───
                  い
                  る
   ─────────────────────────────────────────────────
         試験があるから          読んである
            読んでいる              ↑
                          Resulative aspect with a clear
                          speaker's intention: "have inten-
                          tionally read for some event or
                          situation"
```

As illustrated in the above diagram, in terms of the description of the situation, both ている and てある refer to the same state on the timeline. Both are interpreted as "I'm in the state of having read," i.e., "I have read." The difference is that while ている is more focused on the resultative aspect of the event, which does not include the speaker's intention or any emotional nuances, てある describes the resultative situation with a focus on the speaker's intention and the reason why the speaker has performed the action. Also, the interpretation of ている can be ambiguous, as ている can express an on-going meaning as well, but no such interpretation is applicable to てある. てある is used with the same concept

---

[7] For those who are interested in further discussion of てある, refer to Tsujimura (1991).

as the resultative ている. The following sentences provide more examples that illustrate the meaning of てある and its difference from ている:

(1)　　ドアが開けてある。
　　　The door has been opened with someone's intention and left as it is.
Cf.　　ドアが開いている。
　　　The door is open. (開く is an intransitive verb.)
(2)　　飲み物が買ってある。
　　　A drink has been bought with someone's intention and left as it is.
Cf.　　飲み物を買っている。
　　　Someone is buying a drink (now)./Someone has (already) bought a drink.

Once てある is attached to a verb, the whole compound predicate (e.g., 開ける + ある) functions as a stative-transitive predicate; therefore, the object ドア can be marked by either が or を.[8] However, a slight difference may be detected in the use of が and を. Observe the following examples:

(3)　　a.　　窓 (が) 開けて (ある)。
　　　　　　The window has been opened (with an intention).
　　　b.　　窓 (を) (開けて) ある。
　　　　　　I have opened the window (with an intention).

Theoretically, when が is used to mark 窓, が is tied to the stative attribute of the predicate ある, i.e., the window is in the state of my having opened it.[9] In this case, the resultative state of the window is the main focus of the sentence. On the other hand, when を is used to mark 窓, を is tied to the active attribute of the predicate 開ける. Someone's intention of opening the window is the main focus of the sentence. Although both sentences imply the intention of an individual behind the action, 窓を開けてある conveys a stronger idea of individual intention for

---

[8] Refer to Chapter 4, section 2.2.
[9] If the situation is only in question, ドアが開いています "The door is open" should be used. This sentence does not imply only human intention behind the opening of the door, but simply describes the status of the door.

causing the window to be in the open state. In daily conversation, one may find that が is more commonly used than を.

Although the main activity is conducted prior to the present moment (such that 買う precedes 買ってある), since てある indicates a resultative state continuing to the present moment, and refers to such duration of time including the current moment, the てある predicate is used usually in the non-past form. てあった, on the other hand, means something had been done with an intention at some point in the past (past perfect), but is not necessarily the same at the current moment.

(4)   A: あれ、変だな。ケーキが買ってあったはずだけど・・・。
           Hah? Strange. I am sure that a cake had been bought (but where did it go?)
     B: あ、ごめん。昨日食べちゃったよ。
           Oops, sorry. I ate it up yesterday.

For sentence (4A), ケーキを買っておいた may also be applicable. The difference is that ケーキが買ってあった focuses on the existence of the cake, while ケーキを買っておいた focuses on the speaker's intention (in preparation for something else, such as a party).

Next, let's examine the negative form. First, observe the following examples:

		Formal form	Plain form
(5)	a.	答が書いてありません。	答が書い**てない**。
		The answer has not been written.	
	b.	答を書いてありません。	答を書い**てない**。
		I purposely have not written the answer.	
	c.	答を書いていません。	答を書い**ていない**。
		I am not writing the answer./I have not written the answer.	

As may be seen from the above examples, the negative form of てある and ている is not the same. However, in daily communication, the い in (5c), 答を書いて

いない, is often dropped and pronounced 答を書いてない, which is the same as the casual form in (5b), 答を書いてありません. The meaning can be differentiated only in context.

Sample dialogue

弟： お母さん、何か食べるものない？
Mom, isn't there something to eat?

母： 冷蔵庫にケーキとジュースが買ってあるわ。
I bought cake and juice and put them in the refrigerator.

弟： 冷蔵庫に？入って(い)ないよ・・・。
In the fridge? They aren't there.

母： 変ねえ・・・。今朝買ってきて入れておいたんだけど・・・。
That's strange . . . I bought them this morning and put them in the fridge.
どこに入れてしまったのかしら。
I wonder where I put them.

兄： 何(を)探して(い)るの？
What are you looking for?

母： 今朝買ってきたケーキとジュースよ。
The cake and juice I bought this morning.

兄： あれなら、僕のおなかにしまってあるよ。
Oh, those? I put them away in my stomach.

6. てみる

てみる is used when a speaker tries something to see how it is. The difference between 食べます and 食べてみます is that while 食べます indicates a speaker's will to realize the activity, 食べてみます creates a connotation of a trial: the speaker will try the food to see how it tastes. The result of the trial remains to be seen at the time of speech.

(1) この服を着てみてください。
Please try on this dress and see how you like it.

(2) 1級の試験を受けてみます。
I will take the 1st level exam and see how it goes.
(3) 日本酒を飲んでみましたが、まずかったです。
I tried rice wine to see how it was, but it tasted bad.
(4) 新しくできたレストランに一緒に行ってみませんか。
Would you like to try a new restaurant and see how we like it?

Sample dialogue

私の料理、試食してください

Please sample my food.

女： これ、食べてみてください。
Please sample this and see how you like it.
男： え、ああ、今、食事したばかりだから、おなか、いっぱいなんだ。
Well... I've just finished my meal, so I'm full.
女： ま、失礼ね！まずいと思っているんでしょう。
That's not nice! You think that it tastes bad, don't you?
母が作ったのよ。
My mom made it.
男： あ、そう？じゃ、ちょっと食べてみよう。（う・・・まずい！）
Is that so? Well, then, I will try it. (Wuuu, yuk!)
女： どう？おいしい？ほんとうはね、私が作ったの・・・。
How do you like it? Is it good? To tell you the truth, I made it...
男： やっぱり！
I knew it!

7. てしまう

しまう itself means "to put things away," but when it is attached to the て form of a verb, the compound verb expresses an "unrecoverable event" as a result of being put away. This notion communicates two extended meanings: (1) completion of action, and (2) a regrettable event (since both are completed events that cannot be recovered). Therefore a sentence such as 彼がビールを飲んでしまった can carry the connotation of "He finished up the beer," or "(Unfortunately/

unexpectedly) he finished up (my) portion of beer," or it can be both. The meaning depends on context, but when completion is emphasized, the sentence is often accompanied by adverbs such as すっかり "completely." In casual communication, てしまう is pronounced ちゃう or じゃう as in 書いちゃう and 飲んじゃう. Since てしまう expresses the concept of regret, it often occurs in a passive sentence that exhibits an adversity meaning. Observe the following sentences:

(1) 夕飯は主人が帰る前にもう食べてしまいました。
Speaking of dinner, I had already eaten up before my husband returned.

(2) 戦争でたくさんの人が死んでしまいました。
Many people, it is sad to say, died in the war.

(3) 東京の町はすっかり変わってしまいました。
The city of Tokyo has unfortunately completely changed.

(4) 傘を持っていなかったので、雨に降られて、すっかり濡れてしまいました。
Since I did not have an umbrella, I got rained on and completely soaked.

(5) 今朝電車の中で財布を盗まれてしまいました。
Unfortunately, I got my wallet stolen in the subway this morning.

Sample dialogue

先生: 松田さん、うれしそうですね。何かいいことでもあったんですか。
Ms. Matsuda, you look happy. Did something good happen to you?

松田: いいえ、別に。ただ今日はゆっくりできるので、気分がいいんです。
No, not in particular. I feel good just because I can relax today.

先生: へえ、どうして？
How come?

松田: 宿題をもうしてしまいましたし、レポートも書いてしまいました。それに、本も全部読んでしまいましたから。
I completed my homework, finished writing the term paper, and read all the books.

先生: それはすごい。その調子で頑張ってください。
That's great! Keep up the good work.

[翌日]
先生: 松田さん、今日は元気なさそうですねえ。どうしたんですか？
Ms. Matsuda, you don't look very happy today. What's wrong?

松田: ええ、実は朝から大変だったんです。
Yes, I had a hard time since this morning.

先生: それはまた・・・何があったんですか。
What on earth happened?

松田: 昨日した宿題を犬が食べてしまったんです。それから、書いたレポートをうっかりコンピュータから消してしまったんです・・・。
My dog ate the homework I did yesterday. Then I accidentally erased the term paper from the computer...

先生: ああ、それはかわいそうに・・・。
Oh, poor girl...

ふられちゃったんです
A: 元気ないねぇ。
B: うん、今朝雨にも彼女にもふられちゃったんだ・・・。

8.　ていく/てくる

The motion verbs 行く and 来る do not always correspond to "go" and "come" in English, respectively. 行く and 来る are consistently used in a speaker-centered manner in Japanese. When someone/something approaches the speaker, 来る is used, and when someone/something moves away from the speaker, 行く is used. For example, in English, when you are on the phone and are telling the interlocutor that you are visiting to see him/her, you would say, "I am *coming* to your place." In Japanese, since the speaker will move away from his/her place toward the interlocutor's place, 行く is the appropriate verb, as in これからそちらに行きます "I am *coming* to your place."

行く and 来る can also be used as auxiliaries to form compound verbs such as 持ってくる "to bring" and 帰ってくる "to return." In such cases, they are used to indicate that a situation/event is moving toward the speaker or away from the speaker *temporally, conceptually,* or *physically,* and they are usually written in hiragana. When a situation/event is approaching the speaker, きました in the past tense form is appropriate, since the non-past form きます indicates a future event, which itself temporally and conceptually moves away from the speaker. When a situation/event moves away from the speaker toward the future, いきます is the appropriate verb to use. For these conceptual movements, いきます and きます are usually written in hiragana. The following picture represents the concept of いく and くる.

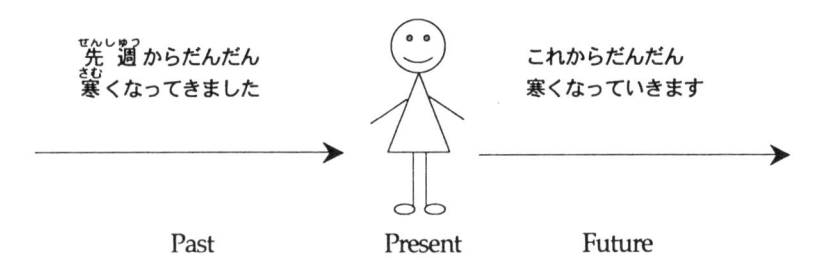

先週からだんだん
寒くなってきました

これからだんだん
寒くなっていきます

Past　　　　Present　　　　Future

In the next section, examples are given in terms of いく／くる for physical movement and for temporal and conceptual movement.

8.1　いく/くる expressing physical movement

いく/くる are added to specify the direction of the physical movement of the preceding verb. Compare the verb with/without いく and くる and visualize where the speaker is in each sentence.

(1) a. 猫が階段を降りました。
   A cat went down the stairs.
   b. 猫が階段を降りてきました。
   A cat came down the stairs toward me.
   c. 猫が階段を降りていきました。
   A cat went down the stairs (moving away from me).

(2) a. ジョンが家へ帰りました。
   John returned home.

b. ジョンが家へ帰ってきました。
John came back to his home (where I am).

c. ジョンが家へ帰っていきました。
John went back home (moving away from me).

(3) a. メリーは花を持ちます。
Mary will hold the flower.

b. メリーは花を持ってきます。
Mary will bring the flower (to me).

c. メリーは花を持っていきます。
Mary will bring the flowers somewhere.

(4) a. 風船が空へ上がりました。
A balloon ascended skyward.

* b. 風船が空へ上がってきました。
A balloon ascended skyward toward me.
(You must be somewhere above the sky.)

c. 風船が空へ上がっていきました。
A balloon ascended to the sky (moving away from me).

8.2 いく/くる expressing temporal/conceptual movement

いく/くる are added to specify the direction of the temporal/conceptual movement of the preceding verb. Compare the verb with/without いく and くる and visualize such temporal/conceptual movement.

(5) a. 空がだんだん暗くなりました。
The sky gradually became dark.

b. 空がだんだん暗くなってきました。
The sky gradually became dark (since a little while ago).

c. 空がだんだん暗くなってきます。
The sky is gradually becoming dark (toward the future).

(6) a. 日本語がわかります。
I understand Japanese.

b. 日本語がわかってきました。
I came to understand Japanese.

		c.	日本語がわかっていくでしょう。[10]
			I will probably start understanding Japanese.
(7)	a.	電話がかかりました。
		The phone rang.
	b.	電話がかかってきました。
		Someone called me.
*	c.	電話がかかっていきました。
(8)	a.	疲れます。
		I get tired.
	b.	疲れてきました。
		I became tired.
*	c.	疲れていきます。
(9)	a.	日本の若者の人口はこれからも減っていくだろうか。
		I wonder if the young population in Japan will become smaller (looking toward the future).
*	b.	日本の若者の人口はこれからも減ってくるだろうか。

As can be observed from the above example sentences, when the verb describes an abstract condition of a state or an event, いきます is not appropriate. いきます is most appropriate and gives a clear picture of the event's movement when it follows an activity verb.

9. てほしい

Although the word ほしい is morphologically an い adjective, ほしい functions like the English verb "want" and takes an object, as in "I want *a car*." ほしい is used only for the speaker him/herself, and does not represent a second or third person's desire. Remember that the object with ほしい is marked by が since ほしい is a pure stative predicate. Observe the following examples:

---

[10] Sentence (6c) is awkward, though it may be encountered in daily communication. In order to describe the change of state, in this case, from not understanding to understanding, わかるようになる is a more appropriate sentence.

(1)　私は新車がほしい。
　　　I want a new car.
(2)　私は自分の家がほしい。
　　　I want my own house.
(3)　母:　誕生日のプレゼントは何がほしい？
　　　　　What do you want for your birthday?
　　　子供:　お金がほしい。
　　　　　　I want money.
　　　母:　じゃあ、クリスマスプレゼントは何がほしい？
　　　　　Well, then what about a Christmas present?
　　　子供:　お金！
　　　　　　Money!

When ほしい follows the て form of a verb, it is used as a request. てほしい expresses that the speaker would like the activity described by the て form of the verb done by someone else: "I want someone to do ~." For example, (あなたに)私のことをわかってほしい means "I want you to understand (about) me." The following are some examples of this pattern.

(4)　ジョンさんにパーティに来てほしいです。
　　　I want John to come to the party.
(5)　ジョンさんにこの英語を日本語に訳してほしいです。
　　　I want John to translate this English into Japanese.
(6)　あなたにそんなこと言ってほしくありません。
　　　I do not want you to say things like that.
(7)　(あなたに)日本で着物を買ってきてほしいのですが・・・。
　　　I want you to buy a kimono in Japan (and bring it to me), but (what do you think . . .)?

Since てほしい is a pattern of request, ほしい can also be replaced by various expressions that indicate different degrees of politeness depending on to whom and in what circumstances the speaker is making the request, as exemplified in the following:

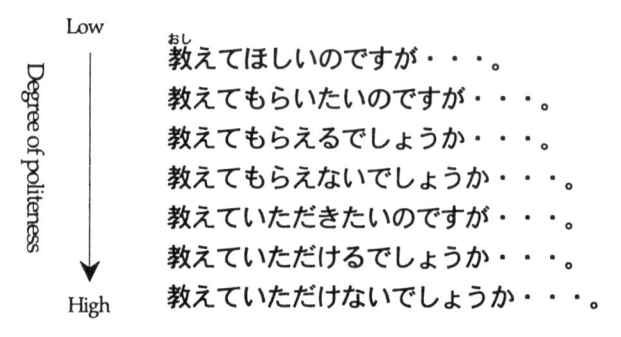

Degree of politeness: Low → High

教えてほしいのですが・・・。
教えてもらいたいのですが・・・。
教えてもらえるでしょうか・・・。
教えてもらえないでしょうか・・・。
教えていただきたいのですが・・・。
教えていただけるでしょうか・・・。
教えていただけないでしょうか・・・。

Since です appears in every expression in the above examples, they are already considered formal. However, ていただけないでしょうか is much more polite than ほしいのですが. The appropriateness of the ordering of the expressions listed above may not receive complete consensus among native speakers of Japanese. However, it is certainly the case that a request made in a negative expression is more polite than the affirmative form. For example, in 教えていただけるでしょうか and 教えていただけないでしょうか, the latter is perceived as more polite than the former.

Sample dialogue

学生: あのう、すみません・・・。CDプレーヤーを貸していただけないでしょうか・・・。
隣人: まあ、音楽をお聞きになるんですか。それなら、家にいらしたら？
学生: いえ、あのう・・・実は明日試験があるんです・・・。
隣人: ？？？

敬語の行方

女の子: ちょっとそこのおじさんとおばさん、悪いけどさ、どいてくれない？写真、撮るのよ。
おじさん: え、おじさん、おばさんって、ぼくたちのこと？
女の子: そうそう、もうちょっと右に動いてほしいんだけどな。

おじさん: 最近の若い人たちは敬語の使い方を知らないねぇ。もっと勉強してほしいと思うんだが、無理かね。

おばさん: 私も彼らにもっと敬語を使ってもらいたいんですけどね。でも、今では敬語の必要性を感じていない人が多いみたいですよ。

おじさん: いや、大学生の時や若いうちはいいかもしれないけど、社会に出て、就職して上司ができたら、やっぱり困るだろう。

おばさん: 本当に。日本語はどうなってしまうんでしょうねぇ。あまり変わらないでほしいけれども・・・。

CHAPTER 11

た Form Compounds

The fundamental notion of the た form is "perfective," which means that an event described by the た form indicates the completion of the event. Such a notion is applicable to an event that has occurred in the past or to an event that will have been completed in the future. In this sense, the た form does not necessarily act as the past tense form, but creates a similar notion to "after."[1] Thus, the た form is used to describe a past event or a future event, both of which indicate the completion of events, regardless of the tense in the main clause.

1. た後で

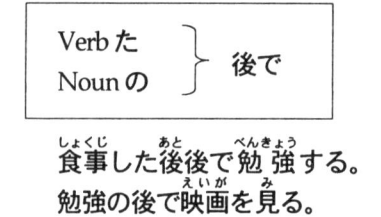

```
Verb た  ⎫
         ⎬  後で
Noun の  ⎭
```

食事した後後で勉強する。　　I study after I eat.
勉強の後で映画を見る。　　　I watch movies after I study.

A verb in the た form followed by 後で has the same meaning as a phrase expressed by the verb + てから. The notion of the completion of the event may be more strongly emphasized when 後で is used. Also, some nouns are linked to 後で by the use of の. Observe the following examples:

---

[1] The notion of "after" is applicable only to activity predicates, not to stative predicates, since stative predicates such as い/な adjectives are not compatible with the notion of sequentiality. "I got tired after busy" is a nonsensical sentence—it should be, "I got tired after swimming a mile," for example. The same concept applies to the notion of "before."

(1) a. お風呂に入ってから食事をする。
I will take a bath, then I will have dinner.

b. お風呂に入った後で食事をする。
After taking a bath, I will have dinner.

c. お風呂の後で食事をする。
After a bath, I will have dinner.

The phrase 後で in sentence (1b) is used to emphasize the meaning "after" as shown in the English equivalent. Neither てから nor た後で is appropriate for describing sequential activities when they are considered activities that naturally occur in a certain order in daily life. For example, 後で in 起きた後で歯を磨く ("After getting up, I brush my teeth") may sound awkward, since brushing teeth cannot happen before one gets up. Consider the following additional examples:

(2) a. 卒業した後で日本へ旅行したいと思っている。
I am thinking of traveling to Japan after I graduate.

b. 卒業の後で日本へ旅行したいと思っている。
I am thinking of traveling to Japan after graduation.

(3) a. 映画を見た後で買い物に行きませんか。
Why don't we go shopping after seeing the movie?

b. 映画の後で買い物に行きませんか。
Why don't we go shopping after the movie?

(4) a. 今日は仕事をした後でゆっくりテレビが見たい。
Today, I want to relax watching TV after I finish working.

b. 今日は仕事の後でゆっくりテレビが見たい。
Today, I want to relax watching TV after work.

(5) a. 新聞を読んだ後でシャワーを浴びるつもりだ。
I'm going to take a shower after reading the newspaper.

* b. 新聞の後でシャワーを浴びるつもりだ。
I'm going to take a shower after the newspaper.

Although nouns accompanied by する can always occur with の後で, such is not necessarily the case for other nouns. As example (5b) demonstrates, the noun 新聞 "newspaper" cannot be used to form the の後で phrase. This is due to the fact that "after the newspaper" can make us think of associating a variety of activities, such as "read," "buy," "subscribe," etc., and does not provide a clear picture of an activity. On the other hand, the phrase "after the movie" can easily be associated with "watching" in ordinary life. If "after *making* the movie" is what the speaker is trying to convey, then the verb 作る has to be included to create the phrase: 映画を作った後で.

2. たり〜たりする/たり〜たりだ

The た form of all parts of speech can be used for this construction.

```
Verb
い adjective        }  たり〜たり する/たり〜たりだ
な adjective
Noun
```

行ったり来たりする	go back and forth
降ったり止んだりだ	it rains on and off
暇だったり忙しかったりする	sometimes free, sometimes busy
本当だったり嘘だったりする	sometimes true, sometimes a lie

たり〜たりする is used when activities and states of things are listed *randomly and are unsolicited*. The predicate used in this construction represents some of the activities or the ways things are. The English equivalents may be that one does things such as X and Y; that things are in ways such as X and Y; and that situations X and Y alternate. Though sentences in this construction usually end with たりする, when states of affairs are described, rather than activities, たり〜たりだ may be used, such as 今週は雨が降ったり止んだりだそうです "I hear that it will rain on and off this week."

When activities are listed randomly, those activities should be able to be conducted in a similar framework and scale in order to carry them out. Going to

Japan from the United States, for example, may require heavy preparation and may not occur on a daily basis, while watching TV can be considered a daily routine activity. 6月には日本へ行ったり、テレビを見たりします "In June, I do things such as going to Japan and watching TV" sounds very awkward. These two activities should not be mixed as random events in the 〜たり〜たり construction. The sentence should be, for example, 6月には家でゆっくり本を読んだりテレビを見たりします "In June, I do things such as reading books and watching television."

(1) 休みの日は掃除をしたり、コンピューターゲームをしたり、音楽を聞いたりします。
On a day off, I do things like cleaning the room, playing computer games, and listening to music.

(2) 日本ではうなぎやうにを食べたり、温泉やカラオケに行ったりして、楽しみました。
In Japan, I enjoyed being there by eating food, such as eel and sea urchin, and doing things such as going to a hot spring and a karaoke bar.

(3) 隣の犬が家の前を行ったり来たりしています。
My neighbor's dog is going back and forth in front of his house.

(4) 試験はできたりできなかったりです。
Speaking of the exam, I sometimes do well and sometimes do not.

(5) マイアミの家はピンクだったり、青だったり、色々な色があって楽しいです。
There are various colors for houses in Miami—some pink, some blue—and it's fun.

Sample essay

日本では運動したりする時間もあまりありません

アメリカにいた時はよく公園を散歩したり運動したりしましたが、日本に帰って来てからは、生活もまたもとに戻ってしまい、毎日家と会社を往復しています。日本でも運動したいと思うのですが、通勤時間が長いので、

そんな余裕もありません。ドライブをしたり、バーベキューをしたりすることもなくなりました。アメリカでの生活が恋しいです。

When I was in America, I often did things like taking a walk in a park and doing exercise, but since I came back to Japan, my life came back to the previous way, and I run between home and office. I think that I want to exercise in Japan, too, but since commuting is so long, I don't have time to spare. I no longer do things such as driving and barbecuing. I miss life in America.

3.　たことがある

Verb + たことがある means "someone has an experience of doing something" or "someone has ever done something" and is used especially when one's *experience* is being emphasized; therefore, activity verbs can occur with ことがある. However, the desiderative form (e.g., 食べたい) or some な adjectives may occasionally be used.

Since an experience is something that has been done, the perfective form た (denoting completion of an event) is used. It can be translated as "I have (ever) done ~," but due to the emphasis on the event as an experience, everyday routine activities may not be described by this construction. 朝ご飯を食べたことがある "I have had an experience of eating breakfast," for example, is ineligible for use with this construction. なっとうを食べたことがある "I have had an experience of eating natto (fermented soy beans)," on the other hand, is an appropriate expression, since eating fermented soybeans may be considered a unique experience for some people. In answering a question, either あります or ありません is repeated. ことがある also follows the verb dictionary form, meaning "I sometimes do ~." Observe the following examples:

(1)　a.　うにを食べたことがありますか。
　　　　 Do you have (Have you had) the experience of eating sea urchin?
　　b.　いいえ、ありません。
　　　　 No, I don't (haven't).
Cf.　c.　うにを食べましたか。
　　　　 Did you eat sea urchin?

d. いいえ、食べませんでした。
No, I didn't.

Sentence (1a) demonstrates that 食べたことがある indicates a particular experience which may be unique to the individual, while in sentence (1c), 食べましたか is not concerned with the individual's experience, but simply asks about the listener's activity in the past.

(2) a. 富士山に登ったことがありますか。
Do you have (Have you had) the experience of climbing Mt. Fuji?
b. はい、あります。
Yes, I do (I have).
Cf. c. (もう)富士山に登りましたか。
Have you (already) climbed Mt. Fuji?
d. いいえ、まだ登っていません。
No, I haven't climbed it yet.

Sentence (2a) 富士山に登ったことがありますか may be translated as "Have you climbed Mt. Fuji?" which seems to be the same as sentence (2c) (もう) 富士山に登りましたか. Although the difference is circumstantial, since both can be interpreted as expressing one's experience, a subtle difference may be that 登ったことがありますか is uttered to see if by chance the listener had the experience of climbing Mt. Fuji, while (もう) 富士山に登りましたか is uttered when the speaker has some expectation that the listener has already climbed Fuji. A negative answer in negative form confirms this observation: ありません conveys that the listener does not have the experience, while まだ登っていません indicates that the listener has not yet climbed Fuji, but suggests that s/he will do so in the near future.

(3) a. 大声で叫んだことがありますか。
Do you have (have you had) the experience of shouting?
b. はい、あります。
Yes, I do (I have).

Cf. c. 大声で叫びたかったことがありますか。
　　　　Do you have the experience of wanting to shout?
　　d. はい、もちろん、あります。
　　　　Yes, of course, I do.

The difference between sentences (3a,b) and (3c,d) is that the individual in (3b) actually did shout at some time in the past and considers that event as an experience, while sentence (3c) is concerned with the *desire* of the listener, and whether the individual actually shouted or not is not an important concern. Thus, the desiderative form たかった may also be used, depending on context.

(4)　試験がだめだったことが何度かある。
　　　I have had the experience of having failed an exam several times.

Sentence (4) is another example where a な adjective is used. だめ can represent various meanings, such as "not good," "fail," "does not work," etc., and in this case, it represents a situation that can be described by the verb 失敗した "failed."

Sample dialogue
木の上で星を見たことはありません
タビ: タマさん、あの木の一番上に登ったことがありますか。
タマ: ええ、あるわ。
タビ: じゃあ、一番上で星 (stars) を見たことがありますか。
タマ: 星？　いいえ、ないわ。
タビ: きれいですよ。今度一緒に見ませんか。
タマ: まあ、タビさんてロマンチックなのね。

4.　たところ

ところ can follow the dictionary form of the verb, the aspectual form (ている), or the た form, and it generally indicates the point in time at which something is about to happen, is happening, or has just happened. For example, 洗濯をするところ, 洗濯をしている/いたところ, 洗濯をしたところ means "I am about to do laundry," "I am/was doing laundry," and "I've just done laundry," respectively.

When ところ follows the た form of the verb, the sentence indicates that the event described by the verb has just been completed, and たところ refers to the time of completion of the event. The verbs used with ところ are mostly transitive verbs over which the speaker has volitional control, but some non-volitional event described by an intransitive verb may also occur with ところ. Observe the following examples:

(1) シャワーを浴びたところへ友達が来た。
My friend came over when I'd just taken a shower.

(2) 今ちょうど食事を済ませたところです。
I've just finished my meal.

(3) 今家へ帰ったところです。
I've come home just now.

(4) 飛行機が空港に着いたところです。
The airplane has just arrived at the airport.

(5) 雨が止んだところです。
It has just stopped raining.

(6) 魚が焼けたところへ猫がやって来た。
A cat came over at the time when the fish was grilled.

Although ところ in the above cases is not a place noun that indicates an actual location, it is still considered a point in space where an activity has been completed. When the predicate of the main clause contains a motion verb, ところ is marked by へ/に, as in example sentences (1) and (6). When ていた is used for an activity verb, ていたところ refers to a point during which the event was in progress.

(7) その件についてはちょうど先生と相談していたところです。
Regarding that issue, I was right in the middle of consulting my teacher.

(8) 電車が駅に止まっていたところへ車がぶつかって来た。
A car came rushing into the streetcar when the streetcar was in the middle of staying at the station.

5. たまま

まま is a dependent morpheme meaning "as it is" and "as it stands." When following a verb in the た form, the phrase means that an activity which previously took place remains unchanged while the same person does something else. For example, an individual turns a light on, then falls asleep without turning off the light; the light remains on. The situation can be described by the たまま construction as 電気をつけたまま寝た "I fell asleep with the lights on." まま can also occur with the imperfective form of a verb or a noun, as in 人の言うままになる "do whatever one tells you to do" and 意のまま "as one pleases," respectively. There are also some fixed phrases that include まま, such as そのまま "as it is."

(1) 時計をしたままお風呂にはいってしまった。
I entered the bathtub with my watch on.

(2) 日本では、くつをはいたまま家へ入ってはいけません。
In Japan, you should not go inside the house with your shoes on.

(3) めがねをかけたまま寝てしまった。
I fell asleep with my glasses on.

(4) 電気をつけたまま家を出た。
I left home with the lights on.

(5) 聞いたままのことをお話ししましょう。
I will tell you exactly what I heard.

(6) A: 窓を閉めしょうか。
　　　Shall I close the window?
　　B: いいえ、開けたままでいいです。
　　　No, it is O.K. with it open.
　　C: いいえ、そのままでけっこうです。
　　　No, leave it as it is (meaning that you don't have to close the window).

CHAPTER 12

おう Form Compounds and ましょう

The おう form is a plain form of ましょう. Both forms are used to mean "Let's" when a speaker tries to have an interlocutor do some activity with him/her such as ねぇ、テニスしよう "Say, let's play tennis (casual situation)" and 食事しましょう "Let's have a meal together (rather formal situation)." The おう form is also used in situations where a speaker might mumble, saying 今日は何をしよう(かな) "What shall I do today...?" In addition, the おう form is also used with other phrases, such as と思う and とする to create patterns that express "I'm thinking of doing ~" and "I am about to do ~," respectively. In this chapter, these two constructions are introduced, followed by a discussion of the use of ましょう in comparison with ませんか.

1. おうと思う

The おう form followed by the verb 思う creates a sentence pattern meaning "I'm thinking of doing ~." Since it is used to express a speaker's intention, there is no reference to the realization of the event. If the sentence describes a past event, it usually expresses a counterfactual meaning.

(1) 今年は日本語を取ろうと思っている。
I'm thinking of taking Japanese this year.

(2) 母に手紙を書こうと思った。
I thought of writing a letter to my mother.

(3) 大学に進学しようと思ったが、お金がなくて、できなかった。
I was thinking of going to college, but I couldn't do so due to lack of money.

(4) a. 来年は結婚しようと思っているが、相手がいない。
I'm thinking of getting married next year, but I don't have a partner.

b. 来年は結婚したいと思っているが、まだ相手がいない。
I'm hoping to get married next year, but I don't have a partner yet.

The difference between (4a) and (4b) is that たいと思う is used to describe a desire which the speaker may not carry out, while the おうと思う construction conveys the speaker's relatively strong intention of realizing the event described by the preceding clause.

Sample dialogue
返そうとは思っているんです

本田: お父さん、新しい車を買おうと思っているんだけどね、ちょっと予算が足りなくて・・・。よかったら10万円くらい貸してもらえないかなって思ってるんだけど・・・。
Dad, I am thinking of buying a new car, but I don't have enough money. If it is O.K., I'm hoping to have you lend me some money, about 100,000 yen...

父: なんだ、10万円でいいのか。
Oh, only 100,000 will do?

本田: うん！ 貸してもらえるの？
Yes! Can I borrow (it)?

父: 貸してあげようと思ったけど、やっぱりやめた。
I thought of lending it, but decided not to.

本田: どうして！？
How come!?

父: だって、結局は「あげる」ことになるからさ。
Because after all the money is to give (not to lend).

本田: え、そんなことないよ。必ず返そうと思ってるんだから。
No, that is not the case. I am thinking of returning the money without fail.

父: ほら、「返すよ」じゃなくて、「返そうと思ってる」だろ。それって返すかどうかわからないっていう意味なんだよ。
See. You don't say "I will return," but say "I'm thinking of returning." That shows you don't know if you are really going to return the money.

本田: お父さん。必ず返します！
Dad, I will return the money without fail!
父: さあ、どうしようかなぁ・・・。
Well...What shall we do...?

人間と結婚しようと思っています
美々子: 私、結婚しようと思ってるの。
アレックス: え、結婚？それ、それはよかった。で、何と？
美々子: 「何と？」ま、失礼ね！人間とに決まってるでしょ。
Of course with a human being!
アレックス: あ、ごめん。また間違えちゃった。

2. おうとする

おうとする means "about to do" or "try to" and is used when someone is/was right at the moment of carrying out or trying to do an activity. It does not indicate that the event was carried out by the speaker; it usually expresses that the speaker failed to carry out an activity at some point, especially when it is used in a past context. The form of する can be either the aspectual form している/た or the past tense form した.

(1) 私はいつもたばこをやめようとするのだが、何回試してもできない。
I always try to quit smoking, but no matter how many times I try, I fail.

(2) 猫が金魚を取ろうとしていたので、あわてて止めた。
My cat was trying to catch a gold fish, so I quickly stopped him.

(3) 中国語を勉強しようとしたが、クラスはもういっぱいだった。
I was going to study Chinese, but the class was already full.

(4) 家を出ようとしたところに電話がかかってきた。
When I was about to leave, the phone rang.

(5) 夕飯を食べようとした所へ友達が来て、結局一緒に食べることにした。
My friend came over when I was about to eat dinner, and I invited him to join me after all.

(6) 僕がゴルフをしようとするところへいつも雨が降り始めるんだ。
When I am about to play golf, it starts to rain without fail.

When the pattern おうとする is combined with ところへ, indicating that the speaker is about to do something, ところ can take に or へ, as is shown above in sentences (4) – (6).

Sample essay

僕は10年前から健康的な生活をしようとしている。一つは肥満の問題だ。今年も何度痩せようとしたか、わからない。マクドナルドへ行かないで家で料理をしてみたが、たくさん作ってしまうので、みんな食べてしまう。それで、食事の量を減らそうとして、小さいお皿を買ってみたが、結局何回もおかわりをしてしまう。甘いものを食べないようにしたが、フライドポテトをたくさん食べてしまう。たばこもやめようとした。コーヒーも減らそうとした。でも、どうしてもできない。ほんとうに泣きたくなってしまう。だれか、助けてください！

この人は健康的な生活をするために、どんなことを試しましたか。

3. ましょう

ましょう is the formal version of the おう form and the equivalent of "Let's" in English when a speaker tries to involve an interlocutor in an activity. Therefore, only an action verb can occur in the ましょう form. おう/ましょう can also be used in a question with the meaning "Shall I/we ~?" when the speaker wonders about the activity or offers something to someone. Although it is used to involve someone in an activity, when used as an invitation, it may give an impression that the interlocutor's intention has already been confirmed. If an invitation is intended, ～ない? with a rising intonation or ませんか "Won't you like to do ~?" may be preferred, since these forms are used to sound out whether or not the interlocutor is interested in the activity. Observe the following examples, which make use of these forms:

(1) a. 今日からまじめに宿題をしよう。
Starting today, I shall do my homework seriously.
b. 成績がCだったら、どうしよう。
What shall I do if I receive a C grade?
c. 図書館まで一緒に歩こうか。
Shall we walk to the library together?
Why don't we walk to the library together?
d. 図書館まで一緒に歩かない？
Would you like to walk to the library with me?

(2) a. 一緒に野球の試合を見に行きましょう。
Let's go to see a baseball game together.
b. 一緒に野球の試合を見に行きましょうか。
Shall we go to see a baseball game together?
c. 一緒に野球の試合を見に行きませんか。
Would you like to go see a baseball game with me?
d. 私たち、これから先どうしましょうか。
What shall we do from now on?

The appropriateness of the use of these forms depends on the relationship between the speaker and the interlocutor, and the environment they are in. The ませんか form is most commonly used for invitation, although the English equivalent "Would you like to do ~?" たいですか is not considered appropriate, especially when the speaker is inviting someone who is older than s/he is. (See Chapter 9, Section 1.)

Sample dialogues
何をあげようか
リサ: 明日は太郎の誕生日ね。何かプレゼントしない？
次郎: そうだね。何をあげようか。
リサ: ポルシェはどう？
次郎: え、ポルシェ！？
リサ: うん、ほら、モデルカーでポルシェがあるじゃない。
次郎: あ、モデルカーね・・・。それなら大丈夫だ。

リサ: 本当の車だと思ったの？
次郎: いや、別に・・・。

私と結婚しませんか—
男: あのう・・・・。もしよかったら、一緒に朝ご飯を食べませんか。
女: あ、あのう・・・、結構です・・・。
男: ・・・。

レストランへ行きましょう
本田: おなかがすきましたね。
鈴木: ええ私も。お昼ご飯、一緒に食べませんか。
本田: ええ、そうしましょう。でもどこで食べましょうか。
鈴木: 「一番」はどうですか。あそこにはいい定食がありますよ。
本田: いいですね。そうしましょう。
鈴木: あ、ちょっと待ってください・・・。あ、私お財布忘れてしまいました。
本田: あ、そうですか。いいですよ。私が立て替えておきますから。
鈴木: そうですか、すみませんねぇ、いつも・・・。じゃ、行きましょう。

先生、召し上がりませんか
先生: ああ、トムさん、ジョンさん、いらっしゃい。どうしたんですか。
トム: 先生、これ僕が作ったんですけど、食べたいですか。
ジョン: (Whispering to Tom) ちょっと、先生は目上の人だから、その言い方は失礼だよ。
トム: あ、そうだった。ありがとう。
先生、これ、いただきたいですか。
ジョン: だ〜めだ、こりゃ・・・。

CHAPTER 13

Demonstrative Pronouns: こ・そ・あ・ど

Japanese has four types of demonstratives that start with こ・そ・あ・ど. These demonstratives can be used in two ways: non-anaphoric (deictic) and anaphoric. The deictic use of こ・そ・あ・ど refers to direct pointing to concrete, visible entities in relation to the speaker's location. The anaphoric use of こ・そ・あ・ど indicates an abstract distance between the speaker and the listener. First we consider the basic non-anaphoric use of the こ・そ・あ・ど pronouns, then the anaphoric use of these こ・そ・あ・ど pronouns.

1. The Non-anaphoric (Pointing) Use of こ・そ・あ・ど

Look at the picture below, which represents the very basic usages of こ・そ・あ・ど. Note that the entity is referred from the speaker's viewpoint.

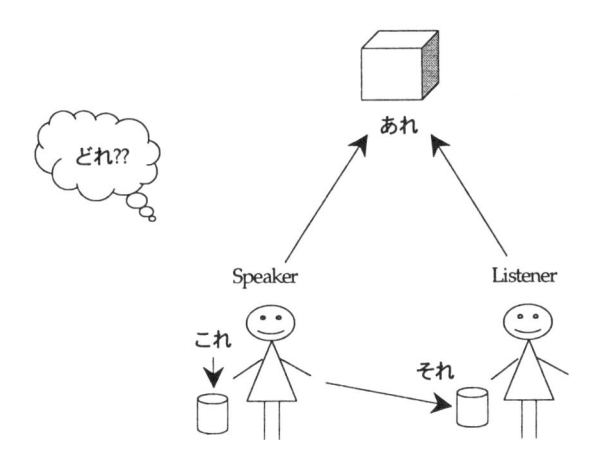

こ: closer to the speaker; usually used in a non-anaphoric way.[1]
そ: closer to the listener than to the speaker.
あ: at a distance both from the speaker and the listener.
ど: which, what type of, where, etc.: location or attribute unknown to both the speaker and the listener.

こ series demonstratives are used when an entity is close to the speaker or in the speaker's hands; そ, when it is close to the listener; あ, when the distance from the speaker and the listener is comparable; and ど, when the location or attribute is unknown to both the speaker and the listener. See the following chart for various usages.

	things	things or person[2]	way[3]	place	person place direction[4]	kind	extent	sort, kind
こ	これ	この	こう	ここ	こちら	こんな	こんなに	こういう
そ	それ	その	そう	そこ	そちら	そんな	そんなに	そういう
あ	あれ	あの	ああ	あそこ	あちら	あんな	あんなに	ああいう
ど	どれ	どの	どう	どこ	どちら	どんな	どんなに	どういう

When the speaker and the listener are next to each other and are pointing to an entity close to the listener, the speaker may use これ to refer to the entity. Thus, the use of こ and そ may sometimes vary depending on the perception and the location of the speaker and the listener. Following are some examples:

---

[1] "Non-anaphoric" means that the speaker is actually pinpointing an entity visible to both speaker and listener. When a speaker talks about an entity that is not physically present, but is referencing it, the usage is called "anaphoric."
[2] この、その、あの、どの are always followed by another noun such as この電話 "this phone (close to me)," その本 "the book (close to you)," あの 車 "that car over there," and どの人 "which person?"
[3] こう、そう、ああ、どう are also usually followed by a word. The typical one is どうやって "how," which is often used in casual communication, such as どうやって来たの？ "How did you get here?"
[4] There are colloquial equivalents of these terms: こっち、そっち、あっち、and どっち.

(1) Two people are sitting together and pointing to a person in a picture:
A: この人、誰？
B: ああ、この方は先生の御主人ですよ。

(2) The listener has a nice bag in her hand, and a nice car is parked on the street at a visible distance from both the speaker and the listener.
A: そのかばん、ブランドは何？
What brand is the bag you have?
B: これ？　グッチ。
This one? It's Gucci.
A: じゃ、あの車は？
(pointing to the car) How about that car over there?
B: あれ？　あれはベンツ。
That is a (Mercedes) Benz.
A: すごいわね。そんなもの買うお金、どうやって稼いだの？
Amazing. How did you earn money to buy things like those?
B: 宝くじに当たったのよ！
I won a lottery ticket!

2. The Anaphoric (Referencing) Use of こ・そ・あ

The demonstratives こ, そ, and あ are used not only to refer to visible entities, but also to indicate the metaphorical distance of an entity from the speaker and the listener. When こ, そ, and あ are used anaphorically, the series still maintains its fundamental behavior, though a concrete entity is not visible in front of the speaker/listener. Of these four, そ and あ are the main demonstratives used in conversation; こ is used much less often.

あ　used to refer to information (at a distance either in time or space) that both the speaker and the listener are aware of.[5]

---

[5] あ may be used where the speaker does not involve an interlocutor, i.e., the speaker does not necessarily share the same information with the listener. For example, a speaker may say あれ、何だったっけ・・・ "what was that...?" when the speaker tries to recall something s/he had in mind. あれ can be used in this isolated communication situation, since the information the speaker is trying to recover is not in his/her mind and there is a spatio-temporal distance from him/her. It is as if the speaker is pointing to the information at a distance, marked by a question mark.

そ used to refer to information that is not known to either the speaker or the listener or has not been part of their shared experience.

こ used to indicate information as if it were visible to both the speaker and the listener during the conversation; it imparts vividness to the conversation.

2.1 あ and そ

(1) Both the speaker and the listener know 花子. The listener uses あの to indicate that he also knows Hanako.

A: きのう花子っていう女の子に会ったよ。
I met a girl called Hanako.

B: ああ、僕もあの子よく知ってるよ。
Yeah, I know that girl well.

(2) Both the speaker and the listener know Ms. Endo.

A: 昨日遠藤さんに会いましたよ。あの人、すてきですね。
I met Ms. Endo yesterday. She is a nice person, don't you think so, too?

B: ええ、本当に。
Yes, indeed.

The use of ね "don't you think so, too?" in the speaker's sentence shows that he/she knows that the listener also knows Ms. Endo.

(3) A: きのうジェフというアメリカ人に会ったんですよ。その人、日本語がわからなくて困っていたので、通訳してあげたんです。
I met an American called Jeff. That man (he) was at a loss not knowing Japanese, so I translated for him.

B: そうですか。それは親切ですね。
Is that so? That's nice of you.

The speaker uses その, assuming that the listener does not know the American called Jeff. The use of demonstratives in reference to things, events, places, time, and manner also shows the same characteristics.

(4) A: きのうダウンタウンで火事があってねぇ。その火事で人が4人死んだんですよ。
There was a fire downtown yesterday. Four people died in that fire.
B: あ、その/あの火事なら、ちょうどダウンタウンにいたものですから、見ましたよ。
Ah, if you are talking about that fire, I witnessed it since I was downtown at that time.

At the time of speech, the speaker does not know if the listener shares the same information regarding the fire and uses その. The listener may use その until he confirms that if they are talking about the same information, or since the listener witnessed the fire, he may use あの in order to let the speaker know that they share the same information. この is awkward. (See この in Section 2.2 below.)

(5) A: 昨日「赤坂」という日本料理店へ行ってきました。
I went to a Japanese restaurant called Akasaka yesterday.
B: そこはどうですか。値段は安いですか。
How did you like it? Is the price affordable?
A: ええ、まあまあです。「一番」よりは安いですよ。
Yeah, it is so-so. It is cheaper than Ichiban.
B: あ、あそこは高いですからねぇ！
That restaurant is expensive, isn't it!

The listener first uses そ indicating that he has never been to Akasaka, but uses あ informing the speaker that he also knows Ichiban. Thus, the use of そ or あ depends on the knowledge the speaker and the listener may share.

2.2 こ

When the こ series is used anaphorically, it can be used for indicating something as if it were visible to both the speaker and the listener at the time of the conversation, and thus it imparts vividness to the conversation. This use is often seen where the speaker wants to emphasize some attribute of the entity.

(6)   The speaker refers to Mr. Sasaki using こ as if he were present.
　　A: 昨日佐々木という人に会ったんだけど、この男、2メートルもあるんだ！
　　　 I met a man called Sasaki yesterday, but this man is two meters tall!
　　B: 2メートル？それはすごい。
　　　 Two meters? That's unbelievable.

(7)   Two people are in a classroom waiting for the class to start. The speaker brings out the placement test he has taken recently.
　　A: この間日本語3年の編入試験を受たんだけど、この試験、超むずかしくて全然できなかったんだ。
　　　 I took a placement test for third-year Japanese the other day, but this exam was extremely difficult, and I could not handle it at all.
　　B: あ、あの試験？僕も受けたけど、全然できなかった。
　　　 That exam? I also took it, but I couldn't do well at all.
　　A: だから僕たちこのクラスにいるのか。
　　　 That's why we are both in this class, isn't it?

The speaker refers to the placement exam using こ as if it were present in front of him. The listener uses あ, since he also took the same exam and shares the same information as the speaker. Thus, あの試験 is appropriate in sentence (7B). Once an understanding about shared information is established between the speaker and the listener, the speaker can no longer use the こ series in referring to the same information.

CHAPTER 14

Conjugation Words and Linking Sentences

The fundamental function of conjunction words is to link words, phrases, and sentences in a way that facilitates coherent and logical communication. Conjunctions may appear as independent words located between sentences, or they may be dependent conjunctions at the end of a sentence and followed by a comma and another sentence. For example:

(1) あのレストランのすしは高かった。 { でも、 / けれども、 / しかし、 } まずかった。
    S1   S2

Sushi at that restaurant was expensive. However, it was bad. =
あのレストランのすしは高かった<u>が</u>、まずかった。
Though sushi at that restaurant was expensive, it was bad.

The following are examples of basic independent and dependent conjunction words that are used to combine sentences.

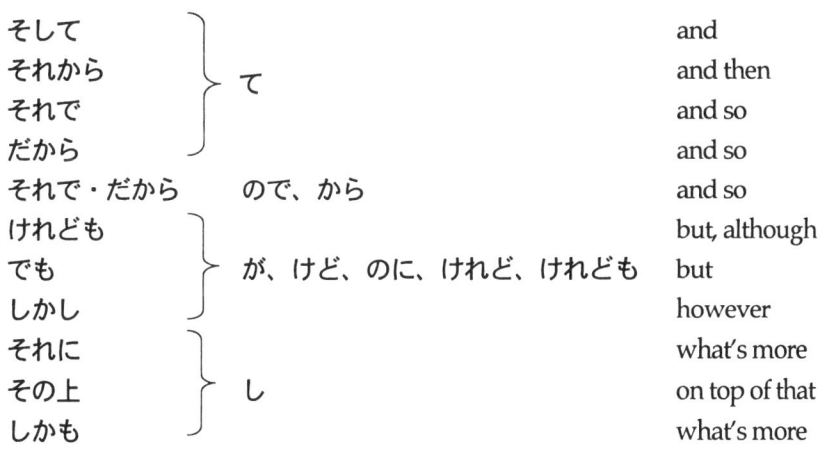

そして	⎫	and
それから	⎬ て	and then
それで	⎪	and so
だから	⎭	and so
それで・だから	ので、から	and so
けれども	⎫	but, although
でも	⎬ が、けど、のに、けれど、けれども	but
しかし	⎭	however
それに	⎫	what's more
その上	⎬ し	on top of that
しかも	⎭	what's more

In this chapter, the functions of basic conjunction words and the way sentences are joined are explained, starting with the て form linkage.

1. The て Form Linkage: そして・それから・それで/だから

The て form of a part of speech itself does not assign any specific meaning, but it does express a meaning when it is used to link words, phrases, and sentences. The meaning of the て form is determined by the relationship between the phrases and/or context. The て form creates the following meanings depending on the type of the predicate:

With verbs

そして	"and"	simple parallel activities
それから	"and then"	sequential activities
それで/だから	"and so"	gives a reason or an explanation

With い adjectives, な adjectives, and nouns

そして	⎤ "and"	simple parallel activities
それで/だから	⎦ "and so"	gives a reason or an explanation

When the て form of *a stative predicate* (い adjectives, な adjectives, or nouns) is used in a sentence, それから becomes inapplicable. Since stative predicates are not used to indicate events in time sequence, the て form carries only the two meanings given above.

    Note that more than two sentences may be combined using the て form. The use of several commas may create a run-on sentence in English, but in Japanese, such parataxis is considered acceptable. Although the て form is a replacement of a conjunction word, when sentences become long due to the multiple use of the て form, the conjunction word may be used after the て form, especially in speaking. In writing, if a sentence becomes long, because of the use of more than three て forms in one sentence, it may be considered awkward.

1.1 The て form of verbs: そして・それから・それで/だから
1.1.1 そして "and"

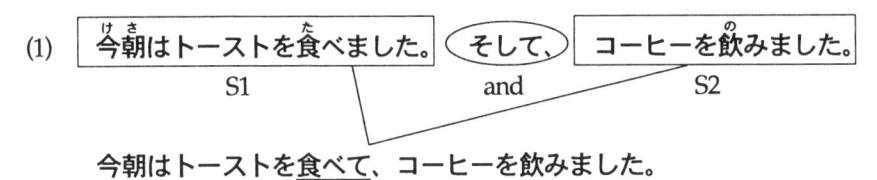

(1) | 今朝はトーストを食べました。| そして、| コーヒーを飲みました。|
           S1   and   S2

今朝はトーストを食べて、コーヒーを飲みました。
This morning, I ate toast and drank coffee.

(2) 豊田さんは天ぷらを注文しました。そして、本田さんはすしを注文しました。
Mr. Toyota ordered tempura. And Ms. Honda ordered sushi.
↓
豊田さんは天ぷらを注文して、本田さんはすしを注文しました。
Mr. Toyota ordered tempura, and Ms. Honda ordered sushi.

(3) 昨日は幸子とお茶を飲みました。そして、今日はメリーとお昼ご飯を食べます。それから、明日は由紀子と動物園へ行きます。
I had tea with Sachiko yesterday. And I had lunch with Mary today. Then, tomorrow, I will go to a zoo with Yukiko. I am busy every day!
↓
昨日は幸子とお茶を飲んで、今日はメリーとお昼ご飯を食べて、明日は由紀子と動物園へ行きます。
I had tea with Sachiko yesterday, lunch with Mary today, and will go to a zoo with Yukiko tomorrow. I am busy every day!

1.1.2 それから "and then"

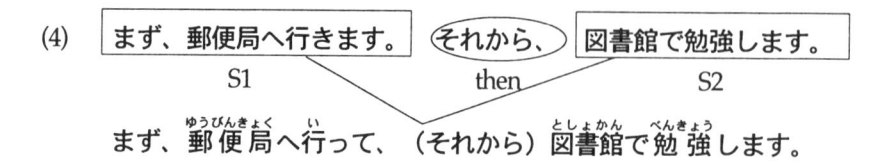

(4) まず、郵便局へ行きます。 それから、 図書館で勉強します。
　　　　　S1　　　　　　　　　then　　　　　　S2

まず、郵便局へ行って、（それから）図書館で勉強します。

First, I will go to the post office; then I will study at the library.

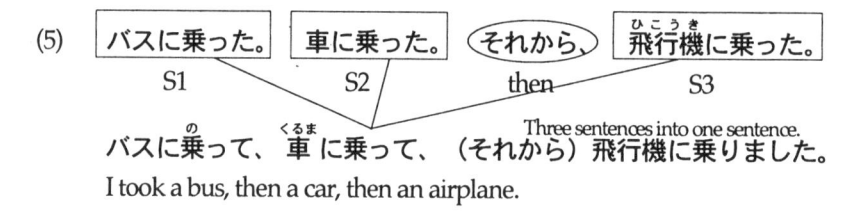

(5) バスに乗った。 車に乗った。 それから、 飛行機に乗った。
　　　S1　　　　　　S2　　　　　　then　　　　　　S3
　　　　　　　　　　　　　　　　　　　Three sentences into one sentence.

バスに乗って、車に乗って、（それから）飛行機に乗りました。

I took a bus, then a car, then an airplane.

1.1.3 それで "and so"

Note that if the verbs in both the first sentence and the second sentence are action verbs, the て form may not carry the meaning "and so." The て form often carries this meaning when the predicate is not active, but stative.

　　　Besides the use of the て form of a predicate, a dependent conjunction word ので or から may also be used to indicate an "and so" meaning. When ので or から is used, the implied relationship between the two sentences is causal. When the て form is used, this may not be the case. ので may be considered a little more polite than から, but there is no difference in terms of their functions. An explanation of the difference between て/から and ので follows the examples.

(6) 家の前には自動販売機があります。 だから、 とても便利です。
　　　　　S1 (cause)　　　　　　　　　so　　　　S2 (effect)

　a. 家の前には自動販売機があって、とても便利です。
　　　There is a vending machine in front of my house, and so it is very convenient.

　b. 家の前には自動販売機があるので、とても便利です。
　　　Since there is a vending machine in front of my house, it is very convenient.

c. 家の前には自動販売機があるから、とても便利です。
Because there is a vending machine in front of my house, it is very convenient.

(7) 日本語のクラスにはいい先生がいます。 だから、 楽しいです。
There are good teachers in the Japanese class. Therefore, it's enjoyable.
↓
a. 日本語のクラスにはいい先生がいて、楽しいです。
There are good teachers in the Japanese class, and so it is enjoyable.
b. 日本語のクラスにはいい先生がいるので、楽しいです。
Since there are good teachers in the Japanese class, it is enjoyable.
c. 日本語のクラスにはいい先生がいるから、楽しいです。
Because there are good teachers in the Japanese class, it is enjoyable.

(8) 遅くなりました。 だから、 すみません。
I'm late. So, I am sorry. (This sentence is awkward in actual use.)
↓
a. 遅くなって、すみません。
I am sorry for being late.
? b. 遅くなったので、すみません。
Since I am late, I am sorry.
? c. 遅くなったから、すみません。
Because I am late, I am sorry.

The reason for something can be expressed by the use of て, ので, or から, as in the above sentences. The て form simply connects two sentences to indicate the "and so" meaning, while ので and から are used to form subordinate clauses indicating the causal relationship between the subordinate clause and the main clause. The use of ので and から is awkward for combining sentences in (8), as 遅くなった and すみません are not exactly tied with the notion of cause and effect. However, if the sentence is restated as 遅くなったので、試験が受けられなかった "Since I was late, I could not take the exam," the causal relationship is logically expressed: the reason for not being able to take the exam was due to the speaker's lateness. Thus, から and ので in combining sentences indicate a strong causal relationship between two sentences, while て may also invite an expression that is considered a comment on the first sentence.

There are two differences between から and ので, one structural and the other pragmatic. In grammar, から can follow either the plain or the formal form of a predicate, as in 嫌いですから、食べませんでした and 嫌いだから、食べませんでした. Both mean "Since I do not like it, I did not eat it." On the other hand, ので normally follows the plain form of a predicate, such as 嫌いなので、食べませんでした, and this is the pattern that is usually introduced as basic Japanese grammar. However, there are some variations in the use of ので, and some may hear 嫌いですので、食べませんでした and 予算がたりませんでしたので、買えませんでした "Since I did not have enough (money in my) budget, I could not buy it," and so on. This use of ので is often considered a device to make the sentence sound more polite. The second difference is often considered a pragmatic one—that ので is more polite than から. Between the sentences 嫌いなので、食べませんでした and 嫌いだから、食べませんでした, most native speakers identify the former sentence as more polite than the latter. It must be mentioned, however, that an individual preference is always seen in the use of から and ので.

Another characteristic that から and ので possess is the fact that they also function to soften the tone of the sentence when they are added at the end. In this case, the meaning "because" or "since" either weakens or disappears. Usually the rest of the sentence is unstated, instead being left implied. For example, observe the following sentences, both of which mean "I will visit your office at 3 o'clock tomorrow." ので in this function can follow a formal form as seen in (9a) and sounds more polite than (9b).

(9) a. 明日3時に先生のオフィスに伺いますので・・・。
　　b. 明日3時に先生のオフィスに伺いますから・・・。

The sentence that may fill in the unstated part varies. It may be that the speaker wants to convey that the listener should not forget the appointment or remind him/her that a recommendation letter should be ready by that time, and so on, depending on context. In fact, in day-to-day communication, unstated elements contain a significant amount of information. Sometimes people avoid stating everything, choosing rather to imply everything. The use of から and ので at the end of the sentence in this fashion is one of many devices that let the listener infer what the speaker intends to convey, avoiding bluntness of a direct statement.

1.2 The て form of nouns, い adjectives, and な adjectives: そして・それで

1.2.1 そして "and"

Note that the interpretation of sentences may differ depending on the attribute of the word and the speaker or listener's understanding of the situation. For nouns, usually the て form is interpreted as expressing an "and" meaning, but for い/な adjectives, it also generates a "what's more" or "not only" meaning. For example, 安くておいしい and きれいで頭もいい may be interpreted as expressing "cheap and, what's more, delicious"[1] and "not only beautiful, but also smart," respectively.

(10)　友達のお父さんは弁護士です。そして、お母さんは医者です。

　　　My friend's father is a lawyer. And his mother is a doctor.
　　　↓
　　　友達のお父さんは弁護士で、お母さんは医者です。

　　　My friend's father is a lawyer, and his mother is a doctor.

(11)　あの店のすしは安いです。そして、おいしいです。

　　　Sushi at that restaurant is cheap. It tastes good.
　　　↓
　　　あの店のすしは安くて、おいしいです。

　　　Sushi at that restaurant is cheap and tasty.

(12)　友達の御主人はハンサムです。そして、背が高いです。

　　　My friend's husband is handsome. He is tall too.
　　　↓
　　　友達の御主人はハンサムで、背が高いです。

　　　My friend's husband is handsome and tall.

---

[1] There are some other ways to express the same meaning, such as 安いし、おいしい and きれいだし、頭もいい. For these linkage patterns, refer to Section 3 in this chapter.

1.2.2 それで "and so"

(13) 気分(きぶん)が悪(わる)いんです。それで、今日(きょう)は授業(じゅぎょう)に出(で)られません。
I am not feeling well. So I cannot attend class today.
↓
- a. 気分が悪くて、今日は授業に出られません。
  I am not feeling well, and so I cannot attend class today.
- b. 気分が悪いので、今日は授業に出られません。
  Since I am not feeling well, I cannot attend class today.
- c. 気分が悪いから、今日は授業に出られません。
  Because I am not feeling well, I cannot attend class today.

(14) 母(はは)が病気(びょうき)です。それで、国(くに)へ帰(かえ)らなくてはなりません。
My mother is ill in bed. So I have to go back to my home country.
↓
- a. 母が病気で、国へ帰らなくてはなりません。
  My mother is ill in bed, and so I have to go back to my home country.
- b. 母が病気なので、国へ帰らなくてはなりません。
  Since my mother is ill in bed, I have to go back to my home country.
- c. 母が病気だから、国へ帰らなくてはなりません。
  Because my mother is ill in bed, I have to go back to my home country.

(15) 試験(しけん)がだめでした。それで、成績(せいせき)がDだったんです。
I did badly on the exam. So I received a D grade.
↓
- a. 試験がだめで、成績がDだったんです。
  I received a D grade because I did badly on the exam.
- b. 試験がだめだったので、成績がDだったんです。
  Since I did badly on the exam, I received a D grade.
- c. 試験がだめだったから、成績がDだったんです。
  Because I did badly on the exam, I received a D grade.

2. Paradoxical Linkage: でも・けれども・しかし

でも, けれども, and しかし function as independent conjunction words that contradict the meaning expressed in the main clause. でも is used in colloquial conversation very frequently; けれども is as well, but not quite so often as でも. しかし is usually used in writing, but may also be used in conversation, often by male-language speakers. The equivalent dependent conjunction words are 〜が, 〜けど, 〜けれど(も), and のに. Independent conjunctions come between sentences, and dependent ones are attached at the end of a sentence and serve to form subordinate clauses.

$$\boxed{S1} \quad \left\{ \begin{array}{l} でも、 \\ けれども、 \\ しかし、 \end{array} \right\} \quad \boxed{S2}$$

(1) 日本に行きました。 $\left\{ \begin{array}{l} でも、 \\ けれども、 \\ しかし、 \end{array} \right\}$ 日本語は上達しませんでした。

I went to Japan. But my Japanese did not improve.

a. 日本に行きましたが、日本語は上達しませんでした。
b. 日本に行ったけど、日本語は上達しませんでした。
c. 日本に行ったけれど(も)、日本語は上達しませんでした。
d. 日本に行ったのに、日本語は上達しませんでした。
   Although I lived in Japan as long as 10 years, my Japanese did not improve.

There are cases where でも and けど do not exactly have paradoxical linkage. They can be used not only between sentences, but also added at the end of a sentence to soften the tone, as in the following examples. In these cases, it does not carry the original paradoxical meaning.

(2) もしもし、佐藤さんですか。ジョンソンですけど・・・。あ、お久しぶりです。
   Hello, is this Ms. Sato? This is Johnson speaking. Long time no hear.

(3) てんぷらとうなぎをお願いしたいんですけど・・・。
I'd like to order tempura and eel.

(4) 東京大学への交換留学生でジョンソンと申しますが、よろしくお願いします。
I'm Johnson, who came to study as an exchange student at the University of Tokyo. Pleased to meet you.

(5) コレステロールですけど、健康な人だとどのくらいですか。
Speaking of cholesterol, what is the right level for a normal healthy person?

2.1 The difference between けれども and のに

The difference between these conjunction words is the involvement of the speaker's empathy. Let us compare the following sentences.

(6) a. せっかく作ったのに、誰も食べてくれませんでした。どうして？そんなにまずいですか。
Although I made a great effort to make this, no one ate it. Why? Is it that bad?

b. 頑張って作ったけれども、誰も食べてくれませんでした。しかたありません。後で私が一人で全部食べましょう。
Although I made a great effort to make this, no one ate it. It cannot be helped. I will eat it later.

(7) a. 何度も説明を聞いているのに、まだわからないんです。どうしてわからないんでしょうか。
Although I am explaining it many times, I still don't seem to understand. I don't understand why I don't understand.

b. 何度も説明しているけれども、まだわからないようです。どうすればわかってもらえるでしょうか。
Although I am explaining it many times, they still don't seem to understand. How can I have them understand?

(8) a. 昨日のパーティ、楽しかったよ。君も来ればよかったのに、どうして来なかったの？
Yesterday's party was fun. You should have come. Why didn't you come?

　*b. 昨日のパーティ、楽しかったよ。君も来ればよかったけれども、どうして来なかったの？
Yesterday's party was fun. Although it was good if you came, why didn't you come?

The difference between けれども and のに is subtle. Depending on the prosody and the environment of the sentence, both words can convey the same shades of meaning. However, のに tends to generate a strong feeling of disappointment regarding the outcome of the event. It often implies that the speaker is/was not satisfied with the way things turn/turned out. Therefore, it is frequently used in a counterfactual situation, as can be seen from sentence (6a). けれども is awkward in this type of situation, since it is best used to describe a paradoxical situation rather objectively by the speaker. The equivalent of both けれども and のに is "although," but けれども is used to describe a factual event without involving too much of the speaker's emotion, while のに involves the speaker's emotion to a great extent, especially when an event does not turn out the way the speaker expects it to.

Sample dialogue
こんなに愛しているのに・・・
チビ：　タマさん、僕はあなたを愛しています。結婚してください。
　　　　たくさん子供を作りませんか。
タマ：　まあ、チビさん、私があなたと？　とんでもない。
　　　　私、デブ (blimp) は好きじゃないの・・・。
チビ：　え、僕そんなに太っていますか。
タマ：　ええ。鏡を見たことないの？
　　　　もっと食事をセーブして (save your food= don't eat)、
　　　　痩せたら結婚してあげてもいいわ。
チビ：　・・・。

妻: ねえ、あなた、チビちゃん、最近変なのよ。気がついた？
夫: どうしたの。
妻: あんなに食べることが好きだったのに、ぜんぜん食べなくなってしまったの。どこか病気なのかしら・・・。病院に連れていった方がいいかしら？
夫: そうだなあ。もう少し様子を見てみれば？

1ヶ月後
チビ: タマさん、見てください。僕、こんなに痩せました。
タマ: まあ、ほんと！
チビ: だから僕と結婚してください！
タマ: まあ、チビさん・・・。せっかく私のために痩せてくれたのに・・・ごめんなさい、実は私先週Thayerのタビさんと結婚する約束をしてしまったの・・・。
チビ: え！そ、そ、そんな・・・。ぼくがこんなに愛しているのに・・・、君はThayerのタビと結婚するの・・・。あんなデブと (to that blimp)！！！？？？

夫: チビは最近どうしてる？
妻: ええ、一時全然食べなくなってしまって、ずいぶん痩せたんだけど、きのうからまた急に食べ始めたのよ。どうしたのかしらねえ・・・。

チビ: ええい！こうなったらもう焼け食いだ！
(Now I've become a compulsive eater)！

3. Additive Linkage: それに・その上・しかも

それに, その上, and しかも share the same attribute in that some event, situation, or characteristic is added to the previously mentioned statement. They mean "on top of ~," "not only~, but also~,"[2] "what's more," and the like. The dependent conjunction word 〜し is used to combine sentences.

---

[2] The exact equivalent of "not only~, but also~" in Japanese is 〜だけではなく、〜だ, as in すしだけじゃなく、てんぷらもおいしい "Not just sushi, but also tempura tastes good."

When these conjunction words are properly used, the added element always carries the same type of quality as the one that was previously stated. For example, if the attribute of something is positive, then another positive attribute is to be added. If positive and negative, for example, are to be mixed, then the situation would be paradoxical, and "but" should be used as a conjunction word. Observe the following examples:

$$\boxed{S1} \left\{ \begin{array}{l} それに、\\ その上、\\ しかも、 \end{array} \right\} \boxed{S2}$$

In S2, も is often used to replace が, は, or を.

(1) あの店のすしはおいしい。 $\left\{ \begin{array}{l} それに、\\ その上、\\ しかも、 \end{array} \right\}$ 値段も安い。

Sushi served at that restaurant is delicious. Not only that, the price is inexpensive.
↓
$\left(\begin{array}{l} あの店のすしはおいしいし、値段も安い。\\ あの店のすしはおいしい上に、値段も安い。 \end{array} \right)$

(2) 日本のアパートは家賃がとても高いです。しかも、狭くて住みにくいです。
The (cost of) rent for apartments in Japan is very high. Not only that, they are small and hard to live in.
↓
日本のアパートは家賃がとても高いし、狭くて住みにくいです。

(3) 先生の奥さんはきれいです。その上、頭もいいです。
The professor's wife is beautiful. On top of that, she is intelligent as well.
↓
先生の奥さんはきれいだし、頭もいいです。

(4) 佐々木さんの息子さんは医者です。しかも、娘さんは弁護士です。
Mr. Sasaki's son is a medical doctor. What's more, his daughter is a lawyer.
↓
佐々木さんの息子さんは医者だし、娘さんは弁護士です。[3]

Cf. 佐々木さんには医者の息子もいるし、弁護士の娘もいる。収入の多い家庭にちがいない。
Mr. Sasaki has a son who is a medical doctor. Not only that, he also has a daughter who is a lawyer. They must be a family of high income.

---

[3] In this sentence, 佐々木さんの息子さんは医者だし、娘さんも弁護士です means "Mr. Sasaki's son is a medical doctor. What's more, his daughter is also a lawyer" and sounds awkward. However, if the sentence includes a phrase that describes an attribute of Mr. Sasaki's children, such as 佐々木さんの息子さんは有名な医者だし、娘さんも有名な弁護士です "Mr. Sasaki's son is a famous medical doctor, but not only that, his daughter is also a famous lawyer," then the sentence becomes appropriate. It seems that if the notion of "also" is applicable in the second half of the sentence, then a noun phrase can be followed by も.

CHAPTER 15

Interrogative Pronouns and Interrogative Sentences

There are two types of question sentences. One is the so-called "yes/no question," and the other is the interrogative question formed by using an interrogative pronoun. In the following, the formation of interrogative sentences as well as the formation of phrases with interrogative pronouns will be discussed.

1. The Functions of か
1.1 Yes/no questions

Yes/no questions are formed simply by adding the equivalent of a question mark か at the end of a sentence in Japanese. There is no change in the sentence's movement on its surface structure. For example, in order to change 田中さんは日本人です "Mr. Tanaka is Japanese" to a question, add か at the end of the sentence and form 田中さんは日本人ですか "Is Mr. Tanaka Japanese?" Since か functions as a question marker, there is no need to add a question mark after か.

The question mark may be used when the sentence is not in the form of a question sentence, but the speaker or the writer wishes to indicate that the sentence is intended to be a question. For example, これ、好き？ "Do you like this?" may occur instead of これ、好きですか. In oral communication, these questions can be identified by the intonation, but in written communication, without the question mark, they may be mistaken for declarative statements.

When answering the yes/no question, a straightforward device for beginners is simply to repeat the predicate in the correct form to practice answering the question. In the following, sentence (a) is a question, (b) is an affirmative answer, and (c) is a negative answer. For the equivalent of yes or no in Japanese, there are some variations.[1]

(1) a. 山下さんは、今日のパーティに来ますか。
Is Ms. Yamashita coming to today's party?
b. はい、来ます。(ええ、来ます is also fine, but may sound a little feminine.)
Yes, she is coming.
c. いいえ、来ません。(いや may also be used, especially by male language speakers.)
No, *she is not*.

(2) a. あの店のてんぷらはおいしかったですか。
Was the tempura served at that restaurant delicious?
b. はい、おいしかったですよ。
Yes, it was delicious.
c. いいえ、おいしくありませんでした。
No, *it wasn't*.

(3) a. あなたの車はきれいですか。
Is your car clean?
b. ええ、きれいです。
Yes, it is clean.
c. いいえ、きれいじゃありません。汚いです。
No, it *is not*. It's dirty.

1.1.1 Negative questions

A question can be formed using a negative predicate, such as "Don't you want to go?" and "Didn't she go to Japan?" In English, regardless of the form of the predicate in the question sentence, if the answer to the affirmative question would be

---

[1] Japanese speakers often use はい as one of あいづち phrases, and in this case, はい does not necessarily mean "yes." They use it as a response to what the interlocutor says, conveying "I'm listening to you." In case of いいえ/いや, however, it does not mean "I'm not listening to you." It means "no" or sometimes means "oh...," such as いや、困りましたよ "Oh... I'm in trouble."

No, then you state No, and if the answer to the affirmative question would be Yes, then you answer with Yes.

In Japanese, however, this is not the case. Observe the following diagram:

| A | か。 |

はい、 | A | Yes. Statement A is not exactly what I meant.

いいえ、 | A (neg.) | No. Statement A is what I meant.

Regardless of the content (negative or affirmative) of the statement A, if the statement is correct, then はい is the right word to use. On the other hand, if the statement A is incorrect, then いいえ is chosen. Now let's look at the examples:

(4) a. 宿題をしませんでした か。
   You did not do your homework, correct?
   b. はい、しませんでした。
   Yes, your statement is correct. I did not do my homework.
   c. いいえ、しました。
   No, your statement is not exactly what I meant. I did my homework.

(5) a. この本はおもしろくありません か。
   This book is not interesting, correct?
   b. はい、おもしろくありません。
   Yes, your statement is correct. This book is not interesting.
   c. いいえ、おもしろいです。
   No, your statement is not correct. It is interesting.

In Japanese, interrogative pronouns do not move around,[2] and か is added at the end of a statement. So, if the statement is correct, one answers indicating the

---

[2] When an interrogative pronoun is moved up to the initial position in a sentence, it is called "WH movement." For example, in English, to form a question sentence from "I went to school," "where" is used to derive "school" as an answer and is placed at the initial position: "Where did you go?" In Japanese, an interrogative pronoun does not have to be moved up to sentence-initial position; instead, it remains in the same position as the original noun phrase.

correctness of the statement. はい、おもしろくありません therefore, does not mean, "Yes, it is not interesting." Rather, it means, "Yes, what you've just stated is correct. It is not interesting."

1.2 Alternate selection

When two questions that are in contrast are next to each other, the か in the first sentence functions to mean "or."

(6) この辞書は便利です<u>か</u>、それとも、役に立ちません<u>か</u>。
   (それとも means "or" and can be inserted between two sentences.)
   Is this dictionary handy or not useful?

(7) あの人は日本人ですか、韓国人ですか、それとも、中国人ですか。
   Is that person Japanese or Korean or Chinese?

(8) 日本語の先生はやさしいですか、厳しいですか。
   Is the Japanese teacher kind or tough?

1.3 か in embedded sentences

When a direct quotation needs to be changed to an indirect quotation or two sentences need to be combined into one sentence, the plain form of parts of speech is always used to combine the two sentences. The formation of the sentence is a little different depending on whether or not the embedded sentence includes an interrogative noun.

When the sentence is combined based on an interrogative question, the plain form followed by か is used, while when the sentence is combined based on a yes/no question, かどうか (the equivalent of "whether or not") is used.

1.3.1 Based on a yes/no question

> かどうか (whether or not ~)

(9) a. 私は本田さんに「日本へ帰りますか」と聞きました。
      I asked Ms. Honda, "Are you going back to Japan?"
   b. 私は本田さんに日本へ帰る<u>かどうか</u>聞きました。
      I asked Ms. Honda *whether* she was going back to Japan.

(10) a. この電話は故障していますか。ご存知ですか。
Is this telephone out of order? Do you know?
b. この電話は故障しているかどうかご存知ですか。
Do you know *if* this telephone is out of order?
(11) a. 本田さんは試験に受かりましたか。お知らせください。
Did Ms. Honda pass the exam? Please let us know.
b. 本田さんが試験に受かったかどうかお知らせください。
Please let us know *if* Ms. Honda passed the exam.

1.3.2 Based on an interrogative question

> Interrogative 〜か + Verb of inquiry, examination

(12) a. 私は本田さんに「いつ日本へ帰りますか」と聞きました。
I asked Ms. Honda, "When are you going back to Japan?"
b. 私は本田さんにいつ日本へ帰るか聞きました。
I asked Ms. Honda when she was going back to Japan.
(13) a. この漢字はどう書きますか。辞書で調べてみましょう。
How do you write this kanji? Let's look it up in the dictionary.
b. この漢字はどう書くか辞書で調べてみましょう。
Let's look up how you write this kanji in the dictionary.
(14) a. 誰が試験に受かりましたか。お知らせください。
Who passed the exam? Let me know.
b. 誰が試験に受かったかお知らせください。
Let me know who passed the exam.

2. The Functions of Interrogative Pronouns

2.1 Formation of a question sentence with an interrogative pronoun

There are a total of six question words, which can be referred to as "5W1H." They are: "who," "what," "when," "where," "why," and "how." See the chart on the following page:

だれ	who	だれが行きましたか。	Who went?
何	what	何で行きましたか。	By what means did he go?
なぜ	why	なぜ行きましたか。	Why did he go?
どこ	where	どこへ行きましたか。	Where did he go?
いつ	when	いつ行きましたか。	When did he go?
どう	how	どうやって行きましたか。	How did he go?

In addition to the basic 5W1H, there are some more interrogative pronouns in the category of こ・そ・あ・ど words, as listed below.

どの noun	which (noun)	どの人がトムさんですか。	Which person is Tom?
どちら/どれ	which one	どちらがトムさんですか。	Which one of these people is Tom?
どんな	what kind of	トムさんはどんな人ですか。	What sort of a person is Tom?
どういう	what type of	トムさんはどういう人ですか。	What is Tom like?

In order to form a question using these interrogative pronouns, the original noun should be replaced with the interrogative pronoun without moving the location of the original noun. For example:

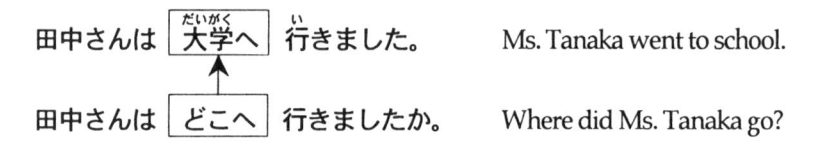

田中さんは 大学へ 行きました。　　Ms. Tanaka went to school.

田中さんは どこへ 行きましたか。　　Where did Ms. Tanaka go?

Unlike English, Japanese can have more than one interrogative pronoun in a sentence requesting information:

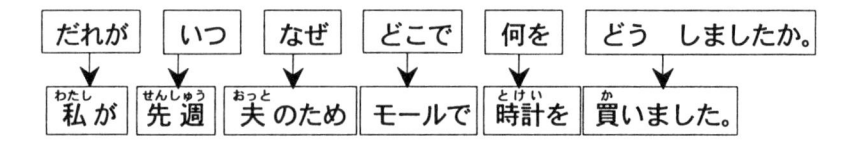

だれが いつ なぜ どこで 何を どう しましたか。
私が 先週 夫のため モールで 時計を 買いました。

If the sentence has more than one interrogative noun, like the above sentence, simply replace the interrogative noun with an answer to create a sentence that answers the question. Do not change the particle following the interrogative pronoun, as you may end up changing the meaning of the sentence as shown in the following example:

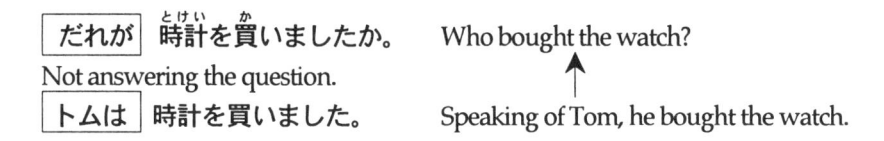

| だれが | 時計を買いましたか。　　Who bought the watch?

Not answering the question.

| トムは | 時計を買いました。　　Speaking of Tom, he bought the watch.

As can be seen from the English translation, if a different particle is used to answer the question, the meaning will be changed. The particle が in だれが is used to find out new information, while は is used to present shared or old information. Even though correct information has been provided, its form jars with the question sentence. So do not change the particle in answering a question.

2.2 Formation of a noun phrase using an interrogative pronoun

Interrogative noun	か (some~) + affirmative predicate
	も (any~) + negative predicate
	でも + いい/かまわない etc.

As the English equivalent with "some" or "any" indicates, when か is attached to an interrogative pronoun, the interrogative noun loses its original meaning as a question word; it becomes an indefinite noun such as "something," "somewhere," and "someone." For example, the equivalent of "Did you go *somewhere*?" is どこかへ行きましたか, and "Did you see *someone*?" is だれかを見ましたか.

In answering such questions, if the answer is negative, such as "nowhere," and "no one," the interrogative follows a negative predicate. Note that the particles に、で、と、へ、から、まで are not dropped, depending on the type of verb used and the meaning of the sentence.

何 / だれ / どこ 〉か	何 / だれに／と／から / どこへ／に／で 〉も
Some/any ~	No ~

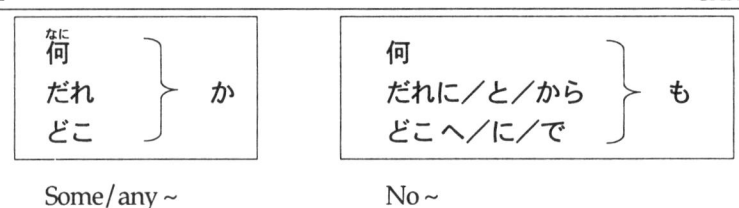

(1) a. 何か食べましたか。
Did you eat something?
b. いいえ、何も食べませんでした。
No, I did not eat anything.

(2) a. どこかへ行きましたか。
Did you go somewhere?
b. いいえ、どこへも行きませんでした。
No, I did not go anywhere.

(3) a. 誰かに会いましたか。
Did you meet someone?
b. いいえ、誰にも会いませんでした。
No, I did not meet anyone.
* c. いいえ、誰も会いませんでした。
No, no one met.

(4) a. どこかにありましたか。
Was it somewhere?
b. いいえ、どこにもありませんでした。
No, it was (found) nowhere.
* c. いいえ、どこもありませんでした。
No, it existed nowhere.

(5) a. 誰からか聞きましたか。
Did you hear (this) from someone?
b. いいえ、誰からも聞きませんでした。
No, I did not hear (this) from anyone.
* c. いいえ、誰もききませんでした。
No, no one heard.

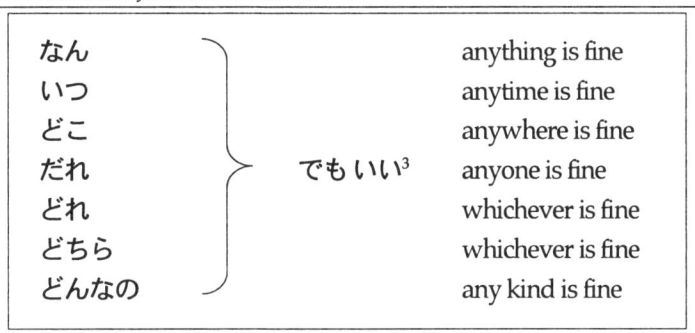

なん		anything is fine
いつ		anytime is fine
どこ		anywhere is fine
だれ	でもいい[3]	anyone is fine
どれ		whichever is fine
どちら		whichever is fine
どんなの		any kind is fine

(6) a. 何が飲みたいですか。
  What would you like to drink?
  b. 何でもいいです。
  Anything would be fine.

(7) a. いつ行きたいですか。
  When would you like to go?
  b. いつでもいいです。
  Anytime is fine.

(8) a. 誰と結婚したいですか。
  To whom would you like to get married?
  b. 誰とでもいいです！
  Anyone is fine!

(9) a. どこでピクニックがしたいですか。
  Where would you like to have a picnic?
  b. どこでもオーケー。
  Anywhere is okay.

(10) a. どんな形がいいですか。
  What kind of shape would you like?
  b. どんなのでもかまいません。
  Any shape is fine with me.

---

[3] In addition to いい "fine," predicates such as かまいません and オーケー that express a positive meaning may be used, as seen from the examples.

CHAPTER 16

Change of State: する・なる Constructions

する "to do" is a transitive verb which takes an object acted upon by an agent (a performer of the action), while なる "to become" is an intransitive verb which does not take an object and which is often used to describe a situation where the agent has no volitional control over the events described (e.g., "I open the door" vs. "The door opens.").[1] する and なる can be used in various constructions to assign different shades of meaning. The fundamental function of する and なる in those constructions is to express a change of state: an event or situation described by the する or なる construction changes. In the discussion that follows, the patterns する/なる "make it to/become" and ことにする/ことになる "one decides to do~/it has been decided that ~" are treated. Both of these carry the connotation of change of state.

1. Predicate + する/なる

When a predicate is followed by する, the sentence indicates that the speaker changes one state into another state described by the predicate. For example, 部屋を暖かくする means "I make the room warm" (by using a heater or something). So the speaker actively changes the state of the room from cold to warm. On the other hand, when a predicate is followed by なる, the sentence indicates that a situation changes from one state into another. A predicate followed by なる can describe a state after some change has been made by a volitional force. For example, 部屋が暖くなった means "the room became warm" since a heater was turned on, for example. The state of the room altering from cold to warm is described as a result of some kind of a volitional act. First, look at the formation of these constructions, then at some examples.

---

[1] Further discussion of する and なる is found in Ikegami (1997).

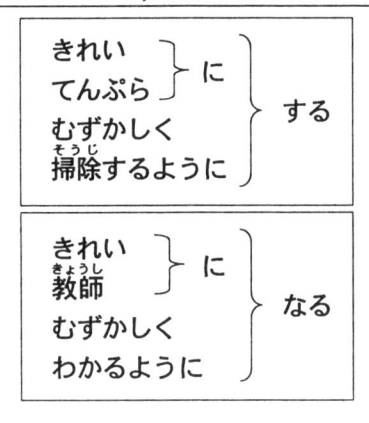

きれい	make it clean
てんぷら }に }する	make it tempura[2]
むずかしく	make it difficult
掃除(そうじ)するように	make (my habit) to clean the room

きれい	become clean
教師(きょうし) }に }なる	become a teacher
むずかしく	become difficult
わかるように	Come to understand (situation changes from not understanding to understanding)

1.1 する

(1) At a restaurant:
　　A: 何(なに)にしますか。
　　　　What are you going to have?
　　B: そうですね。私(わたし)はすきやきにします。
　　　　Let's see... I will have sukiyaki.

(2) A: 試験(しけん)がむずかしすぎるのですが、もっとやさしくしてくださいませんか。
　　　　The exams are too difficult. Could you please make them easier?
　　B: そんなこと言(い)わないで、もっと勉強(べんきょう)するようにしてください。
　　　　Don't say things like that. Try to study harder.

(3) A: 部屋(へや)がきたないですね。もう少(すこ)しちゃんと掃除(そうじ)をするようにしたらどうですか。
　　　　Your room is dirty. Why don't you try to clean the room regularly?
　　B: ええ、きれいにしたいのですが、時間(じかん)がないんです。
　　　　Yes, I would like to clean, but don't have time.

1.2 なる

(4) A: ずいぶん寒(さむ)くなりましたね。
　　　　It became quite cold.

---

[2] When a noun is followed by する, it usually indicates the speaker's selection of the noun. This construction is often translated as "I decide to have ~" or "I choose ~."

(5) B: ええ、ヒーターが要るようになりましたね。
Yes, a heater (be)came to be needed. (I need a heater now.)

文法がやっとわかるようになりました。会話もできるようになりました。漢字も書けるようになりました。いい点数が取れるようになって、先生にもほめられるようになりました。
I finally came to understand grammar. I became able to speak, too. On top of that, I became able to write kanji. So, I became able to get a good score and came to be praised by the teacher.

(6) A: 先生の大学院生は卒業して、こうし(子牛)になったそうですね。
I hear that your graduate student became veal after graduation.

B: いえいえ、違いますよ。こうし(講師)になったんです。抑揚に気をつけるようにしてくださいね。
Oh, no, no. She became an instructor. Try to pay attention to your intonation.

A verb followed by ようにする means that an agent tries to carry out an activity with an intention. Therefore, ようにする can follow the negative form of a verb indicating that the agent tries not to carry out an activity with an intention.

(7) 体に悪いので、たばこを吸わないようにしているのですが、一日に一本は吸いたくなるんです。どうすれば、吸わないようになるでしょうか。
Since it is bad for your health, I am trying not to smoke, but come to want to smoke at least once a day. How can I (be)come not to smoke?

(8) せっかく日本語を習ったのですから、卒業してからも、忘れないようにしてください。
Since you tried hard to learn Japanese, please try not to forget even after graduation.

(9) 甘いものは食べ過ぎないように、お酒は飲みすぎないように、テレビは見過ぎないように、夜更かしはしないようにしてください。
Try not to eat too many sweets, drink too much alcohol, watch too much TV, and stay up too late.

Verb ように can be followed not only by する, but also by other phrases, such as 気をつける "pay attention," 努力する "make an effort," and 頑張る "do one's best." In these cases, the equivalent may change to "so that ~" which may carry a similar meaning to ために "in order to ~." Note the following examples, which are compared with ために sentences:

(10) 大学院へ行けるように、大学生の時一生懸命努力しました。
I made a great effort when I was in college so that I could go on to graduate school.

Cf. 大学院へ行くために、大学生の時一生懸命努力しました。
I made a great effort when I was in college in order to go on to graduate school.

(11) a. トーナメントに勝てるように、みんなで頑張りましょう。
Let's do our best so that we can win the tournament.

b. トーナメントに勝つために、みんなで頑張りましょう。
Let's do our best in order to win the tournament.

(12) a. 発音を間違えないように(発音に)気をつけてください。
Please pay attention (to your pronunciation) so that you don't make mispronunciations.

? b. 発音を間違えないために、漢字には振仮名をふるようにしてください。
Try to put hiragana on kanji words in order not to make any mispronunciation.

(13) a. 虫歯にならないように、毎日何回も歯を磨きました。
I brushed my teeth many times every day so that I would not get cavities.

?? b. 虫歯にならないために、毎日何回も歯を磨きました。
I brushed my teeth many times every day in order not to become a cavity.[3]

---

[3] In reality, one may utter this type of sentence without paying much attention to the grammatical accuracy of the sentence, as the meaning is understood. When you observe the sentence closely, however, you will notice that the sentence conveys that the speaker brushed his teeth so that he does not turn into a cavity, which is nonsensical.

c. 虫歯を作らないために、毎日何回も歯を磨きました。
I brushed my teeth many times every day in order not to make a cavity.

There is a difference between ようにする and ために. Since ために is used to indicate a speaker's purpose in carrying out the event described by the verb, it has to follow a verb that can be executed by the intention of a sentient, animate being. Therefore, non-volitional intransitive verbs, such as なる, cannot occur with ために to express the meaning of purpose, as illustrated by sentence (13). ように does not have this restriction, but tends to occur with a predicate in order to express a situation that cannot be used by ために.

2.　Verb Dictionary Form/ない + ことにする/ことになる

The fundamental notion of ことにする and ことになる is also one of a change of state. Since する is a transitive verb that expresses a speaker's intention, ことにする is used to indicate that a speaker makes up his/her mind to change the situation into the one described by the verb. On the other hand, in the case of なる, an intransitive verb, the speaker has no control over the change of state. When なる is used, the change is assigned to the speaker, and the decision-making process can involve the speaker, as in the case of marriage. Both ことにする and ことになる follow either an affirmative or a negative form of the present casual form. The English equivalent of these constructions is then "I decide (not) to do ~" or "it is decided (not) to do ~," respectively.

　　ことにする and ことになる are often expressed in the aspectual form, ことにしています and ことになっています. When ている is attached, as its function indicates, the speaker made a decision sometime in the past, and the result of making such a decision has continued up to the current moment. For example, the difference between コーヒーは飲まないことにした and コーヒーは飲まないことにしている is that the former sentence points to a time in the past when the decision was made, expressing the meaning "At some point in the past, I made a decision not to drink coffee," whereas the latter refers to a time expanse between when the speaker made the decision and the present moment, expressing the meaning "I'm in the state of having decided not to drink coffee." Such decisions can also be perceived as *habitual*. The difference between 日本へ行くことになった and 日本へ行くことになっている is captured in the same fashion as ことにした and ことにしている, except that the decision is made involving a third person.

2.1 ことにする

(1) a. 健康に悪いから、煙草をやめることにした。
Since it's bad for one's health, I decided to quit smoking.
b. 健康に悪いから、煙草を吸わないことにした。
Since it's bad for one's health, I decided not to smoke.
c. 健康に悪いから、煙草を吸わないことにしている。
Since it's bad for one's health, I don't smoke (by my own decision).

(2) a. 日本語を上達させるために、毎日2時間テープを聞くことにしました。
In order to improve my Japanese, I decided to listen to the tape two hours a day.
b. 日本語を上達させるために、毎日2時間テープを聞くことにしています。
In order to improve my Japanese, I listen to the tape two hours a day (by my own will).

(3) 結婚式は教会で挙げることにしました。でもハネムーンへは行かないことにしました。そのお金を使って、マンションを買うことにしたんです。
We decided to have a wedding ceremony at a church. But we decided not to go on a honeymoon. We decided to buy a condominium using the money for the honeymoon.

2.2 ことになる

(4) 来月から1ヶ月カナダで仕事をすることになりました。
It was decided that I will work in Canada for a month starting next month.

(5) 来年の6月に結婚することになりました。ハネムーンはハワイへ行くことになりました。
It was decided that we will get married next June. Speaking of a honeymoon, it was decided that we will go to Hawaii.

(6) 9月からハーバード大学で大学院生として勉強することになっています。9月が楽しみです。
It has been decided that I am going to study at Harvard University as a graduate student. I am looking forward to September.

(7) アメリカへ出張することになっています。
It has been decided that I will go to America on a business trip.

ことになる may be more appropriate to use for the situations expressed in sentences (6) and (7), where admission to the graduate school or making a business trip to America cannot be decided by the speaker. The decision is made by the school and the company, and there was no control over the acceptance or rejection by the speaker in these situations.

(8) ? 日本語を上達させるために、毎日2時間テープを聞くことになりました。
In order to improve my Japanese, it was decided that I will listen to the tape two hours a day.

Sentence (8) is awkward semantically because the purpose of the speaker described in the subordinate clause and the assignment passively given to the speaker are not conceptually compatible with each other.

Thus, the use of ことにする and ことになる provides crucial information about where the decision-making lies. When ことになる is used, the sentence often creates an impression that the speaker is not responsible for the event described by the verb. When making the decision is not up to the speaker, ことになる is the construction to use.

CHAPTER 17

Modifying Constructions

All the parts of speech—verbs, い adjectives, な adjectives, and nouns—are often modified by other elements for further identification and explication of their attributes and characteristics. Modifiers of these parts of speech are consistently located in front of them in Japanese. (Refer to Chapter 2, Section 1.2, "Left Branching.") Verbs, い adjectives, and な adjectives are modified by an adverb. Most adverbs, however, modify verbs and may also modify some い adjectives and な adjectives that express degree, such as とてもおいしい "very delicious" and かなりむずかしい "fairly difficult." Nouns are modified by a noun, an い adjective, a な adjective, a relative clause or a noun complement clause. In the following, we will examine how modifiers work in Japanese.

1. Noun-Modifying Constructions

Unlike other parts of speech, a noun can be modified not only by a single word, but also by a clause. The clause is either a relative clause (RC) or a noun-complement clause (NC). However a noun may be modified, the noun constitutes a noun phrase (NP) as indicated in the following chart.

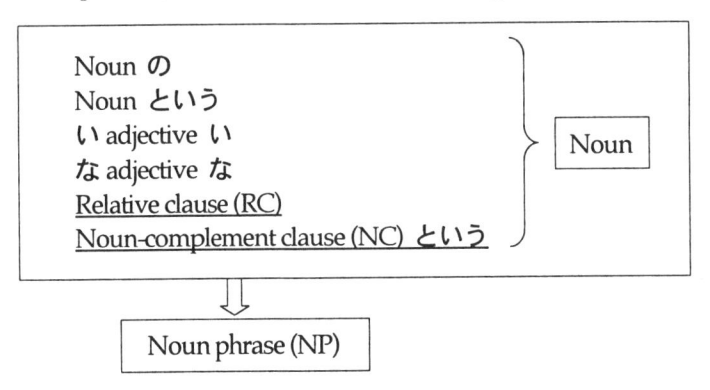

```
┌─────────────────────────────────────┐
│   Noun の                           │
│   Noun という                        ⎫
│   い adjective い                    ⎬  Noun
│   な adjective な                    │
│   Relative clause (RC)              │
│   Noun-complement clause (NC) という ⎭
└─────────────────────────────────────┘
              ⇓
       ┌──────────────────┐
       │ Noun phrase (NP) │
       └──────────────────┘
```

Examples:

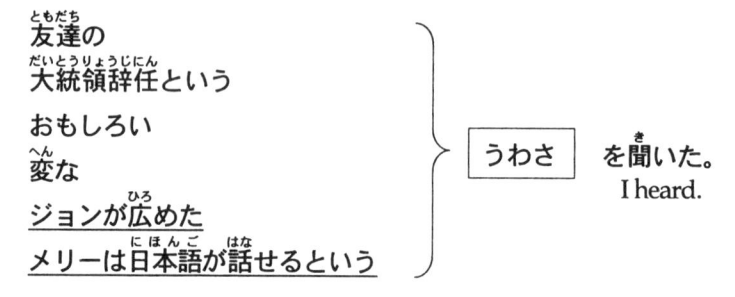

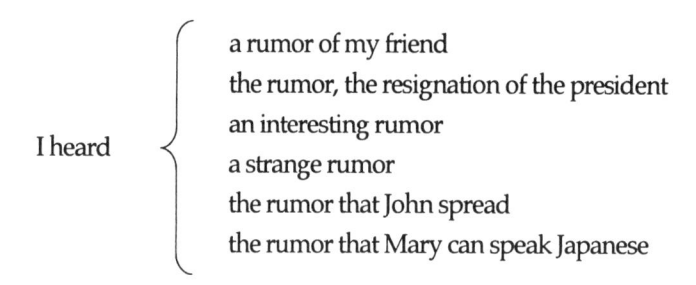

友達の
大統領辞任という
おもしろい
変な
ジョンが広めた
メリーは日本語が話せるという
} うわさ を聞いた。
I heard.

I heard {
a rumor of my friend
the rumor, the resignation of the president
an interesting rumor
a strange rumor
the rumor that John spread
the rumor that Mary can speak Japanese

In the following, noun-modifying constructions will be discussed.

1.1 Noun の noun

Please refer to Chapter 4, Section 10.

1.2 Noun という noun

という is called a *noun complementizer* and is most significantly used to create *apposition*—a syntactic relation in which an element is juxtaposed to another element of the same kind. In Japanese, という is used to express this appositional relationship when the second noun gives/explains the name, content, or attribute of the first noun, indicating a meaning "N2 called/named N1" or "N2 that is N1." The appositional relationship is not a hierarchical one; rather, it links two nouns at an equal rank or status. For example, in ソニーという会社 "a company called Sony," ソニー and 会社 are in apposition, with 会社 identifying the attribute of ソニー. という is generally used when the speaker or the listener may not be familiar with the content or attribute of the second noun. It is also used to link a clause (noun-complement clause) and a noun. (The explanation of this function will be given later in Section 1.5.) Let us first observe some examples where という is used to link nouns.

(1) │ジョージルーカス│ という │映画監督（えいがかんとく）│ がこの映画を作（つく）った。
A movie that the director called George Lucas made.
(ジョージルーカス＝映画監督)

(2) 東京の │渋谷（しぶや）│ という │駅（えき）│ に │ハチ公（こう）│ という │犬（いぬ）の銅像（どうぞう）│ がある。
There is a statue of a dog called "Hachi-ko" at a station called Shibuya in Tokyo.

(3) │OPEC│ という │機関（きかん）│ は何（なん）の略（りゃく）ですか。
What does the organization called "OPEC" stand for?

(4) │「超（ちょう）」│ という │言葉（ことば）│ を若（わか）い人（ひと）の間（あいだ）でよく聞（き）くのですが、どういう意味（いみ）ですか。
I often hear the word "choo" used among young people, but what does it mean?

All of the first nouns followed by という are given as elements regarding which the speaker or listener may not have thorough information. For example, if the speaker is sure that the listener knows 渋谷 station and ハチ公, s/he would not have to use という explaining that 渋谷 is a station and ハチ公 is a statue of a dog, respectively. The speaker would simply say 渋谷にハチ公がある。 という is also used when the speaker does not have all the information or does not know if the listener has the information. Sentences (3) and (4) are such cases. Thus, the appropriateness of using という depends on how the speaker views the source of that information.

1.3　い/な adjective + noun

When an い adjective or a な adjective modifies a noun, it always precedes it, as in いい辞書（じしょ） "good dictionary" and 便利（べんり）な辞書 "handy dictionary" and forms a noun phrase. Here are some more examples:

(5) 背中が痛いので、今は重い物が持てないのです。
Because I have back pain, I cannot lift heavy things.
(6) 不便な所に引っ越してきたことを後悔している。
I regret the fact that I moved to an inconvenient location.
(7) 暗い部屋で本を読むと、目が悪くなるとよく母に言われた。
I was often told by my mother that my eyes would go bad if I read books in a dark room.

Since い adjectives describe attributes, they are usually in the imperfective form when modifying a noun. However, in some cases, the perfective form of an い adjective may be used to modify a noun, as may be seen from the following examples:

(8) 前は遠かったダウンタウンが、高速道路ができて、近くなった。
Downtown, which used to be far from home, became closer because of the highway.
(9) 嫌いだった人がだんだん好きになってきた。
I came to like a person whom I used to dislike.
(10) 昔教師だった母は、今引退して、子供たちに英語を教えている。
My mother, who used to be a teacher in the old days, has now retired and is teaching children English.

The perfective form of an い adjective still precedes a noun to modify it in Japanese, although in English, it has to be expressed by a relative clause indicating how the noun used to be.

1.4 Relative clause (RC) + noun

A relative clause is one that modifies the head of a noun phrase and typically includes other elements. For example, in 知りすぎた男 "the man who knew too much," the relative clause 知りすぎた "who knew too much" modifies "the man." As is evident from the example, in Japanese, relative clauses precede their "antecedents," while English relative clauses follow them. Also, Japanese lacks relative pronouns corresponding to the English "who," "whom," "whose," "which," "that," "where," etc. A noun phrase modified by a relative clause is called a "head noun." A head noun may be either a single noun or a noun that is modified by an い adjective, a な adjective, or a noun. For example:

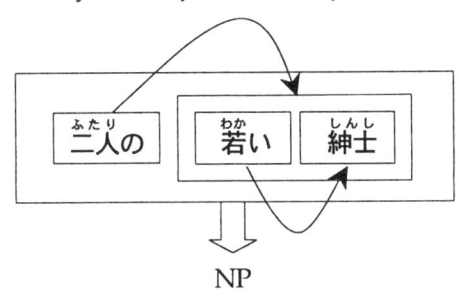

```
┌─────────────────────────────┐
│  二人の    若い    紳士     │
│  ふたりの   わかい   しんし   │
└─────────────────────────────┘
              ↓
             NP
```

In the above diagram, the い adjective 若い "young" modifies the noun 紳士 "gentleman" and constitutes the NP. Then the NP is further modified by the NP 二人の to constitute a longer NP 二人の若い紳士 "two young gentlemen." Since 二人の若い紳士 is a noun phrase, the whole phrase can be modified by a relative clause as seen in the following example:

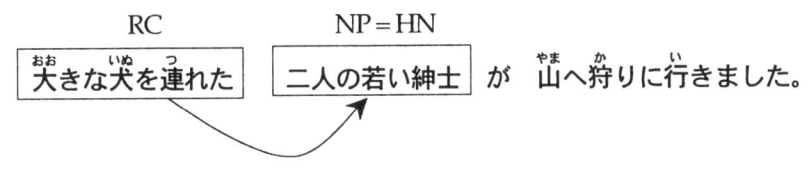

```
      RC                NP = HN
┌──────────────┐  ┌──────────────┐
│ 大きな犬を連れた │  │ 二人の若い紳士 │ が 山へ狩りに行きました。
└──────────────┘  └──────────────┘
```

<u>Two young gentlemen</u> <u>who are taking a big dog</u> went to a mountain to hunt.
     HN = NP   RC

Note that a relative clause has a predicate. The predicate may also be an い adjective or a な adjective. Observe the following sentences.

(11) ［すしがおいしい］店を教えてくださいますか。
Could you tell me a restaurant that serves good sushi?

(12) このクラスには［アニメが好きな］人がたくさんいます。
There are many people who like animation in this class.

(13) ［大学で日本語を勉強した］トムは日本人のように話します。
Tom, who studied Japanese at a university, speaks like a native speaker of Japanese.

(14) a. [歯医者へ行きたがらない]{[子供]の気持ち}はよくわかる。

I understand the feelings of kids who don't want to go to a dentist.

b. [歯医者へ行きたくない] [子供の気持ち] はよくわかる。

I understand the kids' feelings that they don't want to go to a dentist.

(15) a. [私が一緒に住んでいる]{[メリー]の友達}に会った。

I met a friend of Mary, with whom I am living. (Mary and I live together. I met Mary's friend.)

b. [私が一緒に住むことにした] [メリーの友達] に会いに行った。

I went to see Mary's friend, with whom I decided to live (together).

As found in the above sentences, a relative clause can modify a noun regardless of its position in a sentence, as long as the sentence makes sense and is coherent. Proper names and personal pronouns can be freely preceded by relative clauses as well. Also, as seen in sentences (14a) and (15a), 子供の気持ち "kids' feelings" and メリーの友達 "Mary's friend," respectively, there are cases where only the first noun within the noun phrase is identified as the head noun. In the case of the construction "noun の noun," the pattern constitutes a larger noun phrase, and depending on context, this interpretation may apply.

Another difference observed between English and Japanese is that as long as it makes sense, any noun can be modified by a relative clause; therefore there may be more than two relative clauses in a sentence. The following examples exhibit cases of multiple relative clauses:

(16) [紫のシャツを着ている][男]が[誰もいない][駅]で

[東京へ行く][電車]を 待っています。

A man wearing a purple shirt is waiting for a train that goes to Tokyo at a station where no one is. (A man in a purple shirt is waiting for a Tokyo-bound train at an empty station.)

(17) [先週アメリカに来た] 牧野さん は今 [大学に入る] 準備 をしています。

Mr. Makino who came to America last week is now preparing for university admission.

(18) [私が買いたかった] の は [もうだれかに買われてしまった] 赤いジャケット です。

The one I wanted to buy is a red jacket, which was already bought by someone else.

When の functions as a pronoun (as is often seen in the 〜のは〜です sentence pattern), it also functions as a head noun which refers to a concrete meaning based on context.

Note that there is a restriction in constructing a relative clause: the *subject* of a relative clause cannot take は (unless there is a strong contrast). Either が or の should be used. This is due to the fact that は marks a noun as the topic of a sentence, separating it from the rest of the sentence.

(19) ジョンは [∅ 買った] 本 を 読んだ。

ジョンは、買った本を読んだ。 "John read the book [∅] bought."

(20) ∅ [ジョンが/の買った] 本 を 読んだ。

ジョンが/の買った本を読んだ。 "[∅] read the book John bought."

は in sentence (19) is used to mark ジョン, and ジョン is given as the topic/subject of the sentences, with the rest of the sentence as a comment on ジョン.

は automatically locates the marked noun outside the relative clause. Also, in sentence (19), the subject of the relative clause is missing, and from the sentence alone, the listener cannot tell who bought the book. Contrary to this, the subject of the main predicate 読んだ "read" is missing in sentence (20), and the listener cannot tell who read the book which John bought. These missing pieces of information will cause misunderstanding between the speaker and the listener unless both of them are in an environment where they can fill in the missing information. Here are some more examples:

(21) a. 私は | subject ジョンが/の | predicate 住んでいる | | HN ところ | を知っています。

 I know the place where John lives. (ところ = direct object position)
 * b. 私はジョンは住んでいるところを知っています。

(22) a. [ジョンが/の作る] [ケーキ] はとてもおいしいです。
 The cake John makes is very delicious. (ケーキ = subject position)
 * b. ジョンは作るケーキはとてもおいしいです。

(23) a. ジョンは [目が/の見えない] [人] に手をかしてあげました。
 John offered his hand to a person who is blind. (人 = indirect object position)
 * b. ジョンは目は見えない人に手をかしてあげました。

1.4.1 Embedded relative clause

Due to the fact that a head noun modified by a relative clause constitutes a noun phrase, it is technically possible for the noun phrase to be modified by another relative clause. In fact, this is an "embedded relative clause," because one relative clause is located within another. The greater the number of relative clauses are in a coherent way in a sentence, the more complicated the sentence becomes. Although embedded relative clauses are often not used in conversation because the complicated structure may interfere with understanding, the use of embedded relative clauses is often seen in writing. See the following example:

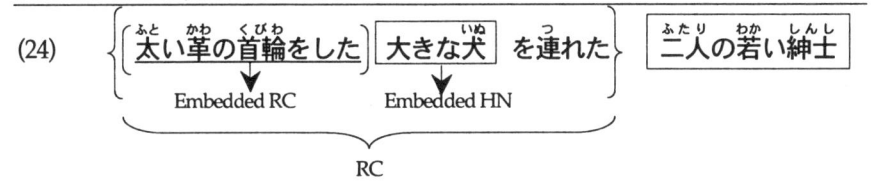

(24) { [太い革の首輪をした] [大きな犬] を連れた } 二人の若い紳士
         Embedded RC   Embedded HN
                    RC

が山へ狩りに行き、道に迷ってしまった。

Two young gentlemen who took a big dog along with them that was wearing a thick leather collar went to a mountain and got lost. (Two gentlemen with a dog with a thick leather collar went to a mountain and got lost.)

(25) { [私が捨てた] [自転車] を拾った } 人 が、
         ERC   EHN
                    RC

その自転車を1,000円で弟に売った。

The person who picked up my bicycle that I abandoned sold the bicycle for 1,000 yen to my brother.

If there is more than one embedded relative clause included in a sentence, the sentence may become difficult to comprehend. However, this happens often in Japanese writing, as a sentence can include a number of such clauses without breaking up the sentence into several short sentences. Try to figure out the meaning of the following sentences, taken from various written materials.

(26) バレンタイン・デーからちょうど一ヶ月後の三月十四日は、バレンタイン・デーにプレゼントをもらった男性が、プレゼントをくれた女性にお返しをあげる「ホワイト・デー」と呼ばれる日になっている。[1]

Sample reading

The following story is based on a fairy tale called 注文の多い料理店 "A Restaurant with Many Orders," originally written by Kenji Miyazawa. It has been

---

[1] Excerpted from Miura and McGloin (1994).

rewritten for the purpose of identifying relative clauses. Once you identify the relative clause, eliminate all the clauses and read only the remaining skeleton structure. You will understand the basic idea of the sentence.

これは、昔、昔の物語です。ある日、大きな犬を連れた若い二人の紳士が山へ狩りに行き、道に迷ってしまいました。その時、二人はこの辺ではあまり見られない一軒の立派な西洋料理店を見つけました。玄関には「西洋料理店－山猫軒」と書いてある札が出ていました。二人が店に入ると、ドアに、「どなたもどうぞお入りください。決してご遠慮いりません。」と書いてあります。こんな所にレストランがあるとは知らなかった二人は喜んで中に入りました。すると、また大きい字で書いた札がありました。それには、「特に太った人や若い人は歓迎いたします。」と書いてあります。若くて太っている二人は大喜びでした。もう少し行くと、またドアに、ここは注文の多い店ですから、どうかご承知ください。と書いてあります。「注文が多いのだから、こんなところでも人がたくさん来るんだろう。」と思いながら、そのドアを開けると、そばに鏡があり、その下には長い柄のついたブラシが置いてあります。そしてまた、「お客様、ここでかみをとかして、それから、靴をきれいにしてください。」と書いた札がありました。二人は「これはもっともだ。きっと立派な人たちがよく来るのだろう」と思って、そうしました。おなかがとてもすいているので、早く温いものを食べたいと思うのですが、二人が入った次の部屋にはまた札がありました。どうぞ、服を脱いでください。そして鉄砲などはここに置いてください。半分はだかになってしまった二人は次の部屋へ入って行きました。そこには、大きな壺があり、それには、「色々注文が多くてすみませんでした。これが最後の注文です。どうぞ体に壺の中の塩をよくつけてください。」今度は二人ともぎょっとして、お互いに顔を見合わせて言いました。「どうもおかしいと思わないか？」「うん、おかしいと思う・・・。」「僕たちが注文しているんじゃなくて、店が僕たちに注文しているんだ。」「つまり店へ来た人に料理を出すのではなくて、来た人を料理する・・・ということなんだ！」ここへ来てやっとそれがわかった二人は、怖くてふるえだしました。「逃よう！」一人の紳士がドアを開けようとしましたが、ドアはぜんぜん動きませんでした・・・。

1.5   Noun-complement clause (NC) + noun

A noun-complement clause is the same as the English subordinate clause used in sentences such as "I know the fact that ~," "I heard a rumor that ~," "I have an idea that ~," "I have an opinion that ~," and "I reached the conclusion that ~." That clause follows a noun that requires a description of the content or attribute of the noun. In Japanese, this formation is realized by the use of という that links a noun and its description.

    A という clause appears to be the same as a relative clause in its surface structure, since a noun-complement clause also comes before a noun in the form of a sentence and explains the noun in further detail. However, as the different terms "relative clause" and "noun-complement clause" suggest, their use is not exactly identical. While a relative clause restricts the attribute or type of the modified noun, a noun-complement clause explains the content of the modified noun. In other words, a relative clause creates a hierarchical relationship, while a noun-complement clause creates an appositional relationship between the clause and the noun by the use of という. As exemplified in Johnson (2005a), という usually precedes a noun such as 事実 "fact," うわさ "rumor," 知らせ "information," 考え "idea," 意見 "opinion," 話 "story," 結果 "result," and 状態 "situation." See the following examples:

(27) 葉子が山田と結婚するという事を僕は今日まで知らなかった。
      Until today, I didn't know that Yoko was going to get married to Yamada.

(28) 大学にフットボールスタジアムができるといううわさを聞いた。
      I heard a rumor that a football stadium will be constructed at the university.

(29) いとこが男の子を産んだという知らせが入った。
      The news came that my cousin gave birth to a baby boy.

(30) 犬が飼い主の命を助けたという話はよく聞く。
      We often hear the story that a dog saved his owner's life.

Sometimes nouns may function as head nouns for a relative clause or a noun-complement clause. The use of という and the context are decisive for determining the meaning of the sentence. See the following sentences:

(31) a. その建物が火事になった理由はまだわかっていない。(RC)
The reason why/for which the building caught fire has not become clear yet.
b. 建物が火事になったという理由でその会社は倒産した。(NC)
For the reason that the building caught fire, the company went bankrupt.

(32) a. 昨日食べ過ぎた結果、今日何も食べられない。(RC)
As a result of eating too much food yesterday, I cannot eat anything today.
b. 昨日食べ過ぎたので、今日何も食べられないという結果になってしまった。(NC)
Since I ate too much yesterday, I came to a result that I cannot eat anything today.

The difference between the RC and the NC may be difficult to detect, but one of the crucial syntactic characteristics is the possible use of は in the NC. The RC cannot include は, but the NC can. This is due to the fact that the NC is a clause that describes the content of the head noun with elements of the same kind as the head noun.

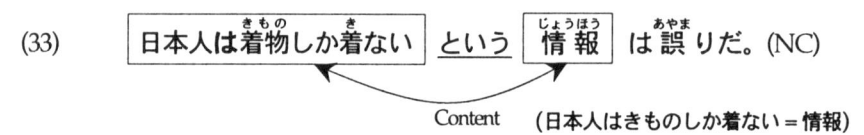

(33) 日本人は着物しか着ない という 情報 は誤りだ。(NC)
　　　　　　　　　　　　　　　　　　Content　(日本人はきものしか着ない=情報)
The piece of information that Japanese wear nothing but kimono is wrong.

Note that が can also be used in a NC, but は cannot be used in a RC.

(34) 日本人が着る 着物 はたいていシルクです。(RC)
The kimono Japanese wear are usually made of silk.

2. Modifying Verbs: Adverbs

A verb is modified by an adverb. There are basically three types of adverbs in Japanese: (1) words that are morphologically and semantically identified as adverbs, including onomatopoeias and mimetics; (2) い adjectives and な adjectives that change their form to modify a verb; and (3) time nouns, such as 明日 "tomorrow" and 毎月 "every month" that explain, for example, when and how often an event described by a verb happens. In any case, the function of these words is consistent in that they all modify a verb. The following are some examples that express the frequency of occurrence of an event, the degree of the situation described by the verb, and the degree of probability that the event described by the verb will come true or be realized.

2.1 Adverbs of frequency

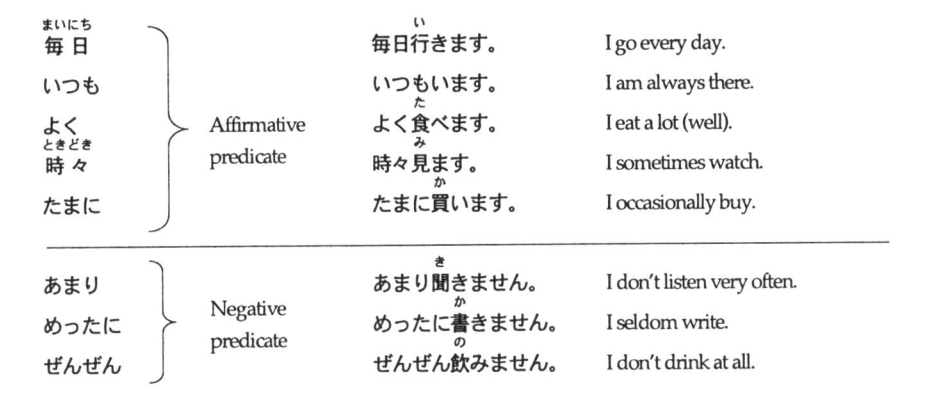

毎日 (まいにち)	⎫	毎日行きます。	I go every day.
いつも	⎬	いつもいます。	I am always there.
よく	Affirmative predicate	よく食べます。	I eat a lot (well).
時々 (ときどき)		時々見ます。	I sometimes watch.
たまに	⎭	たまに買います。	I occasionally buy.
あまり	⎫	あまり聞きません。	I don't listen very often.
めったに	⎬ Negative predicate	めったに書きません。	I seldom write.
ぜんぜん	⎭	ぜんぜん飲みません。	I don't drink at all.

2.2 Adverbs of degree

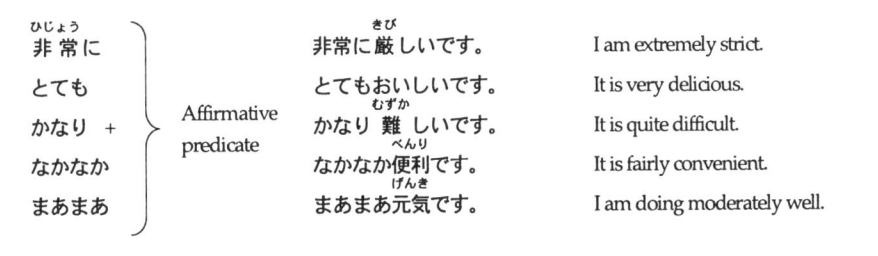

非常に (ひじょう)	⎫	非常に厳しいです。	I am extremely strict.
とても	⎬	とてもおいしいです。	It is very delicious.
かなり +	Affirmative predicate	かなり難しいです。	It is quite difficult.
なかなか		なかなか便利です。	It is fairly convenient.
まあまあ	⎭	まあまあ元気です。	I am doing moderately well.

あまり	Negative	あまり便利じゃありません。	It is not very convenient.
ぜんぜん	predicate	ぜんぜんよくありません。	It is not good at all.

2.3 Adverbs of probability

絶対	絶対来ます。	He will definitely come.
必ず	必ずします。	I will do it without fail.
きっと	きっとできるはずです。	I am sure that I can do it.
恐らく	恐らく雨が降るでしょう。	Perhaps it will rain.
たぶん	たぶん読むでしょう。	I will probably read.
もしかしたら	もしかしたらだめかもしれません。	It may be bad.

2.4 Adverbial forms of い adjectives and な adjectives

い/な adjectives can also function as adverbs.[2] In this case, they change the form in the following way:

```
い adjective く  ⎫
                ⎬ + verb
な adjective + に ⎭
```

(1) あの人はご飯を早く食べます。　　That person eats meals early.
(2) あの人はご飯を速く食べます。　　That person eats meals fast.
(3) 今朝は遅く起きました。　　　　　I woke up late this morning.
(4) 字は丁寧に書いてください。　　　Please write characters neatly.
(5) 手はきれいに洗いましょう。　　　We shall wash our hands clean.
(6) 歯はよく磨きましょう。　　　　　Brush your teeth well.
(7) 点数が極端に悪かったんです。　　My score was extremely bad.

---

[2] い/な adjectives can change their form to function as nouns. In such a case, い changes into さ for adjectives, and さ is added to な adjectives. For example: 寒い→寒さ "coldness," 大きい→大きさ "size," 高い→高さ "height," 深い→深さ "depth," 強い→強さ "strength," 不便→不便さ "inconvenience."

2.5 Onomatopoeia

"Onomatopoeia refers to those conventionalized mimetic expressions of natural sounds" (Shibatani, 1990: 153). Three types of sound-symbolic words under the category of onomatopoeia can be identified in Japanese: 擬声語 (phonomimes); 擬態語 (phenomimes); and 擬情語 (psychomimes). Onomatopoeia is "a word or process of forming words whose phonetic form is perceived as imitating a sound associated with something, that they denote" (Matthews, 1997) and it usually involves reduplication. For example, ワンワン for the sound a dog makes or ドンドン for the sound of a person knocking on a door. Phenomimes "depict states, conditions, or manners of the external world, and "psychomimes symbolize mental conditions or sensations" (Shibatani, 1990: 154). The formation of onomatopoeic words is usually systematic, such as CVCV X 2 (スラスラ), CVCV-ri (スラリ), CVV (スー), and CVV X 2 (スースー), and each sound signifies a specific meaning.[3]

These onomatopoeias are usually treated as adverbs and specify the type of action or state described by the verb. For example, 歩く "to walk" in Japanese covers all the types of walking that are expressed in English by specific verbs such as "trudge along," "wander," and so on. The equivalents of these English verbs in Japanese are expressed by the verb 歩く accompanying the phenomimes とぼとぼ歩く and うろうろ歩く, respectively.

(8) おなかがグウグウなっている。 My stomach is growling. (phonomimes)
(9) 雨がザーザー降っている。 Rain is pouring. (phonomimes)
(10) 日本語がスラスラ読める。 I can read Japanese smoothly. (phenomimes)
(11) もっとゆっくり話してください。 Please speak slowly. (phenomimes)
(12) 頭がズキズキする。 My head is throbbing. (psychomimes)
(13) 涙がジーンとこみあげてきた。 Tears welled up in my eyes. (psychomimes)

---

[3] See Hamano (1988) for a detailed discussion of onomatopoeia.

2.6 もう and まだ

The adverbs もう and まだ carry various meanings as well as constituting important grammar structures.

2.6.1 もう

The fundamental meaning of the adverb もう is to indicate the occurrence of a change in an activity or state.[4] This fundamental meaning extends its function to mean "already" with an affirmative predicate and "no longer" with a negative predicate. In either case, use of もう shows that a change occurred in an event, and the state is not maintained in the same fashion as it was before. Observe the following sentences:

(14) 論文はもう書いてしまった。
　　 I've already finished writing the thesis.
(15) 4時なのに、もう暗い。
　　 Although it is 4:00, it's already dark.
(16) もうだめだ！
　　 I'm already doomed.
(17) 彼はもう彼女に会わないだろう。
　　 He will probably no longer meet her.
(18) おなかが苦しくて、もう食べられない。
　　 I am too full and cannot eat any more.

2.6.2 まだ

The fundamental meaning of まだ is to express a continued, unchanged situation. This attribute contributes to the creation of two interpretations: "still" and "not yet." In either case, a sentence with まだ describes a situation where no change has yet taken place in the situation described. For example, if one says "I still like him," the feelings of the speaker for that person continue in the same manner as

---

[4] The change can be associated with either the onset of the activity or its completion—completion being the attainment of the endpoint (goal) of the activity. See Jacobsen (1983).

before. If one says "I have not eaten yet," the situation of not having eaten continues from a point in the past up to the current moment.

(19)　雪はまだ降っている。
　　　It is still snowing.

(20)　冬は朝7時でも外はまだ暗い。
　　　It is still dark around 7:00 in the morning in winter.

(21)　明日試験なのに、まだ何もしていない。
　　　Even though I have an exam tomorrow, I have not done anything.

(22)　一週間前に母に送った荷物はまだ届いていない。
　　　The package I sent to my mother a week ago has not yet arrived.

When まだ is used with a negative predicate in response to a もう〜ましたか question, ている has to occur with まだ. Simple negative predicates, such as まだ〜ません or まだ〜ませんでした are *inappropriate* responses to a もう〜ましたか question.[5]

(23)　a.　もうばんご飯を食べましたか。
　　　　　Have you already eaten dinner?
　　　b.　はい、もう食べました。
　　　　　Yes, I have.
　　　c.　いいえ、まだ食べていません。
　　　　　No, I haven't eaten yet.
　　　　　(まだ、食べません or まだ、食べませんでした are ungrammatical responses.)

(24)　a.　もう部屋をそうじしましたか。
　　　　　Have you already cleaned your room?
　　　b.　はい、もうしました。
　　　　　Yes, I have.

---

[5] In fact, depending on the type of the verb, the まだ〜しません pattern can be used. However, since the use of ている is always appropriate, it is recommended that beginners use ている with まだ. Further discussion is found in Johnson (2001, 2002).

c. いいえ、まだしていません。
      No, I haven't cleaned the room yet.
(25) a. 外はもう暗くなりましたか。
      Has it become dark outside?
   b. ええ、もう暗くなりましたよ。
      Yes, it has become dark.
   c. いいえ、まだ暗くなっていません。
      No, it hasn't become dark yet.

2.7　だけ and しか

だけ and しか are both dependent constituents that have to follow another word. The English equivalent of だけ and しか is "just" and/or "only," and the primary function of the words is to constitute an adverbial phrase that modifies a verb or an い/な adjective. Although their English equivalent is "only," the syntactic and semantic functions of だけ and しか differ slightly.[6]

だけ may follow a noun and constitutes a nominal phrase, such as 好きな人はあなただけです "The only person I like is you," or it may follow a noun that is used as an adverbial phrase, such as 本田さんだけ来た "Only Mr. Honda came." しか, on the other hand, when used in an adverbial phrase, requires a negative form of the predicate[7] to occur, and emphasizes the fact described by the affirmative of the predicate or that the event, situation, number, and so on is worse or less than what the speaker expected. For example, if しか replaces だけ in 好きな人はあなただけです and 本田さんだけ来た the sentence has to be: 好きな人はあなたしかいません "There is no one except you whom I like" (not with the copula だ but with the verb いる) and 田中さんしか来なかった "No one except Mr. Tanaka came." Compare the following sentences in terms of meaning and structure.

---

[6] Further discussion is found in Kuno (1998a).

[7] In casual communication, however, a word with a negative connotation is sometimes used with しか. This is similar to the phenomenon of the adverbial ぜんぜん "not at all," which is often used with a word with a negative connotation. For example, これしかだめだ "only this is bad" indicates the same meaning as "only this does not work," and ぜんぜんだめだ "it is all bad" indicates the same meaning as "it is not good at all."

(26) a. おすしが一つだけ残っている。
Just one piece of sushi is remaining.
b. おすしが一つしか残っていない。
Nothing is remaining except one piece of sushi./Only one piece of sushi is remaining. (The sentence implies that the speaker expected more sushi to be remaining.)
(27) a. 私にはあなただけいる。
The person I have is just you.
b. 私にはあなたしかいない。
I have no one but you whom I love./The person I have is only you.
(28) a. あの人はおもしろいだけだ。
The attribute of that person is just "interesting." (Implies that there is no other particular characteristic that the person carries.)
b. あの人はきれいなだけだ。
The attribute of that person is just "pretty." (Implies that there is no other particular characteristic that the person carries.)
c. あの人はきれいでしかない。
That person is pretty, but just that.

The use of だけ and しか in sentences (26) conveys what the speaker's expectation was. When しか is used, the speaker's expectation about the number of remaining sushi is clearly indicated, but だけ does not express any strong expectation. だけ states the event/situation rather objectively, indicating the fact without the speaker's evaluative feeling. For this reason, sentence (26b) sounds better than (26a). As may be seen in sentences (28a) and (28b), だけ can occur with both い and な adjectives, while しか can occur only with a な adjective and is located between the copula で and ない.

Sample dialogues

一円玉しかないけど・・・
"I don't have any money, except 10 yen..."
男: 悪いけど、お金、貸してもらえないかな。
女: 悪いけど、10円しか持っていないの・・・。

男： あ、10円でいいんだ。電話するだけだから。
女： 一円玉10個で？　(with ten pennies?)

僕が愛しているのは君だけだ
チビ： タマさん、僕は君しか愛せない。本当だ信じてほしい。
タマ： まあ、何言ってるの！　あそこにいる1ダース(one dozen)の子供たちはいったい誰の子なの？みんなあなたと同じ顔してるわ。
チビ： ・・・。
タマ： あっちこっちで子供作って、何が「君だけだ」よ。笑わせないで。
　　　(You are kidding me, aren't you?)
チビ： でも本当なんだ。僕には君しかいないんだ・・・。
タマ： じゃ、証明してちょうだい。(Prove it.)

CHAPTER 18

Nominalizers: こと・の

"To nominalize" means to change a verb or a sentence into a noun phrase. For example, in order to alter the English verb "eat" into a noun, it has to be changed into either "to eat" (infinitive form) in "I love to eat" or "eating" (gerund form) in "My hobby is eating." Both "to eat" and "eating" function as noun phrases, like the nouns in "I love *cats*" and "My hobby is *tennis*." In order to change a single sentence into a noun phrase, the speaker must embed it in a "that" clause or form a relative clause by adding it to a head noun. For example, sentences, such as "Columbus discovered America," "Columbus was an Italian," and "Columbus was tall and muscular," have to be embedded in a suordinate clause, or constitute a relative clause, as in "that Columbus discovered America," "the fact that Columbus was an Italian," and "the information that Columbus was tall and muscular." Observe the following:

(1) a. I love <u>to eat</u>.
    b. My hobby is <u>eating</u>.
(2) a. I learned <u>that</u> Columbus discovered America.
    b. I found <u>the fact that</u> Columbus was an Italian.
    c. I obtained <u>the information that</u> Columbus was tall and muscular.

In Japanese, こと and の are nominalizers that can change a verb, an い adjective, a な adjective, or a sentence into a noun phrase. They can also act as pronouns, but the pronoun too constitutes a noun phrase. Therefore, in either case, こと and の make the preceding noun or verb phrase into a noun phrase. The fundamental meanings and attributes of こと and の play a crucial role in their different usages.

A summary of the use of こと and の is given at the end of this chapter. You may refer to the chart to grasp the whole picture.

The fundamental meaning of こと(事) is "thing" or "fact," but it is morphologically dependent and constitutes a noun phrase by accompanying another phrase. Although こと is morphologically dependent, because it possesses a concrete meaning, the whole こと phrase can be recognized as a proper, morphologically independent noun phrase that can be used as a title, for example. の is a dependent morpheme, but unlike こと, の itself does not have a concrete meaning. Its function is merely to alter a phrase or a sentence into a morphological noun phrase. Therefore, when a phrase is followed by の, it cannot act as a proper, morphologically independent noun phrase which can be a title.[1] Where の is used as a pronoun, the meaning that the の phrase represents depends on context (Johnson, 2005b).

1. こと
1.1 こと as a pronoun

Based on the characteristics described in the previous paragraphs, the general assumption is that when こと acts as a *pronoun* representing nouns, such as "thing," "fact," "news," "information" "story," "case," "idea," "report," and "rumor," the main predicate of the sentence is one that requires this type of a noun phrase as a sentential object. Such predicates are 学ぶ "to learn," 考える "to think," 知る "to know," 聞く "to ask (and obtain information)," 信じる "to believe," 認める "to approve," 伝える "to notify/convey," 広まる "to be spread," and so on. の is usually not an appropriate option with such verbs.[2] Observe the following examples, which include こと phrases as sentential objects for the verbs mentioned above:

---

[1] For example, 新聞をとること "subscribing to a newspaper" 神様が言うこと "what god says, God's oracle" are independent noun phrases and can be titles, while 新聞をとるの and 神様の言うの are considered noun phrases, but must be used in larger sentences, such as 新聞をとるのをやめた "I quit subscribing to a newspaper," and 神様が言うのを聞いた "I heard what God said," functioning as nominalizer and pronoun, respectively.

[2] However, this observation is not absolute. Perceptions differ from person to person, and which nominalizer is more appropriate sometimes may not receive consensus.

(1) a. コロンブスがアメリカを発見した[こと/*の]を学んだ。
We learned the fact that Columbus discovered America.
b. 日本語を専攻する[こと/*の]を考えた。
I thought of the idea that I major in Japanese.
c. 憲法は男女が平等の権利を持つ[こと/*の]を認める。
The constitution approves the claim that men and women have equal rights.
d. 新しい先生の試験はむずかしい[こと/*の]を学生の間に広めた。
I spread the rumor that the new professor's exams are difficult.
e. 前大統領が亡くなった[こと/?の]を知った。
I came to know (the fact) that the former president passed away.
f. ジョンがドイツ語が話せる[こと/?の]を知っている。
I know (the fact) that John can speak German.
g. 死後の世界がある[こと/?の]を信じている。
I believe (the idea) that there is a world after death.
h. 息子が帰って来る[こと/の]を信じている。
I believe (the luck) that my son will return.

In association with verbs such as 知る and 信じる, which are concerned with an individual's state of mind, the use of こと and の starts to show some variations, though こと remains the primary choice for these verbs. If either may be used, but こと is chosen over の, the sentence exhibits the existence of a head noun, such as "the fact" and "the idea," and the こと phrase is presented as a semantic unit of an independent object. This observation may correspond to the English equivalent in sentences (1e) through (1h) where the sentences are perfectly acceptable without head nouns like "the fact," "the idea," or "the luck." In English too, these nouns give a more concrete representation to what is "known" or "believed" by the speaker.

1.2 こと as a nominalizer

{ Stative-transitive predicate: 食べることが好きです
  〜ことです: 趣味は食べることです

こと acts as a nominalizer: (1) when a stative-transitive predicate, such as 好き "like" or 得意 "be good at," takes an object that involves a verb; and (2) when the copula です follows a verb phrase. In the former case, こと and の are interchangeable, although preference is often given to の. In the latter case, only こと may properly be used. This is due to the fact that です follows a real noun. As explained earlier, the morpheme の itself cannot form a morphologically independent noun phrase. For example, 食べるの "eating" itself cannot be a proper, independent noun phrase; it has to be used in a sentence followed by a particle. On the other hand, 食べること is a complete, morphologically independent noun phrase that can be used as a title. See the following examples:

(2) a. 私は泳ぐ[こと/の]が好きだ。
I like swimming./I like to swim.
b. 太郎は英語を話す[こと/の]が嫌いだ。
Taro does not like speaking English./Taro does not like to speak English.
c. メリーは日本の歌を歌う[こと/の]が得意だ。
Mary is good at singing Japanese songs.
d. メリーは水に潜る[こと/の]が怖いらしい。
Mary seems to be scared of diving into the water.
e. 花子はフランス語を話す[こと/*の]ができる。
Hanako is able to speak French.

Cf. できる invites only a こと phrase as it is a set phrase which means "can do."

(3) a. 趣味はカラオケで歌を歌う[*の/こと]です。
My hobby is <u>singing</u> songs at a karaoke bar.
b. 特技は動物を訓練する[*の/こと]です。
My special ability is <u>to train</u> animals.
c. 頭痛の種は子供が学校を休む[*の/こと]です。
The source of my headache is my kid's <u>skipping</u> class.

The meaning "fact" or "thing" does not quite give the proper nuance for these sentences. こと in sentences like these is a nominalizer, not a word in itself.

2. の
2.1 の as a pronoun：〜のは〜です/〜のは〜ことです

In cleft sentences, such as その男を見たのは私です "The person who saw the man is I (It is I who saw the man)," for example, の is used as a pronoun representing an attribute of a noun in the main predicate. In this example, の refers to "the person," because the main predicate 私 refers to a person.[3] If the sentence is 私が生まれたのは6月です "The month I was born (in) is June," の refers to the month of June indicated in the predicate. This means that the referent for の can be found only in the noun of the main predicate. This observation is supported by usages shown in sentences (1a) through (1f).

However, when the main predicate includes a verb nominalized by こと, it is no longer the case; the verb allows the attachment of こと as well, representing the attribute of the verbal predicate as a pronoun, as seen in 私が毎日しなければならないの/ことは練習です "*The thing* that I must do every day is *to practice*." In this example sentence, the thing corresponds to "to practice," which is a verbal phrase. This observation is supported by sentences (2a) through (2e), where either の or こと is applicable.

(1) a. その男を見た[の/*こと]は私の妹です。(の = the person)
       The person who saw the man is my sister.
     b. 私が生まれた[の/*こと]は東京です。(の = the place)
       The place I was born (in) is Tokyo.
     c. 松田さんに会う[の/*こと]は明日です。(の = the day)
       The day I am meeting Mr. Matsuda is tomorrow.
     d. 私が嫌いな[の/*こと]は黒です。(の = the color)
       The color that I dislike is black.
     e. 母が飼いたかった[の/*こと]は犬です。猫じゃありません。
       (の = the animal/pet)
       The animal that my mother wanted to have is a dog, not a cat.

---

[3] Also, remember if の and こと follow a form other than the dictionary form, they are not used as nominalizers. For example, in 松田さんが書いたのを見た, の is serving as a pronoun, meaning "I saw *something* that Matsuda wrote." の in this sentence cannot be considered a nominalizer, since it follows the た form of the verb. On the other hand, in 松田さんが書くのを見た, の is serving as a nominalizer, meaning "I saw Matsuda write," following the dictionary form of the verb with the verb of seeing.

    f.   クラスを休んだ[の/*こと]は頭がいたかったからです。
        (の = the reason)
        <u>The reason</u> I missed class was that <u>I had a headache</u>.

(2) a.   好きな[の/こと]は食べる<u>こと</u>です。
        <u>What/The thing</u> I love to do is <u>eating</u>.
    b. してはいけない[の/こと]は嘘をつく<u>こと</u>です。
        <u>What/The thing</u> you should not do is <u>to tell a lie</u>.
    c. 太郎が嫌いな[の/こと]は英語を話す<u>こと</u>です。
        <u>What/The thing</u> Taro dislikes is <u>speaking</u>.
    d. メリーが怖い[の/こと]は水に潜る<u>こと</u>です。
        <u>What/The thing</u> Mary is scared of is <u>to dive</u> into the water.
    e. ジョンが日本にいる間にしたかった[の/こと]は富士山に登る<u>こと</u>でした。
        <u>What/The thing</u> John wanted to do while in Japan was <u>to climb</u> Mt. Fuji.

2.2　の as a nominalizer

When the situation described by the main predicate is one that the speaker can directly perceive, partake in, or respond to in terms of something happening right then and there, の is used to nominalize the verb in the object of the sentence. For example, 発見する in 家の前の川で人が溺れているの/*ことを発見した "I found/discovered a person drowning in the river in front of my house" is considered a perception; therefore, 溺れている should be nominalized only by の, and こと is inappropriate.[4] This is due to the fact that the fundamental meaning of こと—"fact" or "thing"—interferes with the notion of perception, i.e., "I discovered/found the thing/fact that a person is drowning in front of me" is not what this sentence is meant to express. Observe some more examples that support the appropriateness of this principle:

---

[4] 発見する can also be used as a discovery of a fact. For example, "I discovered the fact that our professor was married to the chair of our department." In this case, the discovery was a piece of information, not a perception, as is represented by "the fact," こと should be used as a pronoun as in 私達の先生が学部長と結婚していること(事実)を発見した。

(3) a. 私はメリーが歩いている[の/*こと]を見た。
　　　　I saw Mary walking.
　　b. 背筋が冷たくなる[の/*こと]を感じた。
　　　　I felt a cold shiver run down my spine.
　　c. 私はメリーが夕飯を作る[の/*こと]を手伝った。
　　　　I helped Mary make dinner.
　　d. ジョンは老人がバスに乗る[の/*こと]を助けた。
　　　　John helped an elderly person onto the bus.
　　e. ジョンがドイツ語を話している[の/*こと]を聞いた。
　　　　I heard John speaking German.
Cf.　　 ジョンがドイツ語を話す[の/こと]を聞いた。
　　　　I heard/learned that John speaks German. or I heard/learned the fact that John speaks German.

The object of the verb given in the above sentences is not a concrete entity; rather it is an activity or feeling that the speaker can partake in or perceive. As seen in the comparison example following (3e), when the sentential object is presented as a fact that the speaker obtained/learned, こと can be used as a pronoun.

When the main predicate is not concerned with perception or partaking, either の or こと may be used relatively freely. In these cases, こと may be interpreted as a pronoun. Also, since こと makes the noun phrase morphologically independent (and can be used as a title, for example), it creates a more formal interpretation. In colloquial communication, の may be more frequently used. See the following examples:

(4) a. 兄はお酒を飲む[の/こと]をやめた。
　　　　My brother quit drinking./My brother quit an activity that is to drink.
　　b. 今後歩きながらたばこを吸う[の/こと]を禁じます。
　　　　From now on, we prohibit smoking while walking.
　　c. 脂肪分を摂りすぎる[の/こと]は健康によくありません。
　　　　Taking too much fat is bad for your health.

d. 若いうちに多くのことを経験する[の/こと]が大切です。
Experiencing many things while one is young is important.
e. 先生に3時に会う[の/こと]を忘れていた。
I had forgotten that I was supposed to meet my professor at three o'clock. / I had forgotten the appointment I made with my teacher to meet at three o'clock.

As observed thus far, こと and の are sometimes interchangeable, but sometimes only one is applicable to a sentence, making the rules quite complicated. Having a clear picture of the usages of の and こと may be difficult, since the interpretation is dependent on the main predicate of a sentence. Even for the same verb, depending on how it is perceived, the interpretation of の and こと may vary (as mentioned in n.4 regarding the verb 発見する). However, the semantic and morphological features of こと and の should provide at least a comprehensible picture of basic usages.

こと composes a morphologically independent noun phrase representing concrete meanings, such as "fact" and "thing." These meanings often play a crucial role in determining the function and the meaning of a sentence. Due to its morphological features, the copula です follows a noun phrase nominalized by こと without fail, as seen in 趣味は映画を見ることです "My hobby is seeing movies." Because こと represents meanings such as "fact" and "thing," こと is used as an indefinite pronoun with a verb that tends to invite these noun phrases, as seen in コロンブスがアメリカを発見したことを学んだ "We learned the fact that Columbus discovered America." In these cases, の is not an option.

の, on the other hand, cannot compose a morphologically independent noun phrase. It is used as a pronoun in the cleft sentence structure, as seen in 私が生まれたのは東京です "It is Tokyo where I was born (The place I was born is Tokyo)." It is also used as a nominalizer when the main predicate involves human perceptions, as may be seen in 私はメリーが歩いているのを見た "I saw Mary walking." Interpretations other than these have to rely on the meaning of the main predicate in the sentence—sometimes a pronoun, sometimes a nominalizer. The chart on the next page summarizes the uses of こと and の.

こと	1.	Verbs that inherently take a noun "fact," "thing," or a noun related to these meanings. コロンブスがアメリカを発見したことを学んだ。 We learned the fact that Columbus discovered America." 憲法は男女が平等の権利を持つことを認める。 The constitution approves the claim that men and women have equal rights.
	2.	When followed by です. 趣味はカラオケで歌を歌うことです。 My hobby is singing songs at a karaoke bar. 頭痛の種は子供が学校を休むことです。 The source of my headache is my kid's skipping class.
の	1.	Cleft sentence: "It is ~ that ~." 私が生まれたのは東京です。 It is Tokyo where I was born./The place I was born is Tokyo. 母が飼いたかったのは犬です。 It is a dog that my mother wanted to have./The animal that my mother wanted to have is a dog.
	2.	Verbs of perception in the main predicate. 私はメリーが歩いているのを見た。 I saw Mary walking. 背筋が冷たくなるのを感じた。 I felt a cold shiver run down my spine.
こと/の	1.	Object of stative-transitive predicates: 私は泳ぐこと/のが好きだ。 I like swimming./I like to swim. メリーは水に潜ること/のがこわいらしい。 Mary seems to be scared of diving in the water.
	2.	Interpretation of either pronoun or nominalization can apply. 兄はお酒を飲むの/ことをやめた。 My brother quit drinking./My brother quit an activity that is to drink alcohol. 歩きながらたばこを吸うの/ことを禁じます。 We prohibit smoking while walking./We prohibit an activity that is to smoke while walking.

	3.	Used as a pronoun indicating either "what" or "the thing."
		好<ruby>す</ruby>きなの/ことは食<ruby>た</ruby>べることです。
		What/The thing I love to do is eating./My favorite thing is to eat.
		ジョンが日本<ruby>にほん</ruby>にいる間<ruby>あいだ</ruby>にしたかったの/ことは富士山<ruby>ふじさん</ruby>に登<ruby>のぼ</ruby>ることでした。
		What/The thing John wanted to do while in Japan was to climb Mt. Fuji.
		私<ruby>わたし</ruby>が知<ruby>し</ruby>りたかったの/ことは彼<ruby>かれ</ruby>の趣味<ruby>しゅみ</ruby>です。
		What/The thing I wanted to find out is his hobbies.

CHAPTER 19

Modal Auxiliaries (Modals): Propositions and Modality Expressions

---

In Japanese, as opposed to English, proposition and modality expressions are relatively easy to distinguish in a sentence, as modality expressions usually follow the non-past or past tense marker. A proposition is a statement of fact or the substance of a case expressed in a sentence. Modality expressions are constituents of a sentence and are often modal auxiliaries (*modals*) that are used to indicate a speaker's opinion or psychological attitude toward a proposition. Observe the following diagram depicting the structure of propositional content and modal content:

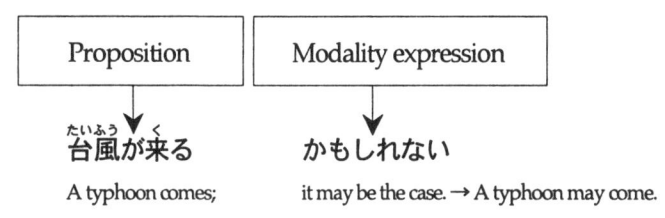

Proposition	Modality expression
台風(たいふう)が来(く)る	かもしれない
A typhoon comes;	it may be the case. → A typhoon may come.

The meanings that the English modal "may" creates are sometimes ambiguous, indicating a speaker's belief or permission, for example. However, in Japanese, there is no modal that represents two different meanings; a speaker's conjecture and permission are expressed by different morphemes. The following sentences exemplify the difference between English structure and Japanese structure.

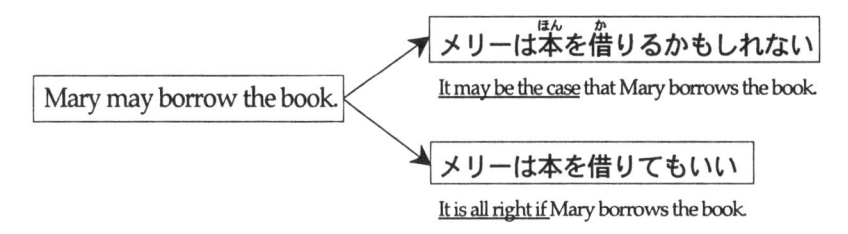

Mary may borrow the book.
→ メリーは本(ほん)を借(か)りるかもしれない
  It may be the case that Mary borrows the book.
→ メリーは本を借りてもいい
  It is all right if Mary borrows the book.

In the above two sentences, かもしれない, which is used to express a low degree of speaker conviction regarding the truth of Mary's borrowing the book, is in the category of true modals, while 借りてもいい falls under the category of propositions.[1]

Expressions that fall into the category of true modals include そうだ "I hear," そうだ "appears to be," らしい "I hear, it seems like," ようだ・みたいだ "it looks like," はずだ "it must be," にちがいない "it must be," だろう "it probably is," かもしれない "it may be," 〜のだ "it is that," わけだ "it is the case that," and so forth (Johnson, 1998b, 2004a). There are some combinations of these modal auxiliaries that may lengthen a sentence, such as だろうというように思う and so forth. This writing style is one of the techniques used to express an author's opinion or attitude toward a proposition more implicitly, as it is often the case that a writer tends to avoid a strong-sounding, definite statement in Japanese.

In analyzing a sentence, first separate a modality expression (if there is any) from the proposition and concentrate on understanding the meaning of the proposition. See the schematic below.

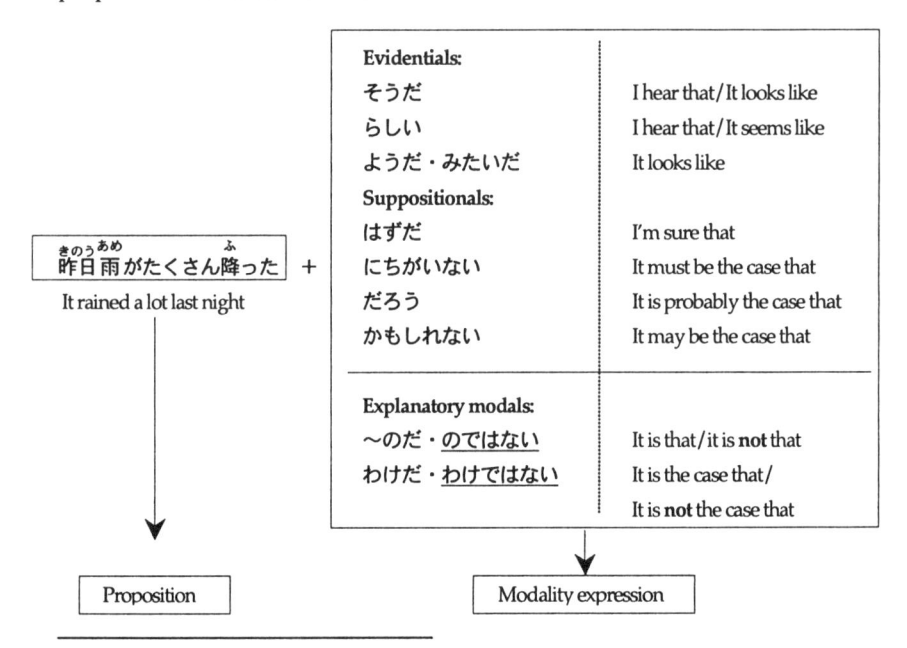

	Evidentials:	
	そうだ	I hear that/It looks like
	らしい	I hear that/It seems like
	ようだ・みたいだ	It looks like
	Suppositionals:	
昨日雨がたくさん降った +	はずだ	I'm sure that
It rained a lot last night	にちがいない	It must be the case that
	だろう	It is probably the case that
	かもしれない	It may be the case that
	Explanatory modals:	
	〜のだ・のではない	It is that/it is **not** that
	わけだ・わけではない	It is the case that/ It is **not** the case that

↓ ↓
Proposition   Modality expression

---

[1] 借りてもいい can invite a modal: 借りてもいい かもしれない "It may be the case that she is allowed to borrow the book."

1. Evidential Modals

そう, よう, and らしい belong to the same category, provisionally called "evidential" that is concerned with a speaker's visual or sensory perceptions.[2]

1.1 そう

そう can function in two ways depending on the preceding form: when そう is preceded by the stem form of the verb, it means "it looks like ~/it is about to ~," the so-called visual そう; when そう is preceded by the casual form of the verb, it means "I hear that ~," the so-called hearsay そう.

1.1.1 Visual そう

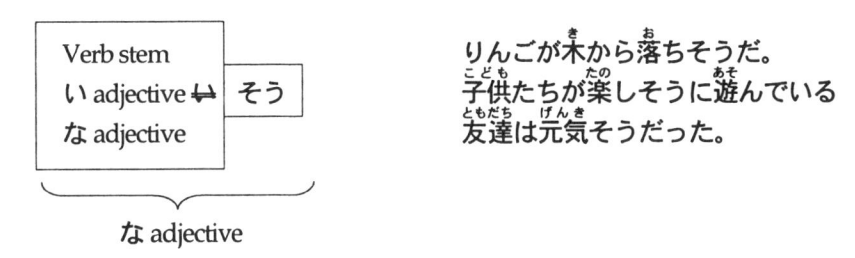

Verb stem	
い adjective ↤	そう
な adjective	

な adjective

りんごが木から落ちそうだ。
子供たちが楽しそうに遊んでいる
友達は元気そうだった。

(Note that そう does not occur with きれい. Also, ない becomes なさそう and いい becomes よさそう.)

そう is used when a speaker makes a judgment based on some visual or sensory impression of a situation; it involves the speaker's conjecture about the truth of the proposition. It is usually interpreted as "It looks like ~," "It feels like ~," or "It smells like ~." For example, おいしそう may be uttered based on the appearance of the food in front of the speaker indicating "It looks delicious," or it may be uttered based on the food smells coming from the kitchen, for example, indicating "It smells delicious." Or it may be the case that someone is describing the food and the listener, picturing it mentally, utters おいしそう！ "The picture I have in mind based on your description of the food looks delicious."

If a speaker is observing an entity that is obviously big, 大きそうだ "it looks big" is an inappropriate expression. For example, standing in front of the

---

[2] See also Kamio (1997a).

Grand Canyon, one might say, "It's big!" but not "It looks big!" 大きそうだ is used when the speaker surmises the size of the entity based on the surrounding sensory evidence.

A description of an event described by a verb, such as 雨が降りそうだ can be interpreted as either "It looks like it is going to rain this afternoon" or "It is about to rain," depending on the speaker's situation. The basic premise underlying the use of そう with a verb is that when a verb, usually an intransitive verb, describes a change of state, such as 倒れる, 落ちる, and 死ぬ, the そう sentence means "something is about to occur/something is almost in ~ state." When the verb is a stative or an action predicate, such as 晴れる "to be sunny," 歩く "to walk," and 勝つ "to win," the そう sentence tends to mean "something looks like ~."

In the case of negatives, preceding い adjectives and な adjectives change form to the negative form, for example, おいしくなさそう and 元気じゃなさそう. For verbs, そうに(も)ない, as in 降りそうに(も)ない, is usually used. Remember that a predicate with そう is a な adjective. See the following examples:

(1) 木が倒れそうだ。
A tree is about to fall (almost falling).

(2) a. おなかがすいて死にそうだ。
I'm about to die (almost dying).[3]
b. 死にそうな人
a person who is almost dead
c. 死にそうもない
It does not look like he is going to die.
d. 死にそうになっている
in the state of almost being dead

(3) 今日は午後から晴れそうだ。
It looks like it's going to be sunny this afternoon.

(4) このケーキはおいしそうだ。
This cake looks delicious.

(5) a. あの人は今日も暇そうだ。
That person looks bored today, too.

---

[3] The speaker is observing the condition of him/herself as a third person. This is a figure of speech.

b. 暇そう<u>な</u>人。
   a person who looks bored
c. 暇じゃ<u>なさそう</u>だ。
   It does not look like s/he is busy.
d. 暇<u>そうに</u>している。
   He looks like he is bored.

Sample dialogues

こわそうな映画は見たくありません
妻: ねえ、今晩この映画見ない？とってもおもしろそうよ。
夫: パンプキンヘッド(Pumpkin Head)？なんかこわそうな映画だなあ・・・。
妻: あらそうなの？私ハロウィーンの映画かと思った。
夫: うん、だからこわいんじゃないの？
妻: あ、そっか。

ばかなどろぼう
妻: ちょっと、ちょっと、あなた来て！男の人がとなりの家の窓から落ちそうになっているわ！
男: 助けて〜！
夫: ちょっと待ってて、今助けるから。

男: はあ・・・助かりました。ありがとうございました。ちょっとよさそうな家だったので、中に入ったら、すごい犬がいましてね・・・。追いかけられて・・・。ああ、死にそうだった・・・。
夫: え？なんでこの家に入ったの？
    あ、お前、どろぼうだろ！
    (to his wife) おい、警察に電話しろ！
男: 助けてぇ！

1.1.2 Hearsay そう

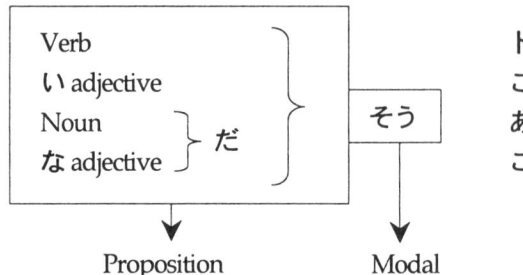

```
┌─────────────┐
│ Verb        │
│ い adjective │          
│ Noun     ┐だ │ ─ そう
│ な adjective┘│
└─────────────┘
      ↓              ↓
 Proposition       Modal
```

トムは日本へ行くそうだ。
このすしはまずいそうだ。
あの人は教授だそうだ。
この辞書は便利だそうだ。

そう following the casual form of a part of speech is used to express something a speaker heard. A そう sentence is semantically the same as 私は〜と聞きました "I heard that ~." Since a そう sentence implicitly includes the subject "I," it should not have an explicit 私は in it. In casual conversation, ですって is often used as a contracted form of だそうです. Remember that only one hiragana character decides the meaning of the sentence.

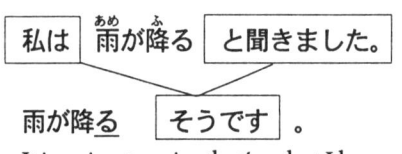

私は | 雨が降る | と聞きました。   I heard that it is going to rain.

雨が降る | そうです | 。
It is going to rain; that's what I hear.

(6) あの店のすしはおいしいそうですが、そのとなりの店のすしはおいしくないそうです。
I hear that sushi at that restaurant is delicious, but sushi at the next restaurant is not good.

(7) 先生の犬は元気だそうですが、猫はあまり元気じゃないそうです。
I hear that the professor's dog is fine, but her cat is not in good health.

(8) 先生のお父さんも大学の物理学の教授だったそうです。
I heard/learned that the professor's father was also a university physics professor.

1.2　よう(みたい)

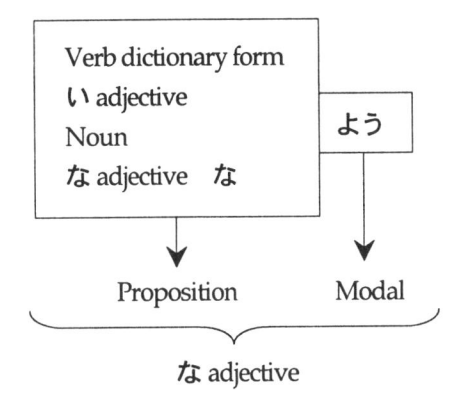

```
┌─────────────────────┐
│ Verb dictionary form │
│ い adjective         │   よう
│ Noun                 │
│ な adjective　な    │
└─────────────────────┘
         │           │
         ▼           ▼
     Proposition   Modal
     ⎵_____⎵
            な adjective
```

彼は日本語ができるようだ。
大阪は物価が安いようだ。
彼は日本人のように話す。
この辞書は便利なようだ。

The visual そう and よう are very similar in that both involve a speaker's visual impression of the situation. よう is also usually translated as "looks like," with the slight difference that よう involves a greater degree of the speaker's conjecture and feelings regarding the truth or realization of the event in question. Therefore, when a situation is about to happen and possesses a sense of urgency, よう is not appropriate. Also, よう usually creates a spatio-temporal distance between the event in question and the speaker. For example, 雨が降りそうだ can mean "It looks like it is about to rain," while 雨が降るようだ means "It looks like, and I feel like, it may rain." 木が倒れそうだ indicates the immediate situation where the tree is about to fall down, but if 木が倒れるようだ is substituted, the event described by the verb is unlikely to be occurring right in front of the speaker's eyes at the time of speech. The adverb どうやら, which shows the speaker's conjecture, often co-occurs with a よう sentence. The use of よう thus creates a certain temporal distance from the event. In casual conversation, みたい often takes over for よう.[4] Let's observe example sentences comparing よう and そう sentences:

---

[4] Please note that みたい and よう are interchangeable in terms of meaning here, although they are not completely interchangeable syntactically. When よう follows a verb or an い adjective, よう can be replaced by みたい in any tense, such as 日本へ行ったようだ/日本へ行ったみたいだ "Looks like s/he went to Japan" and おいしいようだ/おいしいみたいだ "Looks delicious." However, when よう follows a noun or a な adjective, 日本人のようだ "S/he looks [like] Japanese" becomes 日本人みたいだ and 元気なようだ "S/he looks healthy" becomes 元気のようだ.

(9) 明日もクイズがあるようだ。

It looks like (and I feel like) there is a quiz tomorrow too.

Cf. 明日もクイズがありそうだ。

It looks like there is a quiz tomorrow too.

(10) 彼は可愛がっていた犬に死なれて、悲しいようだ。

I surmise that he is sad because his adored dog died on him.

Cf. 彼は可愛がっていた犬に死なれて、悲しそうだ。

He appears to be sad because his adored dog died.

(11) 地下鉄を使うのが一番便利なようだ。

I surmise that using the subway looks like the most convenient way.

Cf. 地下鉄を使うのが一番便利そうだ。

It looks like using the subway is the most convenient way.

(12) どうやらあの人はドイツ人のようだ。[5]

It looks like he is German.

Cf. *どうやらあの人はドイツ人そうだ。

(Since そう cannot occur with a noun, よう has to be used instead.)

1.3 らしい

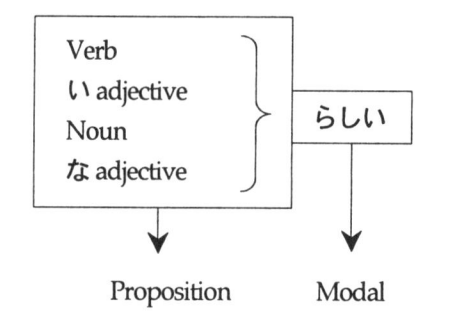

Verb		
い adjective	らしい	
Noun		
な adjective		

先生はオフィスにいるらしい。
あの人は EQ が高いらしい。
新しい先生は日本人らしい。
この建物は有名らしい。

Proposition — Modal

---

[5] When よう follows a noun, it is also used to express a figure of speech "as if ~." For example, あの人はドイツ人のようだ can also mean "that person looks as if he were German" expressing that the person is in fact not German, but looks/behaves/talks, etc. as if he were. Therefore, there are two possible interpretations for あの人はドイツ人のようだ: "Based on the characteristics he presents, I surmise that person is German" or "(Although he is not), that person looks as if he were German." The use of the adverb まるで "as if" or どうやら "somehow/somewhat" explicates these meanings of よう. For example, まるで雪のようだ means "it is as if it is snow (implies that it is not snow)" and どうやら雪のようだ "it somehow feels like snow is coming."

らしい is used when the speaker's subjective judgment is added to what the speaker has heard from an outside source. In this sense, the use of らしい is very similar to that of hearsay そうだ. Although it is hard to find an exact equivalent in English, the most appropriate interpretation of a らしい sentence may be "I hear and I guess it is probably the case" and "It seems like ~." らしい can be located between the following auxiliaries:

雨が降るそう	I hear that it's going to rain.
雨が降るらしい	I hear that it will rain, and I feel like it is going to be the case.
雨がふるよう	It looks like it is going to rain, and I feel like it is going to be the case.
雨が降りそう	It looks like it is going to/about to rain.)

(13) クラスがキャンセルになったらしい。
I hear that the class was canceled, and I feel like it was the case.

(14) カナダは中国人の人口が多いらしい。
Speaking of Canada, I hear that the Chinese population is large, and I feel like it is the case.

(15) その話はどうも嘘らしい。
Speaking of that story, it sounds like a lie.

(16) 彼は今年で100才になるが、まだ元気らしい。
He is going to be 100 years old this year, but it seems that he is still in good health.

1.3.1 Another use of らしい (to express similarity to expectation)

らしい demonstrates another meaning when it links a noun with a repetition of that noun. In this case, らしい is used to express that the attributes of the noun meet a certain image or expectation. For example, 子供らしい子供 means "a kid who behaves like a kid," 先生らしい先生 "the teacher who embodies teacherness." The second noun may sometimes be omitted, as in あの人は本当に日本人らしいねえ "that person creates an atmosphere of true Japanese," "that person seems really Japanese." The meaning should be identified by context.

Sample dialogue

ゴシップ "gossip"

ミミ: ねえ、ご存知？State Street のチビさん、University Street のタマさんに恋をしているらしいですよ。

ミケ: へえ、あのチビさんが？彼は奥さんがあちらこちらにいるらしいですよ。子供も１ダースいるらしいし・・・。それなのに、今度はタマさんですか？ずいぶんプレイボーイですねぇ。

ミミ: 本当に。まあタマさんはきれいだから、好きになるのもわかりますけどね。でもね、それだけじゃないんですよ。Washington Street のタビさんも、どうやらタマさんのことが好きらしいんですよ。

ミケ: へえ、タビさんも？じゃあ、三角関係じゃないですか。でも、チビさんもタビさんもちょっと太っている (fat) でしょう。どうかなあ、タマさんは好きになるかなあ・・・。

2. Suppositional Modals

はず, にちがいない, だろう, and かもしれない belong to a category, provisionally called "suppositional," that is concerned with the degree of the speaker's conviction. はず exhibits the highest degree of speaker conviction that an event is true or realized, and かもしれない, the lowest.

Note that for these modals to function as purely modal, they have to be in the non-past form. If they occur in a clause in the past tense, they do not behave as modals, because they do not express the speaker's supposition. Also, modals do not form interrogative sentences, and はず is no exception.

2.1 はず

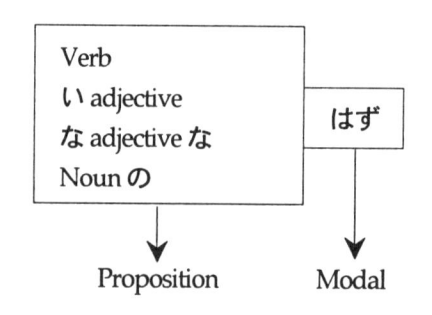

```
┌─────────────────┐
│ Verb            │
│ い adjective    │  はず
│ な adjective な │
│ Noun の         │
└─────────────────┘
      ↓            ↓
  Proposition    Modal
```

彼にはお金があるはずだ。
弟はお金はないはずだ。
この町はにぎやかなはずだ。
トムは学生のはずです。

はず can function as either a suppositional or a nominal, exhibiting meanings such as "must be," "ought to be," "expected to be," or "possibility," "reason," "plan." はず is used when a speaker makes a judgment based on objective grounds, and (used as a modal auxiliary) lies outside a proposition, indicating to the interlocutor that the speaker had firm evidence about the matter in question. Compared to other modal auxiliaries such as にちがいない, だろう, and かもしれない, はず expresses the highest degree of speaker conviction. As mentioned earlier, modals may not be used to form interrogative sentences, and はず is no exception.

(1) きのうは1000円使ったから、Since I spent 1000 yen yesterday,

| 財布には500円残っている | はずだ | 。

| 500 yen is remaining in my wallet | I'm sure. |

Since I spent 1000 yen yesterday, there should be 500 yen remaining in my wallet.

(2) 本田さんはもう帰っているはずです。
Ms. Honda is already home, I'm sure. (= Ms. Honda should already be home.)

(3) 昨日そうじしましたから、まだきれいなはずです。
Since I cleaned yesterday, I'm sure it is still clean.

(4) 彼は日本のパスポートを持っていますから、日本国籍のはずです。
Since he has a Japanese passport, I am sure that he is of Japanese nationality.

はず can also function as a noun, in which case it means "possibility," "reason," or "plan" (see below) and in such cases, it no longer functions as a modal. Since modals are concerned with the degree of speaker conviction toward the realization or truth of a proposition, they may not occur in the negative form. However, when はず is used as a noun, it can occur with negative, interrogative, or past tense forms. In negative contexts, はず<u>は</u>ない "there is no way that ~" rather than はずじゃない is often used.

(5) 私の人生、こんなはずじゃなかったのに・・・。
My life was not supposed to be this way...

(6) きのう論文を出しに来る<u>はずだった</u>んですが、車の事故があって、来られなくなってしまったんです。
I was supposed to come to submit my paper yesterday, but I became unable to do so due to a car accident.

Sample dialogue
そんなはずはありません・・・ (It cannot be that...)
女: あれ、ここに写っている人、堀田さんのお母さんでしょう？
男: え、写真？まさか。堀田さんのお母さんは2年前に亡くなったんだから、写真に写っているはずはないよ。
女: でも、見て、これ堀田さんのお母さんでしょ？
男: あ、そうだよ、これ・・・。
男/女: ぞ〜〜〜〜。

2.1.1 はず vs. ことになっている

When はず is used to indicate a plan, it can often be restated by ことになっている "it has been decided." The difference between these concepts is that while はず reflects the speaker's conjecture about the proposition, ことになっている is a statement concerned with a factual situation, and the statement itself is a proposition that can include another modal. For example, while the double use of the modals 行くはずかもしれない "It must be the case that s/he may go" is ungrammatical, 行くことになっている "It may be the case that s/he is supposed to go" is grammatical. The key to using either of these forms lies in context as well as the degree of the speaker's belief about the proposition. See the following examples:

(7) a. トムは今日はオフィスに来ないはずです。
I'm sure that Tom will not come to the office today.

b. トムは今日はオフィスに来ないことになっています。
It's been scheduled that Tom is not coming to the office today.

(8) ? a. 私は日本へ行くはずです。
I'm sure that I will go to Japan. (sounds as if you do not know about your own schedule)

b. 私は日本へ行くことになっています。
I'm supposed to go to Japan./It has been scheduled that I go to Japan.

(9) ? a. 本田さんは5時に来るはずですか。
Am I sure that Mr. Honda comes at five?

b. 本田さんは5時に来ることになっていますか。
Is Mr. Honda supposed to come at five?

(10) * a. 宿題は今日出すはずですか。
Am I sure that I am submitting the homework today?

b. 宿題は今日出すことになっていますか。
Are we supposed to submit the homework today?

As can be seen from (8a), (9a), and (10a), はず is awkward when used to describe the speaker's own schedule or activity, or to inquire about the validity of the proposition. "I am supposed to" is not necessarily the equivalent of はず; rather, it is the equivalent of ことになっている.

2.2 にちがいない

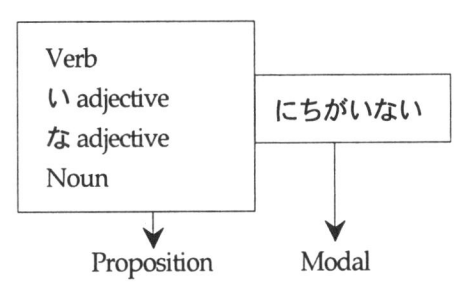

```
┌─────────────┐
│ Verb        │
│ い adjective │ ── にちがいない
│ な adjective │
│ Noun        │
└─────────────┘
      ↓            ↓
  Proposition    Modal
```

彼は物理学者だから、数学もできるにちがいない。
家は駅の前だから、うるさいにちがいない。
家は駅の前だから、便利にちがいない。
ここに写っているのは、幽霊にちがいない。

にちがいない "must be," derived from まちがいない "there is no mistake," is also a modal that expresses a high degree of speaker conviction. While はず has various functions, にちがいない functions only as a modal. It can sometimes express the speaker's belief based not on firm evidence, but on a sixth sense or intuition.

(11) 幽霊はこの世にいるにちがいない。
There must be ghosts in this world. (I believe in the existence of ghosts.)
(12) あの人は韓国人にちがいない。
That person must be Korean.
(13) 妹が変な顔をしているから、弟の作ったカレーはまずかったにちがいない。
Since my sister has a weird look on her face, the curry my brother made must have been bad.
(14) うちの猫は最近あまり食べなくなった。どこか悪いにちがいない。
My cat does not eat much lately. There must be something wrong with him.
(15) もう夜中の1時だ。両親が心配しているにちがいない。
It's already one o'clock in the morning. My parents must be worried about me.

2.3 だろう

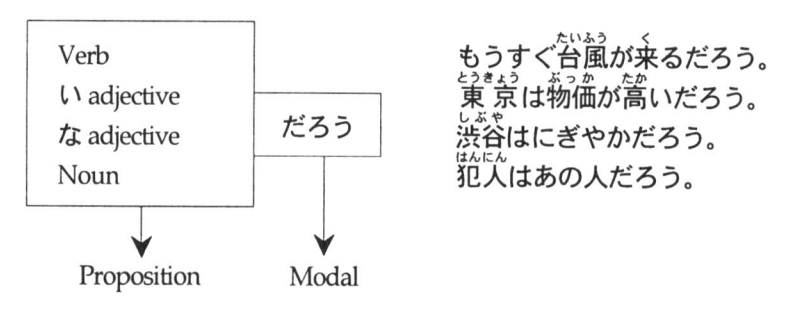

Verb / い adjective / な adjective / Noun	だろう
Proposition	Modal

もうすぐ台風が来るだろう。
東京は物価が高いだろう。
渋谷はにぎやかだろう。
犯人はあの人だろう。

だろう "perhaps," the casual equivalent of でしょう, is the most frequently used modal. It has various functions, such as expressing a marginal degree of speaker conviction and softening the tone of a sentence to avoid making a strong declarative statement. Also, it can occur with a variety of adverbs other than たぶん, and it is sometimes followed by the verb 思う, creating だろうと思う "I think that it is probably ~." Observe the following examples:

(16) 明日もたぶん雪だろう。
Perhaps it will snow tomorrow too.

(17) 山本さんは恐らく会議に出席しないだろう。
Perhaps Ms. Yamamoto won't attend the meeting.

(18) 来年の今頃はもう日本に帰っているだろうと思う。
I think that I probably will have gone back to Japan around this time next year.

(19) 今度の司法試験もあまりできなかった。きっとまただめだろう。
I did not do well on the bar exam this time, either. I guess I won't pass this year, either.

Note that だろう has another function: it is used in tag questions (although でしょう is commonly used as well). Whether だろう is used as a modal or a confirmation marker can be identified by intonation and context.

(20) a. その本は市の図書館にはなかったが、大学の図書館にはあるだろう。
The city library does not have that book, but the university library probably has it.

b. その本、大学の図書館にあるだろう？
Speaking of that book, the university library has it, right?

(21) a. 疲れただろう。
I guess you are tired.

b. 疲れただろう？
Your are tired, aren't you?

Sample dialogue
さあ、どうしよう

父親: アナーバーという町は本当に物価が高い町だね。家賃もきっと高いんだろうねえ。
案内人: ええ、とっても。小さいワンベッドのアパートが700ドルもするんですよ。
父親: 学生は生活が大変だろうなぁ・・・。だめだ。うちの娘はミシガン大学には入れられない。
案内人: でも、寮に住めば、少しは安くなるでしょう。それにアナーバーは安全な町ですから、お父さんも安心でしょう。
父親: そうだろうけど・・・。

2.4　かもしれない

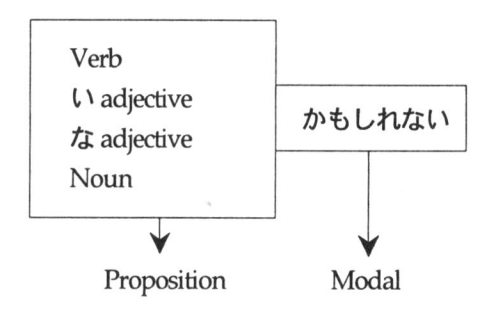

```
┌─────────────┐
│ Verb        │
│ い adjective │ ─── かもしれない
│ な adjective │
│ Noun        │
└─────────────┘
      ↓              ↓
  Proposition      Modal
```

来年は富士山に登るかもしれない。
このカレーはからいかもしれない。
彼は今日は暇かもしれない。
やさしい試験かもしれない。

かもしれない literally means "it cannot be known." Its root form is fundamentally negative, and the phrase acts in much the same way as an い adjective. かもしれない can be used when a speaker does not possess firm evidence, but judges a situation based on his/her intuition and the surrounding environment. Therefore, かもしれない is often used in reference to totally unknowable, imagined situations which are in the domain of epistemic possibility. A sentence with かもしれない can be interpreted as "it is possible that X happens," and it is simultaneously compatible with "it is possible that X does not happen." かもしれない implies neither that X will happen nor that X will not happen, but is compatible with both. For the most part it is used to express situations whose outcome cannot be determined by the speaker, i.e., indeterminable situations. The probability of the proposition's being true is low, since it is based solely on the speaker's intuitive judgment. Therefore, かもしれない reflects the hypotheticality of the proposition.

かもしれない can be attached to both past and non-past forms of verbs and い adjectives, and it selects a zero-form copula (without だ) when attached to nouns and な adjectival predicates. かもしれない cannot invite a question mark, but it can be used in the past.

(22) あしたはクイズがあるかもしれないし、ないかもしれない。
 Tomorrow, a quiz may be given or may not be given.
(23) あの人はインド人かもしれないが、よくわからない。
 That person might be an Indian, but I am not sure.
(24) 家が都会の真中にあるなら交通が便利かもしれないが、うるさいかもしれない。
 If your home is in the middle of the city, transportation may be convenient, but it [your home] may be noisy.
(25) バハマは楽しいかもしれないが、きっと高いだろう。
 The Bahamas may be fun, but they are probably expensive.
(26) お金があったら、[日本へ行った]かもしれない。
 If I had money, I might have gone to Japan. (counterfactual meaning)
(27) 意地悪な人だったら、[行き方を教えてくれなかった]かもしれない。
 If it had been a mean person, s/he might not have given me the directions. (counterfactual meaning)
(28) [その人は背が低かった]かもしれない。
 The person may have been short (but I don't remember.)
(29) [その人は日本人だった]かもしれない。
 The person could have been Japanese (but I am not sure).

As seen in sentences (26) and (27), when the proposition is in a past context and is combined with an "if" clause, かもしれない renders a counterfactual meaning. In general, かもしれない creates the meaning "It may be X, but it may not be X."

Sample dialogue
見たかもしれない、いや、見なかったかもしれない・・・
[警察で]
警部: それで、あなたが見た人というのはどんな人ですか。
男: それが、よく覚えていないんです・・・。背が高い人でしたが・・・。
警部: めがねをかけていましたか。
男: かけていたかもしれません。いや、かけていなかったかもしれない・・・。
警部: 髪の毛は？
男: 長かったかもしれない・・・、いや、短かったかもしれません
警部: 男ですか、女ですか。
男: 男だったかもしれません。いや、男じゃなかったかもしれません。
警官: 警部、だめですね、この人は。全然あてになりませんよ (we cannot count on him at all)。
警部: そうだな。
君はもう帰ってよろしい。
男: すみません、お役に立てなくて・・・。

3. Explanatory Modals
3.1 のだ (んです)

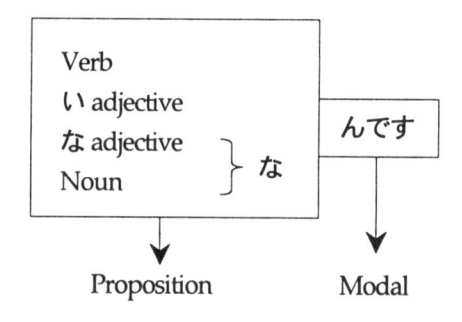

```
┌─────────────────┐
│ Verb            │
│ い adjective    │      ┌──────┐
│ な adjective    │ ─ な │ んです │
│ Noun            │      └──────┘
└─────────────────┘
        ↓                   ↓
    Proposition           Modal
```

私の夫(おっと)はよく食(た)べるんですが、痩(や)せています。
あの店(みせ)は安(やす)いんです。それでよく行(い)くんです。
あの先生(せんせい)は本(ほん)をたくさん書(か)くので、有名(ゆうめい)なんです。
田中(たなか)さんは４０才(よんじゅっさい)ですが、まだ学生(がくせい)なんです。

The phrase のだ／んです, often referred to as an "explanatory ending," has different characteristics from the evidential and suppositional modals. For both evidentials and suppositionals, the proposition is not known to be true or realized from the speaker's viewpoint. The speaker makes a judgment or assumption about the expressed proposition regardless of what the source of information may be. For example, in 彼女(かのじょ)は日本人(にほんじん)らしい "It seems that she is Japanese," らしい is used to indicate that the speaker does not know whether the proposition "She is Japanese" is an absolute truth or not. In other words, the given proposition is presented as being hypothetical.

Contrary to those modals, んです (as well as わけです, which is explained in Section 3.2) follows a proposition that is already known to be true to the speaker. The main function of んです is, then, to explain why the proposition needs to be presented. In addition to this function, んです has another function. The following summarizes its functions:

a. To deliver an explanation of the situation in question or reply to an explanation one receives.
b. To put emphasis on the speaker's emotion. のだ／んです is often used to show the speaker's surprise or irritation.

Also, as seen from the translations below, the use of んです tends to involve the interlocutor in the conversation. Simple です・ます declarative statements may give the impression that the speaker is being short or formal and can create a distance between the speaker and the listener. The use of んです, however, narrows this gap by involving the interlocutor in the conversation.

To understand the meanings of のだ／んです, please look at the following examples:

(1)　あのう、1ドル、借りたいんです
　　　Well, (I am speaking to you because) I want to borrow a dollar.

男：　どうしたんですか。
　　　(Can you explain) what happened to you (as you look troubled)?

女：　あの、お金がないんです。
　　　Well, (the reason I look troubled is that) I don't have money.

男：　ああ、それは困りましたね。少し貸しましょうか。
　　　You sure are in trouble. Shall I lend you some?

女：　え、いいんですか！？　ぜひお願いします。
　　　(Are you telling me that) you don't mind lending me some money? Please, by all means.

男：　いくら貸しましょうか。
　　　How much shall I lend you?

女：　じゃ、1ドルお願いします。
　　　Well, then a dollar will be good.

男：　え、1ドルでいいんですか。
　　　(Are you saying that) a dollar would be good?

(2)　結婚するんです
　　　(I want to tell you) I'm getting married.

女：　あの、実は私、マットさんと結婚するんです。
　　　(I want to explain my situation a bit, but) to tell you the truth, I am getting married to Matt.

男：　え、マットさんと結婚するんですか。あなたは５０才、マットさんは３０才、でしょう・・・？
　　　(Are you saying that) you are getting married to Matt? You are 50 and he is 30 years old... correct?

女：　ええ、でもいいんです。
　　　Yes, but (I'm telling you that) it's O.K. with us.

(3)　きょうはフランス語の試験があるんです
　　　I have a French exam today (so I'm going to skip Japanese class).

トム：　あ、サリーさん、日本語のクラスへ一緒に行きませんか。
　　　Sally, shall we go to Japanese class together?

サリー: あ、今日はちょっと・・・。
Well, today is not a good day...

トム: え、どうして？クラスを休むんですか。
How come? (Are you saying that) you are going to miss class? (If so, explain.)

サリー: フランス語の試験なんです。
I have a French exam (so I am going to skip Japanese class).

トム: あ、そうなんですか。じゃ、また・・・。（日本語も試験なのに、いいのかなあ・・・）
I see (that is the reason). Well, see you later. (There is a test for Japanese, too, but I wonder if it's O.K. with her to skip that...)

The English sentences in parentheses are what the speaker intends to imply by using んです. When a person is surprised or irritated, s/he usually wants to know the reason as well.

3.2 わけ

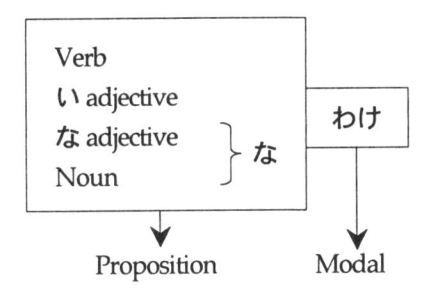

```
┌─────────────┐
│ Verb        │
│ い adjective │      ┌────┐
│ な adjective │ } な │ わけ │
│ Noun        │      └────┘
└─────────────┘
      │              │
      ▼              ▼
  Proposition      Modal
```

日本語を勉強しに、日本へ行くわけです。
料理の鉄人の料理だから、おいしいわけだ。
日本に10年いた。日本語が上手なわけだ。
ソニーか。道理でいい画面がきれいなわけだ。

わけ means "reason," and when it follows a proposition, わけ explains the reason for the proposition to be that way. When combined with どうりで、 it means "no wonder" which shows that the speaker realizes that there is a convincing reason. Although わけ is syntactically a modal, it is different from other modal auxiliaries such as にちがいない and かもしれない in that it is not used to express the degree of speaker conviction, but expresses the speaker's judgment, which is based on confirmed information or knowledge. わけ and はず are interchangeable when はず is used as a noun meaning "reason." Observe the use of わけ in the following dialogues.

(4) アメリカに10年もいれば、英語が上手になるわけだ

She has lived in America as long as 10 years. No wonder her English has improved.

本田: 本当に英語がお上手ですね。どのくらいアメリカにいらっしゃったんですか。

You speak English really well. How long have you been in America?

松田: 10年です。

10 years.

本田: ああ、どうりで上手なわけですよ。[6]

No wonder you speak so well.

(5) どうりで成績が悪かったわけです

No wonder I got a bad grade.

学生1: 哲学のクラスどうだった？

How did you do in the philosophy course?

学生2: Fだった。先輩が書いた論文をコピーして出したんだよ。

I got an F grade. I copied a paper that my senpai wrote and submitted it.

学生1: なんだ、同じ先生が読んだのか。それじゃ単位がもらえないわけだよ。

I see. The same professor (as the senpai) read the paper. No wonder you cannot receive credits.

---

[6] The んです construction can also be used in response to a preceding utterance. In such cases, however, the response will be だからじょうずなんですね "that's why you are so proficient" which means "now it makes sense (based on your explanation) why you speak English well." The same thing applies to sentence (5) どうりで成績が悪かったわけです. It will be だから成績が悪かったんです "That is why you got a bad grade" in the んです construction.

(6) 私の字はこんなにきたないから、道理で誰も読めないはずです。
Since my handwriting is so bad, no wonder no one can read it.

There are other phrases that have a somewhat similar function to modals, such as the following. They are not modals in the strict sense, but are verbs, and constitute a similar structure in that they follow a proposition.

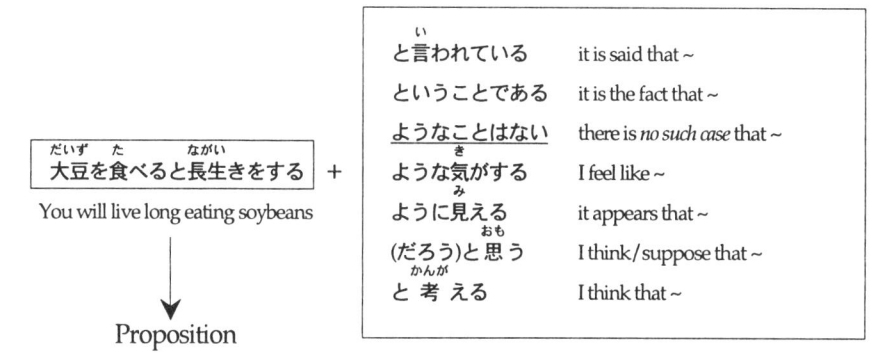

と言われている	it is said that ~
ということである	it is the fact that ~
ようなことはない	there is *no such case* that ~
ような気がする	I feel like ~
ように見える	it appears that ~
(だろう)と思う	I think/suppose that ~
と考える	I think that ~

大豆を食べると長生きをする +
You will live long eating soybeans
↓
Proposition

Although the proposition expresses the main point of the sentence, it does not mean that pseudomodality expressions can be ignored. Some expressions that include a negative morpheme, such as わけではない, and ようなことはない, negate the whole proposition and therefore change the meaning of the entire sentence, as seen in the following:

(7) [彼は自分の間違えを認めている] [のではない。]
He is admitting his own mistake; it is not the case.
→ implies that though he does not seem to admit that he made a mistake, he might be thinking about it.

(8) [若い人が政治に関心がない] [わけではない。]
Young people are not interested in politics; it is not the case.
→ There are young people who are interested in politics.

(9) [学生が先生に対して文句を言う] [ようなことはなかった。]
Students complained about the teacher; there was no such case.
→ Students did not complain about the teacher.

CHAPTER 20

Giving and Receiving

In Japanese, there are three verbs that are roughly equivalent to "give" and "receive" in English: あげる and くれる are equivalents to "give," and もらう to "receive." Since there are two verbs to express "to give," learners have to know the difference between あげる and くれる and make a clear distinction in the use of these verbs. The following diagram summarizes the use of these verbs:

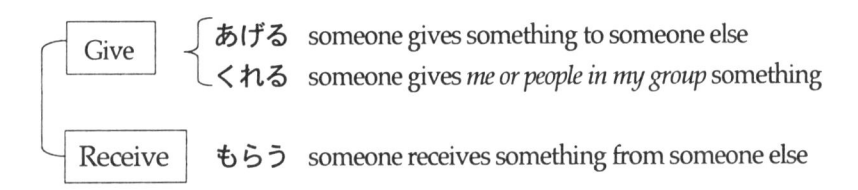

Give	あげる	someone gives something to someone else
	くれる	someone gives *me or people in my group* something
Receive	もらう	someone receives something from someone else

The use of these verbs depends on the speaker's viewpoint. For example, visualize a situation where a gift was sent from X to Y. From X's viewpoint, X gave Y the gift (XはYにプレゼントをあげた), and from Y's viewpoint, Y received a gift from X (YはXにプレゼントをもらった). In language, however, there is always a motivation to choose one sentence over another. The grammatical tendencies for using the three verbs are as follows, though the analysis is not absolute or commonly accepted among native speakers of Japanese, but merely reflects a tendency.

Each of these three verbs, あげる, くれる, and もらう has an honorific equivalent: さしあげる, くださる, and いただく, respectively, to describe the giving and receiving situation depending on the person to whom the speaker is referring.

The pictures below present a general idea of how these verbs are differentiated.

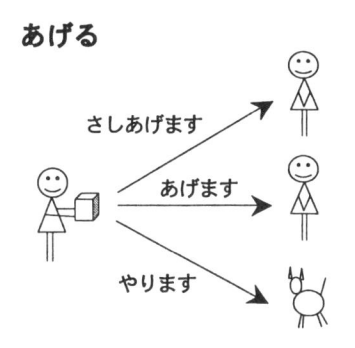

あげる

さしあげます

先生におみやげをさしあげました。
I *gave* a souvenir to my teacher.

あげます

友達におみやげをあげました。
I *gave* a souvenir to my friend.

やります

犬にえさをやりました。
I *gave* food to the dog.

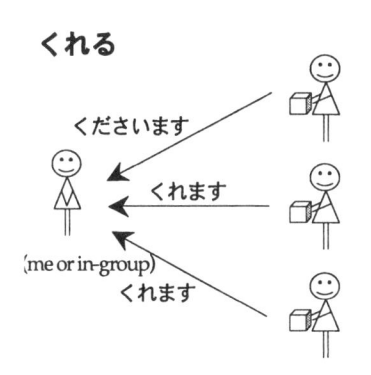

くれる

くださいます

先生が私/弟に日本の雑誌をくださいました。
My teacher *gave me* a Japanese magazine.

くれます

友達が私/妹に花をくれました。
My friend *gave me* a flower.

(me or in-group)
くれます

弟が私にプレゼントをくれました。
My brother *gave me* a present.

もらう

いただきます

友達は先生に本をいただきました。
My friend *received* a book from my teacher.

もらいます

(僕は)友達におみやげをもらいました。
(I) *received* a souvenir from my friend.

もらいます

(私は) 弟にプレゼントをもらいました。
(I) *received* a present from my brother.

1. あげる・くれる・もらう
1.1 やる・あげる・さしあげる

$$X は\ Y に\ Z\ を \begin{cases} さしあげます \\ あげます \\ やります \end{cases} \quad X\ gives\ Z\ to\ Y$$

When an act of giving is conducted between two parties, you can place those two parties in the applicable picture on the preceding page and create a sentence that is appropriate to the situation. The giver can be the first, second, or third person, but the receiver is limited to the second or third person (since くれる should be used when the recipient is the first person). さしあげる, which is an honorific equivalent of あげる, is used when someone gives something to a socially respected person, and やる is used when someone gives something to animals, plants, close friends, family members, and/or people who belong to the speaker's in-group in social settings.

あげる tends to express the flavor of a kind act done by the giver for the receiver.[1] The giver offers something out of his/her goodwill, regardless of the existence or nonexistence of a request from the receiver. Gifts are often given out of goodwill, and usually the giver is recognized as the agent of such an act of goodwill, i.e., the giver becomes the subject of the sentence. Note that this idea becomes clearer when an activity is attached to あげる, which is discussed in Section 2 in this chapter.

(1)　ジョンはメリーにダイヤの指輪(ゆびわ)をあげた。
　　　John was kind enough to give Mary a diamond ring.

The following sentences also create the connotation that the speaker is describing the giver's act as a kind behavior.

---

[1] Of course, this is not always the case, especially when a giver has a negative view of the entity. For example: あのハンバーガー、まずくて食(た)べられなかったから、犬(いぬ)にやった。"I couldn't eat that hamburger because it tasted bad, so I gave it to the dog."

(2) メリーは社長にワインをさしあげました。
Mary gave a bottle of wine to the president.
(3) シュワルツェネッガー氏は奥さんに花束をあげました。
Mr. Schwarzenegger gave a bunch of flowers to his wife.
(4) 大統領はカリフォルニア州に助成金をあげました。
The president gave a subsidy to the state of California.
(5) 母は植木に水をやりました。
My mother gave water to the plant.
(6) a. 弟は妹にコンピュータをあげました。
My brother gave my sister a computer.
b. 弟は妹にコンピュータをやりました。
My brother gave my sister a computer.

あげる in sentence (6a) is used to describe an objective view of the act conducted by the brother, while やる in sentence (6b) may be used based on the speaker's empathy (Kuno, 1987): the speaker is looking at the situation from the brother's viewpoint. When the issue of empathy becomes involved, irregularity in the use of やる may arise. The use of やる varies from person to person, and the generalization of this verb cannot be considered as always pragmatically valid. 犬にご飯をあげた "I fed my dog," 花に水をあげた "I watered the plant" are examples of this. Here, やる or あげる is used depending on personal preference, i.e., how the person feels about the event or situation.[2]

1.2　くれる・くださる

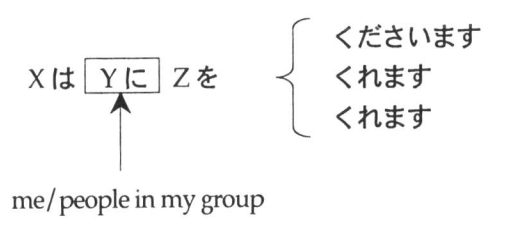

$$X は \boxed{Y に} Z を \begin{cases} くださいます \\ くれます \\ くれます \end{cases}$$

me/people in my group

---

[2] やる is also used as an informal equivalent of する "to do." する and やる are interchangeable when する carries the meaning "to perform." For example, the equivalent of "a movie is showing" is 映画をやっている, and not 映画をしている.

The difference between あげる and くれる is that when someone gives something to the speaker (or someone in the speaker's group) out of goodwill, くれる has to be used. The giver is recognized as the subject of a good deed for me. See the following example:

(7) ジョンが私におみやげをくれた。
　　John was kind enough to give me a souvenir.

The use of くれる is perhaps more complicated and problematic than that of あげる and もらう, because the people in the in-group vary depending on the social setting, the relationship between the speaker and the people in his/her group, the empathy that the speaker shares with the person in question, and so forth. Observe the following examples:

(8) 先生が私に英和辞典をくださいました。
　　The teacher gave me an English-Japanese dictionary.
(9) 先生がクラスの学生全員に英和辞典をくださいました。
　　The teacher gave all the students in her class English-Japanese dictionaries.
　　(The speaker is one of the students and has a sense of camaraderie.)
(10) 大統領が私たちの州知事に助成金をくださいました。
　　The president gave our governor a subsidy.
　　(The speaker's sense of his/her in-group includes the governor.)
(11) ジョンがメリーに花束をくれた。
　　John gave Mary a bunch of flowers.
　　(In order for this sentence to be appropriate, メリー has to be either the speaker's relative or someone with whom the speaker shares a strong empathy. Otherwise, あげた should be used.)
(12) a. その指輪、誰がくれたんですか。
　　　　Who gave you the ring? (I want to know, so please explain.)
　　 b. ボーイフレンドがくれたんです。
　　　　(I will explain it to you.) My boyfriend gave it to me.
　＊ c. あの指輪だれがメリーにくれたんですか？
　　　　Who gave Mary that ring?

* d.   ジョンがくれたんです。
       John gave it (to Mary).

Sentence (12a) may seem awkward, as the speaker is asking who gave *you* the ring. However, the question has to be this way, since the speaker is expecting the answer to be that someone gave the listener (me) the ring. This same observation does not apply to (12c) and (12d), whose subjects are both in the third person. The question should be あの指輪だれがメリーにあげたんですか, and the answer should be ジョンがあげたんです。

1.3   もらう・いただく

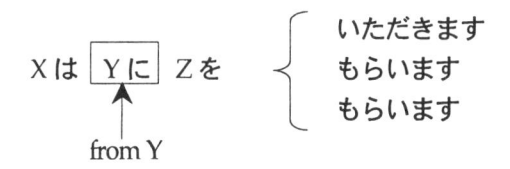

$$X は \boxed{Y に} Z を \begin{cases} いただきます \\ もらいます \\ もらいます \end{cases}$$

↑ from Y

Although the equivalent of もらう is "to receive," it carries the nuance of a favor requested by the receiver. Compare the following sentences:

Between my friend and me
(13)   a.   友達が英和辞典をくれました。
            My friend was kind enough to give me an English-Japanese dictionary.
       b.   (私 は)友達に英和辞典をもらいました。
            I received an English-Japanese dictionary from my friend.

Between John and Mary
(14)   a.   ジョンがメリーに指輪をあげました。
            John gave a ring to Mary.
       b.   メリーはジョンに指輪をもらいました。
            Mary received a ring from John.

The first thing one may notice is the difference in the subject of the sentence. The subject of あげる and くれる is the giver, while the subject of もらう is the receiver, though the result of the activity remains the same. The speaker chooses either sentence depending on whose activity s/he acknowledges. However, a slight nuance may be detected in the way もらう is used, that is, the existence of a request behind the receiving. If the receiver requests something, もらう may be more appropriate. For example, certain people may find that sentence (13b) presumes speaker's request for the dictionary. Observe the following example sentences:

(15) 本田: そのゲーム、もういらなかったら、ちょうだい。
　　　　If you don't need that game anymore, give it to me.
　　　鈴木: うん、いいよ。あげる。
　　　　Sure, I'll give it to you.
　　　Later, Toyota finds Honda playing the game and says:
　　　豊田: 本田、そのゲームどうしたの？
　　　　Honda, where did you get that game?
　　　本田: これ？　鈴木（　　　　　　　）。
　　　　This? Suzuki (　　　　　　　　)。

Though the type of sentence used to fill the space in parentheses depends on individual judgment, 鈴木にもらった "I got it from Suzuki" is most likely the sentence people find appropriate. This observation becomes even more applicable when てもらう is accompanied by an activity verb.

2.　てあげる・てくれる・てもらう

When giving and receiving involve an activity, as when a subject gives an activity such as "buying a ticket" to someone else, あげる functions as an auxiliary verb indicating the subject's giving of a favor.

2.1　てやる・てあげる・てさしあげる

Verb てあげる means that someone does someone the favor of doing something and usually creates the nuance "someone is kind enough to do something." For example:

(1) 弟におとうとコンサートの切符きっぷを買かってあげました。
I did my brother the favor of buying a ticket to the concert = I was kind enough to buy my brother a ticket to the concert.

Because てあげる conveys the connotation of being "kind enough to do ~," てあげる can be pragmatically awkward when it is used for a superior or someone who is older or of higher social status than the speaker. It often creates a condescending connotation since the interpretation "someone is kind enough to do," persists even when the honorific form is used. It should be avoided especially when speaking of physical and/or mental ability. Observe the following examples:

(2) ? 先生せんせいに日本語にほんごで説明せつめいしてさしあげました。[3]
I was kind enough to explain in Japanese to my teacher.
(3) ? 課長かちょうの代かわりに英語えいごで話はしてさしあげました。[4]
I was kind enough to speak in English instead of (making) the section chief (do it).
(4) 先生の荷物にもつが重おもそうだったので、持もってさしあげました。
The teacher's luggage looked heavy, so I kindly carried it.
(5) 先生、荷物、重そうですね。持ってさしあげましょうか/。
お持ちしましょうか。← better
Teacher, your luggage looks heavy. Shall I carry it for you?

The type of verb that あげる follows is crucial in forming an あげる sentence. Depending on the type of verb used with あげる, different particles are required. For example, verbs that can take both a direct object and an indirect (ditransitive verb), such as 紹介しょうかいする、教おしえる、届とどける, can form sentences, including (indirect object) に (direct object) を (give a favor to someone), while regular transitive verbs that take only one object cannot form a sentence in the same manner as those that take two objects. For example, 写真しゃしんを撮とる "to take a picture" and 洗あらう "to wash" cannot involve に since they cannot be used with an indirect object.

---

[3] 先生に日本語で説明いたしました would be better.
[4] 課長の代わりに英語でお話ししました / お話しいたしました would be better.

私に写真を撮ってくれた "someone took me a picture," for example, is an ungrammatical sentence in Japanese. For intransitive verbs, when the person who receives the favor of some action must appear in the sentence, that person is generally marked by のために (for the benefit of ~). Observe the following sentences, which use three types of verbs:

Ditransitive verbs [SOOV]	山田さんは田中さんに荷物を送ってあげました。 Mr. Yamada was kind enough to send Ms. Tanaka a package.
Transitive verbs [SOV]	山田さんは田中さんの車を洗ってあげました。 Mr. Yamada was kind enough to wash Ms. Tanaka's car.
Intransitive verbs [SV]	山田さんは田中さんのために病院に行ってあげました。 Mr. Yamada was kind enough to visit Ms. Tanaka at the hospital.

2.1.1 Ditransitive verbs

田中さんは先生に書類を届けてさしあげました。
Mr. Tanaka was kind enough to take the documents to the teacher.
私は友達に彼女の電話番号を教えてあげました。
I was nice enough to tell my friend the phone number.
私は弟におみやげを買ってきてあげました。
I was nice enough to buy my brother a souvenir.

2.1.2 Transitive verbs

私は先生のオフィスをそうじしてさしあげました。
I was kind enough to clean the teacher's office.
* 私は先生にオフィスをそうじしてさしあげました。
* I was kind enough to clean to the teacher his office.
私は友達の車を洗ってあげました。
I was kind enough to wash my friend's car.

* 私は友達に車を洗ってあげました。
* I was kind enough to wash to my friend the car.

私は妹のコンピュータを直してあげました。
I was kind enough to fix my sister's computer.
* 私は妹にコンピュータを直してあげました。
* I was kind enough to fix to my sister the computer.

2.1.3　Intransitive verbs:

本田さんは課長の<u>ために</u>朝6時に起きてさしあげました。
Mr. Honda was kind enough to wake up at six o'clock for the section chief.
* 本田さんは課長<u>に</u>朝6時に起きてさしあげました。
* Mr. Honda was kind enough to wake up the section chief at six o'clock.)

私は本田さんの<u>ために</u>病院へいっしょに行ってあげました。
I was kind enough to go to the hospital with Mr. Honda for him.
* 私は本田さん<u>に</u>病院へいっしょに行ってあげました。
* I was kind enough to go to Mr. Honda the hospital with him.

2.2　てくれる・てくださる

The standard meaning of くれる continues in てくれる because *only the speaker or people in the in-group* can receive a kind act. てくれる means that someone gives me the favor of doing something. It usually means "someone is kind enough to do *me* something." For example:

(6)　父がコンサートの切符を買ってくれました。
My father did me the favor of buying a ticket to a concert. = My father was kind enough to buy and give me a ticket to a concert.

(7)　本田の社長がうちの課長をパーティに招待してくださいました。
The president at Honda Corporation was kind enough to invite our section chief to a party.

In てくれる as well, the type of verb that くれる follows also creates restrictions in the use of particles. Depending on the type of verb used with くれる, you need to pay attention to the particle. For ditransitive verbs, such as 紹介する, 教える, 届ける, and so forth, this kind of sentence can be formed: indirect object に direct object を give a favor to someone, while transitive verbs can take only one object and cannot form a sentence in the same manner as those taking two objects. For example, 写真を撮る "to take a picture" and 洗う "to wash" cannot involve に, since they cannot involve an indirect object. 私に写真を撮ってくれた "someone took me a picture," for example, is an ungrammatical sentence. For intransitive verbs, when the person who receives the favor of some action must be present in a sentence, that person is often marked by のために "for the benefit of ~".

Ditransitive verbs	山田さんは私に荷物を送ってくれました。
[SOOV]	Mr. Yamada was kind enough to send me a package.
Transitive verbs	山田さんは私の車を洗ってくれました。
[SOV]	Mr. Yamada was kind enough to wash my car.
Intransitive verbs	山田さんは私のために病院に来てくれました。
[SV]	Mr. Yamada was kind enough to come visit me at the hospital.

2.2.1 Ditransitive verbs

先生は弟に日本人を紹介してくださいました。
The teacher was kind enough to introduce a Japanese person to my brother.
友達は私に彼女の電話番号を教えてくれました。
My friend was kind enough to give me her phone number.
弟は私におみやげを買ってきてくれました。
My brother was kind enough to buy me a souvenir.

2.2.2 Transitive verbs

先生は私の写真を撮ってくださいました。
The teacher was kind enough to take my picture.

* 先生は私に写真を撮ってくださいました。
* The teacher took me a picture.

友達は私の車を洗ってくれました。

My friend was kind enough to wash my car.

* 友達は私に車を洗ってくれました。
* My friend was kind enough to wash me the car.

妹は私を見送ってくれました。

My sister was kind enough to see me off.

* 妹は私に見送ってくれました。
* My sister was kind enough to see off to me.

2.2.3 Intransitive verbs

先生は私のために朝6時に起きてくださいました。

The teacher woke up at six o'clock for me.

* 先生は私に朝6時に起きてくださいました。
* The teacher woke up to me at six o'clock.

本田さんは私のために病院へ行ってくれました。

Mr. Honda was kind enough to go to the hospital for me.

* 本田さんは私に病院へ行ってくれました。
* Mr. Honda was kind enough to go to me the hospital.

2.3 てもらう・ていただく

Verb てもらう means that someone receives a favor of doing something from someone, i.e., someone had someone do something.[5] It also carries a connotation that someone asked someone to do something and s/he did so. For example:

(8) 父にコンサートの切符を買ってもらいました。

I received the favor of buying and giving me the ticket to the concert from my father. = I had my father buy me the ticket to the concert.

---

[5] In English, "have" in "I had John do the dishes" carries the connotation of causative, even coercive, which means that I forced John to do the dishes. In Japanese, this meaning is dismissed, although the result of the action may be the same. If coercion is involved, then the proper causative construction should be used, as in "I made John do the dishes."

Note that the English equivalent "have" in this case has the nuance of "favor" rather than of "force."

Since the function of the particle に is to indicate the source of the activity the subject benefits (from), it differs from the indirect object function of に used in あげる/くれる. There are no restrictions on the way a 〜てもらう sentence is used with the particle に.

Ditransitive verbs [SOOV]	山田さんは田中さんに荷物を送ってもらいました。 Mr. Yamada had Ms. Tanaka send him a package.
Transitive verbs [SOV]	山田さんは田中さんに(自分の)車を洗ってもらいました。 Mr. Yamada had Ms. Tanaka wash his car.
Intransitive verbs [SV]	山田さんは田中さんに病院に来てもらいました。 Mr. Yamada had Ms. Tanaka visit him at the hospital.

2.3.1 Ditransitive verbs

先生に日本語を教えていただきました。

I had my teacher teach me Japanese. (I asked my teacher to teach me Japanese and she kindly did so.)

友達に本を貸してもらいました。

I had my friend lend me the book.

兄に新しい時計を買ってもらいました。

I had my brother buy me a new watch.

2.3.2 Transitive verbs

山本さんに夕食代を払っていただきました。

I had Ms. Yamamoto pay for dinner.

友達に妹を待ってもらいました。

I had my friend wait for my sister.

妹に部屋を掃除してもらいました。

I had my sister clean my room.

2.3.3 Intransitive verbs

<ruby>私<rt>わたし</rt></ruby>は<ruby>課長<rt>かちょう</rt></ruby>に<ruby>会議室<rt>かいぎしつ</rt></ruby>に<ruby>来<rt>き</rt></ruby>ていただきました。
I had the section chief come to the meeting room.
<ruby>私<rt>わたし</rt></ruby>は<ruby>後<rt>うし</rt></ruby>ろの<ruby>学生<rt>がくせい</rt></ruby>に<ruby>座<rt>す</rt></ruby>わってもらいました。
I had students in the back sit down.
<ruby>私<rt>わたし</rt></ruby>は<ruby>友達<rt>ともだち</rt></ruby>にわかってもらいました。
I had my friend understand me.

3. てくれる and てもらう Used in the Request Form[6]

The てくれる and てもらう constructions can be used when one makes a request. They are combined with forms such as たい "~want to," the potential form, and the negative form. The degree of politeness may be different depending on the forms used. てもらう has more expressions than てくれる. See the following examples where the speaker asks someone to teach Japanese. Note that the English equivalent is an approximate one.

<ruby>教<rt>おし</rt></ruby>えてくれる？	Can you teach me?
教えてくれますか。	Will you teach me?
教えてくれませんか。	Will you please teach me?
教えてくださいますか。	Could you teach me?
教えてくださいませんか。	Would you please teach me?
教えてもらえますか。	Can you teach me?
教えてもらえませんか。	Can I ask you to teach me?
教えてもらいたいのですが。	I would like you to teach me.
教えていただけますか。	Could I ask you to teach me?
教えていただきたいのですが。	I would like you to teach me.
教えていただけませんか。	Could you please teach me?
教えていただけないでしょうか。	I'd appreciate if it you could teach me.

---

[6] Refer to Chapter 10, Section 9: the verb てほしい "I want (someone) to do (something)."

Sample dialogue

今日中の仕事、あした手伝ってあげます
I will help you work for today tomorrow.

男： 仕事がなかなか終わらなくて困っているんだ・・・。
　　 I cannot finish my work and am in trouble...

女： じゃあ、手伝ってあげましょうか。
　　 Well, shall I help you?

男： ほんと？　助かるなあ。
　　 Really? That will be a great help.

女： そのかわり、私が荷物を一階から三階へ運ぶの、手伝ってくれる？
　　 In return, can you help me carry my stuff from the first floor to the third floor?

男： もちろんさ。
　　 Of course.

女： 今できるかしら。
　　 Can we do it now?

男： いいよ。その後、僕の仕事を手伝ってね。
　　 Yes, I can. Help me work after that, okay?

女： ええ、もちろん。
　　 Yes, of course.

1時間後 [An hour later]

男： ずいぶん時間がかかったねえ。
　　 It took a long time, didn't it!

女： ええ、あら、もうこんな時間！私、今日エアロビクス (aerobics) のクラスがあるの。ごめんなさい、お仕事、あした手伝ってあげるわ。じゃあ、またあしたね。
　　 It sure did. Oops, it is already late. I have an aerobics class today. I'm sorry, but I will help you work tomorrow. See you tomorrow.

男： え、そんな・・・。この仕事今日中なんだ・・・。
　　 Oh, no... This work has to be done today.

切符の行方

Whereabouts of the ticket

　本田さんは豊田課長に歌舞伎の切符をもらいましたが、その日、急用ができて行けなくなってしまいました。それで、その切符を松田さんにあげました。松田さんはガールフレンドとのデートにちょうどいいと思い、さっそく電話をしてみましたが、ガールフレンドは気分が悪いので行きたくないと言いました。困った松田さんは会社で切符をあげられる人を探しました。すると、運よく前に座っている川崎さんが「あ、その切符ぼくにくれる？」と言ったので、喜んで川崎さんにあげました。

　ところが、しばらくして川崎さんのお父さんから電話がありました。お母さんが病気になったのです。それで、川崎さんも行けなくなってしまいました。困った川崎さんが会社の中を見回すと、豊田課長が煙草をすいながら新聞を読んでいました。

　「課長、これ、よろしかったらどうぞ。今晩8時からですが・・・。」と言って課長にさしあげました。豊田課長は切符をしばらく見つめ、そして、言いました。

　「あれぇ、これ、見たことあるなぁ。だれかにあげたなぁ・・・。」

切符の行方は？

(　　)→(　　)→(　　)→(　　)→(　　)

CHAPTER 21

Structures of Imperatives/Commands

The fundamental notion of a command is that one orders others to realize the event described by the verb. Command forms occur in both the affirmative and the negative, as in しろ "Do it" and するな "Don't do it," 自分でしろ "Do it yourself," 止まれ "Stop," 話すな "Don't talk," and 行かないで "Don't go." However, in Japanese these phrases standing alone sound masculine. In conversation, the form なさい is more commonly used by both female and male language speakers since it does not sound as strong as the direct command form.[1] Also, although the equivalent of てください is "please do," this construction should be considered a form of the command, since it has the same function as the direct command. In this section we learn the constructions of the command forms しろ and なさい.

1. しろ

Consonant Verbs		Affirmative	Negative
急ぐ	to hurry	急げ	急ぐな
進む	to advance	進め	進むな
持っていく	to bring	持っていけ	持っていくな

Vowel Verbs (る verbs)			
調べる	to investigate	調べろ	調べるな
考える	to think	考えろ	考えるな
見る	to look	見ろ	見るな

---

[1] For example, one can say 春よ、来い！"Spring, come!" and ゴミよ、燃えろ！"Garbage, burn!" but not 春よ、来なさい and ゴミよ、燃えなさい. なさい is used only from a person to another person (unless personified).

Irregular Verbs		Affirmative	Negative
する	to do	しろ	するな
来る	to come	来い	来るな

In principle, the recipient of the order is an animate entity, who/that can bring about the event as told; therefore, commands are usually made with volitional transitive verbs. However, the command form can also be used toward inanimate entities (which do not have the will to bring a situation into existence), indicating the speaker's strong desire for a situation to be realized, as in 雨よ、降れ "Rain, fall," 春よ、来い "Spring, come," and 焼けろ "Be grilled."

Command forms may be heard alone in casual or extremely informal conversation among male language speakers. Adult female language speakers may not use these forms even during casual conversation. The forms are instead often used in indirect quotations that include some kind of command form, such as 先生が授業中は話すなと言った "The teacher told us not to talk during class," and in written signs seen in public, such as 止まれ "Stop." The direct quotation in this case, may be 先生が「授業中は話してはいけません」と言った "The teacher said, 'You should not talk during class'" or 先生が「授業中は話さないでください」と言った "The teacher said, 'Do not talk during class period.'" Also, when a command form is used alone, it is usually accompanied by a sentence-final particle, such as こっちへ来いよ！"Come here!" and ばかなこと言うなよ "Don't say a stupid thing." Here are some more examples:

(1) Public traffic signs

止まれ	Stop
右へ曲がれ	Turn right
スピード落とせ	Slow down
走るな	Don't run
歩くな	Don't walk
渡るな	Don't cross

(2)
先生: 基本的な言葉は自分で調べなさい。漢字もちゃんと覚えてください。
Check the basic vocabulary by yourself. Memorize kanji correctly.

では、またあした。
Well, I will see you tomorrow.

学生1: 先生が基本的な言葉は自分で調べろと言うけど、どれが基本的な言葉なのかわからない。それに、漢字もちゃんと覚えろと言うけど、どうすればちゃんと覚えられるのかわからない。困ったよ。

The teacher tells us to check the basic vocabulary by ourselves, but I don't know which ones are basic ones. Also, she tells us to memorize kanji correctly, but I don't know how to memorize them correctly. I am in deep trouble.

学生2: 先生のオフィスに行って、聞いて来いよ。

Go to the teacher's office and ask her.

(3) 何してるんだよ。早くしろよ。

What are you doing? Hurry up!

(4) A: うるさいな、ちょっと静かにしてくれる？

You talk too much. Could you be a bit quieter?

B: 黙れと言うのね？

You are telling me to shut up, right?

A: そうじゃないよ。静かにしろと頼んでいるんだ。

No, that's not the case. I'm asking you to be quiet.

(5) 木よ、大きくなれ。そしてたくさん実をつけろ。

Plant, get bigger. And produce lots of fruit.

(6) 明日天気になぁれ！

Be sunny tomorrow!

(7) (To balloons) 上がれ、上がれ、天まで上がれ。

Go up, up, up to the sky.

2. なさい

なさい follows the stem of a verb to form a なさい phrase. The negative form of なさい is created by the ない form of the verb followed by いなさい.

	Affirmative	Negative
急ぐ	急ぎなさい	急がないでいなさい
持って行く	持って行きなさい	持って行かないでいなさい

考える	考えなさい	考えないでいなさい
集める	集めなさい	集めないでいなさい
見る	見なさい	見ないでいなさい

The なさい command form may often be used when an older person or an individual with a higher rank is commanding someone who is younger or in a subordinate position. なさい is a conversational form that can be used by anyone, regardless of the speaker's sex. It is used only in relation to animate entities, such as humans and animals. It may not be seen in signs, and contrary to the しろ form, it may not be used toward an inanimate entity to describe the speaker's desire for an event to become realized. People may find this form used often by parents as they give orders to their very young children. See the following examples:

(1) 真理子、起きなさい。早く学校へ行く支度をしなさい。
Mariko, wake up. Get ready for school as soon as you can.

(2) にんじん、ブロッコリー、ピーマン、全部食べなさい。
Carrots, broccoli, and green peppers—eat them all.s

(3) わからないところがあったら、私のオフィスに聞きに来なさい。
If there is anything you don't understand, come ask me.

(4) 怖い映画は見ないでいなさい。夜トイレに行けなくなるから。
Don't watch scary movies, since you become unable to go to the bathroom at night.

(5) * 明日天気になりなさい。
Be nice weather tomorrow.

(6) * 頭よ、毛がはえなさい。
Head, grow some hair.

CHAPTER 22

Structures of Permission: The ても *Form*

The て form followed by the particle も, the so-called ても form, is used to express an "even if" or an "even though" meaning and constitutes a subordinate clause. The exact meaning of ても is determined by the tense in the main clause. For example, 雨が降っても行きます means "Even if it rains, I will go" and 雨が降っても行きました means "Even though it rained, I went."[1]

The ても construction is quite frequently used to express permission in Japanese.[2] The notion is expressed by a combination of a subordinate clause and a main clause with a few options.

1. Permission and the ても Form
1.1 The structure of the permission sentence

A sentence that expresses a meaning of permission is constructed in the combination of the ても form in the subordinate clause and いい, かまわない, or だいじょうぶ in the main clause.[3] Either the affirmative or the negative form can be used in the subordinate clause, as may be seen from 食べてもいい "It's all right if you eat" and 食べなくてもいい "It's all right even if you don't eat." If the permission occurred in past context, only the predicate of the main clause changes its form to the past tense form. Note that the negative forms of a part of speech all fall under the category of い adjectives in terms of their morphology. A sentence of permission can be structured by all parts of speech in a variety of combinations.

---

[1] A ても sentence in past context can also express a counterfactual situation. For example, 雨が降っても行ったのに means "I would have gone even if it had rained," implying that the speaker did not go.

[2] Permission is also expressed by the use of the potential form of the verb and the phrase ことができる. This structure of permission is, however, exclusively for "permission" and does not possess a dual functions, as the potential form does.

[3] Sometimes も can be optional depending on personal preference.

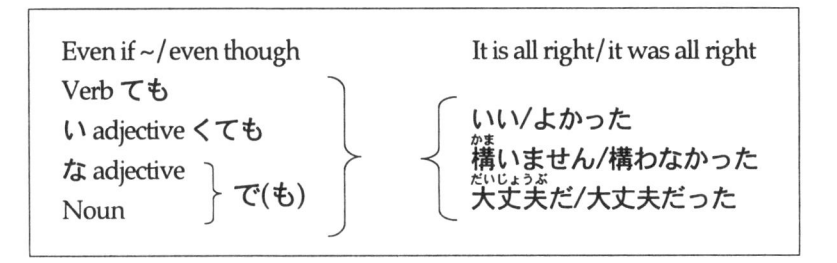

Even if ~ / even though	It is all right / it was all right
Verb ても い adjective くても な adjective ⎱ Noun ⎰ で(も)	いい/よかった 構(かま)いません/構わなかった 大丈夫(だいじょうぶ)だ/大丈夫だった

1.1.1 Permission in non-past contexts:

(1) A: 先生(せんせい)、頭(あたま)が痛(いた)いんです。
    Professor, I have a headache.
  B: そうですか。じゃあ、今日(きょう)は帰(かえ)ってもいいですよ。
    Is that so? Well, you may go home today.
  A: クイズは明日(あした)でもいいですか。
    Is it all right if I take the quiz tomorrow?
  B: ええ、今日は受(う)けなくてもいいです。
    Yes. You don't have to take the quiz today.

(2) A: 「むずかしい」は漢字(かんじ)でどう書(か)くんですか。
    How do you write "difficult" in kanji?
  B: ちょっとむずかしいです。漢字じゃなくても構(かま)いません。ひらがなでいいです。
    It is a little difficult. You don't have to write it in kanji. Hiragana is fine.

(3) 大学(だいがく)の寮(りょう)は場所(ばしょ)が不便(ふべん)でもかまいません。安(やす)ければいいです。
    Speaking of the university dormitory, even if the location is bad, it's all right. If it's cheap, it will do.

1.1.2 Permission in past contexts:

(4) 宝(たから)くじにあたったから、高(たか)いものを買(か)っても構わなかった。
    Since we won the lottery, it was all right even though I bought expensive things. = I could buy expensive things.

(5) 腕の骨を折ったので、試験を受けなくても大丈夫だった。
Since I broke a bone in my arm, it was all right even though I didn't take the exam. = I didn't have to take the exam.

(6) 昨日はクラスが休講だったから、大学へ行かなくてもよかった。
The lecture was canceled yesterday, so it was all right even though I didn't go to the university. = I didn't have to go to the university.

(7) 昨日はクラスが休講だったから、大学へ行かなくてもよかったかもしれない。
Since the lecture was canceled yesterday, it might have been all right even if I didn't go to the university. = I might not have had to go to the university, but actually I went.

A ても sentence with a permissive meaning may express a counterfactual meaning in past context. However, as indicated in sentences (6) and (7), an additional grammatical device like かもしれない is required to differentiate the meaning.

1.2　ても with other main clauses

Since the ても form constitutes a subordinate clause expressing the meaning "even if" or "even though," it can be used with a main clause other than the ones used in sentences of permission. Observe the following examples:

1.2.1　ても sentences in non-past contexts:

(8) 一万円もらっても、芝刈りはいやです。
Even if I receive 10,000 yen, I don't want to mow the lawn.

(9) せっかく作ったのだから、まずくても食べてください。
Since I went to all the trouble to make this, even if it is not delicious, eat it.

(10) だめでも、もう一度やってみてごらんなさい。
Even if it does not work, try one more time.

(11) へたな日本語でも、話せないよりいい。
Even if your Japanese is pathetic, it is better than not being able to speak at all.

1.2.2 ても sentences in past contexts:

(12) 雨が降っても、試合は中止になりませんでした。
Even though it rained, the game was not canceled.

Cf. 雨が降ったけれども、試合は中止になりませんでした。
Although it rained, the game was not canceled. (The speaker is stating a fact involving little of his/her emotion.)

Cf. 雨が降ったのに、試合は中止になりませんでした。
Even though/although it rained, the game was not canceled (against my expectations).

(13) せっかく母が作ってくれたから、まずくても食べた。
Since my mother made it for me with great effort, even though it was not delicious, I ate it.

(14) 先生でも、質問に答えられない時があった。
Even the teacher sometimes could not answer the questions.

(15) 頭が痛くても、我慢した。
Even though I had a headache, I endured.

(16) 本当のことを言わなくても、叱られなかった。
Even though I didn't tell the truth, I was not scolded.

(17) 本当のことを言わなくても、叱られなかっただろう。
Even if I didn't tell the truth, I would not have been scolded.

1.2.3 ても with an interrogative word

An accompanying interrogative changes the meaning of the でも sentence into "no matter how~."

(18) どんなにむずかしくても、頑張ります。
No matter how hard it is, I will do my best.

(19) いくら食べても、おなかがいっぱいにならないんです。
No matter how much I eat, my stomach does not become full.

(20) この映画は何回見ても、おもしろい。
No matter how many times I watch this movie, I can enjoy it.

(21) だれに聞いても、だれも答えがわからない。
No matter whom I ask (no matter how many people I ask), no one knows the answer.

(22) 彼の日本語がどんなにへたでも、そうは言えなかった。
No matter how poor his spoken Japanese was, we could not tell him so.

(23) だれが何と言っても、なっとうは絶対に食べなかった。
No matter what anyone said, I never ate natto.

(24) どんなに悪い点数をもらっても、決して日本語を諦めなかった。
No matter how bad the score I received, I never gave up (learning) Japanese.

(25) どこまで行っても、その店は見つからなかった。
No matter how far we went, we could not find the restaurant.

Sample dialogue

お父さんからのプレゼント
娘: お母さん、そのネックレス、いいなあ。ちょうだい？
母: これはだめなの。だれが欲しいと言っても、いくらもらっても、あげられないのよ。だってお父さんが初めてのデートの時に買ってくれたんですもの。
娘: そう。じゃ、お母さんの形見 (memento) としてしかもらえないのね。
母: いいえ、だめよ。死んでもあげない。
娘: そう。じゃ、その時は私が大切に保管してもいいかしら。
母: ええ、ぜひそうしてちょうだい。

CHAPTER 23

Structures of Prohibition: The ては Form

In English, the notion of prohibition is articulated by modal auxiliaries such as "shouldn't," "cannot," and "mustn't" as well as the negative command "don't" and so on. In Japanese, too, a variety of expressions are used to express the notion—for example, ないでください/ないでほしい "don't do ~/I don't want you to do ~" and negative command phrases, such as するな "don't do" and 行くな "don't go." Sometimes, even the simple な adjective だめ "don't" conveys the meaning "prohibition."

The most common way to express "prohibition" may be to use a sentence that consists of the ては subordinate clause and a main clause meaning "It won't do, if you do ~." The main clause includes a predicate, such as いけません, だめです, and 困ります, expressing that the event described in the subordinate clause is not desired to happen from the viewpoint of the speaker. Note that the negative form is used in the subordinate clause, creating a double negative construction which expresses an obligatory meaning 行かなくてはいけません "must." See Chapter 24 about "obligation" for a more detailed explanation.

If the prohibition conveyed is in past context, only the predicate in the main clause changes its form to the past tense. The ては subordinate in past context, then, expresses a "shouldn't have" meaning (unless referring to a counterfactual situation).

1. The Structure of Sentences of Prohibition

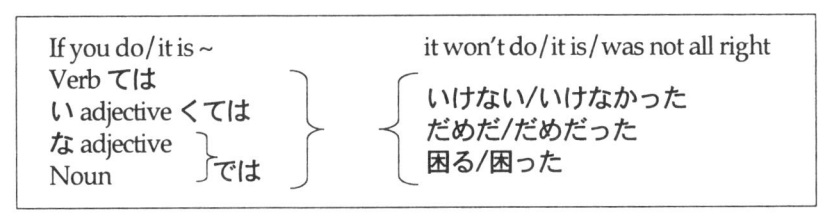

If you do/it is ~	it won't do/it is/was not all right
Verb ては い adjective くては な adjective ｝では Noun	いけない/いけなかった だめだ/だめだった 困る/困った

1.1 Prohibition in non-past contexts

(1) A: 風邪ですね。しばらくお酒を飲んではいけません。それから、煙草も吸ってはだめです。お風呂にも入らないでください。
You have a cold. You shouldn't drink alcohol for a while. Also, you shouldn't smoke. Don't take a bath, either.

B: あのう、コーヒーは飲んでもいいですか。
Well, can I drink coffee?

A: コーヒーもだめですね。早くよくなりたいでしょう。それにはたくさん寝なくてはだめなんですよ。
Coffee is not good, either. You want to get better soon, don't you? For that, you have to sleep a lot.

(2) 答は英語で書いてはいけません。日本語で書いてください。
Speaking of answers, you shouldn't write them in English. Write them in Japanese.

(3) 日本では、家の中を靴で歩いてはいけません。
In Japan, you should not walk around the house with shoes on.

(4) 大学の寮はあまり遠くては困ります。
Speaking of the dormitory, it cannot be too far from the university.

(5) 未成年ではだめです。大人でなければなりません。
It won't do if you are under 20. You have to be an adult.

1.2 Prohibition in past contexts

When a prohibition is conveyed in past context, it can express a counterfactual meaning. Context helps clarify the meaning unless an auxiliary grammatical device appears.

(6) ここで煙草を吸ってはいけなかった。
I could not smoke here. / I shouldn't have smoked a cigarette here. = I was not supposed to smoke here, (but I did).

(7) 答(こたえ)は英語(えいご)で書(か)いてはいけなかった。
Speaking of the answers, we could not use English. / We shouldn't have written the answers in English. = We were not supposed to use English to write the answers, (but we did).

(8) その仕事(しごと)は学生(がくせい)ではだめだった。
Speaking of that job, it wouldn't do if it was a student. = A student could not do the job.

(9) 日本(にほん)では、家(いえ)の中(なか)を靴(くつ)で歩(ある)いてはいけなかった。
In Japan, you could not walk around the house with shoes on.

2. The では Form with Another Main Clause

Since the では form constitutes a subordinate clause expressing an "if" meaning, just like the ば conditional, it can invite a main clause other than the ones used in sentences of prohibition. However, unlike ば, when a では sentence describes a past event, it seldom expresses a counterfactual meaning. Instead, the sentence is interpreted as expressing a "since" meaning. Observe the following examples in both non-past and past contexts:

2.1 Prohibition in non-past contexts

(1) そんなことを言(い)っては、嫌(きら)われてしまいます。[1]
If you say things like that, you will be disliked.

(2) まずくては、売(う)れないでしょう。
If it does not taste good, it won't sell.

(3) 相手(あいて)が子供(こども)では、怒(おこ)ることもできない。
If the person I am dealing with is a child, I cannot even get mad at the child.

(4) お店(みせ)がこんなに暇(ひま)では、人(ひと)を雇(やと)う必要(ひつよう)もないでしょう。
If the restaurant is unpopular to this extent, there is no necessity to hire a waitress.

---

[1] The conditional sentence with the closest meaning is expressed by a たら sentence: 風邪(かぜ)をひいた時(とき)はコーヒーを飲(の)みすぎたら、早(はや)くよくなりません。と and ば conditional sentences express a general, habitual meaning.

2.2 Prohibition in past contexts

(5) しょうゆが嫌いでは、日本のものを食べることができなかったでしょう。
Since I didn't like soy sauce, I could not eat Japanese food.

(6) 相手が子供では、怒ることもできなかった。
Since the person I was dealing with was a child, I could not even get mad at the child.

(7) お店があんなに暇では、人を雇う必要もなかった。
Since the restaurant was so unpopular, there was no necessity to hire a waitress.

(8) 毎日雨では、どこへも行けなかった。
Since it rained every day, I could not go anywhere.

3. The ては Form in Casual Conversation

In colloquial conversation, contracted forms are used instead of ては.

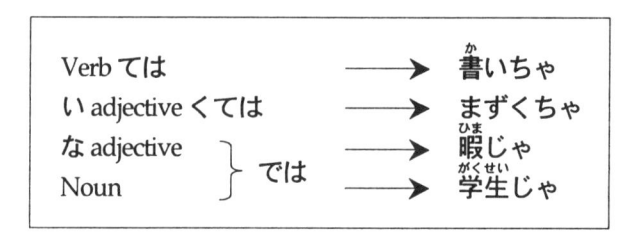

```
Verb ては              ⟶   書いちゃ
い adjective くては    ⟶   まずくちゃ
な adjective  ⎫
              ⎬ では   ⟶   暇じゃ
Noun          ⎭        ⟶   学生じゃ
```

(1) 居眠りをしてはいけない。   → 居眠りをしちゃいけない。
(2) 不便では困ります。   → 不便じゃ、困る。
(3) 小銭ではだめだ。   → 小銭じゃだめだ。
(4) 大学に遠くては困る。   → 大学に遠くちゃ困る。

Sample dialogue

(飛行機の中で)たばこは吸わないでください
Do not smoke in the airplane.

A: あのう、すみませんが、ここは禁煙席です。たばこを吸っては困ります。
B: あ、失礼。じゃ、そこで吸いましょう。
A: あのう、そこも禁煙ですが・・・。
B: あ、そう。じゃ、あそこで。
A: すみません、この便 (flight) は禁煙なんです。
B: あ、そう・・・。
Beep, beep, beep, beep!
C: だれかがトイレでたばこを吸っています！
A: (opening the lavatory door)
たばこは吸ってはいけません！吸うなと言っているんです！
B: すみません・・・。

CHAPTER 24

Structures of Obligation

In English, the meaning of obligation is expressed by auxiliaries such as "should," "ought to," "must," and "have to." For example, if you are obliged to go, "you must go" may be articulated. Since English modal auxiliaries have dual functions, as, for example, "must," which can express meaning both of obligation and of supposition, which meaning the word has in a sentence depends on context.

In Japanese, the two notions expressed by the English auxiliary "must" are expressed, with some variations, by different structures such as なければならない, なくてはいけない, and ないわけにはいかない. See the following example that represents the English sentence "He must go":

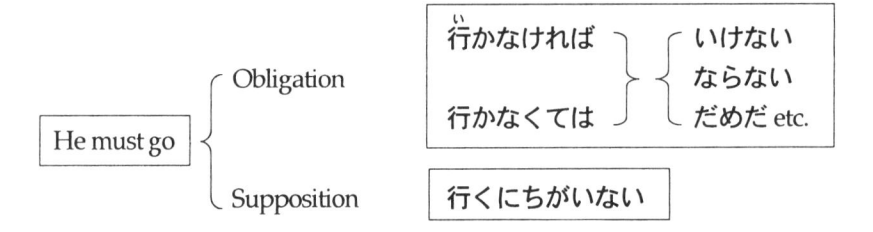

```
                    ┌ 行かなければ ┐   ┌ いけない
         ┌ Obligation                │ ならない
He must go ┤            └ 行かなくては ┘   └ だめだ etc.
         └ Supposition   行くにちがいない
```

行かなければならない, for example, a conditional sentence, is one of the constructions that expresses a meaning of obligation. The ば form is used in this double negative construction and leads to an affirmative meaning, as may be seen from the following representative sentence:

行かない	+	ならない	=	行かなければ ならない
I do *not* go	+	it is *not* all right	=	I must go

There is a phrase ないわけにはいかない "There is *no* way *not* to do~" which also expresses a meaning of obligation. These representative expressions are discussed in what follows.

1. なければならない/なくてはいけない

Any combination presented in the chart above expresses a meaning of obligation. Not only verbs, but also other parts of speech can form a sentence of obligation. Observe the following schematic for a complete listing of ways to form a sentence of obligation:

$$\begin{Bmatrix} \text{Verb} \\ \text{い adjective く} \\ \text{な adjective} \\ \text{Noun} \end{Bmatrix} \text{で/じゃ} \quad \begin{Bmatrix} \text{なければ/なくては} \end{Bmatrix} \quad \begin{Bmatrix} \text{ならない} \\ \text{いけない} \\ \text{だめだ} \\ \text{困る} \end{Bmatrix}$$

As seen in the chart, instead of いけない、ならない、or だめだ, other expressions that express a negative meaning, such as 困る, may also be used. This means that a variety of combinations exist for constructing a sentence of obligation.[1]

The なければならない/なくてはいけない constructions constitute predicates that are morphologically い adjectives; therefore, when they express past events, they alternate to ならなかった/いけなかった. There is no negative form of these predicates, as a triple negative construction is too complicated for listeners to process the meaning immediately in day-to-day conversation. First, observe the following examples that contain these constructions:

(1)　A:　日本へ行ったら、どんなことをしなければなりませんか。
　　　　What kind of thing am I supposed to do when I go to Japan?

---

[1] In fact, there is a grammatical difference between ならない and いけない. When ならない is used, the sentence usually refers to the speaker him/herself, such as "I have to do ~," while いけない tends to refer to another individual's obligation, such as "you have to do~." This is due to the nature of なる and いく, which are generally perceived as inward (coming toward the speaker) and outward (departing from the speaker), respectively. However, in day-to-day communication, such distinctions may not be recognized.

B: まず、家へ入る時はくつを脱がなくてはいけません。
First, you have to take off your shoes when you enter someone's house.
それから、車を運転する時は右側を走らなくてはだめです。
Also, when you drive, you have to drive the car on the right side of the road.
それに、目上の人と話す時は敬語を使わなければなりません。
What's more, when you talk to someone who is older than you are, you have to use honorific language.

(2) 明日までに論文を仕上げなければなりません。
I must finish writing the thesis by tomorrow.

(3) 国民はみな税金を収めなければいけません。
People in the nation all have to pay tax.

(4) 私が結婚する人は、頭がよくなくてはいやです。
The person whom I will marry has to be intelligent.

(5) コーヒーはブルーマウンテンでなくてはだめです。
As for coffee, it won't do if it's not Blue Mountain.

(6) この仕事は健康じゃなければできません。
This job cannot be done if one is not healthy. (One has to be healthy in order to do this job.)

The basic sentence of obligation is formed by using the conditional; therefore, instead of ば, と, or たら may be used to construct a sentence, though the combination of たら and なりません/いけません may be rare. Observe the following examples:

(7) 銀行でお金を借りないとだめです。
I must borrow money at the bank.

(8) 早く帰って来なかったらいけませんよ。
You must come home early.

(9) 薬を飲まなかったらだめです。
You must take medication.

In casual conversation, なくては is often pronounced なくちゃ or なきゃ, and いけない/ならない are often omitted. See examples (10) through (13), which follow.

(10) 手紙を書かなくてはならない。→　書かなくちゃ/書かなきゃ
　　　I have to write a letter.
(11) 小銭じゃなくてはだめだ。→　小銭じゃなくちゃ/小銭じゃなきゃ
　　　I have to write a letter.
(12) 先生に説明しなくてはいけない。→　説明しなくちゃ/説明しなきゃ
　　　I have to explain it to the teacher.
(13) 大学に近くなくては困る。→　近くなくちゃ/近くなきゃ
　　　It has to be close to the University.

2.　ないわけにはいかない

わけにはいかない following a verb in the ない form constitutes a double negative construction, and is a set phrase that also expresses a meaning of obligation. Only verbs are used in this construction. The literal meaning is "There is *no* way *not* to do ~," "it's *not* possible *not* to do ~." わけにはいかない also follows the affirmative form of the verb to express "There is *no* way to do ~" = "One cannot do ~."

　　　Although verb ないわけにはいかない consists of double negative morphemes and has the equivalent meaning to なければならない and なくてはいけない, the difference between these constructions is that verb ないわけにはいかない may express a sense of obligation that is a bit stronger than なければならない and なくてはいけない. It is most typically used to describe an obligation belonging to the speaker him/herself and not an obligation pertaining to a third person. In this sense, it may be said that ないわけにはいかない is used based on the speaker's self-evaluation, while なければならない and なくてはいけない are used when social and moral issues are involved in judgment. The わけにはいかない phrases can be used both in past and non-past contexts as exemplified in the following:

(1) 先生のお別れ会だから、出席しないわけにはいかない。
Since it is a farewell party for my professor, there is no way not to attend the party.

(2) クラスで使う教科書だから、お金はないけど、買わないわけにはいかない。
Since these are textbooks we use in class, though I don't have money, I have to buy them.

(3) 卒業するのに論文が必要だから、書かないわけにはいかなかった。
Since a thesis was necessary in order to graduate, there was no way not to write one.

(4) 父が亡くなったので、学期中だったが、日本へ帰らないわけにはいかなかった。
Because my father passed away, although it was in the middle of a term, I had to return to Japan.

Sample dialogue

結婚式に出ないわけにはいかないんです

女: どうしたの、そんなに急いで。
What happened? You look in a hurry.

男: 急に帰国しなくちゃならなくなったんだ。で、今から空港に行かなくちゃいけなくて・・・。
I came to have to return to my country all of a sudden, and have to go to the airport now....

女: 急に帰国って、何かあったの？
Suddenly returning home? Something happened?

男: 明後日姉と兄が結婚することになったんだ。
My sister and brother are getting married the day after tomorrow.

女: え、お姉さんとお兄さんが結婚するの？　まさか・・・。
What? Your sister and brother are going to get married? No way...

男: 違うよ、二人が同じ日に結婚式をするんだよ。だから帰らないわけにはいかないんだ。
No. They are going to have a wedding ceremony on the same day (with different partners). So, there is no way not to go back.

女： ああ、なんだ、びっくりした。
Phew. You surprised me.
じゃ、クラスを休まなくちゃいけないんでしょ？
Then, you have to miss class, don't you?

男： そうなんだ。あ、先生に報告しなくちゃいけないね。
That's right. Oops, I have to let the teacher know about it.

女： 私が言っておいてあげるわよ。
I will tell the teacher.

男： ほんと？ありがとう。
Are you sure? Thank you.

女： じゃ、お土産、忘れないでね。
Well, don't forget a souvenir.

男： あ、ああ、そうだね。もちろん。
Oh, yes, that's right. Of course.

CHAPTER 25

Terms of Respect: Polite Affixes and Honorific and Humble Forms

---

敬語(けいご) is used to express the speaker's sense of courtesy, respect, and modesty toward the individual. There are three categories, 丁寧語(ていねいご), 尊敬語(そんけいご), and 謙譲語(けんじょうご), all of which fall under the umbrella term 敬語 "honorific language." 丁寧語 is also often referred to as 美化語(びかご) "beautification of words" because its function is to make words sound nice and polite by affixing お or 御 to various parts of speech. 尊敬語(そんけいご) and 謙譲語(けんじょうご) use completely different nouns or verbs with meanings equivalent to the original nouns or verbs, or make use of a particular verbal sentence pattern. Detailed discussion is given in the following sections.

1.　丁寧語：The Polite Affixes お and 御

First, while plain forms, such as 行く "to go" and 見る "to see" are "informal forms" which are used in casual conversation (between friends and family members), です/ます forms are "polite forms" which are used when a speaker talks in public, communicates with people to whom s/he is not close, etc.

In addition to です/ます forms, there are some other ways to elevate words into a polite equivalent. The most common one is the use of the affixes お and 御 that are prefixed to a noun, い adjective, or な adjective, and to make the phrase sound polite or let the speaker feel gracious or, sometimes, feminine. For example, one may say, 私(わたし)はお水(みず)が飲(の)みたいです "I want to drink water." Here, a third person is not involved in the situation, and お is simply there to make 水 sound polite. お and 御 are also used to formulate honorific and humble expressions, such as お借(か)りした先生(せんせい)の御本(ごほん)を拝読(はいどく)しました "I read your book which I borrowed." Thus, since the function of お and 御 is to change a word into its polite equivalent, unlike honorific and humble expressions, phrases with お and 御 do not necessarily refer to a third party or an entity belonging to a third party.

The basic distinction between お and 御 is based on the type of the part of speech. お is prefixed if the word is pronounced in a Japanese way (訓読み), which means that the word is an original Japanese word. If the word is pronounced in a Chinese way (音読み), which means that the word is a Chinese compound, 御 is prefixed. However, there are many exceptions to this basic dichotomy such as 電話 and 返事, which have been assimilated into Japanese words and are prefixed by お: お電話する and お返事する. Here are some examples:

Nouns	い adjectives[1]	な adjectives
お手紙 (letter)	お高い (expensive)	お暇 (time to spare)
お水 (water)	お羨ましい (envious)	お元気 (healthy)
お名前 (name)	お美しい (beautiful)	お上手 (skillful)
御意見 (opinion)	御芳しい (favorable)	御親切 (kind)
御希望 (preference)	御香ばしい (good-smelling)	御不便 (inconvenient)

Few い/な adjectives are prefixed by 御.
One needs to keep in mind that excessive use of お/御 may make sentences sound less graceful.

(1) こちらにお名前、御住所、お電話番号を御記入ください。
Please fill in your name, address, and phone number on this paper.

(2) 御意見がございましたら、どうぞ。
If you have an opinion, please go ahead and tell me.

(3) お高いお料理店でお食事をしてしまいましたので、もうお金がございません。
Since I had a meal at an expensive restaurant, I don't have any money any more.

---

[1] 御芳しい and 御香ばしい are very uncommon compared to their English equivalents.

(4) 何度かお手紙をお出ししましたが、お返事がありません。
Although I sent letters a few times, there has been no response.

Some words may have different polite equivalents. 私 and ございます are good examples. 私 is usually used by female language speakers in day-to-day conversation, but male language speakers also use this word when they make a public speech, on formal occasions, and so on. ございます is a humble equivalent of あります, but it can also be used as a polite equivalent of です or あります. Observe the following examples:

(5) いらっしゃいませ。こちらは東急デパート東館で、家具がございます。
Welcome. This is Tokyu Department Store East Building. We have furniture.

(6) わたくしの主人はアメリカ人でございます。
My husband is an American.

(7) 首相に任命されまして、私は大変光栄でございます。
I am truly honored to be selected as prime minister.

2. Honorific Statements

Honorific forms are used to express a speaker's respect toward the person the speaker is addressing. For example, when an individual whom a speaker respects performs an action, the speaker uses a honorific form to address the individual's activity, as in 先生は今オフィスにいらっしゃいます "The teacher is in his/her office now" and 大統領はお昼ご飯にピザを召し上がりました "The president had pizza for lunch."

In Japan, age and social status are the primary factors behind the use of the honorific forms. If someone is older than the speaker or is at a higher rank in terms of social status, the speaker uses honorific forms when talking about the referent's performance and/or attributes as a mark of respect for and/or courtesy in public situations. The use of the honorific form depends entirely on how the speaker feels about the person and the situation the speaker is in. Honorific forms might not be used if the person in question is not present at the time of the conversation. Or the speaker might use honorific forms to show others that the speaker respects the person in question.

If learners of Japanese are surrounded by college students of a similar age, they may notice that honorific forms are seldom heard. This may be true, as student status occupies a unique period in a person's lifetime and contrasts with the status of people who are employed by some kind of social organization. As soon as young people become responsible members of society, they find that the language they use is no longer the same as the language they used in college. They face the reality of hierarchical social mechanisms in Japan and learn how much they need to know honorific language.

Humble forms are used when a speaker also wishes to show respect toward another person by being humble about the speaker's own activities and/or attributes. The subject of the verb expressed by the humble form therefore is always the speaker him/herself or people in the same group. For example, 先生に明日ご連絡いたします "I will contact the teacher tomorrow" and 父は昨年先生にお目にかかりました "My father met the teacher last year."[2]

Both forms are also used when the speaker and the addressee do not know each other, i.e., are strangers to each other. This is because people try to be polite and respectful to each other, especially when they do not know the other person's age and/or social status. Once they come to know each other, depend-

---

[2] A question may arise as to how one may use an honorific form to describe his/her teacher's activity to a friend for whom s/he can use a plain form to express closeness. When the teacher is not present at the time of the conversation, the speaker might not use the honorific form, but s/he may use the plain form of the honorific form to express the speaker's respect toward the teacher, while simultaneously being casual to his/her friend. The following are examples of such cases in both the honorific and the humble forms:

(1) A: 先生、オフィスにいる？　　　　"Is the teacher in her office?"
    B: ううん、いないよ。　　　　　　"No, she is not."
(2) A: 先生、オフィスにいらっしゃる？
    B: ううん、いらっしゃらないよ。
(3) A: この辞書、先生にもらったんだ。　"I received this dictionary from the teacher."
    B: え、もらったの？いいなぁ。　　　"Did you receive it? I envy you."
(4) A: この辞書、先生にいただいたんだ。
    B: え、いただいたの。いいなぁ。

ing on the relationship into which they develop, they may change the forms they use to each other or maintain the same stance as before.

Some verbs have fixed forms as their honorific and humble forms. For other verbs, there are several patterns for formulating honorific or humble sentencees. First, consider the chart with the verbs that have fixed forms followed by example sentences.

2.1 Verbs with fixed honorific and humble forms

Honorific form	Regular form	Humble form
いらっしゃいます	います	おります
おありです	あります	ございます
〜でいらっしゃいます	〜です	〜でございます
いらっしゃいます お見えになります	行きます 来ます	まいります
なさいます	します	いたします
〜なさいます	〜します 連絡します 電話します	ご/お〜します ご/お〜いたします 御連絡します お電話いたします
召し上がります	食べます 飲みます	いただきます
ご覧になります	見ます	拝見します
御存知です	知っています	存じております[3]
おっしゃいます	言います	申します
(お会いになります)[4]	会います	お目にかかります
(お聞きになります)	聞きます	うかがいます お聞きします
(お訪ねになります)	訪ねます	うかがいます お訪ねします

---

[3] The negative form of 存じております is 存じません.
[4] お会いになります、お聞きになります、お訪ねになります use the お+になります pattern.

(1) A: 学部の住所と電話番号を御存知ですか。
Do you know the address and the phone number of the Department?
B: いいえ、存じません。
No, I don't.

(2) 先生は昨日日本へいらっしゃいました。
The professor went to Japan yesterday.

(3) A: お名前は、なんとおっしゃいますか。
Speaking of your name, what is it (called)?
B: 佐々木と申します。
My name is Sasaki.

(4) 学生: 今日はもうお昼ご飯、召し上がりましたか。
Have you already eaten lunch today?
先生: いいえ、まだ食べていません。
No, I haven't eaten yet.

When communication takes place between a professor and a student, for example, the professor may not necessarily respond using the humble form. The same thing can be said for people with an age difference. This means the honorific form and the humble form are not necessarily paired in communication.

2.2 お/御 + verb stem + になります and お/御 + verb stem + いたします

In order to create the honorific and humble forms for verbs other than those listed above (which have fixed forms), the honorific equivalent お verb stem/ご noun + になります or the humble equivalent お/ご verb stem/noun + いたします may be used. お/ご verb stem/noun + いたします has a similar meaning to "I humbly do/did something for someone whom I respect." Therefore, this pattern is used only when a person the speaker respects is involved in the event described by the verb. For example, in the following instances, 旅行 and 帰宅 do not indicate a humble equivalent, since the activities do not involve a third individual. However, the simple humble form 日本へ旅行いたしました "I humbly tell you that I traveled to Japan" or 父は帰宅いたしました "I humbly tell you that my father humbly went home" are perfectly appropriate.

Honorific お verb stem / ご noun+ になります	Humble お/ご verb stem/noun + します/いたします
先生は本をお送りになりました。	先生に本をお送りいたします。
The professor sent the book.	I will send the professor the book.
田中さんをお待ちになりますか。	先生をお待ちします。
Are you going to wait for Ms. Tanaka?	I will wait for my professor.
先生は図書館で本をお借りになりました。	先生に本をお借りしました。
The professor borrowed a book at the library.	I borrowed a book from the professor.
先生は推薦状をお書きになりました。	先生にお手紙をお書きいたします。
The professor wrote a recommendation letter.	I will write a letter to my professor.
先生は本をお読みになりました。	私は先生の本を拝読いたしました。
The professor read a book.	I read the professor's book.
先生はどちらへ御旅行になりますか。	
Where is the professor going to travel?	
先生はもう御帰宅になりました。	
The professor has already gone home.	
先生が御説明になります。	私が先生に御説明いたします。
The professor will give an explanation.	I will explain it to my professor.

2.3　お + verb stem + です or ご noun + です

There is another way of forming honorific sentences. お + verb stem + です is a sort of contracted version of お + verb stem + になっています, where the event described by the verb is usually progressing. The pattern ご noun + です, where a Chinese compound, such as 御来店 is used, usually expresses a current resultative or a future situation. Observe the following examples:

(5)　失礼ですが、どなたをお待ちですか。(お待ちになっていますか。)
　　　Excuse me, but who are you waiting for?
(6)　課長、お呼びですか。(お呼びになっていましたか/お呼びになりましたか。)
　　　Section chief, are you calling me/did you call me?

(7) 課長は読売新聞をお読みです。(お読みになっています。)
The section chief reads the newspaper *Yomiuri*.

(8) どなたにお手紙をお書きですか。(お書きになっていますか。)
To whom are you writing?

(9) 大統領はあの飛行機に御搭乗(お乗り)です。(お乗りになっています。)
The president is on that airplane.

(10) 本田の社長が御来店です。(お見えになっています。)
The president at Honda has come to the store (and is at the store now).

(11) 社長は来月御帰国(お帰り)です。(お帰りになります。)
Our president will return home next month.

2.4 The passive form

The passive is also used to constitute an honorific sentence. Particles are the key to differentiating the honorific meaning from the passive meaning. Since る verbs share the same form for the passive and the potential, the meaning can be ambiguous, as sentence (14) below shows. Observe the following examples:

(12) 先生がそう言われました。
The professor said so.

Cf. 先生にそう言われました。
I was told so by the professor.

(13) 寺村先生は日記を読まれました。
Professor Teramura read a diary.

Cf. 寺村先生に日記を読まれました。
I was annoyed because Professor Teramura read my diary.

(14) 遠藤先生は子供に日本語を教えられます。
Ms. Endo teaches Japanese to kids./Ms. Endo can teach Japanese to kids.

Cf. 遠藤先生は子供に日本語が教えられます。
Ms. Endo can teach Japanese to kids.

Various manners of creating honorific forms of verbs have thus far been introduced. Most verbs can become honorific by using more than one of the forms listed above. The following is a chart that includes some representative verbs. Fixed forms are the most polite, and passive forms are the least.

	Fixed phrase	お〜になります	御/お〜です	Passive form
い 行きます	いらっしゃいます			行かれます
します	なさいます			されます
りょこう 旅行します	旅行なさいます		御旅行です	旅行されます
た 食べます	めしあがります	お食べになります	おめしあがりです	食べられます
み 見ます	ごらんになります		ごらんです	見られます
あ 会います		お会いになります	お会いです	会われます
か 書きます		お書きになります	お書きです	書かれます
よ 読みます		お読みになります	お読みです	読まれます
はな 話します		お話になります	お話です	話されます
よ 呼びます		お呼びになります	お呼びです	呼ばれます

3. Honorific Requests

Since requests involve a third person, they often make use of honorific forms.

3.1 Regular verbs
3.1.1 お + verb stem + ください

Verb	"Please do" form	English equivalent
と 取る	どうぞ御自由にお取りください。	Please feel free to take one.
はい 入る	どうぞお入りください。	Please come in.
ま 待つ	少々お待ちください。	Please wait for a moment.
すわ 座る	どうぞお座りください。	Please have a seat.
た 食べる	どうぞおめしあがりください。	Please have some.
い 行く	日本へいらっしゃってください。	Please go that way.
い 言う	どうぞお申しつけください。	Don't hesitate to ask.

Verb		English equivalent
<ruby>来<rt>く</rt></ruby>る	どうぞおいでください。	Please come visit.
<ruby>見<rt>み</rt></ruby>る	ぜひ<ruby>ご覧<rt>らん</rt></ruby>ください。	Please look, by all means.
<ruby>寝<rt>ね</rt></ruby>る	ゆっくりお<ruby>休<rt>やす</rt></ruby>みください。	Please have a good rest.
<ruby>帰<rt>かえ</rt></ruby>る	お<ruby>気<rt>き</rt></ruby>をつけてお<ruby>帰<rt>かえ</rt></ruby>りください。	Have a safe trip home.

3.2 する nouns
3.2.1 お/ご + する noun + ください

Verb	"Please do" form	English equivalent
<ruby>連絡<rt>れんらく</rt></ruby>する	<ruby>御<rt>ご</rt></ruby>連絡ください。	Please contact me.
<ruby>説明<rt>せつめい</rt></ruby>する	御説明ください。	Please explain.
<ruby>購入<rt>こうにゅう</rt></ruby>する	御購入ください。	Please purchase.
<ruby>検討<rt>けんとう</rt></ruby>する	御検討ください。	Please consider.
<ruby>推薦<rt>すいせん</rt></ruby>する	御推薦ください。	Please recommend.
<ruby>活躍<rt>かつやく</rt></ruby>する	御活躍ください。	Please take an active role.
<ruby>命令<rt>めいれい</rt></ruby>する	御命令ください。	Please give a command.
<ruby>依頼<rt>いらい</rt></ruby>する	御依頼ください。	Please make a request.
<ruby>電話<rt>でんわ</rt></ruby>する	お電話ください。	Please call me.
<ruby>返事<rt>へんじ</rt></ruby>する	お返事ください。	Please respond.

(1) <ruby>明日<rt>あした</rt></ruby>までに御連絡ください。お<ruby>待<rt>ま</rt></ruby>ちしております。
　　Please contact us by tomorrow. We are looking forward to it.

(2) <ruby>当社<rt>とうしゃ</rt></ruby>の<ruby>教科書<rt>きょうかしょ</rt></ruby>をぜひ御購入ください。
　　Please by all means purchase the textbook of our publisher.

(3) この<ruby>件<rt>けん</rt></ruby>につきまして、ぜひ御検討ください。
　　Please take good consideration regarding this matter.

(4) <ruby>適任者<rt>てきにんしゃ</rt></ruby>を御推薦ください。
　　Please recommend an appropriate person.

(5) これからもどうか御活躍ください。
　　We hope that you will keep playing an active role.

Sample dialogues

Aをください！
学生: 先生、ケーキ、めしあがりませんか。
先生: まあ、リサさんが作ったの？ありがとう、ぜひいただきます。
学生: 先生、これ今日の新聞ですけど、もうご覧になりましたか。
先生: いえ、まだですけど。
学生: あ、じゃあ、どうぞお読みになってください。
　　　あ、それから先生、ゴルフなさいますか。
先生: ええ、しますよ。でも、どうして？
学生: US Openの切符があるんですが、よろしかったらいらっしゃいませんか。
先生: え、いいんですか？
学生: ええ。あの、先生は御結婚なさっていますか。
先生: (Isn't it too personal...?)ええ、していますけど・・・。
学生: じゃ、切符は二枚ありますから、御主人とお出かけください。
先生: あ、そうなんですか・・・。なんか、困っちゃうわ・・・。
学生: 先生。
先生: はい、何でしょうか。
学生: あのう・・・。
先生: どうしたんですか。
学生: あのう、先生・・・。Aをください！！お願いします！！
先生: ・・・。

好きな人に結婚されてしまいました
トム: 松田さんは結婚されているんですか。
松田: そういう質問はちょっと個人的だから、どうかなぁ・・・。
トム: 今日クラスで受身形が敬語として使われることを学んだので、ちょっと使ってみたかったんです。
松田: あ、そうか。それじゃ、練習ですね。じゃ、もう一度、どうぞ。
トム: 松田さんは結婚されていますか。
松田: ええ・・・。好きだった人に結婚されてしまいました・・・。
　　　トホホ・・・。
トム: ？？？

CHAPTER 26

Conditional Sentences: と・たら・ば・なら

There are four conditional forms in Japanese: と, たら, ば, and なら. Together these constitute roughly the same meaning as "when," "whenever/every time," and "if" in English, expressing a causal relation between the antecedent and the consequent.[1]

"When" is used to imply certainty about the occurrence of the event expressed in the antecedent; "every time/whenever" is a plural of "when" indicating that the event in question occurs/occurred repeatedly and can be considered a *habitual* event. The event's realization is thus predictable from the speaker's viewpoint. These notions refer to the domain of the *"non-hypothetical"* world. The event in question is both predictable and known to be true to the speaker.

"If," on the other hand, serves to signal the speaker's supposition about the realization of the event in the antecedent, and the truth of the described event is unknown to the speaker. It refers to the domain of the *"hypothetical"* world (Johnson, 2004a). Note the following, which summarizes the meanings of the conditional forms:

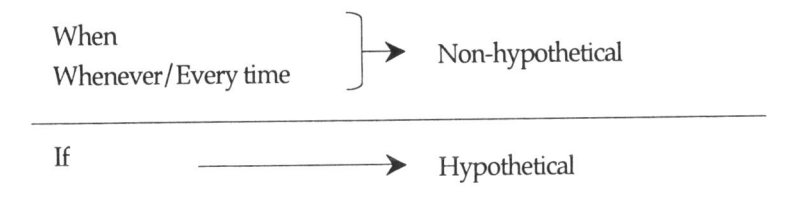

```
When
                        ⟶   Non-hypothetical
Whenever/Every time

If                      ⟶   Hypothetical
```

---

[1] The antecedent generally means that something happens or exists before something else. In grammar, the antecedent is a word or phrase to which a following word refers. For example, in "Please say hello to *John* when you see *him*" "John" is the antecedent of "him." In a logical clause expressing condition, the antecedent refers to the first half of a hypothetical proposition, i.e., the "p" component in a proposition "if *p*, then *q*." The consequent, on the contrary, is found in the second half of a hypothetical proposition, i.e., "q" component. The antecedent is also the same as the subordinate clause in an if-then sentence, and the consequent is the main clause. The terms "antecedent" and "consequent" are used throughout this chapter.

In English, the speaker chooses "when," "if," or "whenever" depending on the meaning s/he tries to express. "If" is given at the beginning of an antecedent and the listener immediately picks up the signal that the speaker is describing a hypothetical situation. In Japanese, however, unlike in English, と, ば, and たら have a dual function—they are used to express two of the three meanings "when/whenever/if," which means that they can be used to indicate either a hypothetical meaning or a non-hypothetical meaning. なら, on the other hand, is used to express only a hypothetical meaning, though it is one that is deeply dependent on the previous context and the flow of communication. Whether a Japanese conditional sentence expresses a non-hypothetical meaning or a hypothetical meaning depends on the nature of the consequent, and on pragmatic judgments made by the speaker.

Thus, the term "conditional" refers to the complete sentence—including both the antecedent and the consequent—that contains any of the conditional forms. For example, let's take the 日本へ行く "Mr. Honda goes" as an antecedent followed by three conditionals と, ば, and たら as examples: 日本へ行くと, 日本へ行けば, 日本へ行ったら. The meaning of each antecedent, however, cannot be determined without a consequent. For example, 日本へ行ったら can be interpreted as "when" or "if" when the consequent is うなぎが食べてみたい "I want to eat eel (and see how it tastes)." Whether "going to Japan" is realized or not is known only to the speaker. If the speaker does not know whether visiting Japan will be realized, then the sentence creates a hypothetical meaning. On the other hand, if the speaker knows that s/he is going to Japan, then the sentence creates a non-hypothetical meaning. Alternately, if the consequent of 日本へ行けば refers to a situation in the past, such as 温泉に入ったものだ "I used to go into a hot spring," then the interpretation of ば is "whenever." If the consequent is いい着物が買える "I can buy a nice kimono" then the ば antecedent indicates most appropriately an "if" meaning.

Thus, Japanese conditional forms have the capability to express either a non-hypothetical or a hypothetical situation depending on the consequent. Such language use is in part due to the fact that, for both temporal "when" and conditional "if," the most frequent relation between antecedent and consequent is causal in nature. Jacobsen (1992) claims that the fundamental feature of conditionals is most appropriately captured if they are viewed in terms of the "contingency" that is expressed in a relationship between two events, whereby one event is contingent on the prior realization of another. Unlike their English counterparts, Japanese conditionals are best grasped if they are treated in terms of whether the antecedent event is actually realized, or not, as an independent feature. The following figure captures the approximate semantics of Japanese conditionals:

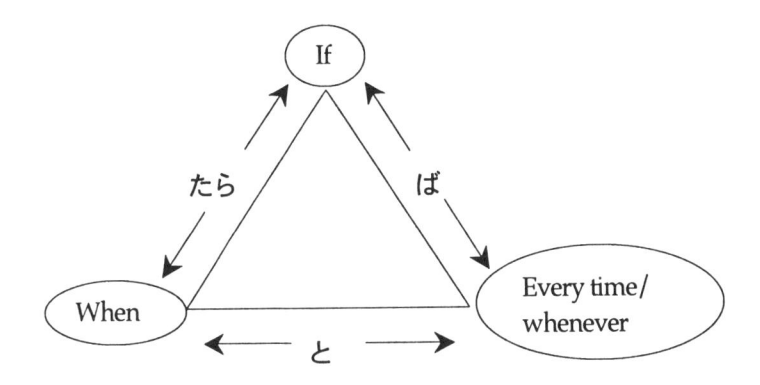

```
                    If
                   / \
                たら   ば
                 /     \
              When ──と── Every time/
                          whenever
```

In the following sections, the functions of each conditional form are explained. The figure above provides approximate meanings of the conditional forms と, たら, ば. (Note that there are always exceptions in their use, such as と being used to express an "if" meaning. The figure gives only fundamental meanings.)

1. と

Verb	行く
	行かない
い adjective	おもしろい
	おもしろくない
な adjective	ひまだ
	ひまじゃない
Noun	学生だ
	学生じゃない

+ と、 [Main clause]

と follows non-past forms of all parts of speech. Although と sentences can be used to express non-hypothetical (when, every time/whenever) or hypothetical (if) situations, depending on context, the fundamental function of と sentences is to describe a situation in which a speaker finds the consequences of an event predictable, such as a natural course of events or general/scientific/mathematical facts whose causal relations are already known to the speaker. Therefore と sentences are used to express mostly a "when/every time" meaning.

と sentences can express an "if" meaning when the antecedent contains an event or a situation that is not controllable or predictable to the speaker, or a described situation is counterfactual. Let us observe the functions of と sentences first in non-past contexts, then in past contexts.

1.1 と sentences in non-past contexts

The most common interpretation of a と sentence in non-past context may be "X, then Y," indicating that Y naturally follows/occurs when X happens. Though future events are not guaranteed to happen as expected, due to the speaker's knowledge based on previous experience and/or scientific events that have been proven to be true, a "when" interpretation is applicable for future events. For example, ミネソタでは１０月になると雪が降る can be interpreted as expressing only a non-hypothetical meaning since October comes every year. The meaning of this sentence is then "October comes, then it snows in Minnesota" = "It snows in October in Minnesota." Observe the following examples:

(1) 私はお酒を飲むと、すぐに顔が赤くなる。
When I drink alcohol, my face immediately turns red.

(2) 娘はエビを食べると、アレルギー症状が出る。
My daughter gets an allergic reaction when she eats shrimp.

(3) 春になると桜が咲く。
When spring comes, cherry flowers bloom./Cherry flowers bloom in the spring.

(4) 赤に青を混ぜると、紫になります。
When you mix red with blue, it becomes purple.

(5) 漢字を知っていると、日本語は読みやすいかもしれない。
If you know Chinese characters, Japanese may be easy to read./Knowing Chinese characters may let you read Japanese easily.

(6) 飛行機の切符は、学生だと安くなりますが、学生じゃないと割引はありません。
Speaking of an airplane ticket, if you are a student, it becomes cheap, but if you are not a student, there is no discount./Airplane tickets are cheap for students, but there is no discount for non-students.

(7) 雨が降ると、試合が中止になってしまう。
If it rains, the game will end up being canceled.

The interpretation of the above sentences varies between hypothetical readings and non-hypothetical readings. When the truth or the realization of the event in the antecedent is uncertain to the speaker, as happens with natural phenomena and other individuals' thoughts and acts, the sentence tends to receive an "if" meaning. On the other hand, when the truth or the realization of the event in the antecedent is certain to the speaker, as happens with activities the speaker him/herself performs and with internalized events, the sentence receives a "when/every time/whenever" meaning. Whether or not the interpretation is a one-time event "when" or a habitual event "every time/whenever" depends on the context and the pragmatic judgment made by the listener.

In addition, the notion of "invited inference" is a great indicator of how strongly a hypothetical meaning is expressed in a sentence. Hypothetical situations often cause a speaker to imply, or an interlocutor to infer, that a result other than that expressed in the antecedent is possible due to the unpredictability of the realization of the expressed antecedent. For example, in the use of natural language, if one says 30ドルくれれば、働いてあげよう "If you give me thirty dollars an hour, I would work for you," it invites an inference about the opposite situation: 30ドルくれなければ、働かない "If you do not give me thirty dollars an hour, I would not work for you." This tendency is referred to as "invited inference," a term proposed by Geis and Zwicky (1971), who pointed out the applicability of biconditionals to natural language phenomena and suggested that a sentence of the form X . . . Y invites an inference of the form ~X . . . ~Y ("~" indicates "negative").

In our daily communication, it is not difficult to perceive that the higher the degree of hypotheticality of a sentence, the stronger the possibility of the proposition's suggesting invited inference. In other words, when a speaker has firm evidence in stating a proposition, the statement does not cause an interlocutor to infer an alternate situation. On the other hand, if the speaker is uncertain of the situation's being true or realized, the interlocutor can scarcely help inferring an alternate situation. To seek a possibility of expressing an invited inference is a good test for discerning whether a conditional sentence expresses a high degree of hypotheticality. と sentences are least likely to create this "invited inference" interpretation, which means that their degree of hypotheticality is low or even nil.

1.1.1 Some grammatical restrictions

When the consequent includes a predicate that expresses human volition, と becomes a grammatically unacceptable option. This is due to the fact that human volition cannot support the establishment of something generally valid. Human volition does not necessarily guarantee the certain realization of an event; therefore, it cannot create a temporal, factual connection between the antecedent and the consequent, which after all contradicts the fundamental function of と sentences. Thus, the unacceptability of these sentences is based on the speaker's volitional involvement in the consequent. Note the following examples:

(8) * わからないと、先生に聞いてみてください。
If you don't understand, please ask your teacher and see (what she says).
(9) * 明日晴れると、ピクニックへ行きましょう。
If it is sunny tomorrow, let's go on a picnic.
(10) * 大学を出ると、コンピュータプログラマーになりたいです。
When I graduate from college, I want to become a computer programmer.
(11) * そのアパートがきれいだと、借りるつもりです。
If the apartment is clean, I will rent it.
(12) * テレビが安いと買おうと思っています。
If the TV is cheap, I am thinking of buying it.

All of the example sentences (8) through (12) have a volitional expression in the consequent and are considered inappropriate. In order to express this meaning, たら is the preferred conditional, because it does not have such restrictions.

1.2 と sentences in past contexts
1.2.1 Non-hypothetical と

The fundamental function of と sentences in non-past contexts, namely, to present natural courses of events, or general/scientific/mathematical facts, is also applicable to と sentences in past contexts. However, since past events have already occurred, unlike future events, they can be externally and objectively observed. と sentences in past context usually create an impression that the situation is descriptive information or is observed from the eyes of a third person. This feature often generates a restriction in the use of と sentences in past contexts, as と becomes awkward when used to describe the speaker's own activities. When a と sentence is used to describe the speaker him/herself, the sentence creates a nuance that s/he is objectively observing him/herself as a third person or presenting his/her activity as descriptive information. This use is often found in novels and essays. Consider, for example, 私はコートを脱ぐと、ハンガーにかけた "I took off my coat and put it on a hanger." This sentence may be used in novels and essays as a descriptive sentence, but it is not used in daily communication. 私はコートを脱いでハンガーにかけた is more appropriate. Let's observe some more example sentences:

(13) ジョンはコートを脱ぐと、ハンガーにかけた。
John took off his coat and put it on a hanger. (This sounds much more natural than it would if 私 were the subject.)

(14) 本田さんは先生を見ると、逃げた。
When/whenever Mr. Honda saw his teacher, he ran away. (one-time/habitual event)

(15) ジョンは家へ帰ると、すぐにシャワーを浴びた。
When John returned home, he took a bath right away.

(16) お酒を飲むと眠くなった。
When I had alcohol, I became sleepy. (descriptive information about the speaker)

(17) メリーは大学を卒業すると、すぐに日本へ行った。
As soon as Mary graduated from college, she went to Japan.
(18) この薬を飲まないと、頭痛が治らなかった。（＝この薬を飲むと、頭痛が治った。）
Unless I was taking this medication, my headache did not get cured. (When I took this medication, my headache was cured.)

1.2.2 Hypothetical と

Although due to the descriptive feature of と sentences in past contexts, one often finds と sentences in written documents rather than in verbal communication, と can be used in colloquial communication to express a hypothetical meaning—in this case, a counterfactual meaning. However, usually some kind of grammatical device is required in order to express such a meaning. Observe the following examples:

(19) 昨日のパーティに来ると<u>よかったのに</u>・・・（どうして来なかったの？）
It would have been good if you had come to yesterday's party. (Why didn't you come?)
(You should have come to yesterday's party. I regret that you did not come.)
(20) 先生に聞くと、よく<u>わかっただろうに</u>・・・。（聞かなかったから、わからなかった）
If you had asked your teacher, you would have understood better.
(You should have asked your teacher to understand better.)
(21) あなたがあんな変なことを言わないと、<u>よかったんだけど</u>・・・。（言ったから困った）
You should not have said weird things like that.

The hypothetical interpretation seems to be created by the use of よかった as a predicate in the consequent and by some other devices, such as けど "but," のに "though," and so forth, that create a counterfactual meaning. In fact, 〜とよかった means "I wish" and is considered a counterfactual set phrase. The chances of

と sentences receiving a hypothetical interpretation in past context is therefore slim due to the fact that the use of conditional と is primarily related to events in the real world.

2. たら

The conditional form たら consists of the past tense suffix た and the mora ら. Unlike と, たら is *not* used to express an "every time/whenever (habitual)" meaning, but is used instead to express a hypothetical meaning "if" or non-hypothetical meaning "when." When a たら sentence is used to express a "when" meaning, it refers to a one-time, specific event. The notion of specificity, in fact, plays a crucial role in determining the meaning of たら sentences, especially in past contexts, and differentiates the meaning of たら sentences from と sentences. In the following, たら sentences in non-past contexts are observed first, followed by sentences in past contexts.

Verb	行った
	行かなかった
い adjective	おもしろかった
	おもしろくなかった
な adjective	ひまだった
	ひまじゃなかった
Noun	学生だった
	学生じゃなかった

+ ら、 　Main clause

2.1 たら sentences in non-past contexts

In non-past contexts, a non-hypothetical interpretation (when) is generated by the speaker's knowledge about the world: if the truth of the event described in the antecedent is known to the speaker, then the sentence receives a non-hypothetical interpretation. A hypothetical interpretation (if), on the other hand, generally originates in certain factors, such as another individual's activity, natural phenomena, and/or events described by non-volitional intransitive verbs.[2] These

---

[2] Non-volitional intransitive verbs are, e.g., 沈む "to sink," 開く "to open," and 消える "to be extinguished," which do not involve the volitional control of an animate entity, while volitional intransitive

events, at root, all communicate the notion of indeterminability and uncontrollability[3] of the event's realization, as viewed by the speaker. When an event is beyond the speaker's volitional control, a たら sentence expresses a hypothetical meaning (if). Observe the following sentences, paying attention to the meaning they express:

(1) 夏になったら、一緒に旅行しましょう。(When)
    When/*If summer comes, let's go on a trip together.
(2) 試験が終わったら、アルバイトを始めるつもりです。(When)
    When/*If the exams are over, I intend to start a part-time job.
(3) 成田に着いたら、電話します。(When)
    I will call you when/*if I arrive at Narita.
(4) 本田さんが来たら、教えてください。(When/If)
    When/If Mr. Honda comes, let me know.
(5) 日本に行ったら、富士山に登りたい。
    When/If I go to Japan, I want to climb Mt. Fuji.
(6) 暇だったら、一緒に映画を見ませんか。(If)
    If/??When you have free time, why don't we go see a movie?
(7) お金があったら、新しい車が買いたいです。(If)
    If/??When I have money, I would like to buy a new car.
(8) 雨が降ったら、遠足は延期になります。(If)
    If/*When it rains, the field trip will be postponed.
(9) 大きい地震が来たら、この家は壊れるだろう。(If)
    If/*When a big earthquake comes, this house will be demolished.

Sentences (1) through (3) describe situations where the speaker knows the realization of the event in the antecedent; therefore, regardless of the type of the predicate, they express a "when" meaning. An "if" interpretation makes the situation

---

verbs, e.g., 歩く "to walk," 泳ぐ "to swim," and 飛ぶ "to fly," do involve the volitional control of animate entity.

[3] The term "indeterminability" means that the truth or realization of the event in question cannot be known from the speaker's viewpoint. The term "uncontrollability" means that the truth or realization of the event in question cannot be manipulated by the speaker's volition.

awkward, because it sounds as if the speaker does not know whether summer is coming, if the exams are going to be over, or if the speaker is going to arrive at Narita or not, respectively. Also, these sentences do not receive an "invited inference" interpretation.

The interpretation of sentences (4) and (5) can depend entirely on the situation of the speaker. If the speaker knows that Mr. Honda is coming, then the interpretation is "when," and if Mr. Honda's coming has not previously been arranged, then the interpretation is "if." The same observation can be applied to sentence (5). Whether or not the interpretation of the sentence is "when" or "if" depends on the situation. The realization and/or the truth of the antecedent is judged based on the environment where the sentences are uttered.

As for sentences (6) and (7), an "if" interpretation is more appropriate, since another individual's schedule and having enough money to buy a car are not determinable, though there may be cases where the speaker can determine the realization of these events. However, sentences (8) and (9) most definitely receive an "if" interpretation, because weather patterns and occurrences of earthquakes are not predictable to the speaker.

Thus, たら can be used to express either an "if" or a "when" meaning, and the speaker's knowledge about the truth and/or the realization of the event in the antecedent is the key to distinguishing one meaning from the other.

2.2 たら sentences in past contexts
2.2.1 Non-hypothetical たら

In past contexts, the "specificity" fundamentally carried by たら communicates the concept of "first-time recognition," which leads たら sentences to receive meanings of "discovery," "surprise," and/or "unexpectedness." Most sentences are interpreted as expressing the speaker's feeling of unexpectedness. Since these notions contradict the speaker's own knowledge, たら sentences are awkward when the speaker him/herself is the subject of both the antecedent and the consequent. Observe the following examples comparing たら and と sentences:

(10) a. 家へ帰ったら、先生が来ていた。
    When I returned home, I was surprised to find my teacher visiting me.
   b. 家へ帰ると、先生が来ていた。
    When I returned home, I found my teacher visiting me.

(11) a. 本当のことを言ったら、頭をぶたれた。
When I told the truth, I was surprised to be hit on the head.
b. 本当のことを言うと、頭をぶたれた。
When I told the truth, I was hit on the head.

(12) a. 時計を見たら、もう10時だった。
When I saw my watch, (I unexpectedly found that) it was already 10 o'clock.
b. 時計を見ると、もう10時だった。
When I saw my watch, I found that it was already 10 o'clock.

(13) a. 部屋がきれいだったら、母が1000円くれた。
When my room was clean, my mother gave me 1000 yen (which I was not expecting).
b. 部屋がきれいだと、母が1000円くれた。
When my room was clean, my mother gave me 1000 yen (as a routine reward).

(14) a. ビールを1杯飲んだら、眠くなった。
When I had a glass of beer, surprisingly, I became sleepy.
b. ビールを1杯飲むと、眠くなった。
When I had a glass of beer, I became sleepy (as a habit).

Both たら and と can be used to express a "when" meaning in past contexts. The interpretation is different because たら sentences express that the speaker discovers the event unexpectedly. たら sentences thus express a speaker's observation internally, and therefore may rarely be seen in a descriptive written document. In such cases と, which is used to express a situation that is externally and objectively viewed by a speaker, is used instead.

2.2.2 Hypothetical たら

In past contexts, たら sentences can also express an "if" meaning, i.e., a counterfactual meaning. However, in order for a たら sentence to receive a counterfactual interpretation, grammatical devices, such as the use of のに and/or aspectual form ている are required. Observe the following examples:

(15) a. 毎日きちんと勉強したら、Aが取れた。
When I studied every day regularly, I was able to get an A grade.
b. 毎日きちんと勉強したら、Aが取れた<u>のに</u>・・・。
If I studied every day regularly, I would have been able to get an A grade.
c. 毎日きちんと勉強<u>していたら</u>、Aが取れ<u>ていた</u>。
If I had studied every day regularly, I would have been able to get an A grade.

(16) a. もっと早く誰かに相談したら、こんなことにならなかった<u>のに</u>。
If you had consulted someone earlier, it would not have turned out this way.
b. もっと早く誰かに相談<u>していたら</u>、こんなことにならなかった。
If I had consulted someone much earlier, it would not have turned out this way.

(17) あんなに深い所で泳がなかったら、溺れなかった<u>だろうに</u>・・・。
If (he) had not swum in such a deep place, he would not have drowned.

Some contexts, such as those in sentences (16) and (17), may naturally create a counterfactual meaning without the necessity of a grammatical device. In sentence (15), のに and ている certainly explicate the meaning of those sentences. Compared to と, たら is more frequently used to express a counterfactual meaning.

2.2.3 たら for advice

たら is frequently used in the set phrase 〜たらいい when one seeks/gives advice. The meaning is "it would be good if you do 〜." Observe the following examples:

(18) a. この問題の答がわからないのですが、誰に聞いたらいいですか。
I cannot figure out the answer to this question. Whom should I ask?
b. 寺村先生に聞いたらいいですよ。
It would be good if you asked Dr. Teramura. (You may want to ask Dr. Teramura.)

(19) a. 鍵をなくしたんですが、どうしたらいいでしょう。
I lost my key. What shall I do?
b. 保安室に行ってみたらどうでしょう。
Why don't you go to the security office and see if they have it?

と and ば are also applicable to this construction, but たら is most frequently used among all conditional forms because it is the safest one to use in terms of the tone of politeness.

3. ば

First, look at the formation of the ば form for all parts of speech.

Consonant verbs	Vowel verbs	Irregular verbs	い adjectives	な adjectives & nouns
読めば	できれば	来れば	安ければ	きれいなら(ば)
歩けば	寝れば	すれば	よければ	日曜日なら(ば)

ば conditional sentences are primarily used to express a hypothetical meaning in both non-past and past contexts. For example, 来ればいい means "it will be good if you come (you should come)" and 来ればよかった "it would have been good if you had come (I wish you had come)." When a ば sentence is used in past contexts, it creates a counterfactual meaning "If it were ~, it would have been ~," but it does not create a "when" meaning.

3.1　ば sentences in non-past contexts

Situations described by ば sentences can alternate between hypothetical and non-hypothetical worlds depending on the speaker's perception and the context. However, a ば sentence expressing a non-hypothetical meaning refers only to a repeated event and does not express a one-time "when" meaning. This means that ば sentences are used to express either an "if" meaning or an "every time/whenever" meaning.

　　When a sentence includes specific information or information that *cannot* be generalized, the ば sentence usually receives an "if" meaning. However, when such information is not provided or cannot be perceived, the sentence can receive an "every time/whenever" interpretation, as it is considered general knowledge common to everyone. Observe the following examples:

(1) a. 風邪をひいた時は、この薬を飲んでよく寝れば、早く治ります。
   When you have caught a cold, if you take this medication and sleep well, you can get better quickly.
   b. 風邪をひいた時は、薬を飲んでよく寝れば、早く治ります。
   When you catch a cold, take medication and sleep well, and you can get better quickly. (General knowledge: taking medication and sleeping well help you get better quickly.)

(2) a. 今度の司法試験に受かれば、弁護士になれる。
   If I pass the bar exam this time, I can be a lawyer.
   b. 司法試験に受かれば、弁護士になれる。
   If one passes the bar exam, s/he can be a lawyer. (General knowledge: one can be a lawyer upon passing the bar exam.)

(3) a. 今日あの店へ行けば、すしが食べ放題で食べられる。
   If you go to that restaurant today, you can have all the sushi you can eat.
   b. あの店へ行けば、すしが食べ放題で食べられる。
   If you go to that restaurant you can have all the sushi you can eat. (General knowledge: that restaurant serves all-you-can-eat sushi.)

(4) ガラスの花瓶は落とせば割れる。
   If you drop a vase made of glass, it will break. (Specific event or general knowledge)

(5) 期末試験が終われば、アルバイトが始められる。
   ?? If the final exams are over, I can start a part-time job.
   I can start a part-time job upon finishing the final exams. (General knowledge)

(6) 春になれば花が咲く。
   * If spring comes, flowers bloom.
   Flowers bloom in spring. (General knowledge)

Sentences (1) through (3) are cases where the interpretation is slightly different depending on the existence of the specific information. When specific information is given, such as in sentence (3b), 今日あの店へ行けば、an "if and only if" interpretation emerges and emphasizes the condition described in the antecedent. When specific information is not provided, the interpretation is also less specific, and the sentence as a whole is presented as general knowledge.

Sentences (5) and (6), on the other hand, are difficult to perceive as expressing an "if" meaning. This observation is especially true for sentence (6), since the coming of spring is a natural phenomenon and cannot be considered a hypothetical event. Thus, ば in non-past context can express either an "if" meaning or an "every time/whenever" meaning which refers to a general event.

3.1.1 Grammatical restrictions on the use of ば

Conditional sentences in non-past contexts have some grammatical restrictions where ば cannot be used. When a predicate in the antecedent is an activity verb, the forms that express a speaker's intention, desire, command, or request cannot be used in the main clause (Johnson 2000, 2004a). However, when a predicate in the antecedent is a stative predicate, this restriction does not apply. Observe the following examples:

(7) * a. 日本へ行けば、うなぎが食べたい。
     If I go to Japan, I want to eat eel.
   * b. その本を読み終われば、この本を読んでください。
     If you finish reading the book, please read this book.
   * c. Alien 5 を見れば、批評を聞かせて欲しい。
     If you see "Alien 5," please let me hear your critique.

(8) a. 安ければぜひ買うつもりだ。
     If it's cheap, I will by all means buy it.
   b. 寒ければ窓を閉めてください。
     If it is cold, please close the window.
   c. 数学の先生ならば、この計算問題の答を教えてほしい。
     If you are a math teacher, I would like you to tell me the answer to this calculation problem.

3.1.2 Comparisons with たら and と

In the previous sections about conditional forms, we have learned that an "if" meaning can also be expressed by たら, and an "every time/whenever" meaning by と. What is then the difference in the use of a different conditional form?

(9) a. 日本へ行けば日本語が上手になる。
   If you go to Japan, your Japanese will improve.
   You will naturally improve your Japanese upon going there. (General knowledge)
   b. 日本へ行ったら日本語が上手になる。
   If you go to Japan, your Japanese will improve.

Sentences (9a) and (9b) do not draw special attention to the way sentences are uttered in day-to-day situations: in them, ば can be replaced by たら without changing the shades of meaning to a great extent. The difference between sentences (9a) and (9b) is that the former emphasizes the *condition* (that is, "to go to Japan") for improving your Japanese, while the latter emphasizes the *consequence* of the action you take (that is, "to go to Japan") receiving an interpretation that "If you go to Japan, *what do you think will happen? Your Japanese will improve.*" Also, while (9a) may be interpreted as expressing general knowledge, (9b) does not give such a picture.

(10) a. 春になれば花が咲く。
   Flowers bloom in spring.
   b. 春になると花が咲く。
   When spring comes, flowers bloom.

Both sentences (10a) and (10b) are expressing a well-known fact and have the same meaning. A slight difference is that while (10b) is a descriptive statement about flowers blooming, (10a) expresses a speaker's expectation/perspective that the whole statement is valid from the speaker's viewpoint. Since the basic meaning of a ば antecedent is "if and only if," which creates an extremely limited condition, it often creates a reverse effect making one hope strongly that the whole statement will be valid.[4]

3.2 ば sentences in past contexts

In past contexts, ば sentences typically express a counterfactual meaning without requiring any further grammatical devices, though the use of のに and ている make the counterfactual meaning much clearer. Also, ば sentences in past contexts create a strong "invited inference" interpretation. Although ば sentences in past contexts can refer to past habitual events, in such cases, additional grammatical devices, such as the use of ものだ "used to ~" may be required to elucidate the meaning. Observe the following examples.

3.2.1 Counterfactual events

(11) a. お金があれば、宝石を買った。
(でも、なかったから買わなかった。)
If I had had money, I would have bought jewelry. (But, since I didn't have money, I didn't buy any.)

b. お金があれば、宝石を<u>買っていた</u>。
(でも、なかったから買わなかった)
If I had money, I would have bought jewelry.

(12) a. もう少し安ければ、よく売れた。(高かったから売れなかった。)
If it had been a bit cheaper, it would have sold well. (It did not sell well because it was expensive.)

b. もう少し安ければ、よく売れた<u>だろうに</u>。
If it had been a bit cheaper, it would have sold well.

(13) きのうのパーティはとても楽しかった。来ればよかった<u>のに</u>。
(どうして来なかったの？)
Yesterday's party was a lot of fun. You should have come. (Why didn't you come?)

---

[4] This observation is not appropriate for a warning, such as 薬を飲まなければよくならない "If you don't take medication, you don't get better." In a warning, the speaker believes that the whole statement is valid from his/her viewpoint.

3.2.2 Past habitual events

(14) 子供の時は、犬を見れば、そばへ行って頭をなでた<u>ものだ</u>。

When I was a child, whenever I saw a dog, I walked up to it and petted it on the head.

(15) 葉子さんのことを考えれば、胸がドキドキした<u>ものだ</u>。

My heart used to beat fast whenever I thought of Yoko.

Sentences (11) through (13) are cases where ば sentences are used to express a counterfactual meaning. It is better in cases like these to have a grammatical device to explicate the meaning. For example, it is possible to interpret sentence (11a) as having a past habitual meaning, such as "whenever I had money, I bought jewelry," depending on context. On the other hand, as seen in sentences (14) and (15), when ものだ is used, it explicitly expresses a past habitual meaning. The use of ものだ creates a somewhat nostalgic atmosphere; the speaker knows that it is no longer possible to experience the same situation at the current time.

4. なら

なら generally follows the plain form of all parts of speech and expresses an "if" meaning. For な adjectives and nouns, なら may be followed by ば, as in 便利なら(ば) "if it is convenient" and 学生なら(ば) "if you are a student." In our day-to-day communication, なら is usually used in non-past contexts to express future hypothetical situations. In some cases, however, なら may follow the た form of a part of speech, indicating a past event or a counterfactual meaning in a past context.

なら is a rather unique conditional form compared to other conditionals, since なら is entirely discourse dependent. なら is often used in a sentence that reiterates, summarizes, and/or advances previously conveyed communication as information belonging to the domain of a third person (Johnson, 1997). Also, the use of なら may differ from that of other conditionals in that the order of the two events in the antecedent and the consequent is not necessarily temporal. For example, in the sentence 日本へ行ったらパスポートを更新しなければならない "When/If I go to Japan, I have to renew my passport," regardless of the interpretation of たら (hypothetical or non-hypothetical), the speaker, going to Japan first, then renews the passport in Japan. The realization of the event in the antecedent is followed by the realization of the event in the consequent. On the contrary, in the sentence described by なら, as in 日本へ行くならパスポートを更新しなければならない "If what I am going/hope to do—visiting Japan—becomes true/realized, I have to renew the passport," the speaker renews the passport before leaving for Japan. Thus the order of two events may not be in the same time sequence in たら sentences and なら sentences.

As discussed earlier, the fundamental feature of conditionals is best viewed in terms of "contingency." Conditional sentences are expressing a relationship between two events whereby one event is contingent on the prior realization of another, as put forward by Jacobsen (1992). When なら is used, however, the event in the consequent might be realized prior to the realization of the event in the antecedent. Thus a なら sentence conveys that, provided that the statement in the antecedent becomes true/realized, then the statement in the consequent becomes true/realized. Therefore, in 日本へ行くならパスポートを更新しなければならない, renewing the passport is contingent on the realization of the speaker's visiting Japan—the speaker's plan has to become feasible. Sentences formed using なら abide by the contingency relationship just as other conditionals do.

Another example that might become an issue is the difference between から and なら, as in あなたがそう言うから、従います "Since (it is the case that) you say so, I will obey you" and あなたがそう言うなら、従います "If (it is the case that) you say so, I will obey you." These two sentences have different meanings. In the former, the speaker has already confirmed and internalized what was said and possesses the information in his own domain. In the latter sentence, however, the speaker has not yet confirmed or internalized what was said, and there is still room for uncertainty, indicating that the information has not yet come entirely into the domain of the speaker. なら is used when a given piece of information based on previous discourse does not entirely belong to the speaker, and the speaker tries to confirm the information by repeating the sentence, summarizing the previous discourse, or presenting a related entity to advance the communication. The interpretation of なら sentences is therefore context dependent, and one needs to fill in a lot in order to understand the meaning of the sentence in English. Now let us observe some example sentences:

(1) 東京のデパートで：
At a department store in Tokyo:
A: あのジャケットは８万円。そのスカートは５万５千円・・・。このドレスは・・・、え、２０万円！？わあ、手が出ないわ。
That jacket over there is 80,000 yen. That skirt is 55,000 yen. And, this dress is . . . Oops, it is 200,000 yen?! I cannot afford it.
B: そんなに高いなら、アメリカでセールの時に買えば？
If it is the case that you think they are so expensive, why don't you buy them when they are on sale in the United States?

In the dialogue above, speaker B uses なら in response to the information that speaker A gives. Speaker B does so by assuming and summarizing what speaker A must be feeling: "if I'm correctly understanding that you are talking about the prices being high, you should buy them in the United States when they are on sale." This is a perfect example of information that has not yet been confirmed, so that there is still room for uncertainty. The information is not yet common to both speaker A and speaker B.

(2) ある女の人が隣の犬にかまれたんです。あなたならそういう時どうしますか。
A woman was bitten by a neighbor's dog. If it were the case of you, (supposing it happened to you), what would you do?

(3) A: お宅のお子さんはしつけができていませんね。
Your son is not disciplined.
B: そんなこと言うなら、お宅のお子さんとうちのを遊ばせないでください。
If it is the case that you say things like that, please don't let your son play with my son.
A: それなら、家の子も悪い影響を受けないでしょう。
If that is the case, suppose we take it that way, I would assume that my son won't receive bad influence (from your son).

(4) 笑ってくれるなら、冗談を一つ言いましょう。
If it is the case that you laugh (If it amuses you), I will tell you a joke.
(5) できた！これなら完璧だ。
It's done! If this is the case of perfection, this is it.
(6) もしも私が家を建てたなら、大きな家を建てたでしょう。
If I had built a house, I would have built a big house.
(7) そんなにおいしかった(の)なら、もっと食べればよかったのに。
If it was that delicious, you should have eaten more.
(8) 彼がハンサムで頭がいいなら、もてるのはあたりまえだ。
If he is handsome and smart, it is natural for others to fall in love with him.

Sentences (6) and (7) express a counterfactual meaning—something did not turn out the way it was supposed to—due to the use of the た form in the antecedent and grammatical devices でしょう and のに. Sentence (8) gives almost the same interpretation as the antecedent with から in 彼がハンサムで頭がいいから "Because he is handsome and smart." The difference is that when なら is used, the information is not in the speaker's domain, and there is still room to hypothesize about the information conveyed. By using なら, the speaker can avoid stating the attributes making the speaker responsible for the statement. On the other hand, when から "since" is used, the information is entirely in the speaker's domain, and there is no room to hypothesize. Thus, placing an event in a hypothetical domain by using なら leaves room for the speaker to avoid making a direct statement and assuming responsibility.

For learners whose first language is English, Japanese conditionals are difficult to understand comprehensively due to the fact that one particular form in the learner's native language corresponds to more than two forms in the target language, a divergent phenomenon pointed out by Inaba (1991). "Give" and "receive," as explained in Chapter 20, are another example of such divergence, as Japanese has two verbs that are equivalent to "give." Although there are always exceptions in the way grammar is described, understanding the basic, fundamental issues of a grammar item should be a great help. It will eventually come naturally if learners have a thorough grasp of the fundamental issues.

CHAPTER 27

Comparative Sentences

The comparative construction is used when two entities are evaluated in relation to each other. Predicates used in the comparative construction are often either an い adjective or な adjective. Verbs are usually accompanied by an adverb, and nouns are accompanied by a modifier indicating degree, quantity, or frequency. Let us first observe the structure for forming a question, then have a look at constructing the answers to the questions. Pay attention to the variations.

1. Creating a Question Sentence

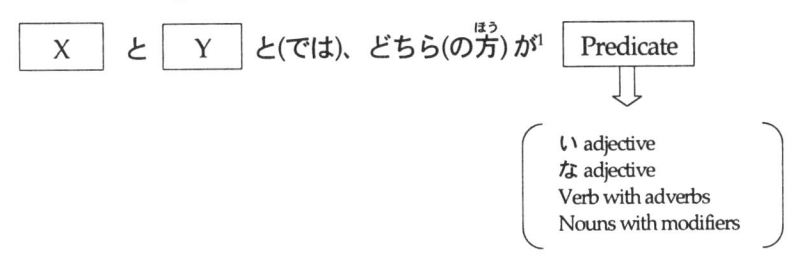

| X | と | Y | と(では)、どちら(の方)が[1] | Predicate |

⇩

```
い adjective
な adjective
Verb with adverbs
Nouns with modifiers
```

(1) カリフォルニア州と日本と(では)、どちら(の方)が大きいですか。
Which is bigger, the state of California or Japan?

(2) 高校と大学と(では)、どちら(の方)が成績がよかったですか。
Which transcript was better, high school or college?

(3) 豊田さんと松田さんと(では)、どちら(の方)が足が速いですか。
Who runs faster, Ms. Toyota or Ms. Matsuda?

(4) 犬と猫と(では)、どちら(の方)が好きですか。
Which do you like better, dogs or cats?

---

[1] が here is used as an example, but the particle does not have to be が. For example, 韓国と中国と、どちらへ行きたいですか "Where (to which) would you like to go, Korea or China?" In this sentence, the particle へ is used. See also example sentences (9) and (12) in the text.

(5) 東京では、電車とバスと(では)、どちら(の方)が便利ですか。
In Tokyo, which is more convenient, the subway or the bus?
(6) 鈴木先生と本田先生と(では)、どちら(の方)がいい医者ですか。
Who is a better doctor, Dr. Suzuki or Dr. Honda?
(7) ジョンとトムと(では)、どちら(の方)が有名な歌手ですか。
Who is a more famous singer, John or Tom?
(8) すしとてんぷらと(では)、どちら(の方)がたくさん食べられますか。
Which can you eat more, sushi or tempura?
(9) レストランと喫茶店と(では)、どちら(の方)へよく行きますか。
Where do you go more often, to a restaurant or to a coffee shop?
(10) チータとひょうと(では)、どちら(の方)が早く走れますか。
Which can run faster, a cheetah or a leopard?

The comparative structure is also used when one chooses between two items. In this case, the sentence is not necessarily comparing the degree, quality, quantity, and/or frequency, but indicating a preference. When the structure is used this way, とでは is not an option.

(11) コーヒーと日本茶、どちら(の方)を飲みますか。
Which are you going to drink, coffee or green tea?
(12) 東京と京都、どちら(の方)へ行くつもりですか。
Which city are you planning to visit, Tokyo or Kyoto?

2. Answering Question Sentences

In answering a comparative sentence, there are several ways to construct a response. Note that as long as the correct particles are used, the order of X の方が and Y より can be reversed.

a. X (の方)が Y より Predicate

b. X (の方)が Predicate

c. X です

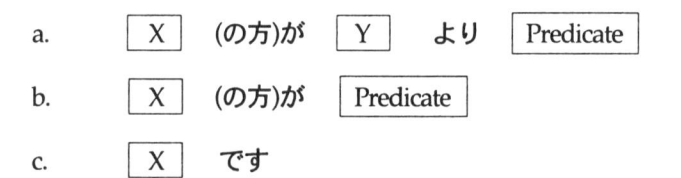

(1) Q:カリフォルニア州と日本と(では)、どちら(の方)が大きいですか。
Which is bigger, the state of California or Japan?
A1: カリフォルニア州の方が 日本より 大きいです。or
日本より カリフォルニア州の方が 大きいです。
The state of California is bigger than Japan.
A2: カリフォルニア州の方が大きいです。
The state of California is bigger.
A3: カリフォルニア州です。
The state of California.

If the sentence is given as a statement (not as an answer to a question), カリフォルニア州は日本より大きいです "The state of California is bigger than Japan" is an appropriate sentence. In the following examples, the sentence in parentheses is a simple statement.

(2) 犬より猫(の方)が好きです。(猫は犬より好きです。)
(3) レストランより喫茶店(の方)へよく行きます。(喫茶店へはレストランよりよく行きます。)
I go to a restaurant more often than to a coffee shop.
(4) 鈴木先生の方が本田先生よりいい医者です。(鈴木先生は本田先生よりいい医者です。)
Dr. Suzuki is a better doctor than Dr. Honda.

When two compared entities are very close based on the evaluation criterion indicated by the predicate, a different construction may be used to exhibit the closeness.

d.　 X も predicate ですが、 Y ほどじゃありません。

For example, when the size of the United States and Canada is compared, though both are big countries, Canada is slightly bigger than the United States. In this case, one may say that America is a big country, but not as big as Canada. See the following examples in Japanese:

(5) 犬も好きですが猫ほどじゃありません。
I like dogs, but not as much as I like cats.
(6) レストラン(へ)もよく行きますが、喫茶店ほどじゃありません。
I often go to a restaurant, but not as often as I go to a coffee shop.
(7) 本田先生もいい医者ですが、鈴木先生ほどじゃありません。
Dr. Honda is also a good doctor, but not as good as Dr. Suzuki.

Due to the availability of diverse structures, there are many ways to create a comparative sentence. As long as the correct particles are used, word order is not a concern to a great extent.

Trivia quiz

Look up the words you do not know in the dictionary.
(1) コーヒーと日本茶と、どちらの方がカフェインが強いですか。
(2) 東京とロスアンゼルスとでは、どちらの方が緯度が高いですか。
(3) ミネソタと北海道とでは、どちらの方が雪がたくさん降りますか。
(4) アメリカのビールとカナダのビールとでは、どちらの方がアルコールが強いですか。
(5) CNタワーとSearsタワーとでは、どちらの方が高いですか。
(6) エジプトと中国とでは、どちらの方が歴史が古いですか。
(7) 馬とグレイハウンド(greyhound)とではどちらの方が速いですか。
(8) スーパーマンとスパイダーマンとでは、どちらの方が強いですか。
(9) ぞうと馬とでは、どちらが長く生きますか。
(10) チキンと卵とでは、どちらが先に創られましたか。

Create questions of your own:

CHAPTER 28

Superlative Sentences

The superlative construction is used to select the most qualified item that suits the evaluation described by the predicate. Unlike the comparative construction, the given entities are not limited to two, but can be an indefinite number. All one needs to do is identify the entity that comes to the top of the list. For this reason, the word 一番 (best, most) is always used before the predicate.[1] Let's consider the creation and answering of a question sentence.

1. Creating and Answering a Question Sentence

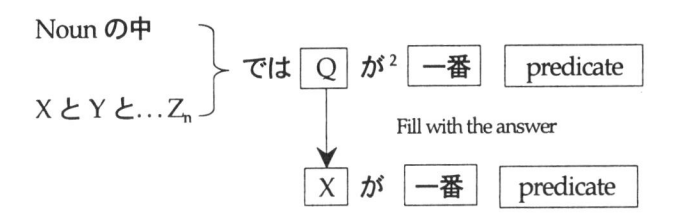

Noun の中
XとYと…Z$_n$ } では [Q] が[2] [一番] [predicate]

Fill with the answer

[X] が [一番] [predicate]

(1) A: 日本の食べ物の中で何が一番好きですか。
Among Japanese food, what do you like best?
B: すしが一番好きです。
I like sushi best.

---

[1] A common mistake is to use どちら and 一番 together in the same sentence, such as どちらが一番好きですか "Which one of two do you like best?" The English equivalent may not sound inappropriate, but in Japanese, どちら is used for a comparative sentence that requires selection of one of two entities, while 一番 is used for a superlative sentence that selects the top item of the list.

[2] が is given as an example here. It may not be が, but may be some other particle, such as を and へ as in 何を一番たくさん食べましたか "What did you eat most?" and どこへ一番行きたいですか "Where would you like to go most?"

(2) A: 家族の中で誰が一番背が高いですか。
Who is the tallest in your family?
B: 妹です。
My sister is.
(3) A: 平仮名とカタカナと漢字の中で、どれが一番むずかしいと思いますか。
Among hiragana, katakana, and kanji, which do you think is the most difficult?
B: カタカナが一番むずかしいと思います。
I think that katakana is most difficult.
(4) A: 東京と香港とニューヨークの中で、どの都市が一番物価が高いですか。
Among Tokyo, Hong Kong, and New York, which city has the highest prices?
B: 東京でしょう。
Perhaps Tokyo.

There are also some variations in the way the notion of a superlative is expressed. They all include 一番.

(5) A: 世界で一番高い山は何ですか。
What is the tallest mountain in the world?
B: (世界で一番高い山は)エベレストです。
It's Mt. Everest.
(6) A: アメリカで一番大きい州はどこですか。
What is the biggest state in America?
B: (アメリカで一番大きい州は)アラスカです。
It's Alaska.
(7) 試験で一番むずかしかったのは物理の試験です。
Among the exams, the most difficult one was the physics exam.
(8) 一番おもしろいと思った映画は「ロード・オブ・ザ・リング」です。
The movie I thought was the most interesting is *The Lord of the Rings.*
(9) 一番悲しかった出来事はペットの死です。
The saddest event was the death of my pet.

(10) 私は研究をしている時が一番充実しています。
The time when I am doing research is the most satisfying time.

Trivia quiz

Look up the words you do not know in the dictionary.

(1) 世界で一番大きい島は何ですか。
(2) 世界で一番深い湖は何ですか。
(3) 世界で一番人口が多い国はどこですか。
(4) 日本で一番大きい湖は何ですか。
(5) 日本で一番大きい県はどこですか。
(6) アメリカで一番人気のあるスポーツは何ですか。
(7) 日本で一番人気のあるスポーツは何ですか。
(8) 世界で一番長い川は何ですか。
(9) 月から一番遠い惑星は何ですか。
(10) 動物の中で一番大きいのは何ですか。
(11) 日本で一番最後の将軍は誰ですか。
(12) 世界で一番裕福(お金持ち)な人は誰ですか。
(13) 石の中で、一番硬い石は何ですか。
(14) 星の中で一番明るい星は何ですか。
(15) 動物の中で一番長く生きるのは何ですか。

Create questions of your own:

CHAPTER 29

Structures of Suggestions

In English, the process of giving and asking for suggestions uses various sentence structures, such as "How about ~?" "Why don't you ~?" and "It may be good if you do ~." In Japanese too, a variety of expressions can be formed using different sentence structures. A representative case is using the conditional forms たら and ば. One may often hear sentences, such as どうすればいい？ "What shall I do?" and 先生に相談したらどう？ "Why don't you consult your teacher?" Suggestions may not be given as a rule to a person at a higher status and/or to someone older than the speaker. Also, since a suggestion is made when a person urges someone to carry out a certain act, the predicate used in the structure of suggestions is a verb.

1. たら/ば

The conditional forms たら or ば can be used to form a sentence of suggestion when followed by どう？, どうですか, いかがですか. The meaning is "It would be good if you do ~." For example, you may say "It would be good if you went home early" when you give such a suggestion to your friend. The Japanese equivalent is 早く家へ帰ったらどうですか. The question sentence that makes such a suggestion then should be derived from the same structure, replacing the verb phrase with an interrogative noun phrase. The question that derives 帰ったら as its answer is どうしたら or どうすれば; therefore どうしたら/どうすれば いいですか "What/How shall I do ~?" is the question. When the question is given in this construction, the answer can be given in various constructions depending on the situation of the speaker, with whom the speaker is interacting, etc. The choices are up to the individual.

(1) 教科書を買いたいんですが、お財布を忘れてしまいました。どうしたらいいでしょう・・・。
I want to buy a textbook, but I forgot my wallet. What shall I do...?

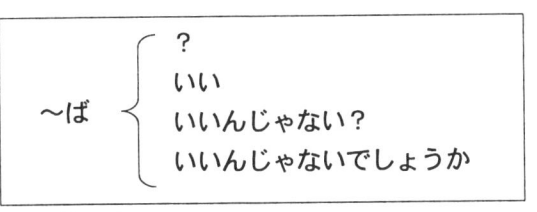

~ば
- ？
- いい
- いいんじゃない？
- いいんじゃないでしょうか

お金を借りれば？[1]
友達に友達にお金を借りればいいよ。
友達にお金を借りればいいんじゃない？
友達にお金を借りればいいんじゃないでしょうか。

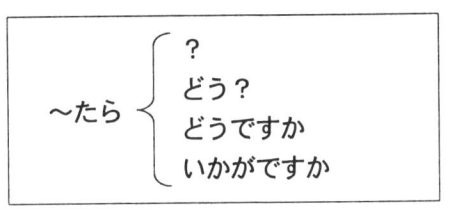

~たら
- ？
- どう？
- どうですか
- いかがですか

友達にお金を借りたら？
友達にお金を借りたらどう？
友達にお金を借りたらどうですか。
友達にお金を借りたらいかがですか。

(2) 友達に借りたコンピュータを壊してしまいました。どうすればいいでしょう。
I broke the computer I borrowed from my friend. What shall I do?

---

[1] The expressions in the forms, ?, ～ばいいよ, ～ばいいんじゃない, which are all in the plain form, are used in casual communications where the speaker speaks to his/her friends and family members, for example. ～ばいいんじゃないでしょうか is formal and is used when the speaker interacts with someone to whom the speaker is not very close emotionally and socially or who is older.

2. 方(ほう)がいい

方(ほう)がいい is another construction that may be used to express suggestion. This is a comparative sentence structure where a speaker selects one situation, event, or entity out of two. When this structure is used to make a suggestion, the person is conveying that "doing A is better than not doing A." 方がいい most frequently follows the perfective た form, but it may also follow the imperfective る form. If one suggests not doing something, ない can be used as well. The English equivalent might be "you may want to ~," "you'd better do ~," and so on.

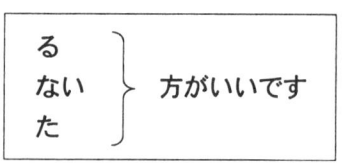

```
る    ⎫
ない  ⎬  方がいいです
た    ⎭
```

クラスは毎日出席(まいにちしゅっせき)する方がいいですよ。
クラスは休(やす)まない方がいいですよ。
クラスは毎日出席した方がいいですよ。

(1) A: 教科書(きょうかしょ)を買(か)いたいんですが、お財布(さいふ)を忘(わす)れてしまいました。どうしたらいいでしょう・・・。
    B: 友達(ともだち)にお金(かね)を借(か)りて、今日買(きょうか)った方がいいかもしれませんよ。もう売(う)り切(き)れそうですから。
    You might as well borrow money from your friend and buy it today. It looks like the textbooks are about to sell out.

(2) A: 友達に借りた本(ほん)をなくしてしまったんです。どうすればいいでしょう。
    I lost the book I borrowed from my friend. What shall I do?
    B: 早(はや)く友達に言(い)った方がいいですよ。それとももう少(すこ)し探(さが)してみますか。
    You may want to tell your friend as soon as possible. Or are you going to look for it a little more?

(3) 今日(きょう)は天気(てんき)が悪(わる)いから釣(つ)りには行(い)かない方(ほう)がいいですよ。
    Since the weather is bad today, you should not go fishing.

(4) 先生は今週忙しそうだから、来週のオフィスアワーの時に質問する方がいいと思います。
Since the teacher looks busy this week, you may want to ask her questions during next week's office hours.

Sample dialogue

空港で
係員： トロント行きの58便ですね。じゃ、パスポート、お願いします。
男： パスポート・・・アアッ！！家に忘れて来ちゃった・・・！！どうしよう・・・。
係員： お客様、パスポートがないと、カナダへは行けないんですが。
男： うん、でもここはデトロイトでしょ。たった40分じゃない、トロントまで。運転免許書じゃだめかなぁ・・・。
係員： 近くても一応外国ですので、パスポートがないと、飛行機には乗れないんです。家に取りにお戻りになるか、どなたかに届けてもらうといいと思いますが。
男： だって、離陸まであと一時間じゃない。無理だよ。
係員： 私の方ではどうすることもできませんが、この後の5時の便にお乗せすることはできます。それまでに御自宅に取りにお戻りになったら、いかがですか。
男： もう〜〜〜！それっきゃないか。じゃ、そうします。ありがとう、色々。

なくした友達のセルフォン
A： ああ、困ったなぁ・・・。友達に借りたセルフォン、どこかに落としちゃったんだ。
B： 拾った人が使い始めたら困るから、早く友達に言った方がいいよ。
A： うん・・・。でも今弁償するお金がないんだ。怒るだろうなぁ・・・。
B： こういうことは正直に話して、謝った方がいいよ。今電話すれば？
A： その電話をなくしちゃったんだよ。

[リーン、リーン]
B: あれ、電話がなってるよ？
A: ほんとだ。誰のだろう。
B: 君のおしりのあたりから聞こえてくるけど・・・。
A: あ、ほんとだ！あ、電話だ！あった、あった！
ポケットに穴があいていて、電話がずれ落ちたんだ。ああ、よかった・・・！
B: その電話、洗った方がいいんじゃない？出る前に・・・。

CHAPTER 30

Potential Sentences

There are two ways to compose sentences with a potential meaning: one may change a verb into its potential form or add ことができる to the verb dictionary form, e.g., 書ける and 書くことができる, respectively. In both cases, only verbs that can be controlled by a speaker's intention can form the potential form.

The function of the two constructions is identical, but ことができる may be more formal and, therefore, less frequently used in casual conversation. The difference between ことができる and られる lies in their syntactic behavior. られる constitutes part of a potential predicate, while ことができる is a complex phrase. The two may not employ the same particle.

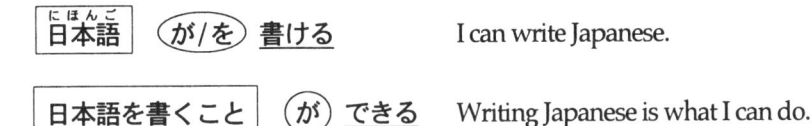

| 日本語 | が/を 書ける | I can write Japanese. |

| 日本語を書くこと | が できる | Writing Japanese is what I can do. |

As seen in the above examples, 書ける is a compound stative predicate consisting of the verb "to write" with the potential "can," while できる is a pure single stative predicate. Further explanation follows.

Potential forms can be used not only to demonstrate ability or possibility, but also permission and request (in combination with verbs of receiving). They share similarities with the potential form in English, as in "You can speak Japanese," which may mean either that you have the ability or the chance to speak Japanese or that you are allowed to speak Japanese, depending on the context and pragmatic judgment made by the speaker. Note that することができる "be able to do" should be contracted to できる "can do." In the following, the 書ける and 書くことができる patterns are observed separately.

1. 書(か)ける

First, one should learn how to inflect a verb in the potential form. Note that only activity verbs that are controlled by an animate entity with volition can be formulated in the potential.

Consonant Verbs (う verbs) → ~u becomes ~e, and る is added

運(はこ)ぶ	hakob-u	運べる	hakob-eru
なおす	naos-u	なおせる	naos-eru
勝(か)つ	kats-u	勝てる	kat-eru

Vowel Verbs (る verbs) → verb stem + られる

起(お)きる	oki-ru	起きられる	oki-rareru
かける	kake-ru	かけられる	kake-rareru
見(み)る	mi-ru	見られる	mi-rareru

Irregular Verbs

| する | | できる | |
| 来(く)る | | 来(こ)られる | |

When the potential suffixes ~*eru* and ~*rareru* are attached to a verb, the verb is considered a compound, stative predicate, and an object of the verb can be marked by either the particle が or the particle を (though が may be considered principal due to the stative nature of the predicate).[1] In theory, when が is used, the potential できる is more emphasized, as in "I *can* speak Japanese," whereas the action of the verb 話(はな)す is emphasized, as in "I can *speak* Japanese" when を is used. The formation of the potential sentence is as follows:

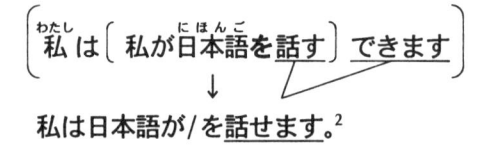

$$私(わたし)は [私が 日本語(にほんご)を 話す] できます$$
$$↓$$
$$私は日本語が/を 話(はな)せます。[2]$$

---

[1] This grammatical regulation is the same as when the desiderative form たい is used. See Chapter 9.
[2] Note that 私には日本語が話せます is also an option if 話せる expresses the ability of the speaker.

Let's observe some examples:

(1) A: スペイン語が/を話せますか。³
　　　Can I speak Spanish? (Is it O.K. if I speak Spanish?)
　　B: ええ、いいですよ、どうぞ。
　　　Yes, you may. Please go ahead (and speak in Spanish.)
(2) A: スペイン語が/を話せますか。
　　　Can you speak Spanish?
　　B: スペイン語は苦手です。英語ならできますけど。
　　　I am bad at Spanish. If it's English, I can speak.
(3) A: 先生、うちの猫、治るでしょうか・・・。
　　　Doctor, will my cat get better?
　　B: 本当にお気の毒ですが、この病気はまだ治せないんです。
　　　I am terribly sorry, but this disease cannot be cured yet.
(4) A: ここでは、花火はあげられません。
　　　You cannot light fireworks here.
　　B: え、だめなんですか。それは知りませんでした。
　　　I can't? Oh, I didn't know that.

Although the questions in examples (1) and (2) are the same, they are functioning differently: the person in sentence (1a) is trying to obtain permission to speak Spanish, while the person in sentence (2a) is questioning whether the listener is able to speak Spanish. Conversation (3) has only a potential meaning, and conversation (4) most likely has only a permissive meaning due to the nature of the verbs and the particular content of the dialogue. If trying to obtain permission, the speaker can also use the てもいい construction that is exclusively used to express a permissive meaning.

---

³ In day-to-day conversation, you will often hear a sentence without a particle. For example, the most natural casually uttered sentence may be スペイン語、話せますか "Can I speak Spanish?" which leaves out が entirely. Although in conversation, ellipsis of particles often occurs when the meaning of the sentence can be conveyed effortlessly without them, it does not mean that they are not needed. Ellipsis can be seen when one truly has a knowledge of the language; therefore learners need to gain knowledge of the functions of the particles thoroughly in order to be able to utilize the language appropriately and accurately. Merely getting the meaning across will not let you improve your language skill to a higher level.

Another feature of potential sentences is that when the subject of the potential verb is animate and the potential form is expressing an ability or a possibility, the subject marker can be replaced by に. In such cases, it is often followed by は to create a contrastive meaning. See the following examples:

(5) 本田さんにはピアノがとても上手にひけます。
Ms. Honda can play piano very well.

(6) マットさんには日本料理が作れます。
Matt can cook Japanese food.

(7) 友達には箸を使って上手に絵が描けます。
My friend can draw pictures skillfully using chopsticks.

2. Verb Dictionary Form + ことができる

Since the phrase ことができる is longer, it is considered a bit more formal, but demonstrates exactly the same functions as the compound potential form. The syntactic difference between these two potential forms is that できる in ことができる is a pure, single stative-transtive predicate; therefore, を is never used to mark the object. See the following examples:

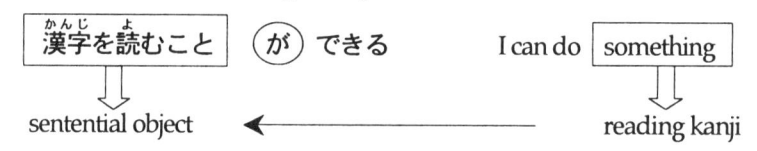

| 漢字を読むこと | (が) | できる | I can do | something |

sentential object ←————————————————— reading kanji

(1) A: ここで煙草を吸うことができますか。(= 煙草が吸えますか)
Can I smoke here? (Is it permissible to smoke here?)
B: いいえ、トイレの中ではできません。
No, you cannot smoke in the bathroom.

(2) 坂本さんは逆立ちして歩くことができます。(= 歩けます)
Mr. Sakamoto can walk on his hands.

(3) 豊田さんは100キロの石を持ち上げることができます。(= 石が持ち上げられます)
Mr. Toyota can lift a 100-kilogram stone.

(4) 私には嘘をつくことはできません。(= 嘘はつけません)
It is impossible for me to lie. (I cannot lie.)

(5) 妹には黙っていることができません。(=黙っていられません)
It is impossible for my sister to remain silent. (My sister cannot remain silent.)

(6) ジョンには納豆を食べることができます。(=納豆が食べられます)
It is possible for John to eat natto. (John can eat natto.)

Note that, as may be seen in most of the above examples, には and は are often interchanged. Sentence (2), for example, could be restated using には (坂本さんには・・・). This rephrasing has the same meaning as "It is possible for Sakamoto to walk." In the same manner, 私には in sentence (4) might be 私は, indicating that 私 is the topic/subject of the sentence.

CHAPTER 31

Passive Constructions

A passive sentence is created when a situation is observed from the viewpoint of the syntactic object of an active sentence. For example, "Mr. Honda invited Ms. Suzuki to a party" is an active sentence where Mr. Honda's activity is described. If one looks at the situation from the viewpoint of Ms. Suzuki (the object of this sentence), the sentence should be changed to the one that describes what happened to Ms. Suzuki—Ms. Suzuki was invited to a party by Mr. Honda, i.e., a passive sentence. The most basic method of constructing a passive sentence is described below.

In the following, the active sentence "Mr. Honda invited Ms. Suzuki to a party" is altered into the passive sentence "Ms. Suzuki was invited to a party by Mr. Honda."

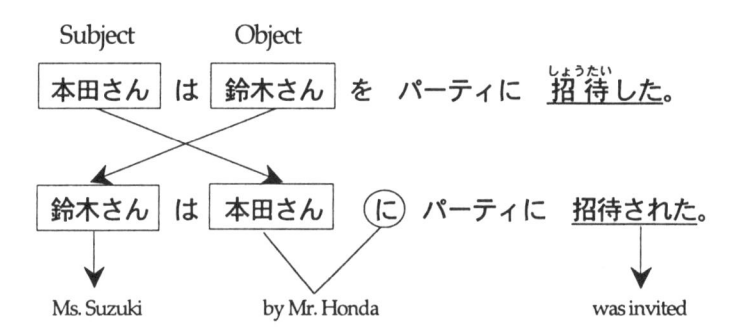

```
  Subject      Object
 ┌─────┐      ┌─────┐
 │本田さん│ は │鈴木さん│ を パーティに 招待した。
 └─────┘      └─────┘

 ┌─────┐      ┌─────┐
 │鈴木さん│ は │本田さん│ (に) パーティに 招待された。
 └─────┘      └─────┘
     ↓            ↓                      ↓
  Ms. Suzuki   by Mr. Honda          was invited
```

1. Formation of the Passive

Japanese is an agglutinative language where constituents are joined together to form predicates, and the passive form is one such example. For example, in English, "was invited" consists of two words, while in Japanese, the equivalent phrase is 招待された, which is considered a predicate consisting of the verb 招待する, the passive morpheme れる, and the past-tense marker た.

a. Consonant Verbs (う verbs) → ~u becomes ~a, and れる is added

断る	kotowar-u	断られる	kotowar-a-reru
盗む	nusum-u	盗まれる	nusum-a-reru
笑う	wara(w)-u	笑われる	waraw-a-reru
書く	kak-u	書かれる	kak-a-reru
切る	kir-u	切られる	kir-a-reru

b. Vowel Verbs (る verbs) → る is dropped and られる is added

食べる	tabe-ru	食べられる	tabe-rareru
育てる	sodate-ru	育てられる	sodate-rareru
ほめる	home-ru	ほめられる	home-rareru
教える	oshie-ru	教えられる	oshie-rareru
着る	ki-ru	着られる	ki-rareru

c. Irregular Verbs

する	される
来る	来られる

2. Structure and Meaning of the Passive Construction

The passive construction in Japanese is unique. There are two types of passive constructions in Japanese: *direct passive* and *indirect passive*. The formation of the direct passive sentence is the same as the English passive, while the formation of the indirect passive sentence is entirely different from English, which has no equivalent to it. In either case, the Japanese passive construction avoids placing an inanimate entity in the subject position unless the passive sentence conveys a factual statement that does not involve a speaker's empathy, a term used in Kuno (1987). Each of the constructions is discussed separately below.

2.1 The direct passive

The direct passive form is equivalent to the English passive form in which the syntactic object of a (di)transitive verb becomes the subject of a sentence. In the direct passive construction, the outcome of the event is the same, but the speaker observes the situation from a different viewpoint. Both active sentences and passive sentences are viewed as objective statements that describe the attribute or the state of the event.

However, when the object in an active sentence is inanimate, the direct passive sentence tends to be avoided. For example, コーヒーは鈴木さんに飲まれた "The coffee was drunk by Ms. Suzuki" is pragmatically awkward, as the speaker is observing the situation from the hypothetical viewpoint of the coffee. This is, however, not the case for sentences that describe historical and scientific facts, involve creation or discovery, or do not involve a speaker's empathy. For example, sentences such as "This building was built in the fifteenth century," "This book was written by Mishima," "A new rocket was launched last night," and so forth, are commonly used without creating awkwardness. This use of the passive construction is due to the fact that historical and scientific facts, for example, are objectively perceptible by the speaker without involving the speaker's empathy. Thus, in the direct passive construction, unless the situation can be objectively perceptible, the subject of the sentence is best with an animate entity.

Another characteristic that the direct passive construction shares with English is omission of "by people," "by them," and so forth. When the subject in the active sentence is plural and is generally understood to be sentient, it can be omitted, as in the English sentence "English is spoken in America (by people)."[1] Now observe the following examples:

(1) 小さい魚が大きい魚に食べられた。
The small fish was eaten by the big fish.

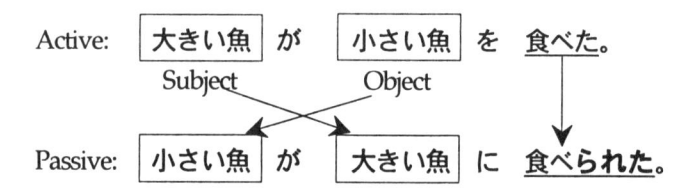

Active: | 大きい魚 | が | 小さい魚 | を　食べた。
　　　　　Subject　　　　　Object

Passive: | 小さい魚 | が | 大きい魚 | に　食べられた。

---

[1] A Japanese equivalent is アメリカでは(人々によって)英語が話されている. 人々によって, indicated in parentheses, is hardly uttered in this type of sentence. It will be mentioned only when the speaker wants to specify the type of people who speak English.

(2)　鈴木さんは本田さんにデートに誘われた。
　　Ms. Suzuki was asked to go on a date by Mr. Honda.

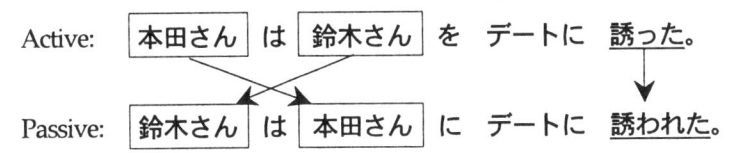

Active:　|本田さん| は |鈴木さん| を　デートに　誘った。

Passive:　|鈴木さん| は |本田さん| に　デートに　誘われた。

(3)　鈴木さんは豊田さんに本田さんに紹介された。
　　Ms. Suzuki was introduced to Mr. Honda by Ms. Toyota.

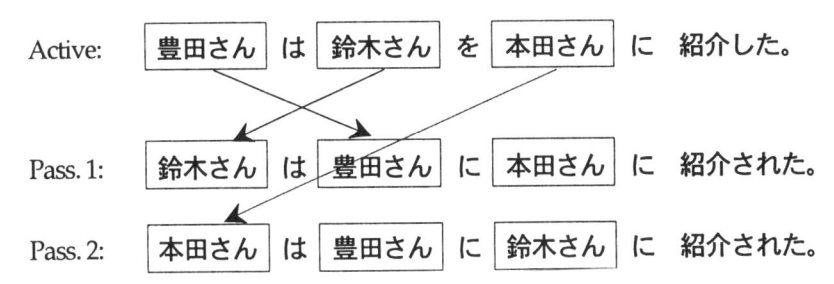

Active:　|豊田さん| は |鈴木さん| を |本田さん| に　紹介した。

Pass. 1:　|鈴木さん| は |豊田さん| に |本田さん| に　紹介された。

Pass. 2:　|本田さん| は |豊田さん| に |鈴木さん| に　紹介された。

(4)　太郎はお父さんに叱られた。
　　Taro was scolded by his father.
　　(お父さんが太郎を叱った。)

(5)　花子は先生にほめられた。
　　Hanako was praised by the teacher.
　　(先生が花子をほめた。)

In the above sentences, where the objects are all animate entities, the speaker is observing the situation from the viewpoint of the given subject. An adversity meaning is not necessarily implied unless a verb such as 叱る "to scold" communicates the concept.

When a verb expresses a notion of "creation," "discovery," and so on, によって is used instead of に.

(6)　このデパートは鹿島建設によって建てられた。
　　This department store was built by Kajima Construction Company.
　　(鹿島建設がこのデパートを建てた。)

(7) アメリカはコロンブスによって発見された。
America was discovered by Columbus.
(コロンブスがアメリカを発見した。)
(8) 「金閣寺」は三島由紀夫によって書かれた。
Golden Pavilion was written by Yukio Mishima.
(三島由紀夫が「金閣寺」を書いた。)

As mentioned earlier, when an event described by the verb is conducted by people in general, 人に "by people" is usually not mentioned.

(9) この国ではフランス語と英語が(人によって)話されている。
French and English are spoken (by people) in this country.
(この国では人はフランス語と英語を話す。)
(10) その話は(多くの人に)知られている。
That story is known (by many people).
(多くの人がその話を知っている。)

2.2 The indirect passive: adversity passive

The indirect passive is a unique construction in Japanese with no structural equivalent in English. The subject of an indirect passive is normally an animate entity to which a speaker can relate by way of empathy. The meaning is quite distinct from that of English passive sentences in that a meaning of adversity is usually created.

An indirect passive sentence usually has a sense of adversity because the animate subject suffers from an activity done by another source.[2] The subject of an indirect passive sentence is therefore typically an animate entity that can express emotion, feelings, and empathy toward the event. For example, if a mother's eating her son's cake annoyed the son, the situation is best described in an indirect

---

[2] However, when a verb such as "praise" that gives a positive interpretation is used, the nature of the verb prevails over any sense of adversity. For example, the passive version of 先生が友達の作文をほめた "The teacher praised my friend's essay" is 友達は作文を先生にほめられた "My friend was praised by the teacher because his essay was well written." Although the structure is in the indirect passive construction, this sentence does not create an adversity meaning.

passive sentence: 僕は母にケーキを食べられた "I was upset because my mother ate the cake" (which was converted from the active sentence 母が(僕の)ケーキを食べた"My mother ate my cake"). The literal translation of the subject and the predicate in the indirect passive sentence, that is, "I was eaten" does not accurately reflect the meaning of the sentence. The sentence is actually constructed as diagrammed below:[3]

$$\left(\ 僕は\ \boxed{母が(僕の)ケーキを食べる}\ \underline{られた}\ \right)$$

    I   [my mother eats my cake]   receive

I received my mother's eating my cake.

⇩

僕は母にケーキを食べられた。

I was upset by my mother's eating my cake.
= I was upset because my mother ate my cake.

This characteristic also extends to intransitive verbs that are normally not used to form passive sentences in English. A Japanese passive sentence with an intransitive verb also produces an adversity meaning. A representative example may be 私は雨に降られた "I was inconvenienced by the rain" = "I got rained on." Also, note that てしまう often accompanies the passive predicate in order to emphasize the adverse meaning.

In the following sections, the formation and meaning of a transitive verb used in an indirect passive, as well as the behavior of intransitive verbs in the indirect passive construction, are explained.

2.2.1 Transitive verbs

In the following sentence, the verb こわす is used. The verb itself already carries a connotation of adversity, but when it is used in an indirect passive sentence, the sentence denotes clearly who suffered by the object's being destroyed.

(11)   妹は弟にカメラをこわされた。

     My sister was upset because my brother broke her camera.

---

[3] This structure is called "bi-clausal." See Kuno (1973, 1983).

In sentence (11), 妹のカメラ "my sister's camera" is the object of the active sentence, and the direct passive structure is 妹のカメラは弟にこわされた "my sister's camera was broken by my brother." This direct passive sentence would be considered a factual statement describing what happened to the camera. However, as has already been mentioned, use of an inanimate entity as a subject tends to be avoided, as such an entity cannot express human empathy. Therefore, 妹のカメラは弟にこわされた is considered pragmatically inappropriate in daily communication because the speaker cannot observe the situation from the viewpoint of the camera with his/her empathy.

Active: 弟は妹のカメラをこわした。
Passive: 妹は弟にカメラをこわされた。

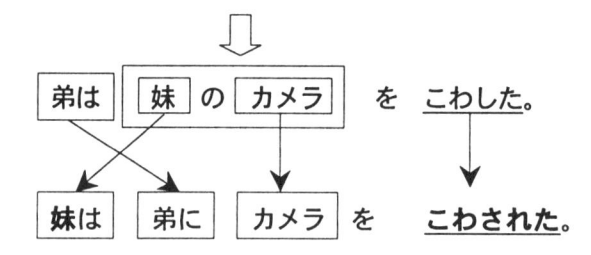

(12) 私はだれかに財布を盗まれた。
I was troubled because someone stole my wallet.

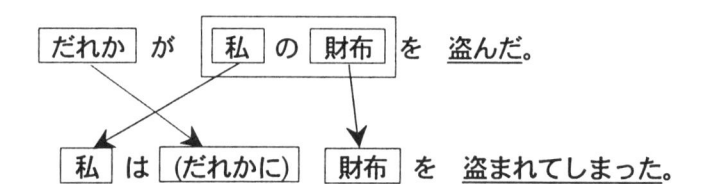

(13) 父が僕のビールを飲んだ。
My father drank my beer.
↓
僕は父にビールを飲まれてしまった。
I was upset because my father drank my beer.

(14) 電車の中でだれかが私の足を踏んだ。
Someone stepped on my foot in the train.
↓
(私は)電車の中で(だれかに)足を踏まれた。
I got hurt because someone stepped on my foot in the train.

(15) 村田さんは山本さんのコンピュータを使った。
Ms. Murata used Mr. Yamamoto's computer.
↓
山本さんは村田さんにコンピュータを使われた。
Mr. Yamamoto was inconvenienced because Ms. Murata used his computer.

As the English equivalent demonstrates in the above sentences, when a sentence is converted into a passive sentence, an extra meaning is appended. For example, sentence (15) describes a simple fact when it is in an active sentence, but as soon as it is converted into a passive sentence, the nuance that Mr. Yamamoto was annoyed by Ms. Murata's using his computer is added.

It should be mentioned that the subject of an indirect passive sentence is one that receives an inconvenience; therefore, the following sentence is also appropriate.

(16) だれかが弟の自転車を盗んでしまったので、妹は困った。
Someone stole my brother's bicycle, and my sister was in trouble.
↓
妹は弟の自転車を盗まれてしまった。
My sister got in trouble because someone stole my brother's bicycle. (My sister is certainly upset, and I feel bad for her too.)

(17) 太郎は次郎が花子に書いたラブレターを見てしまった。
Taro read the love letter that Jiro wrote to Hanako.
↓
花子は太郎に次郎が花子に書いたラブレターを見られてしまった。
Hanako was upset because Taro read a love letter that Jiro wrote for Hanako. (Hanako is certainly upset, and I feel bad for her too.)

In sentences (16), the speaker's sister is the one who was troubled by someone's stealing her brother's bicycle. This would be the case when the sister was asked to see to the brother's bicycle while he was away. The bicycle was stolen during that period, and the sister is responsible for it. Sentence (16) describes this situation in just one sentence expressing both the sister's annoyance at the theft of the bicycle and the sympathetic viewpoint of the speaker. The same observation applies to sentence (17). It is Hanako who was embarrassed by the fact that Taro read the love letter written by Jiro and addressed to Hanako, and the speaker indicates his/her empathy with the situation. Thus, it is always the subject that is inconvenienced or suffers from the event described in the indirect passive form from the speaker's/writer's perspective.

Describe the following situations using the indirect passive construction:

(18) Taro was dog-sitting his teacher's dog while she was away. However, when he took the dog for a walk, the dog got off its leash and ran away. Taro is very upset, but does not know what to do. . . .
(　　　　　　　　　　　　　　　　　　　　　　　)

(19) Taro was asked by Hanako to see to the luggage while she was away at the airport. While he was doing so, someone came and accidentally spilled coffee over the bag. Hanako returned and was very upset. (In this case, write two passive sentences.)
(　　　　　　　　　　　　　　　　　　　　　　　)
(　　　　　　　　　　　　　　　　　　　　　　　)

2.2.2 Intransitive verbs

Another distinctive feature of the Japanese passive construction is that intransitive verbs are also used in passive sentences, expressing a meaning of adversity. For example:

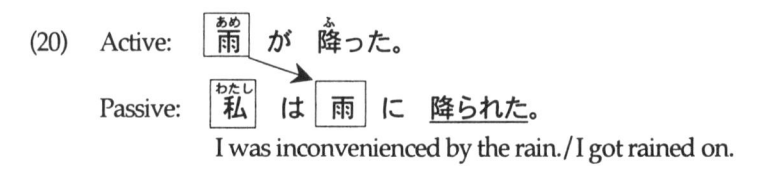

(20) Active: 雨が降った。
Passive: 私は雨に降られた。
I was inconvenienced by the rain./I got rained on.

In the passive sentence above, the subject 私 is the person who suffered from its having rained. In the indirect passive structure as well, regardless of the type of the verb, the subject is always an animate entity that has feelings, and the sentence can express a meaning of adversity.

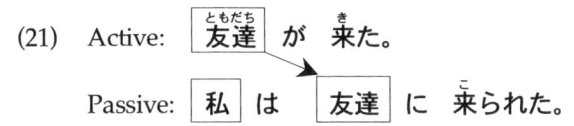

(21) Active: 友達が来た。

Passive: 私は友達に来られた。
     I was troubled because my friend came over.
     (when I was taking a shower, for example)

(22) 何もしないのに、子供が泣いた。それで、私は困った。
Even though I did not do anything to the baby, she cried.
↓
何もしないのに、(私は)子供に泣かれてしまった。

I was troubled because the baby cried even though I did not do anything to her.

(23) 泥棒が家に入った。
A robber entered the house.
↓
(私は)泥棒に家に入られた。

I got my house robbed by a robber.

(24) 泥棒が家の中をくつで歩いた。
A robber walked in the house with his shoes on.
↓
泥棒に家の中をくつで歩かれた。

I got my house walked through with shoes by a robber.

(25) 約束の時間に遅れたので、ガールフレンドは帰ってしまった。
Since I was late for the meeting, my girlfriend ended up going home.
↓
約束の時間に遅れたので、(私は)ガールフレンドに帰られてしまった。

Since I was late for the meeting, my girlfriend went home and I got in trouble.

Sample essays and dialogues

おもしろい一日

　きょうは色々なことがあった。まず日本語のクラスへ来る途中で帽子(hat)を車にひかれた。古い帽子だったから、ひかれてもあまり頭に来なかった (I didn't get upset)。クラスが終わると、僕の気に入っている(my favorite)女の子がそばに来て、宿題を一緒にしてほしいと頼まれた。いい気分だった (I felt good)。夕方図書館で会って勉強して、それから日本の映画を見に行こうと言われた。女の子に誘われるのはあまりないことなので、うれしかった。

　物理(physics)のクラスへ行くと、僕の論文がいいと先生にほめられた。これもめったにないことなので (since it seldom happens)、うれしかった。さて、いよいよ夕方になって図書館へ行った。彼女はまだ来ていなかった。ベンチに座わって待っていると、同じ日本語のクラスにいる他の女の子が来て、「ジュリーは今日来れなくなったの」と言う。「なんだ、ふられたか・・・。」と独り言を言うと (when I mumble)「私もまだ宿題していないんだけど、よかったら一緒にしない？」と彼女が言った。また女の子に誘われた、と思うといい気分だった。そしてその後で映画も見て帰った。映画館を出てからは雨に降られたけど、なかなかいい日だった。

　さて、夜になってジュリーから電話がかかってきた。「今日はごめんなさい。でもサリーが行ったでしょう。彼女どう？あなたのこと、とても気に入っているの。よかったらつきあってあげてくれない？」なんだそういうことだったのか・・・。ぼくはやっぱりジュリーにふられたんだ・・・。あ~あ。

Excerpt the passive sentences and translate them in the manner introduced in the chapter.

誰の足?

本田: 　スミスさん、今日、ちょっと会社を休みたいんですが・・・。
スミス: 　何かあったんですか。
本田: 　ええ、実は妻に足の骨を折られましてねぇ・・・。
　　　　(足の骨を折る= to break a leg)

スミス: え、奥さんがそんなことをなさったんですか。それは大変でしたね。じゃ、病院ですか、今日は。
本田: ええ、今からちょっと行って来ようと思って・・・。
スミス: じゃ、お大事に。
[翌日]
本田: スミスさん、昨日はすみませんでした。
スミス: あれ、本田さん、足の骨を折ったんでしょう？松葉杖 (crutch) はいらないんですか。もう歩けるんですか。
本田: え・・・？

What is the misunderstanding in this story? (Who broke whose leg?)

ついていない日
(Alex's) Unlucky Day

　　　アレックスはその日、朝からついていなかった。それは、目覚し時計 (alarm clock) がこわれていたことから始まる。もちろん寝坊だ(oversleep)。最近大学で取り始めた日本語のクラスは9時に始まる。　　その時はもうすでに8時５０分だった。そこで、車で行こうと思ったが、エンジンがかからなくて (the engine wouldn't start)、バスで行かなければならなかった。バスはいつもよりずっとこんでいて (was crowded)、たくさんの人に足を踏まれた。おまけに (on top of that) シャツに口紅 (lipstick) もつけられた。クラスには遅く着いたので、クイズは受けることができないと先生に言われた。これはルールだから仕方ない (it cannot be helped since this is a policy)。
　　　夜は美々子とデートの約束があった。今日もまた彼女をレストランへ誘い、おいしいものを食べながら、いろいろな話をした。日本語は大学で勉強しているので、ずいぶん上達 (improve)したが、文法はまだ苦手だ。
　　　食事が終わって会計 (check) が来た。彼女にご馳走するつもりだったのだが (I was going to treat her)、なんと、財布がないことに気がついた (I realized that I didn't have my wallet)。あ！　バスの中で盗まれたのだ。あちゃ〜 (Oh, no!)。そこでしかたなく、彼女に払ってほしいと頼んだら、「財布がないことに今まで気がつかなかったの？」と驚かれてしまった。それ

だけではない。その後(あと)はもっと大変(たいへん)だった。シャツについていた口紅を美々子に発見(はっけん)された (was discovered) からだ。

アレックス：　あ、これ？これは今朝(けさ)バスの中(なか)でつけてもらったんだよ。
美々子(みみこ)：　「つけてもらった」？　何(なに)それ、どういう意味(いみ)？「つけてもらった」って。バスの中でそんなこと人(ひと)に頼(たの)んでいるの。変(へん)な人(ひと)ねえ！　私(わたし)もう帰(かえ)るわ。じゃぁね。」
アレックス：　？？？

外(そと)は土砂降(どしゃぶり)だった (outside, it was pouring rain) が、アレックスは傘(かさ)を持(も)っていなかった。

Exercise:
1. Excerpt passive sentences from the essay.
(1)
(2)
(3)
(4)
(5)
(6)

2. Based on the content of the essay, complete the following sentences. (Pay attention to the subject of the sentence and the forms you use.)
(1) アレックスは9時(じ)の日本語(にほんご)のクラスでクイズを＿＿＿＿＿＿＿＿。
(2) 美々子はアレックスにデートに＿＿＿＿＿＿＿＿＿＿＿＿＿。
(3) 美々子はアレックスにお金(かね)を払(はら)ってほしいと＿＿＿＿＿＿＿＿。
(4) 美々子はアレックスのシャツについていた口紅(くちべに)を＿＿＿＿＿＿＿＿。
(5) アレックスは美々子に一人(ひとり)で家(うち)へ＿＿＿＿＿＿＿＿＿＿。
(6) アレックスは傘を持っていなかったので、雨(あめ)に＿＿＿＿＿＿＿＿。

3. Refer to the dialogue between Alex and Mimiko.
Alex made a grammatical mistake that upset Mimiko. How should he have explained what happened on the bus? Write the sentence in Japanese. Also, compare your sentence with 「つけてもらった」 and explain the difference between those two sentences.

CHAPTER 32

Causative Constructions

The fundamental meaning of the causative morpheme せる is to describe that a sentient subject gives rise to some other animate entity to bring about an activity. This means that the causative construction can be used not only to indicate a coerced activity, but also a permissive activity, where the subject allows a second party to bring about the activity. Therefore, Japanese causative constructions can be used to express a meaning of either to "make" or to "let" someone do something (although the permissive case requires extra grammatical devices). The necessity of a grammatical device depends structurally on the type of predicate used in the causative construction. First, observe the basic formation of a causative sentence:

1. Formation

a. Consonant Verbs (う verbs) → ~*u* becomes ~*a*, and せる is added

買う	kaw-u	買わせる	kaw-a-seru
飲む	nom-u	飲ませる	nom-a-seru
帰る	kaer-u	帰らせる	kaer-a-seru

b. Vowel Verbs (る verbs) → る is dropped and させる is added

受ける	uke-ru	受けさせる	uke-saseru
教える	oshie-ru	教えさせる	oshie-saseru
開ける	ake-ru	開けさせる	ake-saseru

c. Irregular Verbs

| する | | させる |
| 来る | | 来させる |

375

2. Structure and Meaning: "Make" vs. "Let"

Pragmatically, a causative meaning usually prevails over a permissive meaning if a causative sentence alone is used in daily communication. In order to express a permissive meaning, an additional grammatical device is required. However, the grammatical device may be slightly different depending on the type of verb used in a causative sentence. When a transitive verb is used, the use of the verb of giving/receiving (てあげる, てくれる, てもらう) or the use of an adverbial phrase, such as 勝手に "at one's own will" and 自由に "freely," is required to express the permissive meaning. When an intransitive verb is used, the use of the verb of giving/receiving is also key to expressing a permissive meaning, but the use of a different particle further differentiates the meaning.

2.1 Causative sentences with transitive verbs

When a causative sentence is formed, the person who is forced to perform an activity is marked by the particle に since the person becomes an indirect object who receives the command/request. For example, in causative sentence (1), 子供 is the entity to whom her mother's command is directed and is marked by に.

2.1.1 Transitive verbs

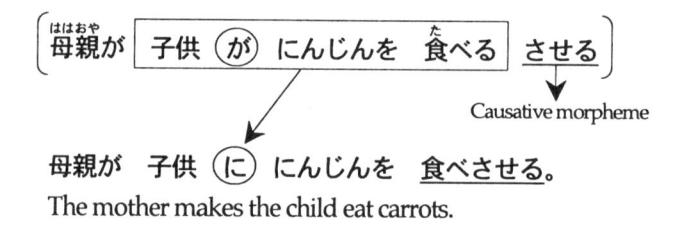

母親が [子供 (が) にんじんを 食べる] させる
　　　　　　　　　　　　　　　　　　　　　　Causative morpheme

母親が 子供 (に) にんじんを 食べさせる。
The mother makes the child eat carrots.

(1) 妹 (が) 車を 洗う。
　　My sister washes the car.

　　弟が 妹 (に) 車を 洗わせる。
　　My brother makes my sister wash the car.

(2) 学生 (が) 先生を 手伝う。
The students help the teacher.
↓
先生が 学生 (に) (自分を) 手伝わせる。
The teacher makes the students help him.

2.1.2 Ditransitive verbs

先生が [ジョン (が) メリー (に) 数学を教える] させる
↓
先生が ジョン (に) メリー (に) 数学を 教えさせる。
The teacher makes John teach Mary mathematics.

(3) メリー (が) ジョン (に) お金を 払った。
Mary paid John money.
↓
先生が メリー (に) ジョン (に) お金を 払わせる。
The teacher made Mary pay money to John.

(4) 鈴木さん (が) 豊田さん (に) 車を 売った。
Mr. Suzuki sold a car to Mr. Toyota.
↓
本田さんが 鈴木さん (に) 豊田さん (に) 車を 売らせた。
Mr. Honda made Mr. Suzuki sell a car to Mr. Toyota.

In order to express a permissive meaning, てあげる, てくれる, or てもらう have to be accompanied at the end of a sentence. See the following examples:

Causative

> 先生が学生に辞書を使わせた。
> The teacher <u>made</u> students use the dictionary.

Permissive

> <ruby>先生<rt>せんせい</rt></ruby>が<ruby>学生<rt>がくせい</rt></ruby>に<ruby>辞書<rt>じしょ</rt></ruby>を<ruby>使<rt>つか</rt></ruby>わせ<u>てあげた</u>。
> The teacher <u>let</u> students use the dictionary.
> 学生は先生に辞書を使わせ<u>てもらった</u>。
> The students had the teacher <u>let</u> them use the dictionary.
> 先生が<ruby>私<rt>わたし</rt></ruby>たちに辞書を使わせ<u>てくれた</u>。
> The teacher was kind enough to <u>let</u> us use the dictionary.
> 先生が私たちに辞書を<ruby>自由<rt>じゆう</rt></ruby>に使わせ<u>てくれた</u>。
> The teacher was kind enough to <u>let</u> us use the dictionary freely.

If one wants to ask for permission, the causative construction can be used as exemplified in the following. Note that the てもいいですか "May I ~?" construction may also be used, but the causative construction is more polite and less casual.

(5) コンピュータを使わせてくださいますか。
Can you let me use the computer?

(6) <ruby>今日<rt>きょう</rt></ruby>は<ruby>気分<rt>きぶん</rt></ruby>が<ruby>悪<rt>わる</rt></ruby>いので、<ruby>仕事<rt>しごと</rt></ruby>を<ruby>休<rt>やす</rt></ruby>ませていただきたいのですが・・・。
Since I'm feeling sick, I would like to get permission to take a day off from work.

(7) 先生の<ruby>論文<rt>ろんぶん</rt></ruby>、<ruby>読<rt>よ</rt></ruby>ませていただけますか。
Would you let me read your thesis?

2.2 The causative construction with an intransitive verb

There are three basic grammatical devices that express a permissive meaning for intransitive verbs. The first is to add the verb of giving/receiving at the end of the sentences just as one does with a transitive verb. The second is to use an adverbial phrase, such as <ruby>勝手<rt>かって</rt></ruby>に "at one's own will" and 自由に "freely." The third is to use the particle に instead of を: に is for permission, while を is for causation. However, the latter is rather pedantic, and the alternating use of the particles may not be very consistent in daily communication. The best way to express a permissive meaning is, after all, the use of the verb of giving/receiving just as in the case of a transitive verb. Also, the change in particles becomes ineffective if the verb of giving/receiving is added at the end of the causative form. Observe the following examples:

Causative

> 父親が 息子 (を) 大学へ行かせた。
> The father <u>made</u> his son go to college.

Permissive

> 父親が 息子 (に) 大学へ 行かせた。[1]
> The father <u>let</u> his son go to college.
> 父親が 息子 (を/に) 大学へ 行かせてあげた。
> The father was kind enough to <u>let</u> his son go to college.
> 父親が 息子 (を/に) 大学へ 自由に行かせた。[2]
> The father was generous enough to <u>let</u> his son choose a college to go to freely.[3]

Pay attention to the use of the particles and the verb of giving/receiving to make sure that the meaning of each sentence is clear.

(8) a. 先生が 学生 (を) 家へ 帰らせた。
　　　　The teacher <u>made</u> the student go home.
　　b. 先生が 学生 (に) 家へ 帰らせた。
　　　　The teacher <u>let</u> the student go home.

---

[1] In the above example, に is used to indicate that permission was granted to the son. Although this is a grammatical device that alters the meaning of a sentence, in practice the use of auxiliary verbs explicate the permissive much more appropriately.

[2] The adverbial phrase can also occur with verbs of giving/receiving, which means that there are many combinations for expressing a single permissive meaning. Following are some examples:
a.　父親が息子を大学へ行かせてあげた。
b.　父親が息子に大学へ行かせてあげた。
c.　父親が息子を大学へ自由に行かせた。
d.　父親が息子に大学へ自由に行かせてあげた。

[3] This sentence may be interpreted that regardless of his financial situation, the father let his son go to a college by paying the tuition. In Japan many parents pay for the cost of their children's education.

c. 先生が 学生 を 家へ 帰らせてあげた。
The teacher was kind enough to <u>let</u> the student go home.
d. 先生が 学生 に 家へ 帰らせてあげた。
The teacher was kind enough to <u>let</u> the student go home.

If one wants to express permission, the causative construction can be used, as is shown in the following examples. Also, the てもいいですか "May I ~?" construction may also be used, but the causative construction is more polite and less casual.

(9) 私に行かせてくださいますか。
Would you please let me go?
(10) 息子にここで泳がせていただけるでしょうか。
Would you please let my son swim here?
(11) 今度のマラソンでは、私に走らせてください。
At the next marathon, let me run.

Note that when a causative sentence with an *intransitive verb* intends to express a permissive meaning, only an animate entity can be the recipient of the permission. See the following examples that support this idea.

(12) a. 父は植木を死なせてしまった。(causative meaning)
My father unfortunately made the plant die (because he did not water the plant for a long time, for example).
  * b. 父は植木に死なせた。(permissive meaning, but nonsensical)
My father let the plant die. (My father gave the plant permission to die.)
(13) a. 僕は野菜を腐らせてしまった。(causative meaning)
I made the vegetables rot (because I forgot to put them in the fridge).
  * b 僕は野菜に腐らせてしまった。(permissive meaning, but nonsensical)
I let the vegetables rot. (I gave the vegetables permission to rot.)

The following is a brief summary of the grammatical devices that express a permissive meaning using the causative form.

2.2.1 Transitive verbs
Two grammatical devices expressing a permissive meaning:

1. The use of あげる、くれる、もらう
   お母さんが子供 (に) アイスクリーム (を) 食べさせてあげた。
   The mother was sweet enough to allow the child to eat ice cream.
2. The use of an adverbial phrase
   (自由に、勝手に、好きなだけ, etc.)
   お母さんが子供 (に) アイスクリーム (を) 好きなだけ食べさせた。
   The mother let the child eat as much ice cream as the child wanted.

2.2.2 Intransitive verbs
Three grammatical devices to express a permissive meaning:

1. The use of あげる、くれる、もらう
   お母さんが子供 (に) 家の中で遊ばせてあげた。
   お母さんが子供 (を) 家の中で遊ばせてあげた。
   The mother was kind enough to allow the children to play inside the house.

   > Both sentences can express a permissive meaning due to the use of あげる regardless of the use of a different particle.

2. The use of an adverbial phrase (自由に、勝手に、好きなだけ, etc.)
   お母さんが子供 (に) 家の中で自由に遊ばせた。
   お母さんが子供 (を) 家の中で自由に遊ばせた。
   The mother let the children play inside the house freely.

   > Both sentences can express a permissive meaning due to the use of 自由に regardless of the use of a different particle.

3. The use of a different particle

お母さんが子供(に)家の中で遊ばせた。[4]

The mother let the children play inside the house.

(Permissive reading)

お母さんが子供(を)家の中で遊ばせた。

The mother made the children play inside the house.

(Causative meaning only)

Describe the following situations in one causative sentence:

課長： 中山君、悪いけど、これ月曜までに翻訳してくれないかな。
中山： え、英語ですか・・・。課長。僕、英語苦手なんですよ。
　　　できるかなぁ、月曜までに・・・。
課長： 仕事だよ、君。頼んだよ。
中山： はぁ・・・。

And...Nakayama pulled three all-nighters and translated the document.

兄： ５００円あげるから、車洗ってくれよ。
弟： ええ、500円じゃ、やだよ。1000円くれなきゃ。
兄： 何言ってんだよ、この前宿題、手伝ってあげただろう？
弟： そうか・・・。じゃまた手伝ってくれる？
兄： うん、車洗ってくれたらね。

And the little brother washed his brother's car for 500 yen.

母： できた、できた。
娘： わあ、お母さん、おいしそう！ちょっと味見してもいい？
母： お父さんが帰って来るまでだめよ。
娘： ちょっとだけ。ねえ、いいでしょう、お母さん。
母： しょうがないわねえ。じゃ、一口だけよ。

And the daughter tasted the cake.

---

[4] Although the use of に is one of the grammatical devices used to express a permissive meaning, in daily communication, the use of the giving/receiving verb or adverbial phrase will let the meaning across more accurately.

CHAPTER 33

Causative-Passive Constructions

A causative construction can combine with a passive construction to form a compound predicate causative passive form, such as "I was made (forced) to eat fish." The causative-passive construction does not carry a permissive meaning, but usually carries an adversity meaning. Since the causative predicates are all る verbs, the formation of the causative passive-predicate is simply to add られる.

1. Formation

	Causative	Causative-passive	
書く	書かせる	書かせられる	is made to write
飲む	飲ませる	飲ませられる	is made to drink
行く	行かせる	行かせられる	is made to go
買う	買わせる	買わせられる	is made to buy
教える	教えさせる	教えさせられる	is made to teach
いる	いさせる	いさせられる	is made to stay
する	させる	させられる	is made to do
来る	来させる	来させられる	is made to come

Causative: 友達が 僕に 納豆を 食べさせた。
My friend made me eat natto.

Caus.-Pass.: 僕は 友達に 納豆を 食べ させ られ た
　　　　　　　　　　　　　　　　　Stem　Causative　Passive　Tense marker

I was made to eat natto by my friend.

In the following sentences, pay attention to the function of the particle に.

(1) 医者に病院に入院させられてしまった。
I was forced to be hospitalized by the doctor.

(2) 先生にオフィスに来させられた。
I was made to come to the office by the teacher.

(3) 子供の時は、よく母に買物に行かせられた。
I was often made to go buy something by my mother when I was a child.

(4) 1週間に3冊も本を読ませられた。
I was made to read as many as three books a week.

(5) 兄に無理やり川を泳がせられた。
I was made to swim the river by force by my brother.

Consonant verbs have a contracted form, which is casual and used in colloquial communication.

買わせられる	kawas – (er) – areru	買わされる
行かせられる	ikas – (er) – areru	行かされる
飲ませられる	nomas – (er) – areru	飲まされる
泣かせられる	nakas – (er) – areru	泣かされる
読ませられる	yomas – (er) – areru	読まされる
歩かせられる	arukas – (er) – areru	歩かされる
泳がせられる	oyogas – (er) – areru	泳がされる

Sample exercise

Describe the following situations in one causative-passive sentence:

ティム: 先生、レポートができました。見ていただけますか。

先生: ああそう。どれどれ・・・。あれえ、何これ、タイポだらけだ (full of typos)。これじゃあだめですね。もう一度書いて来てください。

ティム: あ、そうですか・・・。すみませんでした。
And Tim rewrote the report.

母: 百子お父さんが出張 (business trip) から帰ってくるんだけど、雨が降ってるから駅まで傘持って来てほしいって。
百子: え〜、今忙しいのよ。お母さん行ってよ。
母: お母さんは夕飯作ってるでしょ。
百子: じゃ、隆に行かせれば？
母: 隆はあした試験があるって言うから、勉強させているの。
百子: あ、そう言えば (speaking of which)、私もあした試験があるのよねえ〜。
母: 百子、お父さん、おみやげがたくさんあるそうよ。
百子: え、あ、そうなの？じゃ、行って来ま〜す。

And Momoko brought an umbrella to the station for her father.

課長: アメリカのソニーに電話しなくちゃいけないんだけど、どうも英語が苦手でねぇ。鈴木君、僕の代わりに電話してくれないか。
鈴木: え、課長、僕も英語苦手なんですよ。だめですよ、僕じゃ。
課長: そんなことないよ。この前上手に話していたじゃないか。あれだけ話せればじゅうぶんだよ。ほら、電話して、今。
鈴木: え、今ですか？課長、ちょっと練習させてくださいよ。
課長: だめだめ。急いでいるんだ。早くして。
鈴木: あ、そうなんですか・・・。困ったなぁ・・・。

And Suzuki had to call Sony in America.

美々子: アレックス、これ、何か知ってる？
アレックス: え、何、これ・・・。
美々子: 「梅干し」って言うのよ。梅を長い間塩につけておくの。
アレックス: へえ、じゃ、しょっぱいんだろうね。(It must be salty)
美々子: ええ、とっても。一つ食べてみる？
アレックス: え、いいよ、僕。
美々子: いいから、食べてみなさいよ。ほら。
アレックス: やだよ・・・。
美々子: 日本に来たんでしょ。色々な事経験した方がいいわ。食べなさい。
アレックス: う！しょっぱい！水だ、水がいる！ああ、助けてぇ〜！

Bibliography

Geis, Michael, and A. Zwicky. 1971. "On Invited Inference." *Linguistic Inquiry* 2. 561–566.

Hamano, Shoko. 1998. *The Sound-Symbolic System of Japanese*. Stanford: CSLI Publications.

Ikegami, Yoshihiko. 1997. *Suru to Naru no Gengo-gaku: Gengo to Bunka no Taiporojii e no Shiron*. Tokyo: Taishukan Shoten.

Inaba, Midori. 1991. "Nihongo Jooken-bun no Imi Ryooiki to Chuukan Gengo Koozoo." *Nihongo Kyooiku* 75. 153–163.

Jacobsen, Wesley. 1983. "On the Aspectual Structure of the Adverbs Mada and Moo." *Journal of the Association of Teachers of Japanese* 18. 119–144.

———. 1992. *The Transitive Structure of Events in Japanese*. Tokyo: Kurosio Press.

Johnson, Yuki. 1997. "Hypotheticality and the Conditional Nara." *Princeton Japanese Pedagogy Workshop* 5. 64–72.

———. 1998a. "Birds of a Feather: An Examination of the Aspectual Forms Te-iru and Nai." *Princeton Japanese Pedagogy Workshop* 6. 103–113.

———. 1998b. "Modality Riron no Meikaku-ka o Motomete" (Seeking a better understanding of the theory of modality). *Nihongo-gaku to Nihongo Kyooiku* (Linguistics and Japanese Language Education), 145–160. Tokyo: Kurosio Press.

———. 2000. "Conditionals and Modality: A Reexamination of the Function of Ba and Volitional Expressions." *Japanese-Language Education around the Globe* 10. 165–189.

———. 2001. "Mada~Nai Bun ni okeru Ishisousa no Yakuwari" (The role of agentivity in mada sentences). *Nihongo-gaku to Nihongo Kyooiku 2* (Linguistics and Japanese Language Education 2), 111–126. Tokyo: Kurosio Press.

———. 2002. "The Role of Agentivity in Accusatives, Unergatives, and Unaccusatives: A Japanese Case." *Chicago Linguistics Society* 37. 190–205.

———. 2004a. *Modality and the Japanese Language*. Ann Arbor, Michigan: The University of Michigan Center for Japanese Studies Publications Program.

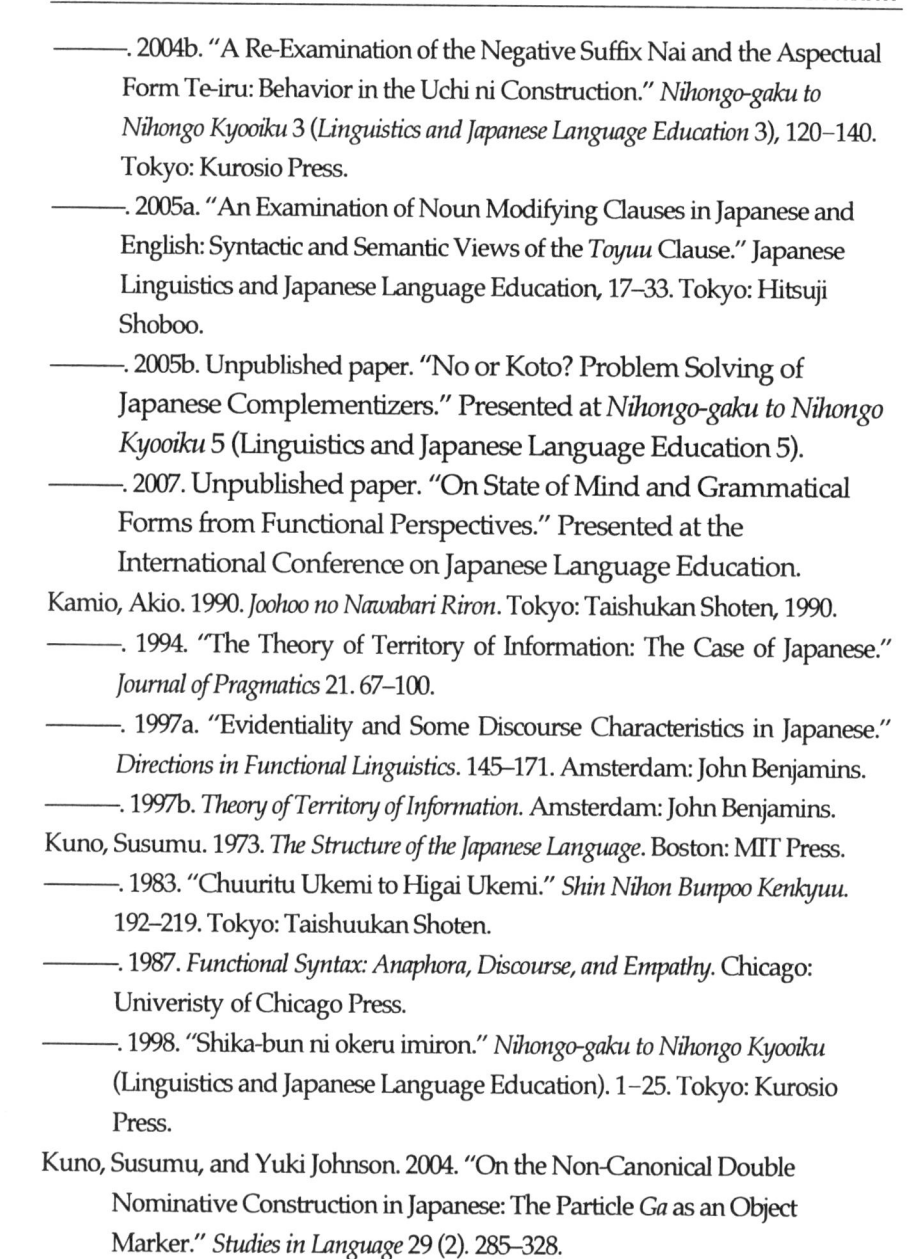

―――. 2004b. "A Re-Examination of the Negative Suffix Nai and the Aspectual Form Te-iru: Behavior in the Uchi ni Construction." *Nihongo-gaku to Nihongo Kyooiku* 3 (*Linguistics and Japanese Language Education* 3), 120–140. Tokyo: Kurosio Press.

―――. 2005a. "An Examination of Noun Modifying Clauses in Japanese and English: Syntactic and Semantic Views of the *Toyuu* Clause." Japanese Linguistics and Japanese Language Education, 17–33. Tokyo: Hitsuji Shoboo.

―――. 2005b. Unpublished paper. "No or Koto? Problem Solving of Japanese Complementizers." Presented at *Nihongo-gaku to Nihongo Kyooiku* 5 (Linguistics and Japanese Language Education 5).

―――. 2007. Unpublished paper. "On State of Mind and Grammatical Forms from Functional Perspectives." Presented at the International Conference on Japanese Language Education.

Kamio, Akio. 1990. *Joohoo no Nawabari Riron*. Tokyo: Taishukan Shoten, 1990.

―――. 1994. "The Theory of Territory of Information: The Case of Japanese." *Journal of Pragmatics* 21. 67–100.

―――. 1997a. "Evidentiality and Some Discourse Characteristics in Japanese." *Directions in Functional Linguistics*. 145–171. Amsterdam: John Benjamins.

―――. 1997b. *Theory of Territory of Information*. Amsterdam: John Benjamins.

Kuno, Susumu. 1973. *The Structure of the Japanese Language*. Boston: MIT Press.

―――. 1983. "Chuuritu Ukemi to Higai Ukemi." *Shin Nihon Bunpoo Kenkyuu*. 192–219. Tokyo: Taishuukan Shoten.

―――. 1987. *Functional Syntax: Anaphora, Discourse, and Empathy*. Chicago: Univeristy of Chicago Press.

―――. 1998. "Shika-bun ni okeru imiron." *Nihongo-gaku to Nihongo Kyooiku* (Linguistics and Japanese Language Education). 1–25. Tokyo: Kurosio Press.

Kuno, Susumu, and Yuki Johnson. 2004. "On the Non-Canonical Double Nominative Construction in Japanese: The Particle *Ga* as an Object Marker." *Studies in Language* 29 (2). 285–328.

———. 2005. "The Syntax of Object." *Nihongo-gaku to Nihongo Kyooiku* 4 (Linguistics and Japanese Language Education 4), 13–24. Tokyo: Kurosio Press.

Kuroda, S-Y. 1978. "Case Marking, Canonical Sentence Patterns, and Counter Equi in Japanese. In *Problems in Japanese Syntax and Semantics*, edited by John Hinds and Howard Irwing, 30–51. Tokyo: Kaitakusha.

Levin, Beth, and Malka Rappaport Havov. 1995. *Unaccusativity*. Boston: MIT Press.

Makino, Seiichi. 1996. *Uchi to Soto no Gengo Bunkagaku*. Tokyo: ALC Press.

Matthews, Peter. 1997. *The Concise Oxford Dictionary of Linguistics*. Oxford: Oxford University Press.

Miura, Akira, and Naimi Hanaoka-McGloin. 1994. *An Integrated Approach to Intermediate Japanese*. Tokyo: Japan Times.

Perlmutter, David. 1978. "Inversional Passives and the Unaccusative Hypothesis." *Berkeley Linguistics Society* 4. 157–189.

Shibatani, Masayoshi. 1990. *The languages of Japan*. Cambridge: Cambridge University Press.

Tsujimura, Natsuko. 1991. "On the Semantic Properties of Unaccusativity." *Journal of Japanese Linguistics* 13. 91–116.

Tsukuba Daigaku Nihongo Kyoiku Kenkyukai. 1983. *Nihongo Hyogen Bunkei Chukyu* 1. Tokyo: Bonjin-sha.

Index

accusatives, 92
additive linkage, 204–205
adjectives, 11, 13–15; compound, 130; conjugation of, 29–30; *i* (い), 11, 13–15; *na* (な), 15, 30–32
adverb: degree of attributes, 233; degree of frequency, 233; degree of probability, 234
adverbial forms of *i* / *na* (い/な) adjectives, 237
after, 173–175, notion of, 109. *See also* perfective
agent (performer of an action), 48, 51–53, 69, 91–95, 147, 216
ageru (あげる), 276–279
agglutination, 16, 105, 362
aida ni / *aida wa* (間に/間は), 120–124
aizuchi (あいづち), 208
anaphoric, 187, 189, 191
antecedent, 226; definition of, 323
apposition, 78, 224, 233
aru (ある), 98–104
aspectual form, 106, 148, 150, 157, 178, 183, 220, 334. See also *te iru* (ている)

ba (ば), 321, 336-341; grammatical restrictions, 338; in non-past context, 336–338; in past context, 340–341
ba ii (ばいい), 352–353; *ba iin janai* (ばいいんじゃない), 353; *ba iin janai deshoo ka* (ばいいんじゃないでしょうか), 353

before, 115; notion of, 109. *See also* imperfective
bi-directional, 63

causal, 196–197, 323–325
change of state, 216–222
choo'on (long vowel) (長音), 7
cohortative form (*oo* [おう] form), 20, 24, 28, 181–184
commands, 144, 292–295, 338, 376
comparative, 345–348
complementizer: of a sentence, 64; of a noun, 224
completion of an event, 15, 105, 148, 117, 163, 172, 176–177. See also *ta* (た) form compound
complex predicate, 16
compound adjective, 130
compound predicate, 51, 114, 143, 160, 383
conditional, 20, 29, 31, 107, 303, 306, 308, 324–344, 353; *ba* (ば), 321, 336–341; *nara* (なら), 321, 341–344; *tara* (たら), 321, 331–336; *to* (と), 321, 325–331
conjugation: of copula *da* (だ), 30–32; of *i* (い) adjectives, 29–30; of verbs, 21–29
conjunction words, 61, 80, 193–205; *dakara* (だから), 193,194, 196–198; *demo* (でも), 193; dependent, 201; *ga* (が), 201; *kara* (から), 197–199; *kedo* (けど), 193, 201–202; *keredo* (けれど), 193;

keredomo (けれども), 193, 201–203; *node* (ので), 193, 197–199; *noni* (のに), 201–203; *shi* (し), 204–206; *shikamo* (しかも), 193, 204–206; *shikashi* (しかし), 193; *sonoue* (その上), 193, 204–206; *sorede* (それで), 193, 194, 195, 196, 199, 200; *sorekara* (それから), 193, 194, 195–196; *soreni* (それに), 193, 204–205; *soshite* (そして), 193–195; *te* (て), 193–198
consequent, 323–325, 328–329, 331, 333, 339; definition of, 323
consonant verb, 21–22
contingency, 325, 342
contracted forms: of *te wa* (ては), 304
contrast, 34, 39–43, 99, 115, 116, 120, 122, 130, 209, 229, 359
counterfactual, 115, 181, 203, 269, 296, 301–303, 330, 334–336, 340–341, 344. See also conditional

dakara (だから), 194, 196–198
dake (だけ), 240–241
dakuon (voiced sound) (濁音), 5
daroo (だろう), 254, 266–268
daroo to omou (だろうと思う), 267, 275
de (で): marking a noun phrase (as a cause), 70; marking a noun phrase (as a tool), 69; marking a noun phrase (as time or quantity), 70; marking a place noun, 67–68
deictic, 188
demo (でも), 88–89
demonstrative pronoun, 187–192

dependent conjunction word, 193, 197, 201, 204
desiderative, 50, 97, 130, 132, 176, 178
dictionary form, 23–25, 26, 28–29, 114, 115, 118, 176, 178, 220, 259, 357, 360
dictionary-form compound: *aida ni/aida wa* (間に/間は), 120–124; *koto ni naru* (ことになる), 216, 220–222; *koto ni suru* (ことにする), 216, 220–222; *mae ni/wa* (前に/は), 115–116, 128; *tame[ni]* (ため[に]), 118–120; *tokoro* (ところ), 117–118; *tsumori* (つもり), 114; *uchi ni/uchi wa* (うちに/うちは), 124–129
direct quotation, 210, 294
discovery, 248, 333, 364
ditransitive verb, 56, 96, 283, 284, 285, 286, 287, 377
dochira (どちら), 188, 212, 215, 318, 345–348; and *ichiban* (一番), 349–351
doo on igigo (同音異義語), 5
dynamic situation, 42, 148, 102, 148. See also *te iru* (ている)

e (へ), 62–63
ellipsis, 359
embedded relative clause, 230–231
embedded sentence, 82, 83, 208, 241
energy input, 148–151
epistemic possibility, 268
evidential modal, 255–262
exhaustive-listing, 42, 46–48
existence verbs, 57, 98–104
explanatory modals, 254, 270–275

first-time recognition, 333
5W1H, 211, 212
fixed forms; honorific and humble, 316
furigana (ふりがな), 2

ga (が), 42–50; as a subject marker (for exhaustive-listing), 46–48; (for neutral description), 43–46; (for new information), 42–48; as an object marker, 48–51
Geis, Michael, 327
gerundive form, (*te* [て] form), 21, 24, 29, 31, 71, 243
giving, 276
go (ご), as a polite affix, 313; –noun *desu* (です), 318
grammatical restrictions, –*ba* (ば), 338; –*to* (と), 328–329

habitual, 106, 115, 116, 132, 151, 155, 221, 323, 327, 329, 331, 340, 341
haiku (俳句), 3
Hamano, Shoko, 237
hazu (はず), 19, 254, 262–265; vs. *koto ni natte-iru*, 264–265
hiragana (平仮名), 1
hodo ja arimasen (ほどじゃありません), 347
honorific: language, 23, 73, 274, 276, 281, 315–319; requests, 320–321. *See also* humble forms; polite affix
hoo ga ii (方がいい), 354–356
humble forms, 312; fixed humble forms, 316–317; *ni narimasu/itashimasu*, 318; *o–desu/go–desu*, 318-319

hypothetical, 269, 271, 323–324, 339, 341, 344, 364, ; *tara* (たら), 331–335; *to* (と), 325–331

i (い) adjective, 11, 13–15; adverbial form of, 234
ichiban (一番), and *dochira* (どちら), 349
Ikegami, Yoshihiko, 216
imperatives, 20, 292–294
imperfective, 15, 23, 105, 107, 109, 114, 115, 180, 226, 354
Inaba, Midori, 344
independent conjunction word, 201
indirect quotation, 210, 293
information: new, 42–47, 102, 104, 213; old, 35, 46, 213; territory of, 86, 253. *See also* Kamio, Akira
in-group, 277, 278, 280, 285
interrogative question, 207, 210, 211
intransitive: 90–92; of verbs, 90–95; of volitional, 52, 53, 92, 93, 95, 331; of non-volitional, 150, 153, 220, 331
invitation, 88, 89, 131, 184, 185
invited inference, 327–328, 333, 340
iru (いる), 49, 98–102
itadaku (いただく), 276, 281, 287

Jacobsen, Wesley, 90, 238, 324, 342

ka (か), 82–85; as "or," 84–85; sentence-final particle (as a question mark), 10, 83–84; with an interrogative noun (creating a word "some–"), 85
Kamio, Akira, 86, 255

kamoshirenai (かもしれない), 19, 253, 254, 262, 263, 264, 268–270
kara (から), 33, 36, 41, 54, 55, 59, 60, 79–80, 81; as sentence-final conjunction, 194, 196–197, 200, 213, 214, ; difference from ので, 197–199
kata (方), 137–138
keiyoodooshi (形容動詞), 13
keiyooshi (形容詞), 13
keredomo (けれども), 193, 201–203; difference from *noni* (のに), 202–203
ko so a do (こ・そ・あ・ど), 187
koto ga dekiru (ことができる), 357
koto ni naru (ことになる), 216, 220, 221–222
koto ni natte-iru (ことになっている), 221; difference from はず, 264–265
koto ni suru (ことにする), 216, 220, 221
kudasaru (くださる), 276–277
Kuno, Susumu, 9, 46, 48, 97, 240, 367
kunyomi (訓読み), 4, 313
kureru (くれる), 96, 278–281, 282, 285–287
Kuroda, Shige-Yuki, 53

Levin, Beth, 92
linkage: additive, 203–204; paradoxical, 201–203

mada (まだ), 177, 238–240
made (まで), 81–82
madeni (までに), 82
mae ni/wa (前に/は), 115–116

Makino, Seiichi, 133
manyoo gana (万葉仮名), 1
manyoo shyuu (万葉集), 1
mashoo (ましょう), 89, 184–186
Matthews, Peter, 237
McGloin, Naomi, 231
mitai (みたい), 19, 254, 259–260
Miura, Akira, 231
mo (も), 70–74; with *i/na* (い/な) adjectives ("not even"), 74–75; with noun phrases ("also," "both," and "neither"), 71; with verb stems ("not even," "in addition"), 72
modal: auxiliary, 19, 253–275, 301, 306; *daroo* (だろう), 19, 254, 262, 263, 266–268; difference from *kotoni natte-iru* (ことになっている), 264–265; evidential, 254, 255–262, 271; explanatory, 254, 270–275; *hazu* (はず), 19, 254, 262–265; *kamoshirenai* (かもしれない), 19, 253, 254, 268–270; *mitai* (みたい), 19, 254, 259; *ni chigainai* (にちがいない), 18, 19, 254, 262, 263, 265–266; *noda* (~n desu) (のだ[~んです]), 254, 255, 270–273; *rashii* (らしい), 19, 254, 260–262; *soo* (そう), 19, 252, 255; *soo* (そう) hearsay, 258; *soo* (そう) visual, 255–257; suppositional, 254, 262, 263, 271; *wake* (わけ), 19, 254, 271, 273–274; *yoo* (よう), 19, 252, 259–260
modifying constructions; embedded relative clause, 230–231; *i/na* (い/な) adjective + noun, 223–224; noun (*no* [の]),

76–78; noun (*to iu* [という]), 224–226; noun-complement clause + noun, 233–234; relative clause + noun, 226–233
monoda (ものだ), 324, 340, 341
moo (もう), 28
morau (もらう), 59, 281–282, 287–289, 376, 377, 381

na (な) adjective, 11, 13–15; adverbial form of, 237
nagara (ながら), 121, 135–137
nai wakeniwa ikanai (ないわけにはいかない), 306, 307, 309–311
nakereba naranai/nakutewa ikenai (なければならない/なくてはいけない), 306, 307–309
nakutewa, nakucha, nakya (なくては, なくちゃ, なきゃ) 309
nara (なら), 323, 324, 341–344
naru (なる), 216–220
nasai (なさい), 292, 294–295
ne (ね), 86–87
negative form: adjective, 16, 29–30; copula *da* (だ), 30–31; verb, 27–28
negative question, 208–209
neutral description, 42, 43–46
new information, 42, 45, 46, 47, 102, 104, 213
ni (に), 55–62; for listing noun phrases, 60–62; marking a place noun, 57–58; marking a time noun, 58–59; marking an indirect object, 55–57; marking the source of an action, 59–60
ni chigainai (にちがいない), 18, 19, 254, 262, 263, 265–266

nikui (にくい), 134
no (の), 76–78; expressing an appositional relationship, 78; linking noun phrases, 76–77; marking a subject in a relative clause, 78–79
noda (~n desu) (のだ[~んです]), 254, 268–273
node (ので), 196, 197–199
nominalizers (*koto/no* [こと/の]), 244–252
non-anaphoric, 187
non-hypothetical, 323, 324, 325; *tara* (たら), 333–334; *to* (と), 326–328
noni (のに), 193, 201–202; difference from *keredomo* (けれども), 202–204
non-past affirmative, 14
non-volitional, 149, 150, 179; intransitive verbs, 150, 153, 220, 333
noun-complement clause, 223, 225, 233
noun modifying, 76, 223

o (を), 51–55; place noun marker (indicating a path), 53–55; object marker (for transitive predicates), 51–52
o (お), as a polite affix, 313
o (お) + verb stem + *desu* (です), 318–319
o (お) + verb stem + *kudasai* (ください), 318
o/go (お/御): + *suru* noun + *kudasai* (+する noun +ください), 321; + verb stem *itashimasu* (いたします), 315; + verb stem –*ni narimasu* (になります), 317

object (syntactic), 9, 10, 31, 32, 33, 35, 42, 48, 50, 51, 52, 53, 55, 56, 71, 77, 90, 92, 93, 94, 95, 97, 101, 130, 131, 160, 168, 216, 230, 246, 248, 249, 251, 282, 283, 358, 360, 362, 363, 364, 365, 367, 368; definition of, 48–49; indirect, 55, 56, 77, 92, 96, 101, 130, 230, 283, 286, 288, 376; sentential, 244, 249, 360
object marker, 41, 42, 48, 51, 52, 93. See also *ga* (が); *o* (を)
obligation, 19, 301, 307–311
o denwa (お電話), 313
o henji (お返事), 313
old information, 35, 46, 213
one-time event, 127, 149, 150, 153, 154, 157, 159, 327, 330, 331, 336. See also *te-iru* (ている)
on-going, 106, 117, 120, 148, 149, 151, 154, 157, 159
onomatopoeia, 1, 235, 237
onyomi (音読み) (sound-reading), 4, 5, 311
oo (おう) form, 24, 28, 182; *to omou* (と思う), 182–183; *to suru* (とする), 183

paradoxical linkage, 201–204
particles, 10, 12; *de* (で), 67–70; *demo* (でも), 88–89; *e* (へ), 62–63; *ga* (が), 42–51; *ka* (か) 83–85; *kara* (から), 79–80; *made* (まで), 81–82; *madeni* (までに), 82; *mo* (も), 70–75; *ne* (ね), 86–87; *ni* (に), 55–62; *no* (の), 76–79; *o* (を), 51–55; *to* (と), 63–67; *wa* (は), 34–42; *ya* (や), 75–76; *yo* (よ), 87–88

passive, 16, 59, 60, 319, 320, 362–374; adversity, 365, 366–371; direct, 364–365; formation of, 362–363; honorific sentences and, 319; indirect, 363, 366–371
past tense: of adjectives, 30; of the copula *da* (だ), 30–31; of verbs, 27
past tense form (*ta* [た] form), 24, 27, 105, 115, 173, 174, 178, 179, 180, 341, 344, 354
perfective, 15, 23, 105, 106, 107, 109, 111, 114, 115, 172, 176, 180, 226, 354
Perlmutter, David, 92
permission, 71, 253, 296–300, 357, 359, 378, 380
plain form. *See* dictionary form
polite affix, 313; *go–* (ご), 310; *o–* (お), 310
postposition, 10, 33
potential, 50, 97, 289, 319, 357–361; *koto ga dekiru* (ことができる), 360–361
predicate: complex, 16; compound, 50, 51, 114, 143, 160, 383; simple, 16; stative-transitive, 43, 49, 50, 52, 92, 97, 160, 251. See also *ga* (が) (as an object marker); potential; *tai* (たい)
progressive, 148, 182
prohibition, 301–305
pronouns, 244, 250, demonstrative, 187–192; interrogative, 12, 207, 209, 211–213; personal, 228; relative, 226
propositions, 18, 19, 253, 254, 255, 260, 263, 264, 265, 269, 271, 273, 275, 328

question: interrogative, 207, 210, 211; negative, 204–205; yes/no, 207, 211
quotation: direct or indirect, 66, 210, 293

Rappaport Havov, Malka, 92
rashii (らしい), 19, 254, 255, 260–262
referencing, 188, 189
relative clause, 11, 12, 76, 78, 224, 226–230; embedded, 230–232, 230; with *no* (の) marking the subject, 78–79
repetition, 148, 149, 150, 151, 153
respect, 312–322
resultative, 92, 117, 148, 149, 151, 154, 155, 157, 159, 160, 161, 318. See also *te aru* (てある); *te iru* (ている)
run-on sentences, 194

sashiageru (さしあげる), 276, 277, 278–281, 282–285
sentence complementation, 66
sequential, 115, 129, 146, 147, 173, 194. See also linkage; *te kara* (てから)
Shibatani, Masayoshi, 237
shika (しか), 73, 238–239
shikamo (しかも), 192, 203–204
shikashi (しかし), 192
shiro (しろ), 290–292
simple predicate, 16
soku-on (促音) (double consonant), 6
sonoue (その上), 192, 203–204
soo (そう), 252; hearsay, 256; visual, 253–255

sorede (それで), 193, 194, 195, 196, 199, 200
sorekara (それから), 61, 146, 147, 193, 194, 195, 196
soreni (それに), 61, 193, 204–206
soshite (そして), 193, 194, 195, 199
sound-reading (*onyomi* [音読み]), 4, 313
speaker-centered, 140, 165
speaker's group (in-group), 133, 277, 278, 279, 280, 285, 315
specificity, 333; notion of, 331
static, 46, 68, 148
stative-transitive predicate, 43, 49, 50, 52, 92, 97, 160, 246, 251. See also *ga* (が) (as an object marker); potential; *tai* (たい)
stativity: 42, 109; existence verb *aru/iru* (ある/いる), 98–104; resultative, 92, 117, 148, 149, 150, 151, 154, 155, 157, 159, 160, 161, 318; static, 46, 68, 148; *te aru* (てある), 159–162; *te iru* (ている), 106, 148–157
stem form, 26, 27, 71, 74, 130–142, 255
stem form compound: *kata* (方), 137–138; *nagara* (ながら), 135–137; *ni* (に) + motion verb, 140–142; *nikui* (にくい), 134; *sugiru* (すぎる), 138–140; *tagaru* (たがる), 132; *tai* (たい), 130–132; *yasui* (やすい), 134
subordinate clause, 23, 105, 107, 108, 109, 120, 121, 123, 124, 125, 126, 127, 128, 129, 135, 136, 197, 201, 222, 235, 296, 298, 301, 303;

aida (間), 120–124; *mae* (前), 115–116; *nagara* (ながら), 121, 135–137; *ta ato de* (た後で), 147, 172–174; *ta mama* (たまま), 180; *tame (ni)* (ため[に]), 118–120; *te kara* (てから), 143, 146–147; *uchi* (うち), 123, 124–129; "when," 107–113. *See also* conditional
suggestion, 352–353
sugiru (すぎる), 138–140
superlative, 349–351
suppositional modal, 254, 262, 263, 271
surface structure, 207, 233
suru (する) nouns, 321

ta (た) form, 23, 27, 115, 172
ta (た) form compound: *ta atode* (た後で), 147, 172–174; *ta koto ga aru* (たことがある), 176–178; *ta mama* (たまま), 180; *ta tokoro* (たところ), 178–180; *tara* (たら), 329–333; *tari tari suru* (たりたりする),174–176
tagaru (たがる), 132–134
tai (たい), 130–132
tame (ni) ため(に), 118–120; difference from *yoo ni suru* (ようにする), 218–219
tara (たら), 321, 331–334; comparison with *to* (と), 333–334; for advice, 335–336
te (て) form, 24, 25–27
te (て) form compound: *te ageru* (てあげる), 282–285; *te aru* (てある), 159–162; *te hoshii* (てほしい), 168–170; *te iku/kuru* (ていく/てくる), 165–168; *te iru* (ている), 148–157; *te kara* (てから), 146–147; *te kudasai* (てください), 143–145; *te kureru* (てくれる), 283–285; *te miru* (てみる), 162–163; *te morau* (てもらう), 96, 282, 287–289; *te oku* (ておく), 157–158; *te shimau* (てしまう), 163–165
teineigo (丁寧語), 312–314
tense, 16, 18, 23, 24, 25, 26, 105–113
to (と): as a conditional, comparison with *tara* (たら), 333–334; as a parallel linkage, 65–66; as quotation marks, 66–67; indicating a mutual action, 64–65; grammatical restrictions on, 328–329; hypothetical, 330–331; non-hypothetical, 329–330
to iu (という): noun という noun, 224–225; noun-complement clause + noun, 233–234
to iu koto de aru (ということである), 275
to iwarete iru (と言われている), 275
toka (とか), 75
to kangaeru (と考える), 275
tokoro (ところ), 117–118
topic, 17, 18, 33, 34, 37, 38, 39, 40, 41, 43, 50, 77, 98, 103, 229, 361; definition of, 35–36; topic-comment structure, 17, 35, 43
topic language, 17
transitive structure, 90
transitive verb, 52, 53, 55, 90, 91, 92, 93, 95, 96, 179, 216, 220, 283, 284, 286, 288, 293, 363, 367, 376, 378, 379, 381
Tsujimura, Natsuko, 159

tsumori (つもり), 114–115

uchi ni / uchi wa (うちに/うちは), 123, 124–129
unaccusatives, 92
unergatives, 92
unexpectedness, 73, 333

verb modifying. *See* adverb
verb phrase deletion, 12
verbs: conjugation, 20–29; consonant, 21, 22, 24, 26, 27, 28, 292, 336, 358, 363, 375, 384; ditransitive, 55, 56, 92, 93, 96, 283, 284, 286, 288, 377; intransitive, 52, 53, 90, 91, 92, 93–96, 149, 150, 153, 160, 179, 216, 220, 256, 284, 285, 286, 287, 288, 289, 331, 367, 370, 376, 378, 380, 381; non volitional intransitive, 150, 153, 220, 331; of leaving, 95; volitional intransitive, 49, 52, 53, 92, 93–96
volitional control, 49, 92, 147, 149, 150, 179, 216, 332

wa (は), 34–42; as a topic marker, 34–39; for contrast, 34, 39–42

wake (わけ), 19, 254, 271, 273–275
wake ni wa ikanai (わけにはいかない), 306, 307, 309, 310
WH movement, 209
when clause, 107–113
writing system: *hiragana* (平仮名), 1; *kanji* (漢字), 1; *katakana* (カタカナ), 1

ya (や), 75–76
yaru (やる), 278–279
yasui (やすい), 134
yes/no question, 207, 210
yo (よ), 87–88
yone (よね), 86–87
yoo da (ようだ), 254, 259–260
yoo na ki ga suru (ような気がする), 275
yoo na koto wa nai (ようなことはない), 275
yoo ni mieru (ように見える), 275
yoo ni suru (ようにする), 218; difference from *tame ni* (ために), 219–220
yoo'on (拗音) (contracted sound), 6

Zwicky, A., 327

About the Author

Yuki Johnson is Associate Professor of Japanese Linguistics and Undergraduate Program Coordinator in the Department of East Asian Studies at the University of Toronto. She received her Ph.D. in linguistics from the University of Minnesota in 1994 and has served on the faculty of International Christian University and Harvard University, and as Director of the Japanese language programs at the University of Michigan and the University of British Columbia. Her field of expertise concerns the functional syntax and semantics of Japanese, focusing on the topic of modality, which she has discussed in numerous articles and a book entitled "Modality and the Japanese Language." Her expertise extends also to second language curriculum and instruction. Dr. Johnson takes great interest in training Japanese language instructors and graduate students with a thorough knowledge of Japanese linguistics, grammar, and pedagogy in the framework of proficiency-oriented instruction. She is a valuable member of various professional linguistics associations, as well as of the Association of Teachers of Japanese (ATJ), where she has served as a board member.